A History of Cyber Literary Criticism in China

This is the first scholarly attempt to write a history of cyber literary criticism in China. The author uses the Internet as the departure point, literature as the horizontal axis, and criticism as the vertical axis, to draw a detailed trajectory of the development of cyber literary criticism in China.

The book comprises two parts. The first part focuses on the representation of historical facts about cyber literary criticism, covering five topics: the evolution of cyber literary criticism in the context of the new media; major types of cyber literary critics and their criticism; academic achievements in cyber literary studies; the form, contents, and rhetorical expressions of so-called netizens' critical commentaries; and important events in the history of cyber literary criticism. The second part discusses the historical changes in literary criticism as responses to cyber literature, covering another five topics: the conceptual transformation in literary criticism of the Internet era; the establishment of evaluation criteria for cyber literature; changes in the function of cyber literary criticism; changes in the constitution of cyber literary critics; and the impact of cyber literary criticism.

This book will be an essential read to students and scholars of East Asian Studies, literary criticism, and those who are interested in cyber literature in general.

Ouyang Youquan is Professor at the School of Literature and Journalism, Central South University, China. His research interests include literary theories and cyber literature. He has published many books, including *The Ontology of Cyber Literature*, *Studies of Literature and Art in the Context of Digitalization*, and *The Transformation of Art in Digital Media*.

A History of Cyber Literary Criticism in China

Ouyang Youquan

Sponsored by Chinese Fund for the Humanities and Social Sciences

First published 2024
by Routledge
4 Park Square, Milton Park, Abingdon, Oxon OX14 4RN

and by Routledge
605 Third Avenue, New York, NY 10158

Routledge is an imprint of the Taylor & Francis Group, an informa business

© 2024 Ouyang Youquan

Translated by Jin Hao and Huang Yingying

The right of Ouyang Youquan to be identified as author of this work has been asserted in accordance with sections 77 and 78 of the Copyright, Designs and Patents Act 1988.

All rights reserved. No part of this book may be reprinted or reproduced or utilised in any form or by any electronic, mechanical, or other means, now known or hereafter invented, including photocopying and recording, or in any information storage or retrieval system, without permission in writing from the publishers.

Trademark notice: Product or corporate names may be trademarks or registered trademarks, and are used only for identification and explanation without intent to infringe.

English Version by permission of China Social Sciences Press.

British Library Cataloguing-in-Publication Data
A catalogue record for this book is available from the British Library

ISBN: 978-1-032-54999-6 (hbk)
ISBN: 978-1-032-55001-5 (pbk)
ISBN: 978-1-003-42848-0 (ebk)

DOI: 10.4324/9781003428480

Typeset in Times New Roman
by Newgen Publishing UK

Contents

List of Tables   *vii*

Introduction: To Write a History of Cyber Literary Criticism   1

PART I

1 New Media and the Evolution of Cyber Literary Criticism   35

2 Major Types of Cyber Literary Critics and Their Criticism   67

3 Academic Achievements in Cyber Literary Studies   91

4 The Forms, Contents, and Rhetorical Expressions of Netizens' Critical Commentaries   120

5 Important Events in the History of Cyber Literary Criticism   148

PART II

6 The Conceptual Transformation in Literary Criticism of the Internet Era   183

7 The Establishment of Evaluation Criteria for Cyber Literature   206

8 Changes in the Function of Cyber Literary Criticism   228

9 Changes in the Constitution of Cyber Literary Critics   250

10 The Impact of Cyber Literary Criticism	270
Coda: Three Follow-up Questions about the Historiography of Cyber Literary Criticism	291
Index	*296*

Tables

0.1	Search results on CNKI, for papers on cyber literary criticism, on March 2, 2016	9
3.1	Fifty representative books on cyber literature (2000–2016)	93
3.2	Fifty representative journal articles on cyber literature (2000–2016)	97
3.3	Fifty representative newspaper articles on cyber literature (2000–2016)	103
5.1	The Ranking List of China's Excellent Web Novels in 2015	157
5.2	The Ranking List of China's New Web Novels in 2015	158
8.1	Representative reviews on *The Story of Wukong* written by scholars and ordinary netizens	235

Introduction
To Write a History of Cyber Literary Criticism

Cyber literary criticism, as this book will discuss, refers to a type of literary criticism that deals with cyber literature, especially original writings posted online. While some texts of cyber literary criticism are published on the Internet, others are published in traditional media as commentaries on writers, works, phenomena, and other issues of cyber literature. Thus, those who write cyber literary criticism include not only ordinary netizens who love literature and write actively online but also scholars and media workers who engage in the study of cyber literature.

As cyber literature is still in its youth, its criticism is also just at the early stage of development. As such a type of literary criticism is still not yet full-blown, its limited academic impact cannot make it adequately acknowledged by scholars in the mainstream of literary studies. It is even regarded by some as not yet officially started and still in a state of preparation. In such a context, our discussion on the construction of a history of cyber literary criticism undoubtedly sounds risky, as we may be talking about something that will only happen in the future and is non-existent today. This will also pose a challenge to us as we need to aptly theorize about cyber literature and its criticism. As we know, literary criticism is always written after literary creation, and a history of literary criticism should never be written before there are numerous works of literary criticism. The writing of a history of China's cyber literary criticism is no exception to this rule.

Nevertheless, we can prove this proposed project to be viable by actually conducting it. Today, if we come to the "site" of literary production and consumption, if we get on the Internet and start to read there, we can hear the critical voices rolling toward us from readers who read the radiant and flourishing cyberwriting, and we can see how scholars make their efforts to analyze and discuss an abundant number of phenomena in cyber literature. We can, from an increasing number of academic publications, gather remarkable resources and conceptions to help us establish a history of cyber literary criticism. Therefore, it is no longer unreasonable and unfounded for us to rethink the necessity and possibility of writing a history of cyber literary criticism: it has become, indeed, a project that is quite valid, or even inevitable; it has become an important part of the general history of literary criticism in China, as there have already been enough meaningful practices of cyberwriting and as there is the need to construct theoretical discourses on such practices. If we are to write a history, we shall always begin with a study of certain facts and then use theories to interpret such historical facts to eventually form a unity between facts and theories. Based on this idea, we can use the Internet as our departure point, literature as the horizontal axis, and criticism as the vertical axis, to start a journey of academic exploration that allows us to go through historical facts all the way into the theoretical discussions on cyber literary criticism.

The Necessity and Possibility of Writing a History of Cyber Literary Criticism

To argue that cyber literature criticism should have a history of its own, we need to discuss the relationship between the development of literature and the development of society in the specific context of the Internet as the new mass media. In my view, the writing of a history of cyber literary criticism both as a part of the general history of literature and as a part of the general history of literary criticism can be fully justified by people's practices and conceptualizations concerning literature, as there have already been abundant resources and achievements in the field of cyber literary criticism. Three points can serve as the theoretical basis for this.

First, cyber literary criticism is a phenomenon of historical significance, and we need to examine it objectively with an awareness of its historicity. There has been a huge body of critical texts on cyber literature, which, altogether, has a great influence on our society: it thus enriches the history of contemporary literature and has become an integral part of China's literary criticism today. Thus, cyber literary criticism, as a cultural existence, deserves a history of its own.

Second, cyber literary criticism is culturally valuable. We can examine cyber literary criticism's socio-cultural values and analyze how it plays a role in today's society and culture. Cyber literary criticism has helped ordinary people to make their voices heard—they can now write literary commentaries online. As a result, the conceptualization of literary criticism is renewed and expanded, and there are more ways for literary criticism to be delivered to readers, which are no longer limited by time and space in the traditional sense. We should have the insight to grasp such a new condition.

Third, cyber literary criticism has new functions. It can provide us with a broader view and constantly change our ideas about the history of literature to a certain degree. Our ways of literary criticism, based on theories since Aristotle's *Poetics* and Liu Xie's *The Literary Mind and the Carving of Dragons* (Wenxin diaolong), can be continuously updated.

Therefore, as we see that different elements—ideas about the development of literature, ideas about literary criticism, ideas about literary history, and ideas about society and history in general—are all necessarily connected, we can not only theoretically justify the writing of a history of cyber literary criticism but also recognize the necessity and significance of doing so. Cyber literary criticism not only has abundant literary resources to support its entry into the history of China's contemporary literary criticism as an integral part but also has enough new intellectual ideas to support the writing of a history of its own. While facing historical materials, facts, and achievements concerning cyber literary criticism, we should be confident: armed with adequate views and theories of history, we can seek to lay a logical basis for the history of cyber literary criticism.

Cyber Literary Criticism as a Historical Fact

While historical facts serve as the premise for the writing of history, the historicity of such facts is the ontological basis on which history is built. As we know, no matter how disorderly and immature today's cyber literary criticism is, it is already objectively existent and historically factual, and there is no doubt about this. If we visit the "site" of cyber literary production and consumption, we can see a large number of historical facts and materials about cyber literary criticism, many of which have been examined and analyzed by various scholars.

First, cyberwriting, which is radiant and flourishing, naturally demands cyber literary criticism; the huge body of literary works and critical texts thus ontologically validates our writing of a history of cyber literary criticism. Since the 1990s, when cyber literature written in Chinese was born in North America, with the quick popularization of the Internet in China and the thriving of literary websites, it has become a cultural trend that people now write with computers in replacement of their pens and post their writings on the Internet. As the Internet, structured like a spiderweb, allowed people to enjoy freedom in a virtual world, stored a huge amount of texts, and circulated them to all parts of the globe, a large body of writers with their countless original works and hundreds of millions of readers flooded into cyberspace. In particular, since the rise of "we media," it has become a part of people's daily life to read, write, and post their words on various apps, with handheld devices, such as smartphones, tablets, and e-readers, via mobile networks. In this way, all technical barriers established and maintained previously by traditional literature for its production, circulation, and criticism have been deconstructed. Scholars' elitist monopoly on literary criticism has come to an end, and ordinary people can enjoy a higher degree of freedom in critiquing literary texts. Literature thus gets off its pedestal and returns to the people. While "serious literature" used to be regarded as the absolute mainstream, today we can observe a phenomenal volume of cyber literature in China.

Meanwhile, as cyber literature is growing wildly, due to the discrepancy in cyber writers' writing abilities and the lack of editors as "gatekeepers," cyberwriting, though huge in volume, is not always good in quality: some works are closely associated with cyberspace, yet they are not literature; others are supposed to be works of literature, yet they are indeed not "literary" enough. This is the major deficiency of cyber literature and has received a lot of criticism. Therefore, it has become historically important for us to ask scholars to use literary criticism to better guide cyberwriting, to make our theoretical studies helpful in explaining and regulating the mechanisms of cyberwriting, and to call for better interaction and communication between traditional literature and cyber literature: it is in such a historical context that our cyber literary criticism was born and is growing up.

However new it is, cyber literature has grown in volume and in its social impact. Its "massiveness" cannot be denied or ignored. This requires us to objectively represent its condition as a historical fact. If we write a history of contemporary literature, we should not ignore the historical facts of cyber literature, including the achievements in cyberwriting. Without a discussion on cyber literature, our history of contemporary literature would be incomplete. By the same token, if we write a general history of literary criticism in contemporary China, we cannot avoid discussing the history of cyber literary criticism.

I made the following argument in an article to support the idea that cyber literature is essential to our writing of a history of contemporary literature:

> Today's cyber literature is …in the interplay between "the peripheral" and "the mainstream." With the increasing number of excellent works, cyber literature is gaining its position in the field of literature and culture and forging a new relationship with the dominant discourse of power in our society. With its unique mode of existence and way of circulation, it creates a certain "field" where it can negotiate with and further change various factors, including the media ecology, the mass culture, cultural theories, the mechanism of political power, and people's demands, thoughts, and ways of life. Such connection and interaction are the premises for us to argue that cyber literature should have a history of its own.[1]

Such a discussion applies not only to cyber literature but also to cyber literary criticism. As an undeniable historical existence, cyber literary criticism effectively intervenes in the interaction between literature and the changing sociocultural/historical condition, thus making it reasonable to have a history of its own.

The Historical Value of Cyber Literary Criticism

Cyber literary criticism's existence is not only a historical fact but is also of historical value. While scholars evaluate and examine cyber literature, they constantly consolidate and enrich the history of cyber literary criticism. As the value of literary criticism depends on critics' interpretations of literary texts, the value of the history of literary criticism originates from the analysis of literary criticism done by the one who writes history. As René Wellek and Austin

Warren remind us: "Values grow out of the historical process of valuation, which they in turn help us to understand."² Cyber literary criticism's cultural value makes it valid as an object to be examined in the historical context. In other words, while trying to validate cyber literary criticism as an integral component in the project of "rewriting literary history," we not only need to make clear its current forms and conditions but also should study its values and significance as a "node" in literary history.

Cyber literary criticism can be viewed as valuable in several different ways. In my opinion, while studying cyber literary criticism, we should first examine the cultural values of our society that are embedded and reflected in cyber literary criticism. We should evaluate how and to what degree cyber literary criticism influences the mainstream cultural values of our society and warn against or eliminate the negative influence if there is any. As we guide cyber literary criticism properly and make it focus more on its cultural values, we also make the history of cyber literary criticism more culturally valuable.

Today, there is a huge volume of cyberwriting and an enormously large body of readers who read cyber literature. Moreover, works of cyber literature have also been adapted into works of various other popular art forms, including films, TV series, theater performances, printed books, pieces of music, video games, cartoons, audiobooks, children's books, etc. For example, *Love Is Not Blind* (Shilian sanshisan tian), which is the top-grossing movie of 2011, *Empresses in the Palace* (Hougong Zhen Huan zhuan), which is the most popular TV series in 2012, *So Young* (Zhi women zhongjiang shiqu de qingchun), which is the top-grossing movie of 2013, and many TV series and films popular in 2015, including *The Journey of Flower* (Huaqiangu), *Nirvana in Fire* (Langyabang), *Grave Robbers' Chronicles* (Daomu biji), *Love Yunge from the Desert* (Yunzhongge), *Ghost Blows Out the Light* (Guichuideng), and *Chronicles of the Ghostly Tribe* (Jiuceng yaota), are all adapted from web novels. This manifests that cyber literature has already changed the overall condition of China's literature and art: it has become one of the most popular among all types of literature and art and a powerhouse in the field of modern Chinese literature; it has made a great contribution to, and had a great influence on, the prosperity of China's literature and art and the enrichment of people's cultural life. Because of this, cyber literature is no longer simply an issue about the Internet or an issue of literature; it has become a significant cultural issue that is directly related to the quality of literature, the cultural trend, the humanistic spirit, and the value orientation of our times: as it is phenomenally influential, it is directly related to the construction of the nation's ideology and culture in the contemporary period, to the country's control over voices in cyberspace and especially voices in new media, to people's consumption of mass culture, their reading of literature, and the education of the youth, and even to the construction of the society's mainstream values, the strengthening of the country's soft power, and improvement of the country's image in the international community. Therefore, critics should take their responsibility to interpret, evaluate, study, and even guide such a phenomenal literary and cultural practice while recognizing such a job as distinctively valuable. Meanwhile, as we clarify and delineate the process and contents of literary criticism, we can construct a history of cyber literary criticism that is also distinctively valuable.

If we focus on the inherent values of literature, we can see that cyber literature and its criticism are also valuable in the context of media technologies as they are aesthetically novel. We should pay special attention to this point as we are building a consensus as to how to study cyber literature. Cyber technology and the new means of production allow cyber literature not only to break literary traditions but also to construct a "poetics" based on the use of new media: in this way, the aesthetics of literature goes through a process of deconstruction and reconstruction. Scholars of cyber literature thus have the duty to clarify how such a new type of literature departs from literary traditions, how it can transform our literary theories and conceptualizations, and how it can gain value for itself through this process.

As cyber literature turns technology into a matter of art and turns art into a matter of technology, it creates a tension between art and technology. The charm of writing literature with a pen and reading literature on paper, as a result, disappears. Meanwhile, a new dimension of "digital poetics," that does not exist in traditional literature, is created. For example, as texts of cyber literature are stored in digital forms, they are not limited in length and can be easily circulated, searched, and duplicated. The fonts can also be freely changed and more than one language may be available as a result of the use of machine translation. Audiobooks allow readers to listen instead of reading. Texts can also be updated in real time and shared among readers without limits. Netizens, as ordinary people, now can participate in the writing and critiquing of literature. All these new conditions make it more convenient for writers to freely create their works as expressions of their thoughts and interests: now, they can "have a broad view of history and reality as if it is right before their eyes" and "express their poetic feelings through typing and clicking"; technology thus has a magical power to help them create an artistic wonderland. This exactly corresponds to what I once argued in an article:

> Multi-media works on the Internet incorporate various aesthetic elements, including pictures, texts, sounds, and moving images, thus being able to attract all our faculties and allow us to comprehensively feel their artistic charms... . Literary texts of such a type cannot be found in traditional literature in the print media. They combine pictures with texts and integrate the visual with the auditory. They can be interactive and constantly evolving. With such characteristics, cyber literary works create a poetic wonderland, and cyber literature itself has become a new art form based on the use of digital technology.[3]

As cyber literature, in the context of new media technology, has new artistic characteristics and aesthetic values, the critical reviews and studies of such a type of literature are valuable in a distinctively new way. Consequently, the writing of a history for such critical reviews and studies of cyber literature can also be of value.

In addition, cyber literature is also different from traditional literature in that it pays more attention to the commercial value of literature in the culture industry. Consequently, we need to consider how cyber literature sells in the market, and this is where our writing of a history of cyber literary criticism does not simply follow the traditional way. While the commercial value of cyber literature may be regarded as a departure from, or even a dissolution of, the traditional humanistic spirit, it has become a factor that cannot be overlooked as literature has come into an era of mass consumption. If traditional literature is an artistic "vocation" to which writers are dedicated, today cyber literature is mainly an "industry" of mass culture that aims to make profits by following the logic of the market. This is also the economic inducement for cyber literature to boom in recent years in China. Cyber literature is a product to be sold in the market shaped by technologies and readers' preferences: unlike traditional literature, it is no longer regulated by "writers associations" of different administrative levels and is not hampered by the current evaluation criteria; instead, it only needs to be acknowledged by readers and be shaped by the industry of multimedia entertainment in cyberspace. Ouyang Ting and I once made a description of this condition in an article:

> Websites run their businesses independently and are responsible for themselves. Thus, only the fittest can survive. Cyber writers depend on the use of new technology and their identities as ordinary people, as two powerful weapons, to fight in the jungle. Initially, they write alone to please themselves. Then, some of them begin to take writing as a career, a way of earning a living, or even a means of becoming rich. What they (mainly) expect is not to make literary achievements or to create works of timeless values. Instead, they aim to receive more clicks and "favorites" from readers, to let websites represent them to sell their works with full copyrights, and to sell the copyrights of their works to certain companies so that these works can be further adapted and make even more profits. This is what writers and businesses of cyber literature deem as the most important.[4]

Literature always has a spiritual dimension and an economic dimension. In the past, we paid more attention to the former, which was not wrong, but now cyber literature puts more emphasis on the latter, and this is obviously subject to critique. Nevertheless, critics of cyber literature can pass fair judgment on this phenomenon, which is significant and quite necessary. This is indeed an important issue cyber literary criticism must face and deal with. It is also an important "historical fact" we must pay attention to while writing a history of cyber literary criticism.

Moreover, as cyberwriting allows ordinary netizens to participate in literary creation, the identity of writers has been changed. This can be seen as a great revolution in literature brought by digital technology. How to evaluate this

8 *Introduction*

phenomenon has become an issue we must deal with in the writing of a history of cyber literary criticism. The inherent structure of the Internet naturally allows all users to be equal, so netizens enjoy a high degree of freedom to write in cyberspace. This corresponds to a description I once made in an article:

> The Internet allows cyber writers to publish their writings without anxiety. As it does not require any qualification, everyone can have the right to publish works online, and no one has any right to prevent others from freely expressing themselves. Everyone with a dream of becoming a famous writer now has a chance. Ordinary people, who are unknown to others, now have an equal opportunity to publish, just like professional writers do.[5]

As a result of this, the era of a "new folk literature" soon came. One does not have to be a professional and qualified writer to write, and the traditional rules in the field of literature are subverted. Thanks to new technologies, literary creation is no longer practiced by an exclusive group of professional writers but by ordinary netizens, and a huge volume of literature comes out. Although this "great leap forward" in literary creation does not necessarily signify progress in literature, as I argued in an article, it is undoubtedly "a rebellion against, and a correction to, the condition that literature has been written exclusively by the elite for thousands of years."[6] As I further argued in this article, this "restores literature to its original condition, as people's 'expressions of sadness and happiness,' as their 'responses to certain incidents,' as 'laborers' songs about their labors,' and as 'hungry people's songs about their desire for food.'"[7] This is historically significant: "it helps literature return to the study of human nature" and "it allows us to experience what happened more than two thousand years ago when common people used poetry to record their labors and describe the change of seasons."[8] Undoubtedly, critics of cyber literature should not and will not ignore such a historical change—indeed, there has already been abundant research on it. The fact that now literature is no longer a domain exclusively for professional writers and that ordinary people can write and publish is the best "gift" given to us by cyber technologies. It is also an opportunity for literature to popularize itself in this period. This is a historical fact that has been discussed by critics of cyber literature. It is also to be further reviewed and written into the history of cyber literary criticism.

Academic Achievements in Cyber Literary Studies

The mainstays of cyber literary criticism, as historical materials that accumulate over time, are academic achievements. At a theoretical level, they give us an overview of critics' practices and thoughts and allow us to see how such thoughts were developed in the process of criticism. A review of academic achievements can also allow us to examine how effective and valuable literary criticism is. If cyber literary criticism is founded on the study of cyberwriting, then the history of cyber literary criticism should be based on the study of such academic achievements, as they are the very "facts" that need to be recorded in history. Since the 1990s, when cyber literature in mandarin Chinese started to develop, cyber literature and its criticism on the Internet have always been closely associated with each other. The literary commentaries posted on the Internet have been powerfully influencing the writing and reading of cyber literature, as well as people's views as to what is good literature and their interactions with writers accordingly. Meanwhile, scholars and media workers have also actively written on cyber literature and published a huge volume of works in print media, such as newspapers.

A Historical Review of Academic Achievements in China's Cyber Literary Studies

Using three sources, including the databases offered by China National Knowledge Infrastructure (CNKI), Cyber Literary Research Archive (Wangluo wenxue wenxian shujuku), and *A General Survey of Cyber Literature Across Five Years (2009–2013)* (Wangluo wenxue wunian pucha erlinglingjiu-erlingyisan), I checked and sorted academic achievements and worked out some statistics to reflect the current status of cyber literary criticism in China.[9]

First, let us look at an overview of the condition of related academic achievements on CNKI (see Table 0.1).

CNKI is the largest database of academic publications in China today. It contains articles in academic journals, selected doctoral dissertations and masters' theses, articles in important newspapers, articles from important

Table 0.1 Search results on CNKI, for papers on cyber literary criticism, on March 2, 2016

Keywords searched for from all contents	Number of articles	Keywords searched for from article titles	Number of articles
"research on cyber literature" (wangluo wenxue yanjiu)	11,389	"cyber literature" (wangluo wenxue)	573,929
"criticism of cyber literature" (wangluo wenxue piping)	4,733	"cyber literature and traditional literature" (wangluo wenxue yu chuantong wenxue)	435,506
"commentary on cyber literature" (wangluo wenxue pinglun)	4,089	"publication of cyber literature" (wangluo wenxue chuban)	3,254
"development of cyber literature" (wangluo wenxue fazhan)	12,273	"industry of cyber literature" (wangluo wenxue chanye)	1,197
"language used in cyber literature" (wangluo wenxue yuyan)	5,834	"influence of cyber literature" (wangluo wenxue yingxiang)	2,919

conferences, yearbooks, and other reference books. It is the infrastructure that provides databases covering a wide range of materials and the search results it gives are quite reliable and authoritative. From the statistics provided above, we can see that the number of academic papers on "cyber literature" written in Chinese has reached 573,929, the number of papers on "criticism of cyber literature" is 4,733, and the number of papers on "commentary on cyber literature" is 4,089. This indicates that the academic research on cyber literature has been quite developed, and it deserves to be studied and reviewed as a historical issue.

Second, I developed the Cyber Literary Research Archive and some statistical information can be found there. The core contents of the archive are the three components as follows.

The first is the book *The Annals of Cyber Literature in China* (Zhongguo wangluo wenxue biannianshi), which records the development of cyber literature written in Chinese from 1991 to 2013, organized by date, month, and year, including important events, people, works, and keywords.[10] To date, it is the work that preserves the most complete and original materials, including a large number of critical texts and discussions on cyber literature.

The second component is the book entitled *A Dictionary of Words about Cyber Literature* (Wangluo wenxue cidian), which is a collection of 1,177 entries about cyber literature, including terms of the Internet, concepts of cyber literature, literary websites, cyber writers (as individuals and groups), computer applications for cyberwriting, literary works and genres, language styles in cyber literature, the industry of cyber literature, academic research on cyber literature, events concerning cyber literature, and yearly buzzwords on the Internet.[11] There is a phonetic index of these entries at the end, which makes it convenient for readers to search. This dictionary includes 13 entries for research institutions, 14 for scholars of cyber literature, 74 for books of cyber literary criticism, 11 for doctoral dissertations, 150 for masters' theses, 500 for newspaper articles, and 280 for cyber literary works.

The third component is the book entitled *Collected Entries of Major Academic Publications on Cyber Literature* (Wangluo wenxue yanjiu chengguo jicheng).[12] It collects entries of important academic publications since the birth of cyber literature, including 908 journal articles, 1,035 newspaper articles, 229 doctoral dissertations and master's theses, 143 conference papers, and 83 books. It also includes entries of 1,081 published works of cyber literature and 3,006 blog articles written by 67 cyber writers.

Apart from CNKI and the Cyber Literary Research Archive, there is another source of information—a book entitled *A General Survey of Cyber Literature Across Five Years: 2009–2013*.[13] This survey, which took one year, was conducted by the research team of cyber literary studies at Central South University. This survey gives a comprehensive overview of the development of China's cyber literature from 2009 to 2013. As the Internet media developed at an unimaginable speed and as a huge volume of information was incessantly circulated on the Internet, it is significant to draw a clear picture of the

Introduction 11

condition of cyber literature and the trajectory of its development: this is a process of "recording history" as it clarifies historical facts and keeps historical materials.

This book covers 16 topics, including literary websites, cyber writers, works of cyber literature, readership of cyber literature, language used in cyber literature, theoretical discussions on cyber literature, the influence of cyber literature, the interaction between cyber literature and traditional literature, the development of cyber literature as an industry, blog/microblog/WeChat literature, online videos and short films, TV and film adaptations from web novels, cyber literature by ethnic minority writers, cyber literature by female writers, cyber literature for children, and cyber literature in foreign languages. It offers a faithful and comprehensive record of the precious historical materials to illustrate how cyber literature has become a spectacular cultural phenomenon.

The sixth chapter of this book, entitled "Cyber Literary Criticism," gives us statistics of academic articles, books, research projects (sponsored by governments of different levels), and research awards, as well as lists of representative works of cyber literary criticism.[14] According to the statistics, from January 2009 to December 2013, 856 journal articles were published, and 179 doctoral dissertations and master's theses were finished. During these 5 years, 59 books were published (10 in 2009, 12 in 2010, 25 in 2011, 8 in 2012, and 4 in 2013), covering a wide range of popular issues concerning cyber literature as follows: 1. theories, criticism, and appreciation of cyber literature; 2. the reading, writing, and teaching of cyber literature; 3. the industry and values of cyber literature; 4. the art of new media and digital technology, and the culture of cyberspace. They are textbooks, monographs, collections of academic papers, collections of public speeches, books about the history of literary theories, and dictionaries.

During these 5 years, research projects on cyber literature were sponsored by the National Social Science Fund, the Ministry of Education, and provincial governments. Among them, one project started to receive support from the National Social Science Fund in 2009, 7 in 2010, 3 in 2011, 3 in 2012, and 8 in 2013. Apart from these, 10 research achievements in cyber literature received awards as "excellent research achievements" on the national and provincial levels. This survey, in the form of a book, also lists 20 incidents from 2009 to 2013 as "important incidents about cyber literary criticism."

This survey indicates a trend that cyber literary research and criticism increase over time, and that such research and criticism are no longer limited to the study of writers and works of cyber literature but gradually become more systematic, specific, and diversified. More and more experts, scholars, and professors got involved in cyber literary criticism; many graduate students wrote dissertations and theses on cyber literature. Overall, there is a growing number of people who are engaged in cyber literary research and criticism.

Meanwhile, there is an increasing amount of articles on cyber literature being published in academic journals on literature and art, such as *Literary Review* (Wenxue pinglun), *Literature and Art Studies* (Wenyi yanjiu), *Theoretical*

Studies in Literature and Art (Wenyi lilun yanjiu), *Literature and Art Contention* (Wenyi zhengming), *Contemporary Writers Review* (Dangdai zuojia pinglun), and *Novel Review* (Xiaoshuo pinglun), and in important generalist journals in the field of social sciences, such as *Social Sciences in China* (Zhongguo shehui kexue), *Academic Monthly* (Xueshu yuekan), and *Social Science Front* (Shehui kexue zhanxian).

We can see that although China's cyber literary criticism is generally in its early stage of development, there is already a complete team of scholars studying a wide spectrum of issues and a huge volume of academic resources and materials in a variety of forms covering various questions, which altogether demonstrate the vitality and sharpness of scholars' thoughts, along with frequent critical activities that exert a far-reaching influence on society. Based on all this, we can argue that writing a history for cyber literary criticism is necessary not only as an act to preserve historical materials but also as an act to help cyber literature better develop itself.

The Ecology of Cyber Literary Criticism

Based on our review of academic achievements in recent years, we can see the "ecology"—the condition and development—of cyber literary criticism in China.

Unlike traditional literary criticism, which is mainly practiced by professional critics and scholars, cyber literary criticism involves three groups of people: netizens who write commentaries on the Internet, media workers who write critical articles for the market, and professional critics and scholars. Among them, netizens' commentaries are the most dynamic: netizens form the broad audience who read works of cyber literature immediately after they are posted; they freely express their thoughts about these works in forums and other online communities; this creates an effect of "heteroglossia" as their critical voices are all mixed up in cyberspace as a public sphere. Netizens, as readers, can leave a few characters, such as "good" and "bump (the thread)," or emojis/emoticons/pictures, as quick and straightforward responses to what they have just read, while writers can also reply to such short comments. Many websites have systems to help them quickly access readers' responses: for example, they let readers click buttons to recommend, save, rate, or give monetary rewards to certain works. Apart from this, there are book rankings of various kinds, such as those for books recommended by most readers, books that are the most popular among VIP readers, books that have received the most reviews, and books that have received the most "votes" from readers. This can also be deemed a means to evaluate books online. Of course, there are also spam posts for commercial purposes. As cyberspace is open to everyone, people can freely and honestly complain about what they read without the need to consider others' feelings or follow any strict rules. Yet, sometimes netizens' remarks are so subjective that they become unfounded and unfair.

The second group of critics are media workers, including journalists, editors, writers, and other cultural celebrities, who write for the market. They are good at exploring the phenomena of cyber literature that can be valuable for reportage. Sometimes they hype up a particular issue and make the whole society pay attention to it. A series of events were hotly discussed online in the past decades, including the controversy over Mu Zimei's diary, the controversy over Zhao Lihua's poems, the debate between Han Han and Bai Ye, and the sudden success of Yu Qiuhua's poetry.[15] All these issues make us see how media workers as literary critics can be quite powerful in leading the public opinion about issues concerning cyber literature.

The third group of critics—professional critics and scholars—are well-trained academically. They are good at using theoretical reasoning to analyze cyber literature, and their works are often seen in academic journals, books, conferences, and seminars. However, they are restrained by the academic system and limited by their academic training. They usually use traditional ways to discuss cyber literature, focusing more on the theoretical part than on the specific cyberwriting. In this sense, their works sometimes keep a certain distance away from the actual practice of literary creation.

In recent years, works of cyber literary criticism have been increasing in number and circulating in multiple ways. Take research articles published in academic journals as an example: according to *Collected Entries of Major Academic Publications on Cyber Literature*, there were nine academic articles on cyber literature published in 2000, 32 in 2001, 48 in 2002, 31 in 2003, 42 in 2004, 25 in 2005, 41 in 2006, 42 in 2007, 79 in 2008, 109 in 2009, 54 in 2010, 160 in 2011, 144 in 2012, and 75 in 2013. We can clearly see the trend that the number increased every year.[16] According to Cyber Literary Research Archive (Wangluo wenxue wenxian shujuku) and *A General Survey of Cyber Literature Across Five Years (2009–2013)*, academic books, newspaper articles, master's theses, and doctoral dissertations that discuss cyber literature have all consistently increased in recent years.

This well indicates that cyber literary studies, just like cyber literature, now prosper and flourish; scholars constantly push forward the conceptual transformation and theoretical construction in this field. Meanwhile, compared with traditional literary criticism that is only to be read in print media, cyber literary criticism can take on various forms and be disseminated through various channels. As we can see, apart from print media (such as journals, newspapers, and books) and TV/radio broadcasts, there are Internet media, especially "we media" (blogs, microblogs, and WeChat), which are faster and more dynamic. Moreover, new media allows information to be transmitted in multiple directions, thus making it possible for people to have "two-way" communication connecting "one to one," "one to many," and "many to one." This significantly alters the unidirectional communication via traditional media. Particularly, critics can interact with each other and give prompt feedback to writers, which makes their criticism practical and relevant to cyberwriting.

Moreover, critics have been exploring how to establish a system of criteria for evaluating cyber literary works. This has become a hotspot in cyber literary studies and is of the greatest academic value. We need to have a set of criteria that are suitable for our study of both the "cyber" and the "literary" aspects of cyber literature. Although cyber literature has a short history and its criticism has just started, there are already many scholars who have done excellent research on the evaluation criteria.

Some scholars responded to the question of how to construct the system of evaluation criteria academically. Wang Guoping pointed out:

> As we discuss cyber literary works, we should stick to the study of its literariness while paying particular attention to its unique characteristics. We should seek and examine the differences between cyber literature and traditional literature. After writing on and discussing cyber literature for a long time, we will gradually form a system for aesthetically evaluating cyber literary works. That system will suit the actual condition of cyber writing and reading and reflect the unique characteristics of such activities.[17]

In an article, I also discussed the uniqueness of cyber literary criticism through a comparison between cyber literature and traditional literature. I summarized the characteristics of cyber literature as follows: "writers are also netizens"; "literary creation is done through interaction"; "literary texts are in digital forms"; "works are circulated online"; "readers read on computers and other electronic devices."[18] Moreover, I also discussed some relevant issues, such as cyber literature's mode of existence and mechanism of writing, and how the changes in the ideas of literature have an impact on the evaluation criteria.

As I searched, the earliest article proposing a set of evaluation criteria for cyber literature is Chen Qirong's "A Call for the Establishment of an Evaluation System for Cyber Literature" published in *People's Daily* in 2013.[19] In the article, the author articulated: "Although there might be various criteria, two of them were the most important: they were 'the ideological value and the aesthetic value' of cyber literature."[20] As to the ideological value, he pointed out: "Cyber literature should first and foremost serve the people. At the ideological level, it should actively shoulder the responsibility for the country and the nation."[21] As to the aesthetic value, he proposed: "Cyber writers should have an elegant and fine aesthetic taste. They should have a feeling of awe toward literature and an ambition to create excellent works in cyberspace."[22]

The theorization of cyber literature is a historical process that takes a long time and requires many scholars' collective efforts. While such a process is like a road with no end, every academic work serves as a road sign, marking the accumulation and development of critical thoughts in history. Today, people have expressed different ideas, but they have not yet reached a consensus as to what criteria we should use for evaluating cyber literature. Nevertheless, their discussions are academically valuable as they lay the foundation of the system of criteria that will eventually be established.

The History of Cyber Literary Criticism and Its Theoretical Discussions

To write a history of cyber literary criticism, we need to not only cover the historical facts, but also give interpretations of such facts, particularly focusing on the interaction between literature, media, and society in recent history. There are various ways to do so: we can sort out critical articles on writers and works, examine events of literary criticism in chronological order, and study the changes in the concept and theory of literature; we may also use the ideas of modernity to interpret the historical development of literature, just like what Kang-i Sun Chang and Stephen Owen did in *The Cambridge History of Chinese Literature*. In *Theory of Literature*, René Wellek and Austin Warren discussed whether it would be possible to write a book that is both about literary history and literary criticism. They argued that to write a book of literary history, the writer should have adequate knowledge of literary criticism: "The whole supposed immunity of the literary historian to criticism and theory is thoroughly false.... 'The literary historian must be a critic even in order to be a historian.'"[23] Meanwhile, they also argued: "Conversely, literary history is also highly important for literary criticism as soon as the latter goes beyond the most subjective pronouncement of likes and dislikes. A critic who is content to be ignorant of all historical relationships would constantly go astray in his judgments."[24] Then, how shall we grasp the progress of cyber literary criticism and use a conceptual framework to write a history of it?

As cyber literature has neither a long history nor a rich and organized archive of critical texts, we can only tentatively use "historical facts" and "theoretical discussions" as the two dimensions to represent both the practice of cyber literary criticism and the progress in the theorization of cyber literature. The whole book will be divided in this way: the first five chapters discuss "historical facts," while the remaining five chapters give "theoretical discussions."

Representation of the History

We shall first give a diachronic representation of the development of cyber literary criticism. In other words, we need to give a historical account of the past and the present of cyber literary criticism, focusing on a few issues that are particularly important in this process. Such issues also correspond with the first five chapters of this book, and the outlines of these chapters are as follows.

New Media and the Evolution of Literary Criticism in Cyberspace

Both the history of literature and the history of literary criticism are closely associated with the changes in media. This is true of cyber literary criticism because its evolution—from its appearance to all events that happened thereafter—is based on the use of Internet media and digital technology. Cyber literary criticism can thus be seen as a cultural byproduct of the new media. Tan Dejing discussed this issue:

> What role does the Internet play in its interaction with literature and literary criticism? What characteristics does it have? We have to make clear these issues before we can adequately study cyber literature and its criticism. The best way to do so is to use a comparative perspective to look into history. By examining the historical changes in media and its relationship with literature and literary criticism, we can clarify the great significance of "media," or "media platform," to literature and criticism and understand how the Internet is particularly important to today's literature and criticism.[25]

The importance of media changes to literature and criticism has been well confirmed in literary history. In ancient times, literature was initially written on bamboo slips and engraved on metals and stones. Later, there came the "movable type" as a technology of printing. In the past few decades, there was "laser phototypesetting." In different historical periods, there were different ideas of literature, and scholars discussed literary works in different ways.

However, in the past, whether carved on animal bones and turtle shells, engraved on bronze bells and cauldrons, brushed on bamboo slips and silk pieces, written on paper, or printed with the use of laser phototypesetting, the words of literary criticism were accessible only to a limited number of people and were belated as responses to literature. Today, as information is transmitted via digital media, the situation is different. As Tan Dejing pointed out, "in the age of digital media, the so-called 'criticism' is always exerting its influence on our reading and even our literary tastes," and the Internet brought a high degree of freedom and "allowed literature and its criticism to enter into a completely new stage of development."[26]

Internet technology directly influences cyber literature and becomes an integral part of it. It also completely renews the media to change the way of writing, publishing, and reviewing. As people's relationship with literature is changed, their aesthetic experience of the world is changed as well. Therefore, we should view the evolution of cyber literary criticism from the perspective of media changes. Three basic issues should be clarified: first, the birth of cyber literature and cyber literary criticism, including the rise of we-media literary criticism; second, the changes and developments embodied by cyber literary criticism as compared with traditional literary criticism; third, the significance and contribution of cyber literary criticism to the general development of literary theories. By studying these issues, we will see how the new media, as new platforms and channels based on digital technology, takes the historical responsibility to serve literary criticism while changing its traditions and norms.

Major Types of Cyber Literary Criticism

In the Internet era, changes happen to the identities of literary critics. There are mainly three groups of them in the field of cyber literary criticism. First, some professional critics, especially those who pay attention to the development of literature and like to comment on current issues, have now started to study cyber literature. As academics and professionals, they promptly change their focus and have the acumen to express thoughts on literature in the new media. They form the most "orthodox" school among all critics of cyber literature.

Another group of critics is media workers who write for the market, including journalists, editors, writers, and other cultural celebrities who pay attention to cybermedia. They are good at discovering works, writers, and phenomena of cyber literature that can be valuable for reportage. Sometimes they hype up a particular issue and make the whole society pay attention to it.

Netizens can also write as critics. They write a wide variety of words that can be viewed as literary criticism, including short comments as expressions of personal thoughts, words that manifest fans' craze for some works, spam posts posted in forums to flood screens, brief messages on literature to exchange thoughts and make friends, appreciative articles that dissect specific works, and promotional writings for commercial purposes.

These three groups of critics have their strengths and weaknesses in their writings of literary criticism. While separate from each other, they work in the same direction to develop a variety of forms and contents for cyber literary criticism. Among them, professional critics are well-trained academically. Some of them have rich experience in research or even have good publications. Academically speaking, their works are the mainstays of cyber literary criticism. Nevertheless, they are restrained by the academic system (e.g., universities may only recognize articles of certain lengths and in certain journals as valid contributions) and limited by their academic way of thinking and writing. They usually use traditional ways to discuss cyber literature, focusing more on the theoretical part than on the specific cyberwriting. They are keen on getting to the "logical essence" of the issue and constructing theories to explain it. In other words, they seek to discover the universal law behind certain literary phenomena. Yet, they do not pay much attention to specific writers, works, and literary phenomena: they either do not talk much about them or remain quite insensitive when discussing them, which makes us feel that they always keep a certain distance away from the actual practice of cyberwriting. Their critical works, therefore, are neither valued by other academics nor cared about by cyber writers.

Media workers as the second type of critic report or comment on incidents about cyber literature. They usually take advantage of the mass media to grasp discursive power in the current cultural sphere. With a wide readership and the authority of the media, they define certain phenomena in cyber literature, pass value judgments on them from the position of mainstream culture, or write critically on them, so as to guide public opinion. These critics are keen on discussing social problems with a strong sense of responsibility. They use clear words to dissect and critique the real conditions and use pertinent language to offer solutions to problems in cyber literature. Nevertheless, if they just give critiques from the perspective of media workers or focus merely on the media that carries literature, then they will be too rash and superficial and unable to go deeper into the issues. Media workers are not good at using theories to help their reasoning. Meanwhile, they have to work for profit and conveniently hype up some issues to better market their writings. Their words may be unfair and inappropriate, unable to give a clear and reasonable evaluation of literary works. Sometimes they may even misguide cyber literature and its readers.

Netizens' comments on cyber literature can best represent the characteristics of cyber literary criticism. This means the online interaction between netizens and authors and among netizens themselves, which is best seen in online forums. Cyberspace allows people to "push" information to others and "draw" information from them. Here, everyone can open a column and write interesting and sometimes strange words to impress readers and to show their unique personalities. People can write whatever they like to comment on whatever they read. There is no need to care about the form, style, and meaning of their expressions. There is no need to consider other people's feelings either. Netizens can write casual words, sometimes just for fun, sometimes to express their thoughts, sometimes to show their disagreement with the works they read, and sometimes even to attack writers personally.

Academic Achievements in Cyber Literary Studies

Academic publications are embodiments of scholars' theoretical discussions and critical thoughts. To be published, articles and books have to be effective and valuable as literary criticism. Thus, they constitute the mainstays of cyber literary criticism as historical materials. Although there are fewer publications on cyber literature than on traditional literature, there are still a considerable number of them. They are often seen in academic journals, books, newspapers, online media, conferences, and seminars. They can be articles, books (including edited collections and translations), postgraduate theses and dissertations, conference papers, and online reviews. Journal articles constitute the bulk of these works. They represent the best contributions to academic studies in this field and are also the most influential. From the 1990s on, there are thousands of them, covering a wide range of topics, including the current status and problems of cyber literary criticism, the importance and necessity to write cyber literary criticism, the characteristics and values of cyber literary criticism, the system of criteria for evaluating cyber literature, the study of critics and their identities, and analyses and reviews of particular websites, writers, works, and phenomena of cyber literature.

In these works, scholars gave theoretical analyses of cyber literature. Some of them are keen to blaze the trail and lead the way in the field of cyber literary studies. Others, however, simply use traditional theoretical frameworks to study cyber literature. In this sense, their discussions cannot keep up with the times. They may have a condescending attitude toward cyber literature or have limited means to address the real issues. What can make up for such a shortcoming are netizens' commentaries posted in forums and in "we media": this is cyber literary criticism in its narrow sense and can also be called "online literary criticism."

The Forms, Contents, and Rhetorical Expressions of Netizens' Critical Commentaries

While academic publications on cyber literature most exist as hard copies, here netizens' critical commentaries exist in electronic forms in cyberspace. We can see the three differences between these two types of cyber literary criticism: their modes of existence, textual forms, and rhetorical expressions.

In terms of the mode of existence, online criticism can be further divided into three types: "texts that are fragmentary," "texts that are interactive," and "commentaries in the form of monologues." The first type—fragmentary texts written by netizens to give their responses to cyberwriting—is the most common. Such texts tend to discuss specific works. They are concise, straightforward, and unrestrained. With just a few words they can accurately hit the targets. By joking, laughing, and cursing, netizens can be blunt enough to let cyber writers feel either embarrassed or enlightened and to make other readers feel amused. The weakness, however, lies in that these netizens do not have deep thoughts and analyses based on a knowledge of literary theories. Rather, they often write casually without a good sense of responsibility.

The second type—"texts that are interactive"—refers to posts in forums and discussion sections on certain web pages that serve as a means of communication for readers and writers to share their views of certain works or literary phenomena. These texts are of the greatest vitality among all texts of cyber literary criticism, as they allow people to come together and directly exchange thoughts.

The third type is "commentaries in the form of monologues." There are review articles (such as blog posts) by professional critics. While relatively long and well-reasoned, they also highlight critics' personalities. There are also well-written commentaries (such as messages posted on microblogs and WeChat, or delivered via e-mails) by netizens. They directly address concrete issues and fully express netizens' opinions, thus being quite effective as cyber literary criticism.

Netizens' critical commentaries often break the conventions and go "beyond paradigms." In terms of content, they can also be divided into several types. First, there are commentaries discussing netizens' direct experiences of the essence of literature. A netizen who delves deep into a story may be able to share his/her personal feelings and understanding of various aspects of a story, including characterization, representation of characters' life, plot, tension, narrative style, and language use. Second, there are commentaries as netizens' casual and unrestrained discussions. They correspond to the fragmentary texts of criticism, which we just mentioned in this section. A commentary of this kind is usually short, with just a few sentences. Third, there are subversive commentaries that break rules and traditions. They assert values and morals that are unconventional and highly personal and deconstruct what has been viewed as sublime and authoritative. Netizens who write these types of commentaries tend to take the stance of postmodernists: they embrace typical postmodern ideas such as "depthlessness," "loss of historicity," "death of the subject," and "abolition of critical distance."[27] Their words are thus superficial and fragmentary. Sometimes they even use spoofing as a way to mock certain literary works and subvert their intended meanings.

As to the language style, there are a few rhetorical strategies to facilitate netizens' freedom of expression. First, netizens use a massive volume of "netspeak" in their critical commentaries. "Martian language" (huoxing wen) is a unique system of characters and symbols used by young netizens. These characters may look childish, fanciful, absurd, and hard to read, but they also make online communication more interesting and can help netizens better express their unique personalities. As a kind of youth subculture, "Martian language" also allows young netizens to have a sense of belonging in terms of culture and language.

Second, netizens use colloquial and vernacular expressions to express their views of certain works. Such a style makes netizens look approachable, unaffected, amiable, and even humorous. It is often seen in forums as dialogues between netizens.

Third, some netizens use vulgar words as a language strategy to convey their thoughts and feelings. As an embodiment of the wisdom in folk culture, vulgar words gradually become an important phenomenon as they are now widely used in cyberwriting and its criticism. Specifically, netizens use slang words and vulgar expressions to deconstruct the sublime, subvert the sacred, despise the authoritative, scorn the grand narrative, and dispel the idea of hierarchy. As I discussed in an article, netizens use vulgar words to "worship the commonplace while dragging down those who are above us, directly touch people's hearts while not hiding desires, straightforwardly express unique personalities instead of being pretentious and affected, freely spread personal feelings rather than use reason to strangle feelings."[28] This is true for both cyber literature and its criticism.

Fourth, netizens use "netspeak" widely in their critical commentaries, including popular buzzwords and language styles. Examples of buzzwords are "give power" (geili, meaning "excellent"), "you know" (nidongde, meaning "I cannot say it, but you know what I mean"), "the gods and horses are all floating clouds" (shenma doushi fuyun, meaning "everything will be alright"), "sell cute" (maimeng, meaning "perform as cute"), "spit complaints" (tucao, meaning "to complain"), and "you are cheating me, your dad" (kengdie, often meaning "you must be kidding"). As to language styles, examples include

"Taobao style" (taobao ti), "roaring style" (paoxiao ti), "harem style" (hougong ti), and "story for dummies" (xiaobai wen). The use of such netspeak makes netizens' commentaries stylistically close to the literary texts under review and can well manifest the linguistic characteristics of today's online literary criticism.

Important Events in the History of Cyber Literary Criticism

As people are more attached to the Internet as a new media platform and as cyber literature is inherently interactive, netizens' critical views concerning cyber literature can draw a lot of public attention and become phenomenal incidents. The history of cyber literary criticism is filled with such incidents. From April 1991, when the first Chinese online magazine *China News Digest* (Huaxia wenzhai) was launched in North America, to December 2015, when the Cyber Literature Committee of China Writers Association (Zhongguo zuoxie wangluo wenxue weiyuanhui) was established, there were many incidents of cyber literature each year. Here are some examples:[29]

a. *The First Intimate Contact* (Diyici de qinmi jiechu) was hotly discussed online after its publication in 1998.
b. *Outside the City* (Chengwai), the first short story to be read on cellphones, attracted a lot of attention and stirred up some debates after its publication in 2004.
c. The first series of books on cyber literary studies—"Professors' Discussions on Cyber Literature" (Wangluo wenxue jiaoshou luncong)—was published in 2004.
d. Zhao Lihua's poetry in "pearl flower style" (lihua ti) was spoofed by netizens in 2006.
e. Professional critics questioned cyber literature and gave it negative reviews, such as Tao Dongfeng's critique of fantasy novels in 2006.
f. The famous work *Stories of the Ming Dynasty* (Mingchao naxie shi'er) caused some controversies after its publication in 2006.
g. Han Han and Bai Ye had an intense debate as to whether the "post-80s generation" writers could write good literature, which happened in 2006.
h. The "Review of Cyber Literature in the Past Ten Years" (Wangluo wenxue shinian pandian) was launched in 2008.
i. The first seminar on cyber literature was held in Beijing in 2012.
j. The academic journal *Internet Literature Review* (Wangluo wenxue pinglun) was established in 2016.

As we study such events' historical significance, there are two things to be done. First, we should analyze their status and value in contemporary cultural ecology. Second, we need to clarify their significance to contemporary literary criticism.

We should put such events of cyber literature into the social and cultural context so as to have a better understanding of them: we need to consider the market economy, mass consumption, the rise of cultural studies, and the strong power of new media. The transition from planned economy to market economy, fully launched in the 1990s, not only liberates the productive forces but also greatly liberates people's minds and gives them new ways of thinking. It also allows them to enjoy more material wealth so that they can participate in mass consumption. Literature in the traditional sense, which used to be worshipped, has begun to lose its aura. Meanwhile, with the economic boom and increasing consumption of cultural commodities, people's daily life has become more filled with aesthetic experiences. As a result, the "marriage" between literature and the Internet not only leads to the rapid development of cyber literature but also gives netizens a perfect media platform to freely express themselves. As we can see, behind every event of cyber literature there is a collaboration between economy, culture, and digital media. In other words, these events are echoes of the spirit of the times: they are shaping and shaped by the contemporary cultural ecology at the same time. Because of these events, people get to know how vital and powerful cyber literature, cyberculture, and cyber media can be, and what role cyber literary criticism can play in contemporary cultural ecology.

Meanwhile, we need to consider how these events contribute to the development of contemporary literary criticism. These events demonstrate how literary criticism can be critical and personal, thus being able to redress and remedy the kind of traditional literary criticism that is too bland: some professional critics tend to rigidly follow fixed patterns to formulate their articles; they do not present a sharp critique of literary works, but write in a mild and pragmatic way; as they blindly praise some literary works, they try to maintain their good relationships with a circle of writers and critics as their friends. Critical articles of this kind are just like clouds drifting across the sky. They cast shadows on the ground but do not help the field of literature thrive. Sometimes they may even affect the growth of literature.

Nevertheless, the aforementioned events of cyber literature also have their negative aspects. For example, many of them just aim to hype up writers and works, so they stir up people's emotions without giving them a chance to do serious thinking. In this sense, they draw many "onlookers" but do not actually give a proper critique of literary works. Sometimes, such events are well packaged and pushed to the front by companies and cultural brokers to make profits. Thus, they can harm cyber literary criticism.

A Review of the Theoretical Discussions

As we study cyber literary criticism, we should not only observe its historical development but also evaluate and analyze the changing ideas of literary criticism that underlie such a historical process so as to establish a basis for further theorizing about the historical facts and make clear the significance of such a history. Such changing ideas can be seen in various aspects of cyber literary criticism, which will be discussed respectively in the second five chapters of this book. The outlines of these chapters are as follows.

The Conceptual Transformation in Literary Criticism in the Internet Era

First, we need to examine how people's ideas of literature changed in the Internet era. According to the famous ancient literary scholar Liu Xie (ca. 465–520), "if it [i.e., literature] changes, it will endure; if it adapts itself to the changing tide, it will lack nothing."[30] Cyber literary criticism inherits ideas of literature from traditional literary criticism in history and further develops such ideas—this signifies a spirit of change and creativity. As literary criticism must adapt to the development of literature, our observation should start from the "evolution" of ideas in the field of cyber literature. Cyber literature has a series of new characteristics: everyone now can write with a high degree of freedom to create works with multiple meanings; they do not follow fixed patterns and rules and tend to avoid the traditional literary idealism that writers must pursue "grand narrative," "truth," and "essence" in their writings; readers' reading experience has become fragmentary yet immersive, and it has become a mass consumption of cultural commodities. All these conditions make writers lose their subjectivity: they no longer make efforts to meticulously design their works; instead, they write more casually and carelessly. Meanwhile, the boundary between literature and non-literature begins to be blurred. Zhao Xianzhang discussed this issue in an article: "Cyberwriting has already entered into our daily life as a new form of writing activity. Such a new form fundamentally differs from traditional writing not only in its technical aspects but also in its ideological aspects. The traditional way of writing cannot compete with it, as its circulation is much faster and wider and its social influence is much stronger."[31]

In the face of these changes, critics must adjust and adapt their ideas of literature. They need to review their positions in relation to the past and the future, so as to decide which ideas in the literary tradition should be kept, modified, suspended, transcended, or even subverted respectively. In recent years, many scholars have already made efforts to do research in this field.

Based on such an understanding of the changing ideas of literature, we also need to further clarify the cultural factors and the important notions of cyber literary criticism. First, we need to pay attention to a series of cultural factors, including media convergence, postmodern culture, aesthetic turn, and the creation of hypertexts. We also need to pay attention to a series of important notions related to cyber literary studies, such as "intersubjectivity," "worship of the mediocre," "the blasphemous tendency," "the parody of classics," "the use of vulgar words," "the spread of feelings," "spoofing," "disenchantment," "posts in forums," and "virtual persona." These factors and notions are the building blocks that we use to construct a conceptual system that guides our cyber literary criticism.[32]

On top of all this, we also need to build up a new theoretical framework to further guide our study of cyber literature. A series of issues have been studied by scholars and need to be further sorted out, including the system of criteria for evaluating cyber literature, the cultural identities of critics, the humanistic positions critics should hold, the new forms of critical texts, the new ways critical texts function, and the significance and value of literary criticism. The creation of a new theoretical framework for cyber literary studies should be revolutionary, and it should be based on a good understanding of digital technologies and Internet media as the context.

The Establishment of Evaluation Criteria for Cyber Literature

Cyber literature has a short history and scholars have just started to study it. There has not been a new system of criteria that is comprehensive and authoritative enough for us to review cyber literary works. Some review articles do not give adequate analyses of the characteristics of cyberwriting and do not present reviews of specific cyber literary works (as there are a massive number of them). Particularly, scholars' academic writings are often not pertinent enough to the actual condition of cyberwriting. In other words, scholars discuss with each other in a small circle without paying attention to the outside world. This situation is well described in an article as follows:

> Many scholars are detached from the actual condition of cyberwriting. Most of them focus on the external factors that influence cyber literature and pay particular attention to the new revolution in media as an issue in communication studies. These scholars obviously do not have a good knowledge of literary theories and lack the ability to give an in-depth analysis of the complex and changing conditions of cyberwriting. Their understanding of the ecology and mechanism of cyber literature is far from sufficient. Their study and criticism of cyber literature thus only circulate among themselves and can hardly be recognized in the broader society of writers, editors, and readers in cyberspace.[33]

Such a review of the condition is objective. Despite this, there are still many scholars who have made efforts to establish a set of criteria for the review of cyber literature. Some of them consciously or unconsciously use some criteria to guide their writing of cyber literary criticism. Their theoretical discussions mainly focus on three issues as follows.

The first is the necessity and possibility of the construction of the evaluation criteria. Cyber literature is booming, but many shoddy works are coming out. To study such a situation, scholars need to develop theories and intervene in cyberwriting through criticism. Scholars such as Huang Mingfen, Ouyang Youquan, Liu Lili, Wang Yichuan, Chen Dingjia, Shao Yanjun, and Yu Jianxiang have published papers to discuss this issue.

The second is the multi-dimensionality of the evaluation criteria. Critics should not only pay attention to the "literary" aspects of cyber literature but also consider its "cyber" aspects. They should not only recognize cyber literature as a new way of entertainment for mass consumption but also keep an eye on its intellectual, artistic, and aesthetic qualities.

A single criterion cannot suit the characteristics and the actual condition of cyber literature, thus being insufficient to guide our literary studies. Instead, there should be a multiplicity of criteria, and they should be more than the old ones used for traditional literature. For example, there should be new criteria focusing on technology and media, user-stickiness, click-through rate, and requirements of commercialization. Nevertheless, as we use these criteria to examine literature, there is still something quintessential to all kinds of literature and not to be altered: Zhang Kangkang called it "literary elements, such as emotion, imagination, moral sense, and language,"[34] while Wang Yichuan called it "experience, imagination, talent, and what is based on all of these—creativity."[35] These are the dimensions we need to pay particular attention to while considering the multiplicity of criteria for the evaluation of cyber literature.

Third, critics should directly answer the question "what evaluation criteria do we need for cyber literature?" and develop their own value judgments. Many scholars proposed their thoughts concerning this issue. For example, Kang Qiao argued that we should review cyber literature by evaluating readers' "reading pleasure and aesthetic experience" because "reading pleasure and aesthetic experience are people's basic needs and should be the basis on which cyber literature develops."[36] According to him, this is the evaluation criterion that suits "cyber writers' literary obligation, writing practice, and readers' expectation."

For another example, Shao Yanjun proposed that we should consider the "cyber" aspects of cyber literature because "the Internet is not just a platform for publishing literature—it is also a space of cultural production."[37] Based on this, Shao further argued that we need to pay attention to three elements: hypertext, fan economy, and the cultural connections between animation, comics, and games. Chen Guoxiong, another scholar, pointed out that we should consider the fact that cyber writers enjoy a high degree of freedom and equality and that cyberspace provides a virtual world in which different voices are allowed. In this sense, we should build "a discourse of universal ethics" in cyber literary criticism.[38] Until today, although scholars have not yet reached a consensus about the evaluation criteria, their theoretical discussions undoubtedly have made great trailblazing contributions to the eventual formation of a system of criteria.

Changes in the Function of Cyber Literary Criticism

As we know, literary criticism can inspire writers, guide readers, facilitate the construction of literary theories, interpret literary phenomena, respond to questions about literature, and build up an environment for people to write and read literature. Cyber literary criticism should and can function as such. Meanwhile, it also extends and alters some of these functions.

First, cyber literature allows people to share the right to literary criticism and subvert the old hierarchy. For a long time, the right to literary criticism has been held by a few intellectuals as the cultural elite. Such critics use a set of criteria that has been widely recognized by academia to review literature. Literary criticism thus has to follow a set of rules and traditions in terms of its academic approach and format. Articles use theories to reason and express ideas and are published in journals only after being reviewed by editors. However, cyber literary criticism subverts such a condition and breaks the monopoly of elite criticism by allowing ordinary people to participate in it. Ordinary netizens can now use various channels, including literary websites, web portals, blogs, microblogs, forums, social networks, and mobile apps, to post their literary commentaries. As a result, everyone can become a literary critic. Such words of netizens are colloquial and casual rather than serious and bookish. As it is so, they disenchant people from the myth that literature is "sacred." While writing such words, netizens stress the reading pleasure, the show of unique personalities, and their readers' emotional identification.

Second, cyber literary criticism has postmodern characteristics. It rejects discourses that stress the importance of "center" and "reason" and values a cultural context that allows a diversity of thoughts to coexist. Growing up in the cradle of postmodernism, cyber literature is remarkably postmodern in terms of its way of functioning. All kinds of critical words, including those based on personal reflections, those full of humor and exaggeration, and even those that are absurd and non-sensical, can be freely posted in cyberspace. As the Internet is a web of multiple centers and nodes and creates a tolerant environment that allows people to speak freely and equally, cyber literary criticism asserts ideas of "decentralization" and "cultural diversity."

Third, cyber literary criticism asserts new meanings and values. If traditional literary criticism aims to shape the collective consciousness, then cyber literary criticism pays more attention to individual preferences. It no longer stays at the level of abstract theories and thoughts based on reasoning but goes directly to discuss specific textual issues based on personal experiences. Cyber literary criticism also allows reviewers to remain anonymous and distant from their readers, so they do not need to be concerned about interpersonal relationships and personal interests. As a result, they are independent, honest, straightforward, and spontaneous, and they do not need to present positive images of themselves or unreasonably praise writers who are their friends.

In addition, online literary criticism is done by ordinary netizens instead of professional critics. As they are not public figures and lack social influence, they feel less pressure when expressing their opinions as long as they respect public order, custom, and morality. In this sense, they are more likely to express their thoughts in an unaffected manner and without reservation. Nevertheless, as cyberspace is tolerant of different points of view, there can be negative and mistaken ideas—even ideas that negate all values—that lead online literary criticism astray and weaken its validity.

Changes in the Constitution of Cyber Literary Critics

As mentioned, there are three groups of cyber literary critics: scholars, media workers, and netizens. While they are generally separated from and even opposed to each other, these three groups also overlap to some degree. As critics, they have different positions, values, and ways of writing. Scholars pay more attention to the theoretical analysis of literature, focusing on big issues and value judgments. Media workers stress the technological aspects of cyber literature in the context of the culture industry. They tend to write more about popular cultural phenomena so as to attract more readers, guide public opinion, and make profits. Netizens' literary commentaries generally manifest a diversity of thoughts and their individual tastes.

With the development of Internet technology, these three groups of critics also changed their ideas about literature and criticism. Before 2002, when most cyber writers did not write for profit, these three groups of critics, though distinct from each other, could still work in the same direction to express their ideas about cyber literature, making a cacophony of voices as if it was a carnival. Later, as cyber literature became rapidly commercialized, scholars became more obviously detached from actual cyberwriting, while critical commentaries written by netizens and media workers continued to thrive. This led to a new condition of cyber literary criticism. On the one hand, academic research on cyber literature has been furthered, and scholars are now studying various aspects of cyber literature. On the other hand, as microblogs and WeChat have more social influence, media workers' and netizens' online literary criticism takes on new and diverse forms.

At the same time, as portal websites and new media gradually replace the traditional media, and as big data, cloud computing, and "Internet plus" emerged one after another, the mass media in the new era almost all operate on the Internet: in a sense, critical articles in print media has gradually been replaced by articles and commentaries online. Correspondingly, the never-ending struggle for discursive power shifted its focus: before, it was mainly between scholars off the Internet and non-scholars on the Internet; now, it is mainly between netizens and media workers who work for literary websites and print media.

The Impact of Cyber Literary Criticism

The impact of cyber literary criticism has a few different aspects. First, there are collisions and collaborations between different groups of critics. This accelerated the public recognition of cyber literature as a new field of study. Second, cyber readers now become participants in cyber literary criticism. They are no longer passively "spectating" but are directly involved in the "carnivalesque" activities of cyber literary criticism with others, thus exerting a great influence on the cultural landscape. Third, the Internet, as a media platform with a huge social impact, has subverted and restructured the ecology of literary criticism. In cyberspace, discursive power is no longer centralized, and ordinary people have the right to write critical commentaries. Literary criticism as a field is thus reshaped.

This is further related to the significance and limitations of cyber literary criticism. On the positive side, authoritative scholars' monopoly on literary criticism is broken, and ordinary people have the chance to review literary works. But cyber literary criticism also has its limitations. First, cyberwriting subverts the traditional concept of literature and blurs the boundary between literature and non-literature and between different genres of literature. This makes the writing of literary criticism a more difficult task to do. Then, as ordinary netizens, scholars, and media workers have different positions and use different ways to review cyber literature, they do not have a consensus on what is good. People generally feel confused as there lacks a set of criteria to guide cyber literary criticism.

In addition, the impact of cyber literary criticism is also manifested in critics' attitudes toward literary classics. We know that literary classics are an important symbol of elite culture. They carry the mainstream ideology and embody the order of literary aesthetics. However, cyberculture breaks the old way of literary criticism and changes people's view of literary classics: it deconstructs what is deemed as authoritative and negates the spirit of humanism. As a result, netizens (as readers and critics) no longer acknowledge the cultural values and aesthetic tastes embodied by literary classics. Particularly, as businesses intervene in cyber literary criticism for profit, some individuals and companies work to "hype up" certain literary works, creating words about literary works that are essentially commercials rather than proper reviews. Literary classics—both as works and as a concept—sink into oblivion. This is how cyber literary criticism had a fundamentally negative influence on the value of literature.

Notes

1 Ouyang, Youquan 欧阳友权, "Chongxie wenxueshi yu wangluo wenxue 'rushi' wenti" 重写文学史与网络文学"入史"问题, *Hebei Academic Journal* 河北学刊 no. 5 (2013): 9.
2 René Wellek and Austin Warren, *Theory of Literature* (New York: Harcourt, Brace & World, 1956), 43.
3 Ouyang, Youquan 欧阳友权, "Yong wangluo dazao wenxue shiyi" 用网络打造文学诗意, *Literary Review* 文学评论 no.1 (2006): 194.
4 Ouyang, Ting 欧阳婷 and Ouyang, Youquan 欧阳友权, "Wangluo wenxue de tizhi puxixue fansi" 网络文学的体制谱系学反思, *Theoretical Studies in Literature and Art* 文艺理论研究 no. 1 (2014): 94.
5 Ouyang, Youquan 欧阳友权, "Wangluo wenxue ziyou benxing de xueli biaozheng" 网络文学自由本性的学理表征, *Criticism and Creation* 理论与创作 no. 5 (2003): 4.

6 Ouyang, Youquan 欧阳友权, "Chongxie wenxueshi yu wangluo wenxue 'rushi' wenti" 重写文学史与网络文学"入史"问题, 10.
7 Ouyang, Youquan 欧阳友权, "Chongxie wenxueshi yu wangluo wenxue 'rushi' wenti" 重写文学史与网络文学"入史"问题, 10.
8 Ouyang, Youquan 欧阳友权, "Chongxie wenxueshi yu wangluo wenxue 'rushi' wenti" 重写文学史与网络文学"入史"问题, 10.
9 Ouyang, Youquan 欧阳友权, *Wangluo wenxue wunian pucha (erlinglingjiu-erlingyisan)* 网络文学五年普查 (2009–2013) (Beijing: Central Compilation & Translation Press, 2014).
10 Ouyang, Youquan 欧阳友权, *Wangluo wenxue yanjiu chengguo jicheng* 网络文学研究成果集成 (Beijing: CFLAC Publishing House, 2015a).
11 Ouyang, Youquan 欧阳友权, *Wangluo wenxue cidian* 网络文学词典 (Beijing: World Publishing Corporation, 2012).
12 Ouyang, Youquan 欧阳友权, *Wangluo wenxue yanjiu chengguo jicheng* 网络文学研究成果集成 (Beijing: CFLAC Publishing House, 2015a).
13 Ouyang, Youquan 欧阳友权, *Wangluo wenxue wunian pucha (erlinglingjiu-erlingyisan)* 网络文学五年普查 (2009–2013).
14 All statistic numbers are from: Ouyang, Youquan 欧阳友权, *Wangluo wenxue wunian pucha (erlinglingjiu-erlingyisan)* 网络文学五年普查 (2009–2013), 98–117.
15 Translator's note: these issues are discussed in more detail in the following chapters. See chapter two, "Editors' 'on-site' criticism" for Yu Xiuhua's case, and chapter five, "Important events of cyber literary criticism" for other cases mentioned here.
16 Ouyang, Youquan 欧阳友权, *Wangluo wenxue yanjiu chengguo jicheng* 网络文学研究成果集成, 1–54.
17 Wang, Guoping 王国平, "Wangluo wenxue jidai queli piping 'zhibiao tixi' 网络文学亟待确立批评'指标体系,'" *Guangming ribao* 光明日报 (Beijing), Jul. 3, 2012.
18 Ouyang, Youquan 欧阳友权, "Wangluo wenxue: tiaozhan chuantong yu gengxin guannian" 网络文学:挑战传统与更新观念, *Social Science Journal of Xiangtan University* 湘潭大学社会科学学报 no. 1 (2001): 36–37.
19 Chen, Qirong 陈崎嵘, "Huyu jianli wangluo wenxue pingjia tixi 呼吁建立网络文学评价体系," *Renmin ribao* 人民日报 (Beijing), Jul. 19, 2013.
20 Chen, Qirong 陈崎嵘, "Huyu jianli wangluo wenxue pingjia tixi 呼吁建立网络文学评价体系."
21 Chen, Qirong 陈崎嵘, "Huyu jianli wangluo wenxue pingjia tixi 呼吁建立网络文学评价体系."
22 Chen, Qirong 陈崎嵘, "Huyu jianli wangluo wenxue pingjia tixi 呼吁建立网络文学评价体系."
23 René Wellek and Austin Warren, *Theory of Literature*, 36. For the sentence in single quotation marks, see: Norman Foerster, *The American Scholar* (Chapel Hill, NC: University of North Carolina Press, 1929), 36.
24 René Wellek and Austin Warren, *Theory of Literature*, 36–37.
25 Tan, Dejing 谭德晶, *Wangluo wenxue piping lun* 网络文学批评论 (Beijing: CFLAC Publishing House, 2004), 1.
26 Tan, Dejing 谭德晶, *Wangluo wenxue piping lun* 网络文学批评论, 18.
27 Translator's note: for the typical characteristics of postmodernism, see: Fredric Jameson, "Postmodernism or the Cultural Logic of Late Capitalism," *New Left Review* no. 146 (1984): 53–92.

28 Ouyang, Youquan 欧阳友权, "Lun wangluo wenxue de cukouxiu xushi" 论网络文学的粗口秀叙事, *Journal of Qujing Normal University* 曲靖师范学院学报 no. 4 (2004): 3.
29 Translator's note: some necessary information is added here to better describe these events; some events are further discussed in the following chapters in detail.
30 Liu, Hsieh (Liu, Xie) 刘勰, *Zengding wenxin diaolong jiaozhu* 增订文心雕龙校注, trans. Vincent Yu-chung Shih (Hong Kong: The Chinese University of Hong Kong Press, 2015), 222.
31 Zhao, Xianzhang 赵宪章, "Lun wangluo xiezuo jiqi dui chuantong xiezuo de tiaozhan" 论网络写作及其对传统写作的挑战, *Journal of Southeast University: Philosophy and Social Sciences Edition* 东南大学学报（哲学社会科学版）no. 1 (2002): 105.
32 Translator's note: more detailed discussions on these factors and notions are given in chapter six.
33 "Zhubu jianli wangluo wenxue pingjia tixi, jiji yindao wangluo wenxue jiankang fazhan" 逐步建立网络文学评价体系，积极引导网络文学健康发展, in *Wangluo wenxue pingjia tixi xushitan* 网络文学评价体系虚实谈, ed. Creation and Research Department of China Writers Association 中国作家协会创作研究部 (Beijing: Writers Publishing House, 2014), 339.
34 Zhang, Kangkang 张抗抗, "Wangluo wenxue zagan 网络文学杂感," *Zhonghua dushu bao* 中华读书报 (Beijing), Mar. 1, 2000.
35 Wang, Yichuan 王一川, "Wangluo shidai de wenxue: shenme shi buneng shao de?" 网络时代的文学：什么是不能少的? *Master* 大家 no. 3 (2000): 202.
36 Kang, Qiao 康桥, "Wangluo wenxue piping biaozhun chuyi 网络文学批评标准刍议," *Guangming ribao* 光明日报 (Beijing), Sep. 3, 2013.
37 Shao, Yanjun 邵燕君, "Meijie geming shiye xia de wangluo wenxue 'jingdianhua'" 媒介革命视野下的网络文学"经典化," in *Wangluo wenxue pingjia tixi xushitan* 网络文学评价体系虚实谈, ed. Creation and Research Department of China Writers Association 中国作家协会创作研究部 (Beijing: Writers Publishing House, 2014), 129–132.
38 Chen, Guoxiong 陈国雄, "Shuzi meijie yu wenxue piping de bianjie" 数字媒介与文学批评的边界, *Academic Journal of Zhongzhou* 中州学刊 no. 2 (2010): 252.

Bibliography

Chen, Guoxiong 陈国雄. "Shuzi meijie yu wenxue piping de bianjie" 数字媒介与文学批评的边界. *Academic Journal of Zhongzhou* 中州学刊 no. 2 (2010): 251–252.
Chen, Qirong 陈崎荣. "Huyu jianli wangluo wenxue pingjia tixi 呼吁建立网络文学评价体系." *Renmin ribao* 人民日报 (Beijing), Jul. 19, 2013.
Foerster, Norman. *The American Scholar*. Chapel Hill, NC: University of North Carolina Press, 1929.
Jameson, Fredric. "Postmodernism or the Cultural Logic of Late Capitalism." *New Left Review* no. 146 (1984): 53–92.
Kang, Qiao 康桥. "Wangluo wenxue piping biaozhun chuyi 网络文学批评标准刍议." *Guangming ribao* 光明日报 (Beijing), Sep. 3, 2013.
Liu, Hsieh (Liu Xie) 刘勰. *The Literary Mind and the Carving of Dragons*. Translated by Vincent Yu-chung Shih. Hong Kong: The Chinese University of Hong Kong Press, 2015.

Ouyang, Ting 欧阳婷 and Ouyang, Youquan 欧阳友权. "Wangluo wenxue de tizhi puxixue fansi" 网络文学的体制谱系学反思. *Theoretical Studies in Literature and Art* 文艺理论研究 no. 1 (2014): 90–98.

Ouyang, Youquan 欧阳友权. "Wangluo wenxue: tiaozhan chuantong yu gengxin guannian" 网络文学:挑战传统与更新观念. *Social Science Journal of Xiangtan University* 湘潭大学社会科学学报 no. 1 (2001): 36–40.

Ouyang, Youquan 欧阳友权. "Wangluo wenxue ziyou benxing de xueli biaozheng" 网络文学自由本性的学理表征. *Criticism and Creation* 理论与创作 no. 5 (2003): 4–8.

Ouyang, Youquan 欧阳友权. "Lun wangluo wenxue de cukouxiu xushi" 论网络文学的粗口秀叙事. *Journal of Qujing Normal University* 曲靖师范学院学报 no. 4 (2004): 1–6.

Ouyang, Youquan 欧阳友权. "Yong wangluo dazao wenxue shiyi" 用网络打造文学诗意. *Literary Review* 文学评论 no. 1 (2006): 193–196.

Ouyang, Youquan 欧阳友权. *Wangluo wenxue cidian* 网络文学词典. Beijing: World Publishing Corporation, 2012.

Ouyang, Youquan 欧阳友权. "Chongxie wenxueshi yu wangluo wenxue 'rushi' wenti" 重写文学史与网络文学"入史"问题. *Hebei Academic Journal* 河北学刊 no. 5 (2013): 8–12.

Ouyang, Youquan 欧阳友权. *Wangluo wenxue wunian pucha (erlinglingjiu-erlingyisan)* 网络文学五年普查 (2009–2013). Beijing: Central Compilation & Translation Press, 2014.

Ouyang, Youquan 欧阳友权. *Wangluo wenxue yanjiu chengguo jicheng* 网络文学研究成果集成. Beijing: CFLAC Publishing House, 2015a.

Ouyang, Youquan 欧阳友权. *Zhongguo wangluo wenxue biannianshi* 中国网络文学编年史. Beijing: CFLAC Publishing House, 2015b.

Shao, Yanjun 邵燕君. "Meijie geming shiye xia de wangluo wenxue 'jingdianhua'" 媒介革命视野下的网络文学"经典化." In *Wangluo wenxue pingjia tixi xushitan* 网络文学评价体系虚实谈, edited by Creation and Research Department of China Writers Association 中国作家协会创研部, 127–133. Beijing: Writers Publishing House, 2014.

Tan, Dejing 谭德晶. *Wangluo wenxue pipinglun* 网络文学批评论. Beijing: CFLAC Publishing House, 2004.

Wang, Guoping 王国平. "Wangluo wenxue jidai queli piping 'zhibiao tixi' 网络文学亟待确立批评'指标体系.'" *Guangming ribao* 光明日报 (Beijing), Jul. 3, 2012.

Wang, Yichuan 王一川. "Wangluo shidai de wenxue: shenme shi buneng shao de?" 网络时代的文学：什么是不能少的?, *Master* 大家 no. 3 (2000): 200–202.

Wellek, René and Austin Warren. *Theory of Literature*. New York: Harcourt, Brace & World, 1956.

Zhang, Kangkang 张抗抗. "Wangluo wenxue zagan 网络文学杂感." *Zhonghua dushu bao* 中华读书报 (Beijing), Mar. 1, 2000.

Zhao, Xianzhang 赵宪章. "Lun wangluo xiezuo jiqi dui chuantong xiezuo de tiaozhan" 论网络写作及其对传统写作的挑战. *Journal of Southeast University: Philosophy and Social Sciences Edition* 东南大学学报(哲学社会科学版) no. 1 (2002): 102–105.

"Zhubu jianli wangluo wenxue pingjia tixi, jiji yindao wangluo wenxue jiankang fazhan" 逐步建立网络文学评价体系，积极引导网络文学健康发展. In *Wangluo wenxue pingjia tixi xushitan* 网络文学评价体系虚实谈, edited by Creation and Research Department of China Writers Association 中国作家协会创研部, 335–340. Beijing: Writers Publishing House, 2014.

Part I

1 New Media and the Evolution of Cyber Literary Criticism

The word "medium" refers to a vehicle by which people can communicate with each other and with the external world, while "the media" is the collective name for communication platforms based on such vehicles. In communication studies, a medium can mean an object of a particular kind, together with the related organization, that stores and transmits information, such as books, newspapers, television and radio broadcasts, the Internet, and computers. Meanwhile, the "new media" is a new form of media relying on digital technologies: it serves users with information and entertainment on terminals such as computers, cellphones, and digital televisions; the services are delivered via the Internet, broadband local area networks, wireless networks, and satellites. Compared with traditional media such as newspapers and radio/television broadcasts, the new media is particularly "new": based on digital technologies, it incorporates multiple forms of media and allows people to interact with each other.

The long history of communication can be roughly divided into three major periods: the period of oral communication, the period of written communication, and the period of electronic communication. The invention and application of each new medium in history brought fundamental changes to society. For example, the invention of paper and the development of printing technology made it easier for written words to be circulated. As it became possible for information to be massively reproduced and disseminated, our civilization stepped into a new era. Likewise, the development of photographic technologies and telecommunication technologies allowed people to listen to radio broadcasts and watch TV programs. This brought fundamental changes to individual life and greatly reshaped the whole society. Then, the advent of the Internet had an even more significant impact on our life and society: today, our life and society are totally immersed in digital information. Therefore, the development of media does not merely mean changes in the method of communication. It can impact the overall socio-cultural condition and even the progress of history.

The development of media also impacts literature in various aspects. The form of media that carries literature, the language used in literature, as well as

DOI: 10.4324/9781003428480-3

literature's aesthetic features, mode of existence, values, and functions are all subject to change. This also leads to an alteration of literary criticism because "technical change alters not only habits of life, but patterns of thought and valuation."[1] In this sense, digital technologies can influence literary criticism: they immediately alter patterns of thought and valuation, as they provide literary criticism not only with new media platforms but also with new forms and ideas. Compared with traditional literary criticism, cyber literary criticism is unique in that it no longer depends solely on print media. Instead, it appears abundantly on the Internet, especially in "we media." In recent years we could see the birth of cyber literary criticism and the rise of literary criticism in we media. Subsequently, the identity of literary critics, the way of writing criticism, the criteria for evaluating literary works, and the function of literary criticism are all changed.

The Birth of Cyber Literature and Cyber Literary Criticism

Cyber Literature and Its Criticism

The prototype of the Internet was invented in the United States in the 1960s. In the 1990s, the Internet started to spread to all parts of the globe. Based on digital technologies, the Internet connects computers all over the world and has become a huge system of networks. As a form of medium that carries information for the purpose of communication, the Internet is now deemed as "the fourth major medium" after newspaper, radio, and television. As it is so essential, Nicholas Negroponte argues: "Computing is not about computers anymore. It is about living."[2] The most remarkable literary phenomenon in the Internet era is the appearance and rapid development of cyber literature. Cyber literature in Mandarin Chinese first appeared in North America. The first online weekly in Chinese, *China News Digest* (Huaxia wenzhai), was born in America in 1991. In the same year, *Online Newsletter for Chinese Poems Written Overseas* (Haiwai zhongwen shige tongxunwang, chpoem-1@listserv.acsu.buffalo.edu) came into being, which marked the burgeoning of creative cyberwriting in Chinese.[3] After China was connected to the Internet in April 1994, cyber literature started to develop quickly in China. More than twenty years later, creative writing in cyberspace has become a huge cultural phenomenon. According to the 38th Statistical Report on Internet Development in China, released by China Internet Network Information Center (CNNIC), as of June 2016, there were already 710 million Internet users in China, amounting to 51.7 percent of the total population in the country, and 656 million of them used cellphones to access the Internet.[4] The report also tells us that 308 million (or 46.6 percent) Internet users read literature online. In this sense, cyber literature has grown so powerful and influential that its presence in contemporary Chinese literature should by no means be overlooked. Today, there is already a massive body of writers on the Internet, with myriads of works and hundreds of millions of readers. Cyberwriting thus has become a phenomenon distinctive in China. It can be viewed as one of the "four cultural wonders" in our contemporary world, together with Hollywood films, Japanese cartoons, and Korean dramas. Although people still have different ideas as to what cyber literature is and how we should view such a new type of literature, there is no denying that cyber literature has become hugely important, and its future development will be unlimited.

With the development of literature in cyberspace, criticism of such literature also came into existence. We recognize two major types of cyber literary criticism. The first type is published in journals, magazines, and newspapers, mainly by literary scholars, as well as editors and journalists working for newspapers and magazines. We shall call it "offline criticism." The second type is published directly on the Internet, so we shall call it "online criticism." The writers of online criticism are usually common readers of cyber literature, but there are also scholars in the traditional sense who actively write online. Online criticism, or cyber literary criticism in its narrow sense, is a new type of literary criticism that came into existence with the birth of cyber literature. Our study here will only cover cyber literary criticism in its narrow sense: in this condition, both critical texts and literary works are published online. Of course, when our discussion in this book touches upon issues such as critics' identities, their critical writings and intellectual achievements, as well as the changes of ideas in literary criticism, we will also look into "offline criticism," or cyber literary criticism in the broad sense, to better elucidate the development of cyber literary criticism in history.

Apparently, compared with traditional literary criticism, cyber literary criticism is unique in that it relies on the Internet and mainly concerns literature in cyberspace. Traditional criteria and methods for evaluating literary works are not quite effective in dealing with the new literature in cyberspace. As new criteria and methods were needed, cyber literary criticism came into being. As Chinese cyber literature burgeoned in the West, cyber literary criticism in its early stage appeared mainly on overseas literary websites, such as *New Threads of Thought* (Xin Yu Si) and *Olive Tree* (Ganlan shu). In this period, most cyber literary critics, such as Fang Zhouzi and Tu Ya, were also writers of cyber literature. Early texts of cyber literary criticism are quite rare. They are scattered in various places and most of them are just random thoughts. However, as most cyber literary critics in this period had personal experience in cyberwriting and a good knowledge of the condition of cyber literature, some of their articles are valuable as historical materials. Articles by Fang Zhouzi, such as "The Rise of ACT" (ACT de xingqi), "The Success of ACT" (ACT de fanrong), "The Decline of ACT" (ACT de shuaibai), and "Overseas Electronic Publications in Chinese" (Haiwai de zhongwen dianzi kanwu), are all important in the history of cyber literary criticism.[5]

Many literary websites appeared in mainland China in the late 1990s. Early sites of this kind were established on free platforms provided by major portals such as *NetEase* and *Yahoo!*, but there were also independent sites, such as *Under the Banyan Tree* (Rongshuxia), that started to introduce

Chinese creative writing in cyberspace. Besides, the literature sections of some forums, such as those on *Skyline Community* (Tianya shequ), *Xici hutong*, and *Xilu*, were also quite popular with people who loved cyberwriting. The publication of the Taiwanese writer Cai Zhiheng's book, *The First Intimate Contact* (Diyici de qinmi jiechu), ignited mainlanders' enthusiasm for writing online. As more people could access the Internet and read cyber literature, articles of cyber literary criticism began to appear in large numbers. The forums of the above-mentioned literary websites became the main venues for publishing such articles. In various places, such as *Under the Banyan Tree*, *Skyline Community*, the "Literary Review" column on *Qingyun Library* (Qingyun shuyuan), and the forum on *Sohu*, many writers and common netizens published an abundance of words to exchange, share, and discuss their views of cyber literature. During this period, articles by Wu Guo, Yuan Chen, Xing Yusen, and Chen Cun became noticeable. Wu Guo wrote a series of articles collectively named "Random Comments on Cyber Literature" (Luantan wangluo wenxue), which included "What Does the Internet Bring to Literature?" (Wangluo gei wenxue dailai le shenme?), "Another Meaning of Cyberwriting" (Wangluo xiezuo de lingyizhong yiyi), and "Internet: A Double-edged Sword of Literature" (Wangluo: wenxue de shuangrenjian). These articles, together with Yuan Chen's "My Opinions on Cyber Literature" (Wangluo wenxue zhi wojian), Xing Yusen's "How I View Cyber Literature" (Wo kan wangluo wenxue), "What Is the Purpose of Creative Writing in Cyberspace" (Wangluo yuanchuang wenxue de zongzhi shi shenme), and Chen Cun's preface for books of the "Internet Star Series," tracked the early development of cyber literature and discussed related issues. They are precious materials for the study of early cyber literary criticism. Wu Guo also conducted exclusive interviews with early well-known cyber writers such as "Ning, the God of Wealth" (Ning caishen), Xing Yusen, Li Xunhuan, and "Annie Baby" (Anni baobei). Chen Cun entered the field of cyber literature as a traditional writer. He hosted the forum called "Lie Down and Read" (Tangzhe dushu) on the website *Under the Banyan Tree* and published a series of articles commenting on cyber literature in the column called "Whispers in the Wind" (Fengyan fengyu), which attracted a lot of readers. Of course, in this early stage of cyber literary criticism, many critical words also appeared as comments and replies in the abovementioned literary sections. Readers could directly express their views on the works they read, in the dialog boxes often marked as "Let me say a few words" at the bottom of the webpages. In this way, they could also communicate directly with other readers and authors. Reading, following, and replying to posts became the most popular among netizens. These posts were usually casual, with only a few words, and lacked professionalism. However, as there were a large number of them reflecting readers' different views, they still attracted the attention of many people. In this way, these posts greatly increased the popularity of cyber literature and boosted the development of such a type of literature. Many of these posts are quite insightful and can be read as texts of literary criticism.

While the writing of this new type of literary criticism as an activity attracted an increasing number of netizens, literary scholars started to pay attention to it as well. In June 2011, the seminar "Literary Criticism in Cyberspace, in Media, and in Academia" was hosted by the Research Department of Beijing Federation of Literary and Art Circles and co-hosted by *Chinese Youth • Digital Youth* weekly. In this seminar, the concept of "cyber literary criticism" was put forward by scholars. Some experts classified contemporary literary criticism into three types, including "criticism in academia," "criticism in media," and "criticism in cyberspace," as each type is done by a particular group of people as critics. The practice of dividing contemporary literary criticism into three types has continued since then. In 2009, Bai Ye, in his article "New Circumstances and Challenges of Literary Criticism" (Wenxue piping de xin yujing yu xin tiaozhan), once again summarized that there were three types of criticism: "criticism in academia, written by scholars in the traditional sense; criticism in media, which mainly consists of articles published in traditional media and written by media workers; criticism in cyberspace, mainly including blog posts written by cyber writers."[6] Although there is ambiguity in the term "criticism in cyberspace"—because the Internet itself is a kind of media, this classification may not be rigorous—yet at least such a categorization shows that cyber literary criticism has been recognized as an important part of contemporary literary criticism.

The Forms of Online Literary Criticism

At present, various literary websites provide technical support and platforms for online literary criticism. As a result, online literary criticism mainly exists on such websites. Of course, it can also be seen in literary sections of some forums and BBSes (Bulletin Board Systems), as well as in personal blogs, but the number of critical texts in these places is comparatively smaller. Generally, readers, after reading a certain literary work, can directly post comments in the comments section at the bottom of the page, or they can post their opinions on the work in the forum attached to the literary website. For example, the website *Starting Points Chinese Net* (Qidian zhongwen wang) has a forum for people to communicate. *Jinjiang Literature City* (Jinjiang wenxuecheng) also has a special comments area, where some active commentators are selected and highlighted by the website so as to encourage people to write comments. Some websites also have "Readers' Recommendation List" and "Experts' Recommendation List" to guide readers. At the same time, readers can also express their interest in and support for works by sending monetary rewards to authors and voting to recommend the pieces to other readers. Still, posting is the most common form of online literary criticism. This includes the writing of short and long comments. A comment can be as short as a few words or even only one character or emoji/emoticon. It can also be hundreds or thousands of words or even tens of thousands. Of course, there are also comments in the form of moving images, such as some spoof videos and cartoonish pictures as responses to literary works. As to its content, online literary criticism includes comments on cyber writing and related literary phenomena, as well as some random words that are not even related to the works and have little real significance. Of course, the former is more meaningful and valuable.

Online literary criticism has several styles, such as casual short notes, personal reflections, and long appreciative reviews.

Casual short notes are readers' brief expressions of immediate feelings about the works. They are often only a few words or even one word, such as "good," "very good," "bump (the thread)," "nice job," "not bad," and "keep up the good work," or just an emoji/emoticon. Because of their shortness, such comments seldom analyze the content of the work. Instead, they only express readers' first impressions and intuitive feelings about the works. In this sense, they are quite different from traditional literary criticism that emphasizes logical thinking and academic methodologies. Let us take readers' comments on the popular web novel *Stories of Witchcraft in Miao People's Territory* (Miaojiang gushi) as an example. The novel was originally published on the website *Starting Points Chinese Net*. The pseudonym of the author is "Namo Kasaya Science Buddha" (Nanwu jiasha li ke fo), commonly known as "Little Buddha." There have been thousands of readers' posts after the novel. The following are some comments on the novel posted on another website, *Baidu Post Bar* (Baidu tieba):

[Netizen 1]:	The first one is Xiao Mei, a shop assistant working for Lu Zuo. She likes Lu, but because Lu does not have strong power in the beginning, Xiao Mei dies, so she is not the main character.
[Netizen 2]:	How boring I am. Next time I will go to find out if there is Lu Zuo.[7]
[Netizen 3]:	I suddenly feel sad because they are not villains. If they were pig's feet [Internet slang words for protagonists], and if the story were written from their perspectives, would Zuo Dao be completely righteous? Alas, they just die like this!
[Netizen 4]:	So far, I have almost finished reading *Stories of Witchcraft in Miao People's Territory*, with only a few hundred pages left. I also feel that the author is quite imaginative, and the writing style is just fantastic. He created many vivid characters, which impressed me a lot. As he didn't mention their appearances in the novel, we can only use our imagination. This is just like how we see the historical figure Cao Cao as portrayed in the Chinese classic novel *Romance of the Three Kingdoms*: in the eyes of 10,000 readers, there are 10,000 images of him. This is how I imagine these characters in my heart. Don't attack me if you disagree.
[Netizen 5]:	This novel made me mad. It occurs to me that I often play online dubbing games for videos. I am not sure if there are

	people interested in this game here. I would like to play with gurus like you.
[Netizen 6]:	I'm an ethnic Miao person living in Guizhou Province. A part of the story written by Little Buddha is set in my hometown. We do have legends about *gu*, a venomous insect able to enchant people, but it's not as powerful as Little Buddha described. Many older people told me they did see *gu*, and nowadays, there are still legends about it, especially among Buyi people. I haven't seen this kind of thing anyway. We, Qing Miao people (the Miao people have many branches, and our branch is called Qing Miao), call it "yao po," which translates into Mandarin as *gu*.[8]

These casual short notes rarely discuss the specific text of the novel. Most of them are just about readers' immediate reading experience, and some of them are not even related to the novel at all. Of course, this is also the characteristic of short notes: as they reflect the readers' immediate reading experience to a considerable extent, they are honest, fresh, and vivid, thus being quite capable of attracting more people to read the novel. In other words, a web novel cannot become popular without a large number of recommendations in the form of casual short notes.

The second type of online literary criticism can be called "personal reflections." Personal reflections are readers' expressions of their understanding of a certain part of the work they read, or of the work as a whole. They can touch upon the work's narrative style, language features, socio-political meanings, etc. Compared with casual short notes, personal reflections have more words and focus more specifically on certain elements in the work. Some of them can be seen as developments of casual short notes. In this way, readers can express their immediate thoughts and feelings after reading a work. A good review of this kind, with just a few words, can elucidate the work's essence buried in textual details. It can be simple but wonderful, providing a unique perspective and way of thinking to enrich people's understanding of a certain work. Here are some examples.

Full of passion and hot-bloodedness, the words are very catching! The first half is lively and exciting, but the second half is a little pretentious. It is good overall, and it is worth reading!
(Comments by Bai Jiuhe on the novel *Battle Through the Heavens* (Doupo cangqiong), posted on *Starting Points Chinese Net*)

In face of this materialistic society, a couple who get married without enough money may eventually lose their love for each other. But even if love has gone sour, it is at least called love. It used to be love. With love, what are you afraid of? As long as you ever loved each other, it is enough. The result is determined by too many external factors, and you cannot control it. Thus, if you have the courage to get married without enough money, you should also have the courage to maintain your marriage.

(Comments by "Red-tailed Fish" (Hongweibayu) on the novel Marriage without Money (Luohun), posted on Reading with Beauty (Hongxiu tianxiang))

I like this one better than any other work by "Longan" (Guiyuan). Some people who have been deceived and hurt no longer believe in family affection, friendship, and romantic love, but there are always people who still believe in such beautiful things, even though they have been deceived and hurt. PS: The love between Taishi and Rong Chu is perfect! They don't talk much, but they trust and care about each other. I really like the chapter "You Are My Incomparable."

(Comments by "Hanlian julia" on the novel Phenix to the End of the Sky (Feng qing tianlan), posted on Xiaoxiang Library (Xiaoxiang shuyuan))

Although the comments above, as expressions of readers' feelings and reflections, are brief, they are especially sincere and precious. They sometimes even go beyond the evaluation of the contents of the works to express readers' thoughts of society and life in general, which are often accurate and brilliant. For this reason, some scholars have associated this type of review with the traditional literary review in ancient China, such as Jin Shengtan's critical commentary on literary works. They argue that this is the "revival" of traditional criticism, which focuses on "romantic charm in literature and art."[9]

Long appreciative reviews refer to relatively systematic and detailed comments on a work's intellectual connotation, characterization, language feature, aesthetic value, etc. They often contain hundreds, thousands, or even tens of thousands of words. Such reviews are usually comprehensive expressions of reviewers' thoughts after reading, and they can help other readers better understand the literary works. In some sense, the number of long reviews is also one of the signs indicating whether a web novel has drawn enough attention from readers, so literary websites and authors often pay special attention to long reviews from readers. Quite a few websites reserve a section for readers to publish their long reviews of literary works, and authors of these works usually write responses to such long reviews. The following is a reader's review of *The Killing of Three Thousand Crows* (Sanqian yasha), a novel by Shisi Lang. It was posted on *Jinjiang Literature City*:

Shisi's style is not exquisite. The setting is often not grand enough, and the plot is often very simple. His story is often very simple, cheesy, and hackneyed if condensed into a summary. However, under Shisi's pen, there are always a few very vivid characters who make this kind of simple, stupid, cheesy, and hackneyed story particularly attractive.

A novel is a form of literature that reflects people's life experiences through the description of characters, plots, and environments. The creation of characters, with their "blood and flesh" vividly and emotionally depicted, is the foundation of a good novel. Through the representation of characters, the author can communicate with readers. The plot must be structured on the basis of an accurate understanding of characters and serve the portrayal of characters. Only by doing this can the author let the characters become vivid and lively. In terms of characterization, Shisi has done a very good job.

For example, in *The Killing of Three Thousand Crows*, the male protagonist Jiuyun, also known as Gongzi Qi, has a strong personality and a heart of sincerity, gentleness, and persistence. He thus becomes a round character that is true to life...

Initially, the novel gives us a "long shot" of Jiuyun from the heroine's perspective. Jiuyun always looks lazy, leisurely, and careless about everything. He pretends to be an ordinary playboy. Later, as the novel gives us a close-up of him, we see that he is actually quite tolerant toward the heroine and cares much about her. The heroine's secret has always been well hidden. Even her former lover does not recognize her when they meet. On the entire Xiangqu Mountain, except for this mysterious figure Fu Jiuyun, no one has paid close attention to the heroine. Does Jiuyun treat the heroine with tolerance and care just because he has discovered her secret, or is there any other reason for this? The completely changing attitudes he shows to the heroine make him even more mysterious and unpredictable. As a result, the heroine is in fear and panic. She constantly tries to guard herself and escape.

From the perspective of Jiuyun, he has been patiently waiting for the heroine to fall in love with him. He uses his passion, his indifference, his hugs, his chases, his kisses, his warm hands, his smiles, and his paintings...

In this series of conflicts, Shisi makes full use of the interactions between Jiuyun and the heroine to reveal Jiuyun's personality layer by layer from multiple angles. Jiuyun is initially amorous and powerful; he is then gentle and affectionate; later, he becomes tolerant toward the heroine and persists in caring about her. In the end, he turns out to be a person who lives and dies for love's sake. In this way, the character is fully developed and well represented. It can be said that Jiuyun perfectly exemplifies the ideal image of a male protagonist. While the plot is ordinary, the novel depicts Jiuyun's personality as extraordinary, which not only deeply moves the heroine, but also deeply touches readers. This well-portrayed character, placed in such an environment and condition, has his acts and thoughts consistently in line with his personality. His personality also determines the development of events and pushes forward the smooth progress of the story. If Jiuyun has no deep affection for the heroine and behaves just like the heroine's former lover, who easily gives her up, how can the heroine eventually love Jiuyun so deeply and whole-heartedly? If Jiuyun does not choose to die for love without complaint and regret, how can the heroine finally let go of her hatred and fall in love with him? Such a plot, in turn, reveals the character's personality and finally completes a stunning image of the character. In this way, the story can deeply move its readers.

Despite the cheesy plot, the story is still successful as it conveys deep emotions.

(From "The Portrayal of Characters Through Their Interactions: On The Killing of Three Thousand Crows" (Cong hudong zhong tixian xingge: ping Sanqian yasha), by "Three Six" (Sanliu) on Jinjiang Literature City)

This passage is abridged when quoted. The original text is nearly 4,000 Chinese characters. It tries to illustrate how the novel portrays characters through the writing of their interactions. Although the language is still rather casual, it is quite sincere, denoting a close reading of the story. It can help readers understand the novel's artistic skills and values. Compared with casual short notes and personal reflections, long appreciative reviews are fewer in number. Nevertheless, they embody deeper and sometimes professional analyses of literary works. They are, therefore, the mainstay of online literary criticism.

The Characteristics of Online Literary Criticism

The emergence and rapid development of the Internet heralded a new era of literary criticism. Compared with traditional literary criticism, online literary criticism has its distinctive features. The Internet is not only the technical prerequisite for this emerging type of literary criticism. It also serves as the cultural background for such criticism. Meanwhile, online literary criticism still belongs to the category of literary criticism and thus has commonalities with traditional literary criticism. It not only pays attention to the technical aspects of the Internet but also cares about the innate artistic values of literary works. In this way, online literary criticism is not only about the study of the unique characteristics of cyber literature but also shares some characteristics with cyber literature.

First, online literary criticism is written by ordinary people on the Internet. The most important feature of cyberspace is that people are free to express themselves. Here, as long as people have the most basic computer skills, they can conveniently travel between major websites and exchange information with others. People's freedom on the Internet also lies in their anonymity. They can roam cyberspace with false identities rather than reveal their real names. This means that any netizen interested in cyber literature and willing to express opinions can freely write and publish comments without being restricted by factors such as personal identity and social status. Therefore, compared with the situation "off" the Internet, in which only a few privileged scholars can write and publish literary criticism, cyberspace makes it much easier for people to engage in such an activity. The vast majority of these people are not professional literary critics. In most cases, they are just amateurs who love literature. They generally do not have professional knowledge of literary theories, and most of their evaluations of works are simply based on personal preferences. On the one hand, this allows much more people to write literary criticism; on the other hand, it also puts online literary criticism in a state where there is no authority, no center, and where we hear a cacophony of voices from different people.

Second, the language used in online literary criticism is plain and simple. As ordinary people can now write critical reviews online, their language is vastly different from that used in traditional literary criticism. As we can see, netizens' reviews rarely use specialized theoretical terms. Netizens do not pay attention to their articles' layout, nor do they like to quote classic works. They only intend to express their feelings after reading, and sometimes they just write to release their emotions that are not so much related to the literary works they read. They do not, therefore, try to give comprehensive interpretations and reviews of the works. As they are just ordinary people, their words are plain and simple. For example, a large number of cyber critical reviews have only one or a few words, such as "good," "very good," "excellent," "awesome," "boring," and "very awful." Some have no word at all, but only simple emoticons or emojis such as smiley faces and thumbs up. Even for those long articles of several thousand words, the language is usually colloquial rather than formal. Such a use of language redresses the problem that traditional literary criticism is often too esoteric, obscure, and difficult for the public to read. As a result, ordinary readers can write and read their own critical reviews. At the same time, however, the casual use of language also makes these reviews less rational, objective, and in-depth. Since there is no editor to check the reviews, most of these netizens, as critics, publish their words rashly and causally, without a sense of responsibility for their readers. As a result, exaggerations, spoofs, and words of playfulness and absurdity all appear in these reviews. There are even problems such as grammatical errors, typos, and mistakes due to the lack of common sense. To a certain extent, this makes such a type of literary criticism less scientific and valid.

Third, online literary criticism is interactive. The Internet has broken the constraints of time and space, enabling users in different regions to have two-way and even multi-directional communication easily and quickly. This is a revolutionary change in information dissemination brought about by digital technologies. It is also a significant feature of the Internet compared with traditional media. Online literary criticism fully takes advantage of the Internet so that people can quickly exchange their ideas after reading. Traditionally, literary reviews are published in journals, newspapers, and books. It usually takes a long time for an article to be written, submitted, reviewed, edited, printed, and circulated. It is difficult to have instant communication between writers and critics and between critics themselves. Therefore, it is generally difficult for traditional literary criticism to influence writers' literary creations. But online literary criticism is different. One of the most common situations of cyberwriting is like this: On the one hand, the author keeps writing and posting—in other words, the author has to regularly add more episodes to the story; on the other hand, readers express their thoughts and opinions after reading the newest episodes and immediately share their ideas with the author and other readers. Sometimes, readers can even give the author suggestions on how to arrange the storyline or represent the characters so that the author can continue the writing based on readers' feedback. In this way, online literary criticism directly participates in the process of literary creation. Excellent comments can often become the author's source of inspiration and help push the story forward. While readers can interact with the author, readers can communicate with each other more easily as well. They can discuss a particular work or a specific aspect of a work by creating a thread on a webpage. As the number of discussants is not limited, there can be even thousands of replies in a thread. A good topic for discussion is very helpful for readers to deepen their understanding of a work.

Fourth, online literary criticism embodies diversified values. Traditional literary criticism has a set of criteria mainly for evaluating works of "high culture" written by intellectuals. Critics are required to be objective and fair, following the way of reasoning and the criteria for evaluating works as established by convention. They are supposed to use rigorously accurate words to carefully analyze writers, works, and certain literary phenomena and make value judgments on the intellectual and artistic aspects of literary works. In comparison, online literary criticism is mostly spontaneous. Critics often evaluate works according to their personal preferences. They do not care much about rigorous reasoning and clear thinking, and their language is often colloquial. Therefore, so far, online literary criticism does not follow an established set of criteria for the evaluation of works. Instead, it demonstrates a diversity of values, which undoubtedly helps break the exclusiveness of traditional literary criticism, puts an end to authoritative scholars' monopoly on literary criticism, and gives literary criticism a higher degree of freedom and accessibility. However, the divergence of ideas and the dissonance of voices may also cause a problem: there is no consensus on the criteria for evaluating literary works in cyberspace. While some netizens can review works with a sense of seriousness and responsibility, others may willfully and randomly criticize or attack works in their posts. In this sense, their reviews are no longer meaningful, and as literary critics, they are going down the wrong path.

The Rise of We-media Literary Criticism

We Media and We-media Literary Criticism

"We Media" is originally a term in English used by Western scholars in journalism and communication studies. It was originally proposed by Dan Gillmor, an American columnist known for writing about information technology. In a blog post in 2001, Gillmor said print media and broadcasts are traditional media, or "old media." He also called them "media 1.0." Meanwhile, media 2.0 refers to the media that relies on new technologies, such as digital newspapers, mobile phones, and digital televisions. It is also called cross-media or "new media." Now we also have media 3.0, or "we media," which includes blogs, microblogs, and personal homepages. At the end of 2002, Gillmor officially put forward the concept of we media. In a 2003 article entitled "News for the Next Generation: Here Comes We Media," he pointed out that we media would be the mainstream media in the future.[10] In July 2003, the Media Center at the American Press Institute published the world's first report on we media, "We Media: How Audiences are Shaping the Future of News and Information," co-authored by media scholars Shayne Bowman and Chris Willis. The report points out that we media is "a way to begin to understand how ordinary citizens, empowered by digital technologies that connect knowledge throughout the globe, are contributing to and participating in their own truths, their own kind of news."[11] An article in the American magazine *Wired* believes that we media enables communication from everyone to everyone.[12] In this sense, we media as a concept means that ordinary people can now become "media": people use information technologies and digital technologies to publish information and spread news independently. The rapid development and broad application of we media have become the most significant social and cultural phenomenon in the information society of the 21st century.

In daily life, "we media" and another well-known term, "new media," are often used interchangeably. Some scholars believe that we media is equivalent to new media, or it means a new stage in the development of new media. For example, an article mentions: "We media is new media in its latest stage of development."[13] The concept of "new media" first appeared in the United States in the late 1960s. In 1967, P. Goldmark, director of CBS Technology Center, proposed this term. Although it specifically referred to Electronic Video Recording at the time, the concept of new media then spread widely in the United States and worldwide. Today, the generally accepted idea in the academic circle is that new media is regarded as "means and forms of communication relying on digital technologies, network technologies, and other high-tech achievements in the information age."[14] New media is "new" as it differs from traditional or old media such as newspapers, radio, and television broadcasts. In the information age, new media mainly refers to the media on the Internet, especially the media accessed via smartphones. "We media" and "new media" as concepts emphasize different aspects of the media. "We media" mainly stresses that it is the ordinary people who spontaneously produce and disseminate information; "new media" mainly emphasizes the forms of media as "new" compared with traditional media. We media and new media both rely on the use of new technologies, but new media is more inclusive as a term. We may regard we media as the most typical form of new media today.

As a type of media relying on digital technologies and the Internet, we media enables ordinary people to provide and share information independently. In this sense, just like the Internet traditionally accessed via PC, we media allows users to be free, equal, anonymous, and interactive with each other, and often much more so than before. Its most representative forms include blogs in the past and microblogs and WeChat at present. In recent years, with the rapid development of mobile networks, we media's influence increased day by day. Today, we media applications are the most popular among all mobile applications in China. Taking WeChat as an example, data shows that the number of monthly active users of WeChat in March 2016 exceeded 700 million, which was a 29% increase over the same month in 2015.[15]

The word "we" in the term "we media" emphasizes freedom and autonomy. In other words, we media is easier to use and can disseminate information more quickly and conveniently than before. With a smartphone connected to the Internet, people can now spread their messages anytime and anywhere. In terms of the transmission path, the most prominent feature of we media is that it is no longer limited to the one-way communication mode adopted by traditional media. Instead, the communication can be more flexible and autonomous, as the transmission path can be "one-to-one," "one-to-many," and "many-to-one." The status of the audience is completely changed: an individual can assume multiple roles, not only as the receiver of the information but also as the producer and disseminator of the information. In this sense, an individual's voice can be more easily heard by others. We media also allows people to select their targets of communication. Ordinary people can choose to spread their messages either to a specified small group of people or to broader audiences. However, it is worth noting that we-media communication also has drawbacks. For example, the information can be fragmentary, vulgar, disorderly, and not easily controlled and regulated by the government.

The wide application of we media has brought changes to cyber literature and its criticism. On the one hand, the emergence of we media platforms, such as blogging and microblogging websites and WeChat, has spawned new literary forms such as blog literature, microblog literature, and WeChat literature, which can be regarded as new extensions of cyber literature. These forms of literature are accompanied respectively by blog literary criticism, microblog literary criticism, and WeChat literary criticism, which specifically refer to criticism of literary works published on we media platforms. On the other hand, on such we media platforms, there are also articles or comments on cyber literature published on non-we-media platforms. As we media allows users to express their thoughts freely, quickly, and conveniently, many people post their reviews of various types of literary works there (including works originally published on literary websites and even in paper media). Many of such reviews can be seen in personal blogs. Therefore, we-media literary criticism, in a broad sense, refers to all critical texts published on we media platforms that discuss literature in general and cyber literature in particular.

"Boke" is the Chinese transliteration of the English word "blog," which is short for "weblog." To write blogs means to record and publish messages on the Internet in chronological order. "Boke" in Chinese also refers to a person who writes a web log (i.e., a blogger). The term blog originated in the United States in the 1990s and became widely popular after September 11, 2001. The first blogging platform in China is the website *Blog China* (Boke Zhongguo), established in 2002. Blogs in the early stage were mainly platforms for Internet users to communicate and disseminate information. Later, a large number of literature lovers started to post their works on blogging platforms, as blogs were easy-to-operate, interactive, and personalized. Well-known writers and literary critics, such as Yu Hua, Yu Qiuyu, Wang Shuo, Feng Jicai, Lei Da, and Bai Ye, also started to use blogs for their literary activities. Blog literature thus thrived. At the end of 2005, some major domestic portals, such as *Sina*, *Sohu*, and *NetEase*, established their blogging platforms and opened literary columns. The year 2005 is thus known as China's "first year of the blog era."

The emergence of blog literature led to the birth of blog literary criticism. In a broad sense, blog literary criticism should include all interpretations and comments published on blogging platforms in response to literary works. The targets of criticism include all writers, works, and literary phenomena both in and outside cyberspace. A considerable number of critics reposted their published articles on blogging platforms, but essentially, these are still traditional literary reviews, though they are now accessible as blog posts. As blog literature is originally published in the form of blog posts, what best reflects the uniqueness of blog literary criticism is ordinary readers' replies to such blog posts. There are many readers' comments of this kind on popular blog literary works such as *Random Comments on Outlaws of the Marsh* (Luantan Shuihu) by a writer named "Stuff the squid" (Tianxia wuzei) and *The Book of Illness and Forgetting* (Bing wang shu) by "Female patient in Beijing" (Beijing nübingren). Besides, there were also some bloggers who focused on cyber literature. They recommended cyber literary works to readers and published thoughts and opinions on these works. In so doing, they played an important role in blog literary criticism. Blogging platforms such as *Sina* often proposed controversial topics for people to debate, such as "literature is dead," "the debate between Han Han and Bei Ye," and "the pear flower style." This attracted many literary scholars and amateurs, sparked hot discussions, and further increased the influence of blogs as a new space for literary criticism. Because blogs could easily attract public attention, Kong Qingdong, a literary scholar, described personal blogs as "'man-portable laser-guided missiles'" in contemporary literature.[16]

"Weibo," short for "microblog" in Chinese, is a new type of blog that is mini in size. Users can upload texts, sounds, images, and other information to create their microblogs through computers and mobile phones. A microblog post is usually required to be within 140 Chinese characters, and it can be open either to all netizens or only to a selected group of people. Microblog posts are shorter but more time-sensitive and spontaneous than regular blog posts. The first website in the world to provide microblogging services is Twitter, which was founded in 2006 in the United States. In 2007, *Fanfou.com* introduced the concept of microblog to China. *Sina Weibo*, launched in August 2009, is currently the most widely used and influential microblogging platform in China.

As microblog is personal, instant, interactive, and concise, it is welcomed by users in the information age, who expect to read words fast and freely express themselves. As a result, microblog literature develops and attracts people's attention as a new literary form. Some well-known websites and traditional media held microblog writing contests, such as the "Microblog Story Contest" launched by the microblogging platform "9911 Microblog" (9911 weiboke), which was itself run by *MySpace.com*, and "China's First Microstory Contest" hosted by *Sina Weibo*. Microblog stories, such as "Love in the Microblog Era" (Weibo shiqi de aiqing), also became popular. Typically, microblog literary criticism comes after these microblog stories, as readers post their comments and replies to express their thoughts and opinions of such stories. Meanwhile, authors of microblog literary works also desire to get public attention and have fans. A very popular microblog post says: "If you have no followers, your microblog is just a diary; if you have one follower, it is a chat; if you have ten followers, it is a forum; if you have a hundred followers, it is the place where you give public speeches."[17] This not only indicates how powerful fans can be but also shows how much writers hope to get fans' applauses and suggestions. Microblog thus has become "a brand-new platform for the interaction between writers and readers."[18] Of course, in addition to reviewing microblog literature, micro-bloggers comment on traditional literary works. Alternatively, they can introduce and recommend works of non-microblog cyber literature and express their opinions on these works. Such comments should also belong to the category of microblog literary criticism. For example, *Sina Weibo* has a microblog account called "Cyber Literature Observation Station" (Wangluo wenxue guancha zhan), which focuses on cyber literature in general.

"Weixin" is known as "WeChat" in English. It is a mobile instant messaging application launched by Tencent in January 2011. Using the mobile network, WeChat can quickly deliver texts, voices, pictures, videos, and other information. It has many functions, such as "official accounts" (gongzhong hao) and "moments" (pengyou quan). It has a huge impact on the public after its invention. The number of its users increased significantly, and it has now become an important part of life for many people. WeChat provides a new space for literature: people can create literary works on it, and then publish the works either on "moments" for a certain group of people (their friends) to read, or on their "official accounts" targeting a broader audience. It is also quite easy to incorporate multimedia materials, such as pictures, voices, and videos. WeChat literature can, therefore, take a diversity of forms. I discussed WeChat literature in a journal article, which I quote here:

> The so-called WeChat literature is a new form of literature that uses WeChat as a platform to create, spread, and share literary texts, mainly among a circle of friends. A user can share a particular literary work on "moments" for friends to read. In this sense, WeChat literature is an extension of cyber literature... Its forms include original works created and published on

WeChat, traditional works shared via WeChat, and stories representing people's experiences of using WeChat.[19]

Early influential works of WeChat literature include popular stories, such as "I Shake My Phone Not Because I Feel Lonely, But Because I Want to Find You" ("Yaode shi ni, bushi nimo," written by "Vice-president of NBC," or "NBC Erdangjiade"), "There Are Ghosts in WeChat" ("Weixin yougui," by Moyu'ai), "The Roses in WeChat" ("Weixin lide meigui," by "As women we should be strong," or "Nüzi dangziqiang"), and "The Girl on WeChat Whom I Encountered by Shaking My Phone" ("Wo he Weixin shang yaodao de nühai," by "Spread honey and look at each other," or "Momi xiangwang"). Some cyber writers, such as "The third uncle of the southern school" (Nanpai Sanshu), have set up WeChat "official accounts." Their subscribers and friends on WeChat can directly give "likes" and leave messages in response to their works. Once excellent works are reviewed and shared by many people, they will inevitably have a greater influence over the general public. The "official account," as a function, allows readers to post their opinions after reading. Once selected by the owner of the official account, readers' comments become visible to everyone. If you type "cyber literature" (wangluo wenxue) in the "add friend" box on WeChat and search, you will find scores of official accounts, which contain many original works of literature and texts of literary criticism. A noteworthy phenomenon is that quite a few traditional literary periodicals, such as *Poetry* (Shikan), *People's Literature* (Renmin wenxue), *Literary Review* (Wenxue pinglun), *Harvest* (Shouhuo), *Novel Monthly* (Xiaoshuo yuebao), and *Grain in Ear* (Mangzhong), have opened their own WeChat "official accounts," as editors of these periodicals are now aware of the huge influence of WeChat. Traditional periodicals, in this way, actively explore new methods of publication and make efforts to adapt themselves when facing the impact of new media.

The Characteristics of We-media Literary Criticism

We-media literary criticism relies on we-media platforms. As its technical basis is digital and network technologies, it still belongs to the broad category of cyber literary criticism. In this sense, in we-media literary criticism, we can see all the characteristics of cyber literary criticism, which we discussed previously in this chapter. Such characteristics are often stronger in we-media literary criticism than in earlier types of cyber literary criticism. Meanwhile, compared with literary websites accessed via traditional PC, we-media platforms are unique in their ways of communication. As a result, we-media literary criticism also has characteristics of its own.

First, critics of we-media literature have a higher degree of autonomy and freedom. In the Chinese language, the word *zi* (we) in *zimeiti* (we media) emphasizes that now common people, as creators and disseminators of information, have control over such information: *zi* here not only refers to *ziji* (self), but also means *ziyou* (freedom) and *zizhu* (autonomy). As Zhao Yong, a scholar, pointed out, in the era of we media, "individuals have become independent media outlets as they have the right to release news and spread messages, and it is these individuals who make up 'we' in 'we media.'"[20] This means that individuals in we media have a stronger sense of subjectivity and a higher degree of freedom. In this context, there is also an increasing number of people who participate in we-media literary criticism. The popularity of mobile terminals, such as smartphones, has made it easier for people to "become" we media. According to the data from the 37th Statistical Report on Internet Development in China, released by the China Internet Network Information Center (CNNIC), as of December 2015, the number of mobile Internet users in China reached 620 million and the number of people using mobile phones to access the Internet accounted for 90.1% of the total number of netizens.[21] Today, when "writing microblog posts" and "browsing WeChat 'moments'" have become an integral part of people's daily lives, Internet users are all likely to participate in we-media literary criticism.

Second, we-media literary criticism targets specific readers and allows critics and readers to interact with each other better. We-media literary criticism has complicated modes of communication, as the transmission path can be "one-to-one," "one-to-many," and "many-to-one." In this way, we-media literary criticism facilitates the interaction between critics and readers and between readers themselves. It can sometimes go viral and thus have broader audiences. As critics cannot be totally anonymous, their literary reviews enjoy a higher degree of validity and credibility and can better impress readers. In particular, a piece of literary criticism can be delivered to a specific group of readers (the critic's friends) via WeChat "moments"; it can also be written for and sent to a specific reader to convey the critic's ideas on a particular work. In this sense, WeChat literary criticism can be specially tailored and effective. This is also its most significant advantage over other forms of literary criticism. Thus, WeChat does not only deliver and share information but also allows critics to select their readers and define their relationship with readers. A critic can send texts to a limited group of friends or post texts on "moments" for friends to read. Alternatively, the critic can find more readers by using "official accounts." As a result, the critic's words will be read by more people and become more influential. In an article, I made the following argument when discussing the advantages of WeChat:

> Compared with blog literature, WeChat literature has stronger user-stickiness and is suitable for continuous reading and precision marketing. Compared with microblog literature, WeChat literature is more user-friendly and can more effectively reach target readers. Compared with mobile phone literature,[22] WeChat literature has no word limit and is more flexible to incorporate multi-media materials. Its cost is lower as well.[23]

Third, texts of WeChat literary criticism are often fragmentary and simple to read. The activities of writing, reading, and reviewing are fragmented in the era of digital media. As a writer publishes only an episode of a story each time, the story becomes fragmented. Reading, consequently, is fragmented as well. Literary criticism also becomes fragmented, as a critic may just write a few words to express random thoughts after reading. Thus, fragmentation, as a trend, is inevitable in the information age. The rapid development of mobile Internet technology and the widespread use of we media have made this trend even more powerful. In the we-media era, people carry mobile terminals such as phones and tablets to read news, microblogs, WeChat "moments," and e-books during fragments of time as they wait for buses and have meals. In this era, as "everyone is we media," a large amount of information is produced and disseminated at all times. According to the data, as early as 2013, "Chinese netizens posted and forwarded 250 million microblog messages and sent more than 20 billion messages on WeChat and other instant messaging applications every day."[24] While people are reading on mobile phones, such a large amount of information makes it difficult for them to concentrate on a certain piece of text without being distracted. On microblogging platforms and WeChat "moments," articles published by friends and those by subscribed accounts are all put together, so users may only read fragments of these articles. Even on regular blogging platforms, where longer articles are posted, readers often quickly browse different blogs, and the information they receive is still fragmentary. This also leads to the fragmentation of literary criticism. In the face of the flood of information, people have no time to think deeply and carefully. Instead, they make quick and simple responses. When talking about his use of the microblog, the writer Bei Cun once said that he rarely responded to readers' comments in order not to disturb readers and to avoid discussions with them. He explained this situation: "Because of the word limit, you cannot discuss many issues. It is hard to exchange critical thoughts of literature via microblog messages."[25] When people read we media, they often just browse topics and pictures and generally do not read texts carefully. Even if they open an article, with their fingers constantly touching the screen, it is still difficult for them to read the article as carefully as they read articles published in paper media. Many people even give "likes" to an article without reading it. On the WeChat "official account" named "Micro-magazine" (Weizazhi, ID: weixinzazhi), hosted by a writer named "Vice-president of NBC" (NBC erdangjiade), a reader named "The Almighty Monkey King" (Wannengde Sun Wukong) wrote a reply to the writer's WeChat story "Internet Celebrities Design Bureau" (Wanghong shejiju). This reply well reflects the randomness of WeChat literary criticism: "Actually, I haven't read this official account for a long time. I subscribed to your account because of your stories, but later I thought, why could not I see your account? Then I realized it was because I did not use WeChat correctly. Afterward, I was too busy to read your stories as I did before. Good night."

These readers are not professional critics. They write because they have thoughts and feelings about authors or works; sometimes what they write is not even related to the works. Nevertheless, on WeChat "official accounts" hosted by literature websites, there are some critical reviews and promotional articles for literary works published on such websites, which can be more extended and insightful.

The fragmentation of we-media literary criticism reflects the condition of the information era: Readers now read extensively and widely; they have a closer relationship with writers, so everyone has the opportunity to become a literary critic. Meanwhile, such a condition makes their criticism lacking in depth to a considerable extent. They often use only a few words (one or two hundred characters) or only pictures and emojis/emoticons to praise or question the works. This cannot give the works their due in-depth analysis or discussion. From this perspective, Bei Cun's worries may be reasonable. When talking about microblog's influence on literature and literary criticism, he once said: "Microblog is good as it is convenient and can attract readers' attention. But such a relaxing way of communication is easily addictive and can cost readers too much time. Besides, as microblog is 'fragmentary,' it will make our thoughts superficial in the long run."[26] This commentary applies to other types of we-media literary criticism as well.

As we-media literary criticism is written mainly by ordinary people, the language is often plain and simple. The writings are generally short and straightforward but not so logical and intellectually sophisticated. To show appreciation of an article, one can simply give it a "like" on WeChat without writing anything. Even traditional writers and critics, while writing blog and microblog posts, would consciously or unconsciously adjust their language styles to attract ordinary readers and make it easier for readers to understand their views. Kong Qingdong pointed out:

> While many celebrities write blogs, their writings can give us the impression that they are "grassroots" of society just like us. All writers—whether they be young people born in the 1980s, such as Han Han and Guo Jingming, or those who have been well known for decades, such as Yu Hua and Zheng Yuanjie—must make themselves look just like ordinary people before readers can accept them. The particular means of publication makes blog literature no longer as "sacred" as traditional literature.[27]

Wen Huajian once talked about the writing process of his work, "Love in the Era of Microblog" (Weibo shiqi de aiqing), which is the first Chinese microblog story. According to him, while several main characters in the story are fictitious, others are based on real readers who followed the story on *Sina Weibo*. Their discussions and comments as responses to the ongoing story are eventually incorporated into the work; even the actual links to their microblog accounts are given so that later readers can click to visit them.[28] This clearly shows how readers participate in the author's literary creation. Traditional literary criticism has a relatively consistent set of criteria for evaluating works, focusing on their intellectual and artistic qualities. However, in we-media literary criticism, critics sometimes make value judgments based on their preferences rather than on logical reasoning or scholarly methodologies. This is an important reason why we-media literary criticism tends to be plain and simple to read.

Cyber Literary Criticism in Traditional Media

The Development of Cyber Literary Criticism in Traditional Media

Traditional media refer to newspapers, books, and radio/TV broadcasts. They are "traditional" compared with the emerging media on the Internet. In history, they significantly contributed to the development of human civilization. In the information age, while under pressure from new media, they still play an important role in people's lives. Such traditional media, especially literary and academic journals, newspapers, and books, also carry criticism of cyber literature. There are a series of questions concerning this situation. How did cyber literary criticism develop in traditional media? What issues does such a unique type of cyber literary criticism cover, and what characteristics does it have?

In fact, traditional media did not react to cyber literature as quickly as Internet media did in the beginning. In other words, the early cyber literature did not attract the attention of traditional media workers and professional critics. Cyber literary criticism first appeared on the Internet, and the critics were mainly cyber writers and ordinary netizens. However, with Cai Zhiheng's *The First Intimate Contact* becoming phenomenally popular on the Internet and the subsequent upsurge of cyber literature in mainland China, some articles as commentaries on and recommendations of cyber literary works appeared in traditional media. Initially, these articles were published in magazines focusing on computers and the Internet, such as *Popular Computer Weekly* (Diannao bao), *World of Internet Information* (Internet xinxi shijie), and *Computer Fan* (Diannao aihao zhe). They generally introduced the condition of cyber literature, and such introductions were relatively simple.

Later, some articles appeared in academic journals and newspapers that focused on literature and culture. They discussed the concept, value, and significance of cyber literature. Critics who wrote such articles included Huang Mingfen, Ma Ji, Chen Haiyan, Yang Xinmin, and I. In 2000, Huang Mingfen published his article entitled "Nüwa, Venus, or the Terminator: Computer, Cyber Art, and Theory of Cyber Art."[29] It is the first review article on cyber literature published in an authoritative academic journal in China. It discusses how the computer has its impact on people's life, on literature and art, and on literary criticism. It argues that we do not need to feel anxious about computer and Internet technologies, as this does not oppose the humanistic spirit in literature and art. My article, "The Landscape of Literature on the Internet: A Review and Trend Analysis of Cyber Literature in China," published in 2001, is the first long research report on the development of Chinese cyber literature.[30] It studies literary websites, works, and readership and offers suggestions for further developing cyber literature. These two articles are representatives of early cyber literary criticism published in traditional media.

After 2000, more articles that introduced and studied cyber literature appeared in academic journals and newspapers. A considerable number of scholarly books on cyber literature were also published. Some master's theses and doctoral dissertations also focused on cyber literature. Meanwhile, the academic community held many conferences on cyber literature. Some articles presented at these conferences were collected and published as books, while others were published in academic journals. Cyber literature thus became a research hotspot among academics. We can use the "Web Literature Research Database" (Wangluo wenxue yanjiu shujuku) on *China Web Literature Research Website* (Zhongguo wangluo wenxue yanjiu wang) to observe the condition.[31] The database collects numerous research materials about cyber literature from 1991 to 2013. Among them, eight research articles on cyber literature were published in academic journals in 1999. There were nine in 2000, 31 in 2001, 46 in 2003, and 166 in 2011. As to newspaper articles on cyber literature, there were 22 in 2000, 47 in 2001, and 158 in 2009. There were three master theses in 2001, six in 2002, four in 2003, and 68 in 2012. Besides, there were nearly 20 doctoral dissertations between 2002 and 2013, nearly 80 academic books published between 1997 and 2013, and 10 academic conferences between 2004 and 2013.

The "Cyber Literature and Digital Culture Conference" (Wangluo wenxue yu shuzi wenhua xueshu yantaohui) was jointly organized by the College of Literature at Central South University, the editorial department of *Literary Review*, and the editorial department of *Theory and Criticism of Literature and Art* (Wenyi lilun yu piping) in June 2004. It attracted nearly a hundred scholars from universities and research institutes. It was the first high-level conference in the field of cyber literary research, described in a report as "the 'grassroots' cyber literature's first encounter with academics who form the establishment."[32] News on this conference was published in journals including *Literary Review*, *Criticism and Creation* (Lilun yu chuangzuo), and *Theory and Criticism of Literature and Art*. From then on, various types of conferences that focused on works, criticism, and theories of cyber literature were organized by academics, critics, and traditional media. China Writers Association, Writers Associations of various provinces and cities, colleges, universities, and other research organizations (research groups, associations, societies, committees, etc.) held seminars and meetings to discuss cyber literature, new media literature, and cyberculture.

Although it is difficult for us to exhaust all relevant research materials, it is undoubted that research articles published in traditional media increased year by year. We can also check the academic database "China National Knowledge Infrastructure" (www.cnki.net). If we input "cyber literature" (wangluo wenxue) in the search box on its homepage and click the "search" button, we can find 3,660 results, including articles in academic journals and newspapers, master's theses, and doctoral dissertations, all published between 1999 and

2015. In recent years, a large number of articles that study theories and works of cyber literature were published in various journals and newspapers, including *Literary Review*, *Literature and Art Studies* (Wenyi yanjiu), *Literature and Art Contention* (Wenyi zhengming), *Contemporary Writers Review* (Dangdai zuojia pinglun), *Southern Cultural Forum* (Nanfang wentan), *People's Daily* (Renmin ribao), *Guangming Daily* (Guangming ribao), and *Newspaper of Literature and Art* (Wenyi bao). Meanwhile, academic books in this field also increased every year. Thus, traditional media has significantly contributed to the development of cyber literary research with a series of influential publications.

Major Issues Discussed in Cyber Literary Criticism in Traditional Media

Initially, articles in traditional media mainly discussed the concept, characteristics, values, and drawbacks of cyber literature as a new literary form. The first thing critics needed to do was answer some basic yet fundamental questions. For example, what is cyber literature? Is the Internet only a platform—so there is no such thing as "cyber literature" at all? In an article in *Literature Press* (Wenxue bao), Li Jingze argued:

> Literature comes from human minds, not from the Internet. The particular problem we face now is that a shocking illusion leads people to regard the Internet—instead of human minds—as what produces the content and form of literature. It is because of this that we have so-called "cyber literature" today.[33]

Meanwhile, some scholars believed that cyber literature was just a "phenomenon," not a "type" of literature.[34] However, the rapid development of cyber literature and its characteristics that became increasingly noticeable in this process made it necessary for people to recognize it as a new type of literature. The question remained: should we view all literary works appearing on the Internet as cyber literature? Quite a few papers discussed this issue, and they mostly agreed that "cyber literature" should refer to works originally created and published on the Internet.

The Internet caused significant changes in the production and dissemination of literature. Some academic works studied the Internet's influence on literature and cyber literature's artistic characteristics. Huang Mingfen's article, published on April 13, 1999, summarizes the characteristics of cyber literature and art from six aspects: the artist, art form, method of production, intended audience, the origin of the content, and the environment for artistic creation and consumption.[35] Jin Zhenbang's article, published in 2001, proposes that the artistic characteristics of cyber literature exist in "the blurring of genre boundaries, the multimedia way of creating images, the non-linear narration of the story, the holographic openness in the narrative structure, the endless change in art form, the interaction between writers and readers, and the sharing of works online."[36] My article, published in 2001, summarizes the characteristics of cyber literature and art as: "writers are also netizens"; "literary creation is done through interaction"; "literary texts are in digital forms"; "works are circulated online"; "readers read on computers and other electronic devices."[37]

The values and drawbacks of cyber literature are another critical issue. Critics mostly compared cyber literature with traditional literature and praised the new literature for its spirit of freedom, equality, and openness. They believed that it embodied a post-modern zeitgeist and represented a new direction for the development of literature. For example, Nie Qingpu proposed that cyber literature would become the "mainstream form of literature in the future."[38] However, other critics noticed that since everyone could write and publish in cyberspace, the qualities of their writings vary considerably. Some works were not real literature. As authors lacked a sense of responsibility, their subject matters were too narrow, and the contents were too casual. As an example, a critical article discussing such a problem was written by Si Ningda and published in 2003.[39]

In October 2003, *Starting Points Chinese Net* launched a new service that allowed users to access certain works with paid subscriptions. Major websites followed suit, and paid subscriptions became the basic profit model for literary websites. In 2004, Shanda Group acquired *Starting Points Chinese Net*. After that, a series of acquisitions, mergers, cooperative projects, resource integrations, and other activities were carried out among literary websites. This paved the way for the large-scale industrialization of cyber literature, and the commercial nature of cyber literature became increasingly apparent. Some critics wrote articles in academic journals to study this phenomenon. Mainstream media, such as *People's Daily* and *Guangming Daily*, also published many articles to discuss such issues. At this time, the discussion mainly focused on the excessive commercialization of cyber literature. Critics generally suggested that cyber writers should seek a balance between the artistic and the commercial. These articles on the values and shortcomings of cyber literature indicated that cyber literary studies had become mature and rational.

In addition, critics also focused on the construction of an evaluation system for cyber literature. They generally felt that the criteria and methods used in traditional criticism were insufficient, and we should not simply use them to evaluate cyber literature. Meanwhile, ordinary netizens posted many impressive and intriguing ideas on the Internet, yet due to their lack of academic training, their critical words are often fragmentary, emotional, playful, and not systematic or logical enough. Their argumentations are thus unable to be fully developed. Therefore, how to establish a set of criteria for evaluating cyber literature has become a hot issue discussed by scholars in traditional media. From very early on, critics paid attention to the changes in literature and the corresponding challenges to literary criticism in the new context of cyberculture. They published articles to discuss this issue. Examples include my article "High Technology's Challenges to the Research on Basic Theoretical Issues of Literature," published in 2001,[40] and Liu Lili and Li Yuping's "Cyber Literature's Challenges to Literary Theories," published in 2004.[41] Tan Dejing's

On Cyber Literary Criticism is the first monograph that comprehensively discusses various issues of cyber literary criticism, including its aesthetic characteristics and revolutionary significance.[42] Many other articles published in newspapers and academic journals also called for establishing an adequate evaluation system for cyber literature.[43] However, what kind of system was suitable, as a question, was still under discussion among academics.

The Significance and Limitations of Cyber Literary Criticism in Traditional Media

While cyber literary criticism published on the Internet is often personal, casual, and fragmentary, cyber literary criticism in traditional media—mainly print media such as books, newspapers, and journals—pays more attention to logical reasoning and is more academic and in-depth: the former is mainly written by ordinary netizens, and the latter is primarily by university teachers, doctoral and master students, researchers from other research institutes, and editors and reporters working for traditional media. Most of them have academic backgrounds and received specialized training in doing research. They have clear targets and goals for their criticism, knowing what specific issues they are examining. They maintain a rational, objective, and fair attitude toward literary works and rarely put personal emotions into their critical writing. They are also more willing to use relevant theories and methods in the fields of literature and art, aesthetics, sociology, and psychology to explore various issues concerning cyber literature, such as its production, communication, artistic characteristics, and aesthetic significance.

Interestingly, these literary critics usually do not choose to publish critical articles on the Internet. This may be related to the mechanism for evaluating scholars' academic contributions used widely by universities and research institutes in China. Universities and other research institutes generally require scholars to make research achievements, but these organizations only recognize articles published in academic journals as valid scholarly contributions, as only in this way can they effectively evaluate such works. Scholars' reluctance to publish their critical articles online is also related to their arrogance toward cyber literature and cyber literary criticism. As they are accustomed to publishing and reading works in print media, they are not familiar with or interested in the Internet as a new platform for academic publication. They assume that criticism published online is not in-depth enough and that exchanging opinions with ordinary netizens may benefit little and even degrade them. Therefore, many of them disdain publishing literary criticism on the Internet.

More importantly, cyber literature is different from traditional literature in terms of production, dissemination, and artistic characteristics. Many critics who publish in traditional media still adopt old research methods and criteria to view and evaluate cyber literature. As their evaluation criteria are no longer suitable, they cannot adequately analyze this new literature. The writers of cyber literature are a diversified group of people. Most of them are ordinary literature amateurs, not professional writers, and their writing skills vary significantly. In cyber literature, click volume is usually the measure of the value of a work. A work thus must cater to ordinary readers' aesthetic taste. To make a story more attractive, an author must pay more attention to the storyline and the characters rather than the rich connotation and narrative/rhetoric skills valued by traditional literature. Meanwhile, the current evaluation criteria are set for serious literature in the conventional sense. Critics will encounter problems if they use old criteria to examine new literature.

Apart from this, as a web novel is usually massive in volume, with up to tens of millions of Chinese characters, critics are unwilling to make efforts to analyze it. Instead, they would rather stay at the periphery and give generalized discussions on cyber literature. In addition, as authors and readers of cyber literature can interact quickly and conveniently at any time on the Internet, cyber literary criticism can influence and even guide an author's literary creation. In contrast, the circulation of print media is slow, so it is difficult for traditional critics to have dialogues through books and journals. Although some newspapers and periodicals contain sections to show readers' and scholars' opinions, the words are edited and rearranged to reflect editors' will to a large extent rather than ordinary readers' thoughts. In this sense, the paper media has its limitations.

Thus, critical works published in traditional media have a series of problems: they keep a distance away from specific texts of cyber literature and maintain a set of criteria that are not suitable for evaluating this new form of literature. Critics now pay much attention to such problems. He Ping posed such a question: when cyber literature has become a force that cannot be ignored in contemporary literature, "if critics nowadays still adhere to the old perspective that is used to examine works published in print media, will they be able to draw sound conclusions about today's Chinese literature?"[44] Li Jingze argued: "We cannot force cyber literature to model itself on serious literature and make it read like literary classics."[45] Ma Ji pointed out that "we still lack effective theories to guide the creation of cyber literature."[46] Therefore, how to establish an effective evaluation system for cyber literature has become a hot topic for articles published in print media.

Some scholars argue that traditional literary critics should be truly involved in the activities concerning cyber literature. As I proposed in an article, critics should have more of their presence on the Internet, base their research on actual reading, and give theoretical analyses of specific texts—this should be the primary method of cyber literary research.[47] However, it is still challenging to do so in actual practice. Meanwhile, cyber writers also look forward to reasonable criteria to guide their literary creation. "Dust under the Sky" (Tianxia chen'ai, real name Xiang Juan), a cyber writer, described such good criticism as a "lamp" that sheds light on the path to guide cyber writers who walk in the dark.[48] "Bright and Wavy Purple" (Liulianzi, real name Wu Xuelan) said: "If more professional critics and researchers take the initiative to enter the online communities and have dialogues with writers via blogs, microblogs, and other channels, I believe it will definitely have a positive impact on these writers' literary creation."[49]

In any case, cyber literary criticism in traditional media and cyber literary criticism on the Internet do not oppose each other. Instead, they should learn from and complement each other. Most critics in traditional media have professional knowledge of literary theories and rich experience in academic research. Their analysis is often lucid and thorough. Comparatively, literary criticism on the Internet is more vivid, flexible, and closer to the actual context of cyber literature. Thus, we need to combine these two types of criticism into one. Only by doing this can we truly create a cyber literary criticism that has a reciprocal relationship with cyber literary creation—criticism and literary creation thus can work together, just like the two wings of a bird.

Notes

1 Marshall McLuhan, *Understanding Media: The Extensions of Man* (Cambridge, MA: The MIT Press, 1994), 63.
2 Nicholas Negroponte, *Being Digital* (New York: Vintage, 1996), 2.
3 This website was established by Wang Xiaofei outside China in 1991. It was closed later and was only mentioned in related research articles.
4 China Internet Network Information Center (CNNIC), "The 38th Statistical Report on Internet Development in China," *CNNIC*, last modified September 28, 2016b, www.cnnic.com.cn/IDR/ReportDownloads/201611/P020161114573409551742.pdf.
5 Translator's note: ACT is short for alt.chinese.text. It is the earliest newsgroup (a type of forum) where people posted texts in Chinese.
6 Bai, Ye 白烨, "Wenxue piping de xin jingyu yu xin tiaozhan" 文学批评的新境遇与新挑战, *Literature & Arts Studies* 文艺研究 no. 8 (2009): 8.
7 Translator's note: the sentence here does not make much sense, and this is how a reader's comment can be.
8 From "Miaojiang gushi ba" 苗疆蛊事吧, a section on tieba.baidu.com. Translator's note: The original link is already defunct and is thus not given here.
9 Tan, Dejing 谭德晶, *Wangluo wenxue piping lun* 网络文学批评论 (Beijing: CFLAC Publishing House, 2004), 157.
10 Ren, Changhui 任昌辉and Zheng, Zhibin 郑智斌, "Zimeiti shidai xia chuantong meiti xinwen shengchan de shanbian yu fazhan" 自媒体时代下传统媒体新闻生产的嬗变与发展, *News Reporting and Editing* 新闻采编 no. 5 (2014): 40.
11 Deng, Xinmin 邓新民, "Zimeiti: xinmeiti fazhan de zuixin jieduan jiqi tedian" 自媒体：新媒体发展的最新阶段及其特点, *Exploration* 探索 no. 2 (2006): 135.
12 Zhang, Chenyang 张晨阳, "Zimeiti shidai weibo re de xi yu you" 自媒体时代微博热的喜与忧, *China Publishing Journal* 中国出版 October, no. 2 (2011): 18.
13 Deng, Xinmin 邓新民, "Zimeiti: xinmeiti fazhan de zuixin jieduan jiqi tedian" 自媒体：新媒体发展的最新阶段及其特点, 134.
14 Wu, Chao 吴潮, "Xinmeiti yu zimeiti de dingyi shuli ji erzhe guanxi bianxi" 新媒体与自媒体的定义梳理及二者关系辨析, *Journal of Zhejiang University of Media & Communications* 浙江传媒学院学报 no. 5 (2014): 34.
15 *"Jinji de weixin weixin yuehuoyue yonghushu tupo qiyi"* "进击的微信"微信月活跃用户数突破7亿, Souhu 搜狐, 2016. www.sohu.com/a/70824398_115266.
16 Kong, Qingdong 孔庆东, "Boke, dangdai wenxue de xin wenti" 博客, 当代文学的新文体, *Literary Contestations* 文艺争鸣 no. 4 (2007): 43.

17 Wang, Ji 王蓟 and Yang, Yi 杨艺, "Renren fenwo wo fen renren weibo shuijun xiongmeng 人人粉我 我粉人人 微博水军凶猛," *Chengdu shangbao* 成都商报 (Chengdu), Mar. 13, 2012.
18 Chen, Jing 陈竞, "Weibo cheng zuojia duzhe hudong xin pingtai 微博成作家读者互动新平台," *Wenxue bao* 文学报 (Shanghai), Feb. 17, 2011.
19 Ouyang, Youquan 欧阳友权, "Weixin wenxue de cunzai fangshi yu gongneng quxiang" 微信文学的存在方式与功能取向, *Jianghai Academic Journal* 江海学刊 no. 1 (2015a): 198.
20 Zhao, Yong 赵勇, "'Zimeiti' shidai de gongshi yindao" "自媒体"时代的共识引导, *Chinese Public Administration* 中国行政管理 no. 11 (2011): 103.
21 China Internet Network Information Center (CNNIC), "The 37th Statistical Report on Internet Development in China," *CNNIC*, last modified January 22, 2016a, www.cnnic.com.cn/IDR/ReportDownloads/201604/P020160419390562421055.pdf.
22 Translator's note: this refers to literature sent via text messages.
23 Ouyang, Youquan 欧阳友权, "Weixin wenxue de cunzai fangshi yu gongneng quxiang" 微信文学的存在方式与功能取向, 199.
24 Tang, Liang 唐亮, "Suipianhua yuedu: yizhong huoqu zhishi de tujing 碎片化阅读：一种获取知识的途径," *Zhongguo shehui kexue bao* 中国社会科学报 (Beijing), Nov. 19, 2015.
25 Su, Ya 苏娅, "Women zai xie shenme? 我们在写什么？" *Diyi caijing ribao* 第一财经日报 (Shanghai), Mar. 3, 2011.
26 Su, Ya 苏娅, "Women zai xie shenme? 我们在写什么？"
27 Kong, Qingdong 孔庆东, "Boke, dangdai wenxue de xin wenti" 博客，当代文学的新文体, 42.
28 Deng, Taoying 邓桃英, "Wangyou zai weibo shang shishi zaixian xiezuo yinfa guanzhu 网友在微博上实时在线写作引发关注," *Yangzi wanbao* 扬子晚报 (Nanjing), Mar. 21, 2010.
29 Huang, Mingfen 黄鸣奋, "Nüwa, weinasi, yihuo mogui zhongjiezhe?—diannao, diannaowenyi yu diannao wenyixue" 女娲、维纳斯、亦或魔鬼终结者？—电脑、电脑文艺与电脑文艺学, *Literary Review* 文学评论 no. 5 (2000): 77–86.
30 Ouyang, Youquan 欧阳友权, "Hulianwang shang de wenxue fengjing: woguo wangluo wenxue xianzhuang diaocha yu zoushi fenxi" 互联网上的文学风景：我国网络文学现状调查与走势分析, *Journal of China Three Gorges University: The Humanities and Social Sciences Edition* 三峡大学学报（人文社会科学版）no. 6 (2001b): 5–9.
31 Translator's note: the website and the database are no longer accessible.
32 Ouyang 欧阳 and Aiguo 艾国, "Wangluo wenxue yu shuzi wenhua xueshu yantaohui zai changsha zhaokai" 网络文学与数字文化学术研讨会在长沙召开, *Literary Review* 文学评论 no. 5 (2004): 197.
33 Li, Jingze 李敬泽, "Wangluo wenxue: yaodian he yiwen 网络文学：要点和疑问," *Wenxue bao* 文学报 (Shanghai), Apr. 20, 2000.
34 Dun, Yulin 敦玉林, "Wangluo wenxue: wenxue de xinbianqian" 网络文学：文学的新变迁, *Tianjin Social Sciences* 天津社会科学 no. 4 (2002): 110.
35 Huang, Mingfen 黄鸣奋, "Xinxi keji jinbu yu yishu biange 信息科技进步与艺术变革," *Wenyi bao* 文艺报 (Beijing), Apr. 13, 1999.
36 Jin, Zhenbang 金振邦, "Wangluo wenxue: xinshiji wenxue de liebian" 网络文学：新世纪文学的裂变, *Journal of Northeast University: Philosophy and Social Sciences Edition* 东北师大学报（哲学社会科学版）no. 1 (2001): 1–8.

37 Ouyang, Youquan 欧阳友权, "Wangluo wenxue: tiaozhan chuantong yu gengxin guannian" 网络文学：挑战传统与更新观念, *Social Science Journal of Xiangtan University* 湘潭大学社会科学学报 no. 1 (2001c): 36–37.
38 Nie, Qingpu 聂庆璞, "Wangluo wenxue: weilai wenxue de zhuliu xingtai" 网络文学：未来文学的主流形态, *Social Science Front* 社会科学战线 no. 4 (2002): 105.
39 Si, Ningda 司宁达, "Wangluo wenxue de juxianxing yu fazhan qushi" 网络文学的局限性与发展趋势, *Academic Forum of Nandu* 南都学刊 no. 4 (2003): 68–71.
40 Ouyang, Youquan 欧阳友权, "Gaokeji dui wenxue jiben lilun yanjiu de tiaozhan" 高科技对文学基本理论研究的挑战, *Social Science Front* 社会科学战线 no. 2 (2001a): 95–98.
41 Liu, Lili 刘俐俐 and Li, Yuping 李玉平, "Wangluo wenxue dui wenxue piping lilun de tiaozhan" 网络文学对文学批评理论的挑战, *Journal of Lanzhou University: Social Sciences Edition* 兰州大学学报（社会科学版）no. 5 (2004): 1–8.
42 Tan, Dejing 谭德晶, *Wangluo wenxue piping lun* 网络文学批评论 (Beijing: CFLAC Publishing House, 2004).
43 See: Yu, Jianxiang 禹建湘, "Kongjian zhuanxiang: jiangou wangluo wenxue piping xin fanshi" 空间转向：建构网络文学批评新范式, *Exploration and Free Views* 探索与争鸣 no. 11 (2010): 67–70.
Zhang, Wendong 张文东, "Xinmeiti yu xinpiping: wangluo wenxue piping de 'shixing' lijie" 新媒体与新批评：网络文学批评的"诗性"理解, *Contemporary Literary Criticism* 当代文坛 no. 6 (2015): 4–8.
Guo, Guochang 郭国昌, "Wangluo wenxue huhuan wenxue piping 网络文学呼唤文学批评," *Renmin ribao* 人民日报 (Beijing), Feb. 5, 2010.
Wu, Yan 吴艳, "Jiaqiang wangluo wenxue de zaixian piping 加强网络文学的在线批评," *Wenyi bao* 文艺报 (Beijing), Apr. 11, 2012.
Wang, Guoping 王国平, "Wangluo wenxue jidai queli piping 'zhibiao tixi' 网络文学亟待确立批评'指标体系,'" *Guangming ribao* 光明日报 (Beijing), Jul. 3, 2012.
Chen, Qirong 陈崎嵘, "Huyu jianli wangluo wenxue pingjia tixi 呼唤建立网络文学评价体系," *Renmin ribao* 人民日报 (Beijing), Jul. 19, 2013.
Wu, Changqing 吴长青, "Shilun wangluo wenxue piping de kunjing 试论网络文学批评的困境," *Guangming ribao* 光明日报 (Beijing), Oct. 15, 2013.
Shi, Shiping 时世平, "Wangluo wenxue: piping de mimang yu qingxing 网络文学：批评的迷茫与清醒," *Zhongguo shehui kexue bao* 中国社会科学报 (Beijing), Sep. 14, 2015.
44 He, Ping 何平, "Wangluo wanxue zai renshi: duihua he xieshang de 'xinpiping' 网络文学再认识：对话和协商的'新批评,'" *Renmin ribao* 人民日报 (Beijing), May. 23, 2014.
45 Ma, Ji 马季, "Kuajie hezuo huigui zhuliu—erling yisi nian wangluo wenxue zongshu 跨界合作回归主流—2014 年网络文学综述," *Guangming ribao* 光明日报 (Beijing), Feb. 2, 2015.
46 Ma, Ji 马季, "Kuajie hezuo huigui zhuliu—erling yisi nian wangluo wenxue zongshu 跨界合作回归主流—2014年网络文学综述."
47 Ouyang, Youquan 欧阳友权, "Zhongguo wangluo wenxue yanjiu jidian jiqi yujing xuanze" 中国网络文学研究基点及其语境选择, *Hebei Academic Journal* 河北学刊 no. 4 (2015b): 96.
48 Xiang, Juan 向娟, "Xunmi yizhandeng—huhuan goujian wangluo wenxue pingjia tixi 寻觅一盏灯—呼唤构建网络文学评价体系," *Guangming ribao* 光明日报 (Beijing), Feb. 24, 2014.

49 Yimeng 怡梦, "Wangluo wenxue xuyao shenmeyang de zhuanye piping? 网络文学需要什么样的专业批评？," *Zhongguo yishu bao* 中国艺术报 (Beijing), Jul. 15, 2013.

Bibliography

Bai, Ye 白烨. "Wenxue piping de xin jingyu yu xin tiaozhan" 文学批评的新境遇与新挑战. *Literature & Arts Studies* 文艺研究 no. 8 (2009): 5–11.

Chen, Jing 陈竞. "Weibo cheng zuojia duzhe hudong xin pingtai 微博成作家读者互动新平台." *Wenxuebao* 文学报 (Shanghai), Feb. 17, 2011.

Chen, Qirong 陈崎嵘. "Huyu jianli wangluo wenxue pingjia tixi 呼吁建立网络文学评价体系." *Renmin ribao* 人民日报 (Beijing), Jul. 19, 2013.

China Internet Network Information Center (CNNIC). "The 37th Statistical Report on Internet Development in China." *CNNIC*. Last modified January 22, 2016a, www.cnnic.com.cn/IDR/ReportDownloads/201604/P020160419390562421055.pdf.

China Internet Network Information Center (CNNIC). "The 38th Statistical Report on Internet Development in China." *CNNIC*. Last modified November 14, 2016b. www.cnnic.com.cn/IDR/ReportDownloads/201611/P020161114573409551742.pdf.

Deng, Taoying 邓桃英. "Wangyou zai weibo shang shishi zaixian xiezuo yinfa guanzhu 网友在微博上实时在线写作引发关注." *Yangzi wanbao* 扬子晚报 (Nanjing), Mar. 21, 2010.

Deng, Xinmin 邓新民. "Zimeiti: xinmeiti fazhan de zuixin jieduan jiqi tedian" 自媒体：新媒体发展的最新阶段及其特点. *Exploration* 探索 no. 2 (2006): 134–138.

Dun, Yulin 敦玉林. "Wangluo wenxue: wenxue de xinbianqian" 网络文学：文学的新变迁. *Tianjin Social Sciences* 天津社会科学 no. 4 (2002): 110–114.

Guo, Guochang 郭国昌. "Wangluo wenxue huhuan wenxue piping 网络文学呼唤文学批评." *Renmin ribao* 人民日报 (Beijing), Feb. 5, 2010.

He, Ping 何平. "Wangluo wenxue zai renshi: duihua he xieshang de 'xinpiping' 网络文学再认识：对话和协商的'新批评.'" *Renmin ribao* 人民日报 (Beijing), May. 23, 2014.

Huang, Mingfen 黄鸣奋. "Xinxi keji jinbu yu yishu biange 信息科技进步与艺术变革." *Wenyi bao* 文艺报 (Beijing), Apr. 13, 1999.

Huang, Mingfen 黄鸣奋. "Nüwa, weinasi, yihuo mogui zhongjiezhe?—diannao, diannaowenyi yu diannao wenyixue" 女娲、维纳斯，亦或魔鬼终结者？—电脑、电脑文艺与电脑文艺学. *Literary Review* 文学评论 no. 5 (2000): 77–86.

Jin, Zhenbang 金振邦. "Wangluo wenxue: xinshiji wenxue de liebian" 网络文学：新世纪文学的裂变. *Journal of Northeast University: Philosophy and Social Sciences Edition* 东北师大学报（哲学社会科学版） no. 1 (2001): 70–76.

"Jinji de weixin weixin" yuehuoyue yonghushu tupo qiyi "进击的微信"微信月活跃用户数突破7亿. Souhu 搜狐, 2016. www.sohu.com/a/70824398_115266.

Kong, Qingdong 孔庆东. "Boke, dangdai wenxue de xin wenti" 博客，当代文学的新文体. *Literary Contestations* 文艺争鸣 no. 4 (2007): 41–43.

Li, Jingze 李敬泽. "'Wangluo wenxue': yaodian he yiwen '网络文学'：要点和疑问." *Wenxue bao* 文学报 (Shanghai), Apr. 20, 2000.

Liu, Lili 刘俐俐 and Li, Yuping 李玉平. "Wangluo wenxue dui wenxue piping lilun de tiaozhan" 网络文学对文学批评理论的挑战. *Journal of Lanzhou University: Social Sciences Edition* 兰州大学学报（社会科学版） no. 5 (2004): 1–8.

Ma, Ji 马季. "Kuajie hezuo huigui zhuliu—erling yisi nian wnagluo wenxue zongshu 跨界合作回归主流——2014年网络文学综述." *Guangming ribao* 光明日报 (Beijing), Feb. 2, 2015.

McLuhan, Marshall. *Understanding Media: The Extensions of Man*. Cambridge, MA: The MIT Press, 1994.

Negroponte, Nicholas. *Being Digital*. New York: Vintage, 1996.

Nie, Qingpu 聂庆璞. "Wangluo wenxue: weilai wenxue de zhuliu xingtai" 网络文学：未来文学的主流形态. *Social Science Front* 社会科学战线 no. 4 (2002): 105–109.

Ouyang 欧阳 and Aiguo 艾国. "'Wangluo wenxue yu shuzi wenhua' xueshu yantaohui zai changsha zhaokai" "网络文学与数字文化"学术研讨会在长沙召开. *Literary Review* 文学评论 no. 5 (2004): 197.

Ouyang, Youquan 欧阳友权. "Gaokeji dui wenxue jiben lilun yanjiu de tiaozhan" 高科技对文学基本理论研究的挑战. *Social Science Front* 社会科学战线 no. 2 (2001a): 95–98.

Ouyang, Youquan 欧阳友权. "Hulianwang shang de wenxue fengjing: woguo wangluo wenxue xianzhuang diaocha yu zoushi fenxi" 互联网上的文学风景：我国网络文学现状调查与走势分析. *Journal of China Three Gorges University: The Humanities and Social Sciences Edition* 三峡大学学报（人文社会科学版）no. 6 (2001b): 5–9.

Ouyang, Youquan 欧阳友权. "Wangluo wenxue: tiaozhan chuantong yu gengxin guannian" 网络文学：挑战传统与更新观念. *Social Science Journal of Xiangtan University* 湘潭大学社会科学学报 no. 1 (2001c): 36–40.

Ouyang, Youquan 欧阳友权. "Weixin wenxue de cunzai fangshi yu gongneng quxiang" 微信文学的存在方式与功能取向. *Jianghai Academic Journal* 江海学刊 no. 1 (2015a): 195–200.

Ouyang, Youquan 欧阳友权. "Zhongguo wangluo wenxue yanjiu jidian jiqi yujing xuanze" 中国网络文学研究基点及其语境选择. *Hebei Academic Journal* 河北学刊 no. 4 (2015b): 96–99.

Ren, Changhui 任昌辉 and Zheng, Zhibin 郑智斌. "Zimeiti shidai xia chuantong meiti xinwen shengchan de shanbian yu fazhan" 自媒体时代下传统媒体新闻生产的嬗变与发展. *News Reporting and Editing* 新闻采编 no. 5 (2014): 40–41.

Shi, Shiping 时世平. "Wangluo wenxue: piping de mimang yu qingxing 网络文学：批评的迷茫与清醒." *Zhongguo shehui kexue bao* 中国社会科学报 (Beijing), Sep. 14, 2015.

Si, Ningda 司宁达. "Wangluo wenxue de juxianxing yu fazhan qushi" 网络文学的局限性与发展趋势. *Academic Forum of Nandu* 南都学刊 no. 4 (2003): 68–71.

Su, Ya 苏娅. "Women zai xie shenme 我们在写什么." *Diyi caijing ribao* 第一财经日报 (Shanghai), Mar. 3, 2011.

Tan, Dejing 谭德晶. *Wangluo wenxue piping lun* 网络文学批评论. Beijing: CFLAC Publishing House, 2004.

Tang, Liang 唐亮. "Suipianhua yuedu: yizhong huoqu zhishi de tujing 碎片化阅读：一种获取知识的途径." *Zhongguo shehui kexue bao* 中国社会科学报 (Beijing), Nov. 19, 2015.

Wang, Guoping 王国平. "Wangluo wenxue jidai queli piping 'zhibiao tixi' 网络文学亟待确立批评'指标体系.'" *Guangming ribao* 光明日报 (Beijing), Jul. 3, 2012.

Wang, Ji 王蓟 and Yang, Yi 杨艺. "Renren fenwo wo fen renren weibo shuijun xiongmeng 人人粉我 我粉人人 微博水军凶猛." *Chengdu shangbao* 成都商报 (Chengdu), Mar. 13, 2012.

Wu, Changqing 吴长青. "Shilun wangluo wenxue piping de kunjing 试论网络文学批评的困境." *Guangming ribao* 光明日报 (Beijing), Oct. 15, 2013.

Wu, Chao 吴潮. "Xinmeiti yu zimeiti de dingyi shuli ji erzhe guanxi bianxi" 新媒体与自媒体的定义梳理及二者关系辨析. *Journal of Zhejiang University of Media & Communications* 浙江传媒学院学报 no. 5 (2014): 33–37.

Wu, Yan 吴艳. "Jiaqiang wangluo wenxue de zaixian piping 加强网络文学的在线批评." *Wenyi bao* 文艺报 (Beijing), Apr. 11, 2012.

Xiang, Juan 向娟. "Xunmi yizhandeng—huhuan goujian wangluo wenxue pingjia tixi 寻觅一盏灯——呼唤构建网络文学评价体系." *Guangming ribao* 光明日报 (Beijing), Feb. 24, 2014.

Yimeng 怡梦. "Wangluo wenxue xuyao shenmeyang de zhuanye piping? 网络文学需要什么样的专业批评？" *Zhongguo yishu bao* 中国艺术报 (Beijing), Jul. 15, 2013.

Yu, Jianxiang 禹建湘. "Kongjian zhuanxiang: jiangou wangluo wenxue piping xin fanshi" 空间转向：建构网络文学批评新范式. *Exploration and Free Views* 探索与争鸣 no. 11 (2010): 67–70.

Zhang, Chenyang 张晨阳. "Zimeiti shidai weibo re de xi yu you" 自媒体时代微博热的喜与忧. *China Publishing Journal* 中国出版 October no. 2 (2011): 18–21.

Zhang, Wendong 张文东. "Xinmeiti yu xinpiping: wangluo wenxue piping de 'shixing' lijie" 新媒体与新批评：网络文学批评的"诗性"理解. *Contemporary Literary Criticism* 当代文坛 no. 6 (2015): 4–8.

Zhao, Yong 赵勇. "'Zimeiti' shidai de gongshi yindao" "自媒体"时代的共识引导. *Chinese Public Administration* 中国行政管理 no. 11 (2011): 103–104.

2 Major Types of Cyber Literary Critics and Their Criticism

From the 1990s, China's cyber literature boomed with massive output and attracted a lot of readers' attention. An increasing number of people began to read and write literature online. Critics of such a new type of literature also grew in number and developed different schools of thought. These critics can be divided into three groups: ordinary readers who freely express their views online, market-oriented media that publish criticism to serve the audience, and scholars who base their criticism on literary theories. The works of the three groups of people are complementary to each other. Together, they form the main body of cyber literary criticism.

Free Voices of Ordinary Readers on the Internet

Ordinary readers on the Internet are the main force of cyber literary criticism. Being the first to enter this field, they spoke freely with different voices in cyberspace. In 1991, the first Chinese online magazine *China News Digest* (Huaxia wenzhai) was launched in North America, which marked the birth of cyber literature in Chinese. Subsequently, a series of Chinese online magazines, such as *New World* (Xindalu), *Maple Garden* (Fengshu yuan), *Northeast Wind* (Dongbeifeng), and *Tulip* (Yujinxiang), were established in North America, Asia, and Europe. Literary websites sprung up, including *New Threads of Thought* (Xin Yu Si), *Olive Tree* (Ganlan shu), *Trick* (Huazhao), *Shuimu Tsinghua BBS*, and *Under the Banyan Tree* (Rongshuxia). Cyber writers such as Fang Zhouzi, San Yisheng, Yi Wei, Tu Ya, Shao Jun, "Banly," Yuan Chen, Wu Guo, Li Xunhuan, Xing Yusen, Zhang Yuanshan, and Ge Tao rose to fame. They were quite active in major forums in the early period of cyber literature.

Cyber literary criticism gained strong vitality due to its unique characteristics, such as anonymity, interactivity, connectivity, convenience, and openness. As all ordinary readers could publish their views and cyberspace had unlimited data storage, the group of netizens who read literature and wrote literary criticism continued to expand. In the 21st century, major websites and forums continued to develop, including *Under the Banyan Tree*, *Skyline Community* (Tianya shequ), *Mop.com*, *Netease*, *Sohu*, *Sina*, and *Reading with Beauty*

(Hongxiu tianxiang). Literary websites also rose quickly, including *Book Union for Swordsmen's Legends* (Huanjian shumeng), *Starting Points Chinese Net* (Qidian zhongwen wang), *Jinjiang Literature City* (Jinjiang wenxuecheng), *17K Novels* (17K xiaoshuo wang), and *Crisscross Chinese Net* (Zongheng zhongwenwang). Cyber literary criticism started to develop on these websites and gradually matured. Netizens wrote a massive volume of words, producing countless posts every day. Online literary criticism thus became a significant form of cyber literary criticism. According to the Statistical Report released by China Internet Network Information Center (CNNIC), as of June 2016, there were already 710 million Internet users in China, and 308 million (or 46.6 percent) of them read literature online. 656 million people used cellphones to access the Internet, and 281 million read literature on their cellphones.[1] With the popularization of 4G/5G mobile networks and Wi-Fi, people now no longer have to use a regular computer to access the Internet. With various portable devices, such as cellphones, iPads, and Kindles, and with new media apps, people can freely express their views on literature in a way that is more convenient, faster, and more flexible than before.

Netizens' Short Replies and Clicks

Netizens who express their attitudes toward literary works make the most direct and quickest online literary criticism. Such netizens use concise and clear words and phrases to comment on works they have read, such as "good," "bump (the thread)," "well done," and "I don't like it." Some netizens use emoticons or pictures. Today, such expressions are common on various forums, including *Baidu Post Bar* (Baidu tieba). These readers usually use a few simple words or sentences to express their opinions without excessive analysis or explanation. This is because cyber literature does not encourage readers to think deeply: as people's life becomes fast-paced, they do not go deep into their reading; most readers find it difficult to focus on reading and writing for a long time. Consequently, they usually only talk about their overall impression of the works and give an intuitive evaluation of them. Thus, their writing is conversational, brief, and casual.

There are also other ways that allow readers to express their attitudes instantly. At present, major literary websites have systems for the rapid evaluation of works: readers can respond to a work directly by clicking on a few buttons such as "recommend," "like," "bookmark," "rate," and "reward." There are also book rankings, often based on readers' clicks, recommendations, bookmarks, and ratings. Works that receive the most reviews from ordinary readers and professional critics can also form ranking lists. All these indicators visually show the readership and popularity of the works. The click-through rate indicates a work's popularity, but it does not mean that all those who clicked on a work have read it, so the click-through rate is only for a preliminary evaluation of a work's popularity. As readers have a chance to "rate," "bookmark," "recommend," and "like" a particular work after reading each chapter of it, such a webpage setting collects a more valuable kind of readers' feedback. The instant evaluation system will then display the results in the form of book rankings on a literary website. As an example, there was a list entitled "the rankings of works that received most likes" on *Starting Points Chinese Net* in November, 2015, with the top five novels being Hudie Lan's *Legend of Awakening* (Tianxing zhilu), Er Gen's *I Desire to Rise to the Top of the World* (Woyu fengtian), Yuan Tong's *A Witness's Record of Strange Creatures* (Yichang shengwu jianwenlu), and Wang Yu's *A Legend of Devils* (Motianji).[2] While readers give instantaneous evaluations of literary works with just a few clicks, the rankings synthesize various types of data to create statistical numbers. In this way, the original text-based criticism is replaced by readers' clicks, which can be collected and quantified. The data-based evaluation has become a new form of online literary criticism, and more readers are encouraged to participate as it is so convenient.

Netizens' Dialogues and Posts

Among readers on the Internet, those who like to interact with others tend to cause a chain effect that draws more people into a "field" of criticism. After someone starts a thread on a forum, others refer to the thread starter as the "host" (louzhu) and follow the thread with their own posts. The relationship between the "host" and other posters is not hierarchical but equal. Such threads are like rows of dominoes: a chain effect brings more people into the "field" of criticism, where they can have dialogues with others. With so many different voices mixed in cyberspace, an individual's fragmented comment can quickly go unnoticed. With the influx of new posts that contain so much information, a post made an hour or a day ago is likely to continue to fall lower in the listing, but the chain effect created by posts in a single thread may heat a discussion again. In this way, the bumping up of a thread highlights the tremendous importance of posting as a form of literary criticism.

Most posters are also readers. Some of them discuss their reading preferences and textual details. They express how they feel about reading particular works. Some other posters chat about trivial matters in daily life and their feelings. Some choose to read other people's discussions and have fun mainly as mere onlookers. In a thread, people exchange words and have dialogues: some hotly argue with each other, while others are more friendly. The interaction between an author and readers is also indispensable to this type of literary criticism. In forums, an author can post to tell readers about the date for the release of a new episode, chapter arrangement, and new works. An author often exchanges ideas and even gifts with readers. While readers often ask about a story's progress or ending, an author can also talk about his/her creative motives and thoughts. The author's responses increase the work's popularity and create a dialogue with readers. Meanwhile, readers' encouragement and support are crucial to an author's continuous literary creation. The author's timely understanding of readers' reading experiences and psychological needs is conducive to creating excellent works.

The interactivity of the Internet allows literary criticism to influence literary creation. Readers can tell an author about their demands and opinions to influence the author's writing. They can even directly post their own writing: some rewrite the original ending of a novel, while others continue a novel or expand it. For example, a netizen named "Young Lord Kuan" (Kuan gongzi) posted in the book review area on *Starting Points Chinese Net* to give an alternative ending to *Spies* (Jianke), a novel originally written by "Trick" (Maoni).[3] Some readers work together to create their own story based on an existent web novel: in this process, each reader writes and posts an episode. Representative works of this kind include *Rose in the Wind* (Fengzhong meigui), *Running Dalmatians on the Internet* (Wangshang paoguo bandiangou), *Urban Green Space* (Chengshi de lüdi), and *In Love Women Struggle* (Aiqing shi nüren de jianghu).

This type of criticism is diverse, on-site, interactive, and unrestrained. It breaks free from the tradition of literary criticism. While traditional literary criticism is unidirectional, the interactive criticism in cyberspace draws many readers into multiple dialogues focusing on specific literary works. As this criticism consists of various readers' posts in a thread, it as a whole is constantly using different perspectives to discuss a literary work. As readers interact through these posts, the confrontation and diversion in their discussions will produce different ideas and new topics.

Netizens' Appreciative and Critical Reviews

Those who write appreciative and critical reviews are heavyweights among all netizens. Compared with others, their posts are the most powerful literary critiques and can best reflect netizens' personalities. Such posts are usually long articles with clear topics, and their styles vary: they can be analytical and intellectual, poetic and emotional, humorous and hilarious, or critical and pungent. Some critical articles may be called "brick posts."[4] Some are marked as "excellent posts" in post listings by moderators and administrators of literary forums.[5]

Posters have to write well and meet the requirements of forums to have their posts highlighted in the listing. Usually, a post that contains excellent comments, or a post that is hotly discussed, will have its title marked as "excellent," or colored red, or stuck to the top of the listing. There is never a shortage of talented commentators on the Internet, and forums are a place for them to show their talents. In terms of style, such posts can be divided into several types. We can conveniently call them "posts based on personal reflection" (*tiwushi piping*), "posts based on argumentation" (*shuolishi piping*), "posts for fun" (*quweishi piping*), and "spoofs" (*egaoshi piping*).

"Posts based on personal reflections" (*tiwushi piping*) inherit their essence from ancient criticism that focuses on the romantic charm in literature. They pay particular attention to individuals' reading experiences and emotional expressions. We have many examples of this kind, including a series of posts collectively entitled "Comments on Mao Zedong and His Poems" (Ping Mao shuo shi) by San Yisheng, reviews of Chinese American writers' works by Fang Zhouzi, a series of posts entitled "Sword Competition on the Internet" (Wangluo lunjian) by "Yu, the White-browed" (Yu baimei), "Flowers Blooming in the Dark" (Hei'anzhong zhanfang de huaguduo) by "Ning, the God of Wealth" (Ning caishen), and a series of essays on classic poetry by An Yiru. They are all based on reviewers' personal feelings. The language they use is vivid, straightforward, and quite literary. In particular, San Yisheng, one of the "Eight Masters of Cyber Literature" (wangwen badajia) in the early days, was interested in writing about the overall charm of literary works. His *A Collection of Early Blossoms* (Zha tu ji) contains commentaries on literary works of many writers in history, including Lao Tzu, Cao Cao, Jiang Kui (and his followers), Wang Guowei, Mao Zedong, and Mu Dan.[6] He points out that Jiang Kui "writes about tender love with strength" in his lyric poetry (*ci*) and is not burdened by the political responsibility to "recover the lost territory for the country from scratch." He argues that Mu Dan's poetry has a "universal applicability that transcends the transient life." With just a few words, San Yisheng delineates the charm and essence of such literary works.

"Posts based on argumentation" (*shuolishi piping*) are generally clear and rigorous in logical thinking. They quote other works extensively and proceed with their argumentations tirelessly and vividly. In the early days of cyber literature, most posts were based on personal reflections. Later, with more people writing literary criticism online, "posts based on argumentation" became more common. For example, in the forum attached to *Jinjiang Literature City*, a netizen named Gu Kou posted an article of nearly 10,000 characters entitled "Understanding 'Beautiful Boys': A Discussion on 'the Beauty of Gender Neutrality' and 'the Subculture of Tanbi' in Japanese Culture."[7] In this article, the author examines various cultural phenomena in history to explain the culture of *tanbi* in Japan: the author goes from the rise of *shudō*[8], to the culture of *kabuki* and the concept of "the Beauty of Gender Neutrality," to European aestheticism at the end of the 19th century, to *tanbi* and its association with female imagery in Japan, and then to the development, dissemination, and limitations of *tanbi*. The article quotes many references and gives a detailed analysis. Its academic and intellectual rigor makes it no less than an excellent academic paper.

In recent years, many large literary websites have also set up columns for literary theory and criticism. *Skyline Literature* (Tianya wenxue), a subsidiary of *Skyline Community*, has a section called "Academic Discussion in China" (Xueshu Zhongguo). It has 10,450 members, about 30,000 threads, and 300,000 follow-up posts. The posts in this section are well based on academic reasoning. They cover a wide range of topics, including "Classics Written by Literary Masters," "Debates over Heated Issues," "Culture and Society," "Literary Criticism," "Thoughts about History," and "Faith and Cultivation." There are countless academic articles of theoretical discussions, such as "The Conjecture about When 'Guaci' and 'Yaoci' in *Book of Changes* Were

Created" (Zhouyi guayaoci chuangzuo niandai caixiang), "An Investigation Report on the Current Status of Amateur Philosophers in China" (Zhongguo minjian zhexuejie xianzhuang de kaocha baogao), "Morality is the Denial of the Will to Live: Two Basic Questions in Schopenhauer's Ethics" (Daode shi dui shengming yizhi de fouding: Shubenhua lunlixue de liangge jiben wenti), and "An Analysis of and Thoughts on the Logical Defects of *Foundations of Aesthetics*: A Discussion with Professor Ye Lang" (*Meizai yixiang* luoji quexian fenxi ji sikao: yu Ye Lang jiaoshou shangque).[9]

"Posts for fun" (*quwei shi piping*) and "spoofs" (*egao shi piping*) are lighthearted and amusing. There is a difference between them. While "posts for fun" use witty words and reject complicated theories to entertain readers, "spoofs" aim at criticizing or ridiculing writers and works.

Many cyber critics are masters of humor. They include "Cold Face Dog Shit" (Lengmian goushi), "Munai'er," "Ten Thousand Catties per Mu of Land" (Muchan wanjin), Li Xunhuan, "Stupid Raccoon" (Benli), "Devil Instructor" (Mogui jiaoguan), Xing Yusen, and "sbygd." For example, when "Stupid Raccoon" commented on the novel *The First Intimate Contact* (Diyici de qinmi jiechu), he said that the reason why it became a masterpiece in cyberspace could be explained by a Chinese proverb: "When there is no tiger in the mountains, the monkey becomes the king." This kind of humorous and witty criticism also appears in his other articles, such as "It Is Still a Green Onion Even if It Is Dyed Red" (Ranhongle yeshi yigencong) and "Weaving Texts into a Net" (Zhiwenchengwang).

"Spoofs" use humor as a way to belittle, mock, parody, and subvert. Cyberspace has always been a place for spoofs. The movie *The Promise* (Wuji), directed by Chen Kaige, was spoofed by a netizen named Hu Ge. The spoof video is entitled *A Murder Caused by a Steamed Bun* (Yige mantou yinfa de xue'an). After that, many spoof videos based on *The Promise* appeared, including one that uses pictures from the video game *Age of Empires* and one in the form of comic strips. Spoof literature on the Internet has become a common practice. Many stories subvert and deconstruct the classics to entertain the public. They include *Tall Tales of The Journey to the West* (Dahua xiyou), *Boiled Three Kingdoms* (Shui zhu sanguo), *An Alternative Story to A Dream of Red Mansions* (Fan hongloumeng), *New Strange Tales from a Chinese Studio* (Xin liaozhai zhiyi), and *The Cute Edition of a Chinese Textbook* (Q ban yuwen). It is worth noticing that once a spoof exceeds the boundaries of morality, it will become an act of vulgarity and malevolence. It can even be used for personal abuse and cyberbullying. Such a state of anomie and violation of people's rights should be forbidden, criticized, and corrected.

Spam Posts and Their Possible Commercial Purposes

Cyberspace is filled with spam posts, which are either meaningless or for marketing purposes. There are people who use anonymous identities to create many posts of this kind or even flood the screen in a forum.

Spam posts are generally meaningless and valueless to readers. Nevertheless, as they quickly replace other posts and take up a lot of space, they defy established rules and dissolve the meanings of words. Thus, writing spam posts allows posters to enjoy a feeling of freedom and to get other people's attention. There are mainly six reasons for such postings: 1. to kill time and dispel boredom; 2. to vent feelings of dissatisfaction; 3. to cheer up readers; 4. to say hello to friends online; 5. to gain experience points; 6. to draw others' attention and let them remember the poster.

Although such posts are not meaningful to readers, they still vary in quality. Spam posts of poor quality are mostly symbols, emoticons, pictures, repetitive words, or short sentences. These posts usually do not receive replies from others. Even though they may occupy large spaces in forums, they will soon fall lower in post listings. Some spam posts are only a little better: they may ask questions and sometimes give answers; they may deliberately make ridiculous mistakes or simply complain and moan for no reason. By doing this, they seek other people's replies: some warm-hearted netizens may come to point out the mistakes or answer the questions. These threads will grow in length or even flood a whole screen with questions and answers that are not quite meaningful.

Meanwhile, there are also spam posts of higher quality. Posters who write such posts are often good at cheering up readers with just a few words. By joking, laughing, and cursing, a post of this kind arouses netizens' desire to reply. In this way, it can finally collect a lot of replies.

Some posters work together to flood the screen with spam posts—we call them "water army," or *shuijun* in Chinese. They can be further divided into two types. Posters of the first type gather because they have the same or similar hobbies, interests, and thoughts. While not for monetary profits, these groups are more stable and united. Fans of cyber writers and Internet celebrities typically form groups of this kind.

In contrast, posters of the second type are recruited by PR agencies for commercial purposes. Such groups are less stable, as members are hired. A poster of this type usually has multiple account names, which allows the poster to confuse readers and hide his/her real intention. Such posts have specific purposes and interests. Posters may act as promoters to hype, market, and popularize a particular object or event. They may also work as "bully boys" to slander and abuse their employer's competitor(s). Still, some may flood the screen to block posts on a particular topic as they harm their employer. By creating new threads and replying to old threads, they flood the screen and intend to lead the public opinions in a particular direction. This will serve the purposes of their employer or the intended beneficiary.

As everyone is free to publish in cyberspace, different types of people all write to discuss literature. These ordinary people's perspectives thus become the birthmark of online literary criticism. Mikhail Bakhtin's concept of "carnival in a town square" is thus well exemplified here. However, what deserves our serious thinking is whether the evaluation systems based on quantified data—clicks and rankings—can faithfully assess literary works. As spam posts for commercial purposes now dominate cyberspace, whither is literary criticism bound?

When wanton personal abuse and deliberate defamation occupy the space of online literary criticism, is cyberspace still a home for people to have peace of mind, or has it become a prison cell that incarcerates people with walls made of negative public opinions? Words can be playful, nonsensical, fragmentary, unclear, and full of negative values: they do not only waste readers' time, energy, and resources in cyberspace; they also cause trouble to the development of online literary criticism. While being rebellious to tradition and defiant to authoritative discourses, online literary criticism does not intend to shoulder its social responsibility. This paradox has made more and more people realize that it is urgent to establish rules for evaluating cyber literature and a system to guide cyber literary criticism.

Literary Criticism in the Mass Media

Criticism in the mass media is circulated widely and caters to ordinary readers. Its carriers include newspapers, magazines, journals, books, and radio and television programs. In addition, there are new media platforms on the Internet, such as web portals, blogs, and microblogs. As such media platforms have a wide range of audiences, literary criticism published in the mass media can powerfully shape public opinion. It thus is an important form of cyber literary criticism.

McLuhan once said: "[T]he personal and social consequences of any medium—that is, of any extension of ourselves—result from the new scale that is introduced into our affairs by each extension of ourselves, or by any new technology."[10] The mass media not only influences people's perceptions of the world and modes of thinking but also reshapes their worldviews and values. Criticism in the mass media has penetrated people's daily lives and exerted a subtle influence.

Cyber literary criticism in the mass media mainly focuses on cyber writers, their works, and literary activities in cyberspace. While expanding its scope, it has gradually become more connected to the market and media production and consumption. Following the tide of the market economy, the media must work for higher circulations, audience ratings, and click-through rates to survive the competition. As a result, cyber literary criticism is delivered to a broad audience through media channels as a cultural commodity or a means of entertainment. The critics mainly include journalists, editors, writers, and cultural celebrities.

Journalists' Information-based Criticism

When journalists write about cyber literature, their focus often shifts from literary texts and their artistic value to cultural aspects directly related to ordinary people's daily life. Most articles of this kind are published as news reports and

Major Types of Cyber Literary Critics and Their Criticism 75

interviews. There are two reasons for this. First, to cater to the general public and maximize market share, journalists must abandon academic and theoretical discussions often seen in traditional literary criticism. They must make articles popular and attractive to readers so that they can sell better. Second, journalists naturally pay more attention to interviews and news reporting. When they write about cyber literature, they focus more on the parts that can be viewed as valuable news.

Journalists are good at capturing hot topics. Some journalists report on cyber literary works and related activities. Others give in-depth discussions on popular issues, phenomena, and events concerning cyber literature. Their articles are authentic, accurate, timely, concise, and vivid. Different from traditional literary criticism, these articles are more information-based. They can be further divided into several types, including "brief reports," "reports on hot issues," "reports that expose problems," and "reports on writers' life."

The first type—"brief reports"—describes and promotes cyber writers, their works, and related events. These articles often summarize the plots of some famous web novels without deeply analyzing them. Some journalists will report on seminars, press conferences, and award ceremonies. They also summarize scholars' comments on cyber literary works on these occasions. Others will directly use the press releases provided by organizers of such activities as their own reports. Thus, such a type of literary criticism is actually news reports that deliver messages. For example, there are reports on the following events: *The Mighty River Flows Eastward* (Dajiang dongqu) won the National "Five-One Project Award"; *Caught in the Web* (Wangshi) was longlisted for the Lu Xun Literature Prize; A "Seminar on Cyber Literary Works" was held by China Writers Association. These reports give summaries of literary works. They deliver information concerning related activities and events, such as time, location, people, cause, process, and result.

The second type of information-based criticism—"reports on hot issues"—is more extensive and developed. It also focuses on popular topics—including phenomena, people, and events. In recent years, a series of issues concerning cyber literature attracted people's attention. We have a few examples here: Cyber writers entered the China Writers Rich List; Internet giants, such as Baidu, Sina, Tencent, and Alibaba, entered the industry of cyber literature; Tencent Literature and Shanda Literature merged to form China Literature (Yuewen jituan); many works of cyber literature were adapted to films and other forms; stories and characters based on popular novels began to have much commercial value (which is commonly known as "the heat of intellectual property," or *IP re*). Journalists' articles on these hot issues, as a type of cyber literary criticism, occupied headlines and columns of the mass media and attracted a lot of public attention.

Here are two articles of this type as examples: "Tencent Literature and Shanda Literature Merged; Wu Wenhui at the Helm of the 'Empire of Literature'" by Liu Xia from *Beijing News*, "Fan Economy: Hot Movies and TV Dramas Adapted from Web Novels in China" by Su Yuanwen and Ji

Shaoting from *Xinhuanet*, and "Seventy Percent of Middle School Students Prefer Web Novels over the Classics" by Chen Muyi from *Southeast Express*.[11] Articles of this kind report on phenomena and events of cyber literature that are closely related to people's daily life. Some of them are merely to entertain readers. After all, they are cultural commodities for mass consumption.

The third type of criticism exposes problems concerning cyber literature—especially incidents that violate public morality, laws, and regulations. Many of such cases are about piracy, copyright infringement, and pornography. Since the birth of cyber literature, copyright disputes have repeatedly occurred. Here are two examples: 50 writers jointly published an article entitled "Chinese Writers' Public Accusation Against *Baidu* on March 15th" (San yiwu Zhongguo zuojia tao baidu shu); *Shanda Literature* filed a lawsuit against *Baidu* for copyright infringement. As people can share resources on the Internet, piracy and other acts of infringement can be rampant. In such a context, articles exposing such problems attract public attention and help raise people's awareness of the importance of copyright.

In recent years, the government launched the "Project for the Purification of Cyberspace" (jingwang xingdong) to eliminate pornography and other illegal information. Meanwhile, the media exposed various incidents in which major websites and forums, including *Baidu*, *Sina*, *Skyline Community*, and well-known cyber writers, such as "Pharmacist Lan of *Skyline Community*" (Tianya lanyaoshi) and "Gray Wolf with Wings" (Zhangzhe chibang de dahuilang), spread pornographic and obscene information. By exposing the problems of cyber literature, these articles contributed to the purification of cyberspace and the promotion of positive social values.

The fourth type of criticism investigates the life experience of cyber writers and the stories behind their works. It intends to satisfy readers' curiosity so that they will pay for more of such stories. Journalists focus on a series of issues concerning cyber literature, including the production process, the industrial chain, the fan economy, and the cyber writers' work, income, and living conditions.

Examples of such articles include "Does It Require a Lot of Talent for People to Write Cyber Literature?" by Zhou Yafei from *People's Daily*, "Cyber Literature: A Huge Business Built on a Paywall of Two Cents Per Thousand Characters" by He Liu from *China Report* (Zhongguo baodao), and "Demystify the Fan Economy in the Industry of Cyber Literature: A Writer Earned More than Ten Million RMB Yuan from Fans" by Chen Jie from *Beijing Business Today* (Beijing shangbao).[12] All these articles follow a fixed pattern: seeking an exciting topic, searching for clues, and digging deep to find the "secrets." Some use sensational titles, promotional stunts, and the revelation of secrets to attract readers. Such articles thus report on actual events in popular culture instead of focusing on the literary and aesthetic aspects of literature. Some of them dramatize the issues to entertain readers. Therefore, they are more valuable as news reports than literary criticism.

Editors' "On-site" Criticism

Editors are responsible for selecting topics, soliciting contributions, and reviewing manuscripts. Being the "gatekeeper" in the publication business, editors usually have a good knowledge of literature, excellent writing skills, and extensive experience in reading. While selecting and evaluating works, they must consider the market and cater to readers' expectations. Yet, they also have to pay attention to the literary and aesthetic qualities of works. Thus, they are required to read many of today's literary works and have a good knowledge of new writers, new works, and the overall development of today's literature. As a result, they are capable of writing criticism "on the site" of literary production. Such criticism can be further divided into "visible criticism" and "invisible criticism."

"Visible criticism" refers to articles and books written by editors. By writing such articles and books, editors go from behind the scenes to the front. Some of these editors have multiple identities: they can be critics, writers, and scholars. They can be further divided into two types: those who pay attention to cyber literature in general and those who pay attention to a literary issue in particular. Editors who focus on the overall situation have read literary works of all kinds in terms of genre, topic, content, and form. They have a good knowledge of both literature and literary theory. For example, Ma Ji has been working as an editor for the journal *Selected Novels* (Changpian xiaoshuo xuankan) for more than 20 years. He did not simply follow the discourses and patterns of literary theories but directly approached the "site" of literary production in cyberspace. He tracked the development of cyber literature and gave comments on its past, present, and future. He also examined cyber literature in the grand context of digital reading, cross-cultural communication, and China's national strategy for cultural development. Because of this, his articles are very popular among readers. In addition to articles published in *Guangming Daily* (Guangming ribao), *People's Daily* (Renmin ribao), *Newspaper* of *Literature and Art* (Wenyi bao) and other media, Ma Ji also published books, including *Writing in the Era When People Read on Screens: A Ten-Year History of Cyber Literature* (Duping shidai de xiezuo: wangluo wenxue shinianshi), *A Study and Record of Cyber Literature* (Wangluo wenxue toushi yu beiwang), and *Rankings of Cyber Literary Works in the 21st Century* (Ershiyi shiji wangluo wenxue paihangbang).

Meanwhile, some other editors focus on specific issues concerning cyber literature. There are many editors of this kind, and they have written a large number of articles covering a wide range of topics. Some of them are good at reviewing particular works, while others like to comment on cyber literature as a whole from different angles. An example is Shu Jinyu, editor of *China Reading Weekly* (Zhonghua dushu bao), pen-named Lu Dazhi. Most of her articles are in-depth discussions on hot issues about cyber literature, and they follow a way of reasoning that can be summarized as "finding problems—analyzing problems—solving problems—predicting trends." Her articles are not only firmly based on logical reasoning and critical thinking but also contain a lot of ideas that work together to make her research quite extensive and expansive. Her representative articles include "Ringing the Alarm for Web Novels about School Life,"[13] "Cyber Literature as an Origin of Young Adult Fiction,"[14] "Fantasy Novels of Great Lengths Will Be Booming,"[15] "Will Novels about Video Gaming Become the Next Goldmine?"[16] These articles focus on major types of popular web novels and analyze them from different aspects, including their origins, trajectories, problems, and trends. These specific discussions can help us envision a detailed future of cyber literature.

There is a type of literary criticism that is "invisible." This refers to the critical effect produced by editors, as they intervene in, or even manipulate, the publication of works as "gatekeepers" behind the scenes. Editors make plans for publication, select topics, and solicit, pick, and recommend manuscripts. The power granted to them as the "gatekeeper" requires them not to judge literary works solely based on their personal preferences and interests. Instead, they have to pay attention to the market as the "invisible hand" that pushes and drives. Editors need to choose works that can attract readers. They also have to further create selling points for these works and make them more influential.

For example, in 2015, the cyber poet Yu Xiuhua's poem "I Travelled Across More than Half of China to Sleep with You" (Chuanguo dabange Zhongguo qu shui ni) became famous overnight. More than 100,000 copies of her collection of poems were sold, and the book was out of stock in many bookstores. It was a miracle for the sale of poetry books in the past 20 years. The planning and marketing done by editors were the main reason for such a miracle. Yu Xiuhua's identity as a peasant woman suffering from cerebral palsy, as well as her bold expression of sexual desires in her poems, aroused public curiosity. The pain and warmth felt by the poet—a peasant and sick woman—was the cause for the popularity of her poems. Editors, such as Liu Nian from *Poetry* (Shikan), strongly promoted Yu Xiuhua's poems. They carefully selected the best poems from a number of them in Yu's blog posts and organized a series of promotional activities. As a result, mainstream media, such as *People's Daily*, *Guangming Daily*, and *China Central Television*, rushed to report Yu and her poetry. Yu's poetry-writing then became a phenomenon hotly discussed by literary critics. In recent years, with the rise of new media and the trend of media integration, editors' "invisible" criticism became a unique form of literary criticism. It is "on-site" for its direct intervention in and manipulation of literary activities. It becomes increasingly effective in generating economic profits and gaining social influence for literary works.

Criticism by Writers and Other Cultural Celebrities

Writers and other cultural celebrities often become guests of the media and appear in public. Their literary criticism is not so heavily based on theoretical discussions or argumentations but is more about their individual reflections. This type of literary criticism, among others published in the mass media, highlights critics' personalities the most.

When writers discuss literary works as critics, they maintain a perspective as creators of literature and put emotions and personal experiences into their discussions. Their literary criticism thus clashes with or complements scholars' theoretical discussions.

While some writer-critics are based in cyberspace, others are traditional writers. The former group includes Xing Yusen, "Ning, the God of Wealth" (Ning caishen), Wu Guo, Ge Tao, "Black Cocoa" (Hei keke), Han Haoyue, "The Third Young Master of the Tang Sect" (Tangjia sanshao), "Old Bull Eating Tender Grass" (Laoniu chi nencao), "Lily Magnolia Dock" (Xinyiwu), Li Xiaomin, "The Best in the Whole World" (Tianxia bachang), "The Whole World Returns to Its Origin" (Tianxia guiyuan), "Dust under the Sky" (Tianxia chen'ai), Zhou Xiaoping, and Hua Qianfang. These cyber writers published a series of articles as literary criticism. For example, Xing Yusen's article categorizes female cyber writers as "coquettish urbanites," "those who write plain words with wisdom," and "those who express true feelings."[17] Wu Guo's articles, including "Random Talks on Ning Caishen" (Shuizhu Ning caishen), "Xin Yusen and Novels about Heroes in Cyberspace" (Xing Yusen yu wangxiaxiaoshuo), and "Panning for Gold out of Gravel: A Brief Discussion on the Current Condition of Cyber Literature" (Shalitaojin: Qiantan wangluo wenxue xianzhuang), directly contributed to the formation of an array of early cyber writers as celebrities. Zhou Xiaoping's book *Please Don't Fail This Era* (Qing buyao gufu zhege shidai) is a collection of his articles previously published as blog posts. The collection covers many controversial topics and contains a lot of critical thoughts. It also promotes positive social values and encourages young readers to shoulder their responsibilities for the nation in this era. As a result, it caused many critical responses from a wide range of readers.

Traditional writers also write literary criticism. Some are known for their creative writing, including Mo Yan, Wang Meng, Liu Zhenyun, Xiao Fuxing, Wang Anyi, Zhang Kangkang, Hai Yan, and Tie Ning. Others are known for argumentative writing, including Li Jingze, Chen Qirong, Wang Ying, Hu Ping, He Jianming, Yu Aicheng, Kang Qiao, and Suo Luo. Some writers are freelancers. Others work at organizations such as the Writers Association, the Federation of Literary and Art Circles, and the Lu Xun Literary Institute. These traditional writers maintain mainstream values and have a keen aesthetic sensibility. Their critical articles often make comparisons between cyber literature and classic literature. While demonstrating writers' good knowledge of literary theory, these articles also have an artistic quality for readers to appreciate.

For example, Mo Yan said frankly that "cyber literature is a good phenomenon," but because most of his readers still read print media, Mo Yan did not consider writing online.[18] He believed that writers were diversified, and so were readers. Zhang Kangkang, another writer, discovered that cyber literature was not entirely "non-traditional" and "non-mainstream": instead, it was more rational and modest than many traditional writers imagined.[19] Xiao Fuxing believed that cyber literature had many advantages, as it was democratic, convenient, and interactive. Still, there were also disadvantages, as most works lacked artistic and intellectual value.[20] As a result, he proposed that cyber literature and traditional literature should learn from each other and develop together.

With the rapid development of digital technology, news portals, such as *Sina*, *Sohu*, *NetEase*, and *Tencent*, took the initiative to develop themselves. Traditional media also followed the trend and built up their websites. As a result, electronic magazines, newspapers, and video platforms all came into existence. Blog, microblog, WeChat, and Qzone ushered people into the era of "we media." Internet celebrities, including opinion leaders and public intellectuals, formed the backbone of such media in cyberspace. Their articles became a new literary criticism that combines personal insights with public opinions. Among these cultural celebrities are writers, scholars, and popular book reviewers. Writers of this kind include Ye Yonglie, Lei Da, Qiu Huadong, Chen Cun, Murong Xuecun, "Annie Baby" (Anni baobei), Fang Zhouzi, Han Han, Guo Jingming, Sun Rui, Gu Man, Liu Liu, Cai Jun, and "Bright Moon in That Year" (Dangnian mingyue). Scholars include Chen Xiaoming, Tao Dongfeng, Zhang Yiwu, Zhang Ning, Bai Ye, Ge Hongbing, Zhu Dake, and Xie Youshun. Renowned book reviewers include "Wisdom of the Emperor" (Chenzhitao), Xia Zekui, "Grass of the Ancient Times" (Guzhicao), Mu Kong, Lu Guoping, Jiangshan, "A Paddle Skiff" (Yizhao pianzhou), "Pacific Island Silvergrass" (Wujiemang), and "Lazy Panda" (Lan xiongmao).

As a form of cyber literary criticism in the mass media, cultural celebrities' articles differ from ordinary netizens' writings. First, they are not scribbled quickly and casually but are a result of careful deliberation. Second, writers and cultural celebrities write these articles not only to express themselves but also to attract readers and more broadly circulate their thoughts. As a result, such articles caused a series of incidents heatedly discussed on the Internet in recent years. The following incidents are examples: the debate between Han Han and Bai Ye;[21] the debate between Tao Dongfeng and Xiao Ding;[22] Ye Kuangzheng made an argument that "literature is dead";[23] short stories in the form of microblog posts became a fad;[24] Fang Zhouzi suspected that Han Han's works were ghostwritten.[25] These articles attracted a lot of public attention: they were usually described by readers as "cool" and "sharp," with "jokes" and "insults," and full of "personality," "freshness," "liveliness," and "strength." As such articles could effectively draw public attention to particular issues, cultural celebrities had great potential to further exert their influence over literature.

Scholars' Contributions

Scholars are professionals at universities and research institutes. They have received higher education and have a lot of potential in academic research. Scholars pay more attention to critical thinking and reasoning than other people who write literary criticism, and they try to answer fundamental questions through studies of literary works and phenomena. Based on their studies, they intend to establish criteria and theories for evaluating cyber literature. Their articles are often found in academic journals, books, and conferences, and their writing style is academic and professional. Their studies play an essential role in guiding and regulating the development of cyber literature. Specifically, scholars can be further divided into three types.

The Exploration of "Pioneers"

In the early days of cyber literature, a group of scholars with keen academic insight entered this field of research. As pioneers, they explored this new field with limited resources but strong determinations and published many academic books and papers. In so doing, they made significant contributions to the theorization on cyber literature.

In 1998, the immediate success of the novel *The First Intimate Contact* led to the first wave of development in cyber literature. Huang Mingfen, Nan Fan, Ge Hongbing, Yang Xinmin, and I were among the first group of scholars who started to write criticism on cyber literature.

I, Ouyang Youquan, a professor at Central South University, was called "a pioneer in the study of cyber literature" in an article published in *Newspaper of Literature and Art*.[26] I have been studying cyber literature for more than ten years and have published various articles and books. I examined various aspects of cyber literature, including its ontological basis, the transformation of literature and art in the context of digital technology, the relationship between technologies and the humanities, and the construction of archives for cyber literary research. I attempt to construct a system of theories for cyber literary criticism and introduce cyber literary studies into higher education as a discipline. Chen Dingjia, another scholar, commented on my work in an article: "Ouyang Youquan is the founder and a leading figure in China's cyber literary studies. He has been whole-heartedly, assiduously, and tirelessly devoting himself to this field of research for more than ten years."[27] I published more than ten books and a series of articles in some important academic journals to theorize on cyber literature. I also completed a series of research projects sponsored respectively by the National Social Science Fund, the Ministry of Education, and Hunan Province. Moreover, I also led a group of scholars to write and publish five sets of books on cyber literature. I worked to establish several organizations for the study of cyber literature, including Cyber Literary Research Base in Hunan Province (Hunan sheng wangluo wenxue yanjiu jidi), Cyber Literary Research Association in Hunan Province (Hunan sheng wangluo wenxue yanjiuhui), and National Cyber Literary Research Association (Quanguo wangluo wenxue yanjiuhui). According to statistics, by the end of 2015, the cyber literary research team at Central South University, led by myself, had published 43 books and 257 articles on cyber literary criticism.

Huang Mingfen, a professor at Xiamen University, is the first scholar in China to study and theorize about digital literature and art. As early as 1997,

82   Part I

he started publishing articles to explore information technology's influence on literature and art theories. He published many academic books and nearly a hundred academic papers in total. His works include a six-volume book, *A History of Theories of Digital Art in the West* (Xifang shuma yishu lilun shi), and a four-volume book, *A Study of New Disciplines Concerning Digital Art* (Shuma yishu qian xuekequn yanjiu). These huge volumes are significant contributions to the establishment of these new fields of research. Moreover, he also completed several research projects sponsored, respectively, by the National Social Science Fund, the Ministry of Education, and Fujian Province.

Scholars such as Nan Fan, Ge Hongbing, Yang Xinmin, and Chen Dingjia, with a keen insight into research, were also pioneers in the field. Nan Fan proposed that cyber literature was a new cultural phenomenon not to be ignored. Since 1998, he has been focusing on the study of cyber literature's genre and quality, as well as the construction of a system of criteria for evaluating cyber literary works. Ge Hongbing also affirmed the value of cyber literature. His research on the typology of novels and his teaching of creative writing greatly inspired cyber writers and critics. Yang Xinmin published an article, entitled "A Discussion on Cyber Literature" (Wangluo wenxue chuyi), in which he recognizes two types of cyber literature: the first type is originally published in print media but later published on the Internet, and the second type is originally published on the Internet.[28] He further divides the latter type of cyber literature into three sub-types in terms of content and form. This is a very useful theoretical discussion on the definition and classification of cyber literature. Chen Dingjia is also among the earliest scholars who entered the field of cyber literary criticism. He has published a series of articles discussing cyber literature and its social context since 2000, focusing on the intertextuality in cyber literature. He wrote two important books—*The World of Bits: A Study of the Literary Production in the Internet Era* (Bite zhijing: wangluo shidai de wenxue shengchan yanjiu) and *The Dance of Words: A Study of Cyber Literature and Intertextuality* (Wenzhiwu: wangluo wenxue yu huwenxing yanjiu).

In-depth Research by More Scholars

In the 21st century, with the emergence of new cyber writers and the publication of a huge amount of works, cyber literature started to develop rapidly and attracted many scholars' attention. More scholars at universities and research institutes entered this field. They followed the steps of the aforementioned "pioneers" and formed a mighty army. From then on, the number of research papers published in journals increased year by year. Many academic books were also published. The study of cyber literature thus became more systematic and specialized. Moreover, several research organizations were established to study cyber literature.

Many scholars took advantage of existent theories and examined the changing social condition to deepen and expand this field of research. The "Review of Cyber Literature in the Past Ten Years" (Wangluo wenxue shinian pandian) in 2008 is a historically significant event. Before it, from 2001 to 2008, many scholars had already started to publish articles in academic journals. The representatives of early researchers include Nan Fan, Tan Dejing, Ma Longqian, Yang Xinmin, Ma Ji, Chen Dingjia, Jin Zhenbang, Liu Lili, Wang Qiang, and Ge Hongbing, among others. After 2009, an even larger number of scholars—including professors and writers—entered this field and made many academic achievements. The representatives include Jiang Shuzhuo, Li Fengliang, Ouyang Wenfeng, Li Chaoquan, Zhou Zhixiong, Xia Lie, Zhuang Yong, Wang Xiang, Shao Yanjun, and Huang Fayou. These scholars were armed with a solid knowledge of theories of literature and art. With theoretical resources and broad visions, they found good research questions and gave excellent interpretations. While they cherished the values of traditional literature as cultural heritage, their scholarly articles often contained anxiety, contemplation, and expectations about the development of literature and art in this new era. Their research touched upon a series of issues, including cyber literature's definition, creation, content, characteristics, genres, ways of circulation, reception, significance, and limitations. In so doing, they contributed to the further development of theories on cyber literature.

Cyber literature went through more than 20 years of development. Accordingly, while cyber literary criticism was initially not popular as a field of research, it later became quite significant. Academic organizations dedicated to the study of cyber literature appeared in places such as Hunan, Guangdong, Zhejiang, Shanghai, Jiangsu, Guizhou, Sichuan, and Shandong. Among them, the Cyber Literary Research Base at Central South University (Zhongnan daxue wangluo wenxue yanjiu jidi) is the earliest and one of the most important. It was established by the Cyber Literature Committee of China Writers Association (Zhongguo zuoxie wangluo wenxue weiyuanhui) in April 2006. Under my leadership, the base gathered more than 20 professors, associate professors, doctors, and post-doctoral fellows, such as Yu Jianxiang, Ouyang Wenfeng, Zeng Fanting, Tan Dejing, Yan Zhen, and Lan Aiguo. They wrote many critical articles to examine cyber literature from various aspects, including how it comes into existence, its social context, textual analysis, genres and forms, media platforms, etc. They wrote comprehensive commentaries on representative works, writers, and websites. For example, Professor Tan Dejing studied cyber writers' "spiritual dimension" and the forms of online literary criticism. Professor Yang Yu used ancient literary theories as a basis to interpret web poetry's "return to traditional poetics." Professor Lan Aiguo studied spoofs on the Internet from the perspective of folk culture. Such comprehensive research yielded more than 40 books and more than 250 papers published in major academic journals, including the most authoritative ones. A series of research organizations were also established, including the first research institute of cyber literature, the first website for cyber literary criticism, and the first national research association of cyber literature. Scholars also successfully launched the first research project on cyber literature sponsored by the National Social Science Fund and the first one sponsored by the Ministry of Education. Moreover, they established the most comprehensive research archive for cyber literary studies. These achievements brought great honor to the group of researchers at the Cyber Literary Research Base at Central South University in Hunan Province.

In recent years, many other research organizations and groups were established and developed all over China, including the Research Institution of Cyber Literature in Guangdong Province (Guangdong wangluo wenxue yuan), the Research Center of Cyber Literature at Shandong Normal University (Shandong shifan daxue wangluo wenxue yanjiu zhongxin) in Shandong Province, a group of researchers based at the Communication University of Zhejiang in Zhejiang Province, the Cyber Literature Association in Guizhou Province (Guizhou wangluo wenxue xuehui), and the Research Center of Cyber Literature at Southwest University of Science and Technology (Xinan keji daxue wangluo wenxue yanjiu zhendi) in Sichuan Province. There were also some other governmental and academic organizations, such as the National Joint Meeting for Key Producers of Cyber Literature organized by China Writers Association (Zhongguo zuoxie quanguo wangluo wenxue zhongdian yuandi gongzuo lianxihui), Cyber Literature Committee of China Writers Association (Zhongguo zuoxie wangluo wenxue weiyuanhui), and Cyber Literature and Art Committee attached to China Literature and Art Critics Association (Zhongguo wenyi pinglunjia xiehui wangluo wenyi weiyuanhui).

Emerging Critical Voices of Young Scholars

Graduate students and young scholars in their 30s are the "reserve force" for cyber literary studies. Having grown up in the Internet era, they are very familiar with and interested in cyber literature. Many graduate students, guided by their advisors and teachers, make academic achievements at school: they may participate in their advisors' research projects or choose cyber literature as their research field for postgraduate degrees. Some became university teachers after graduation and continued to study cyber literature.

In recent years, more graduate students have joined the "reserve team" for cyber literary studies. When we search the database on China National Knowledge Infrastructure (CNKI), we can find 1,905 master's theses and doctoral dissertations on "Internet Literature" (wangluo wenxue), including one in 2000, 12 in 2001, 38 in 2002, 43 in 2003, and 65 in 2005, 95 in 2006, 154 in 2007, 151 in 2008, 138 in 2009, 159 in 2010, 199 in 2011, 228 in 2012, 262 in 2013, 224 in 2014, and 74 in 2015.[29] Their research closely followed the trend of the times and covered a wide range of issues. Initially, they studied the basics of cyber literature, including the texts, media platforms, aesthetic values, criticism, and language styles. Later, their research expanded to cover more issues concerning cyber literature, such as popular culture, consumer market, writers' writing process, writers' living conditions, youth readership, integration and reformation of media, and culture industry. Such research thus involved multiple disciplines, including sociology, psychology, communication studies, and management science. Some young scholars focused on other specific topics, such as cyber literature written by women, foreigners, and ethnic minorities, genres of cyberwriting, microblog literature, and cellphone literature. They also studied the adaptation of web novels into films and video games, the industrial chain of cyber literature, and the publishing industry for books and digital products. As their research has covered a wide range of topics and become so professional and meticulous, we can see that young people are quite innovative and insightful. They are quickly growing up to become mature scholars.

For example, Zhang Yu, a student at Shaanxi Normal University, completed a master's thesis in 2006 entitled "A Comparative Analysis of Cyber Literature in China and Abroad."[30] From a multi-lingual and cross-cultural perspective, it gives a comparative study of cyber literature in different countries and regions, including China, Korea, Europe, and America, focusing on cyber literature's current conditions, social contexts, genres, and topics. Meng Xingyu, a doctoral student at Jinan University, completed a dissertation in 2010 entitled "A Study of Chinese Cyber Literature in North America Across Twenty Years (1988–2008)."[31] This work traces the origin and the trajectory of Chinese cyber literature in North America from 1988 to 2008. It uses a perspective of comparative literature to interpret such a mode of writing that is Chinese in language but Western in spirit. In so doing, it is valuable both as a study of literary history and an examination of literary texts. Cui Zairong completed a doctoral dissertation at Peking University in 2011, entitled "The Dilemma and Breakthrough of Chinese Cyber Literary Studies."[32] Cui proposes two concepts in this dissertation, namely "vernacular theory" and "networkedness."[33] Using these concepts, Cui analyzes hot issues concerning cyber literature at that time. Particularly, the dissertation examines a series of phenomena, such as "time-space travel fiction," "fan activity," "wakeng," and "spoiler."[34]

It is worth noting that although these young students are new blood in the field of cyber literary studies, not all of them will become professional researchers. Granted, some became young scholars working at universities and research institutes after graduation. They are committed to cyber literary studies and are the backbone of this field of research. However, many graduate students did not engage in cyber literature after graduation. Like shooting stars in the night sky, their names quickly disappeared in this field. Many postgraduate students leave academia after graduation, but many new students join this research field every year as they come to universities and colleges for higher education.

Now let us take an overview of cyber literary studies in China. In the early days of cyber literature, scholars disagreed on many issues, including cyber literature's origin, naming, related concepts, characteristics, and values. Among these, the legitimacy of this new form of literature is the most hotly discussed. Scholars such as Huang Mingfen and I pioneered the research in this field and opened up a new space for it. Subsequently, many scholars working at universities and research institutes joined and contributed to the further theorization on cyber literature. In recent years, more young scholars and postgraduate students came to develop this field further and made many academic achievements on various topics. These scholars' research, solidly founded on theories, serves as a beacon to guide the creation and evaluation of cyber literature. Nevertheless, we must pay attention to the fact that theories can only work through practice.

While many scholars still use the theoretical framework initially designed for the study of traditional literature to study cyber literature, others are eager to construct new theories. Nevertheless, as they do not pay enough attention to the reading of actual texts of cyber literature, their theorizations are too arbitrary and inflexible, thus not being able to help the study of new phenomena in cyber literature. On top of this, while we lack an evaluation system for cyber literature, scholars often maintain a sense of condescension that makes their literary criticism not appreciated by ordinary netizens and the mass media. A series of problems concerning cyber literary criticism occurred as a result of this. Scholars thus need to change their condescending posture. They should engage in textual analysis and write specific reviews. They should actively examine and respond to the new works, phenomena, and problems of cyber literature. They are also responsible for cultivating readers' aesthetic tastes and maintaining positive and healthy cyberculture. If they can do so, we can expect a new era for cyber literary criticism to flourish.

We have discussed three types of cyber literary criticism in this chapter: 1. free voices of ordinary readers on the Internet, which are all mixed into a "heteroglossia"; 2. articles by journalists, editors, writers, and other cultural celebrities published in traditional media, which are market-oriented and cater to the general public; 3. academic writings by professional scholars and postgraduate students, which contribute to the theorization on cyber literature. What is gratifying is that the three types of cyber literary criticism have penetrated each other. More writers and scholars are now writing online. Professors walk out of their offices and enter the mass media to express their views of cyber literature. Editors and writers today publish articles of cyber literary criticism in authoritative academic journals. In this way, the three types merge and complement each other to form a complex picture of cyber literary criticism.

Notes

1 China Internet Network Information Center (CNNIC), "The 38th Statistical Report on Internet Development in China," *CNNIC*, last modified November 14, 2016. www.cnnic.com.cn/IDR/ReportDownloads/201611/P020161114573409551742.pdf.
2 Translator's note: for the newest rankings on *Starting Points Chinese Net* (Qidian zhongwen wang), see www.qidian.com/rank.
3 Kuan gongzi 宽公子, *Jiming nüzhu de butong jieju* 几名女主的不同结局, Qidian zhongwen wang 起点中文网, 2015. Translator's note: the original link is already defunct and is thus not given here.

4 Translator's note: the Chinese name for these posts is *banzhuan tie* 板砖帖, or *paizhuan tie* 拍砖帖, meaning a post intended to criticize something or someone. Such a name jokingly compares a post with a brick thrown at a person.
5 Translator's note: the Chinese name for "highlighted posts" is *jinghua tie* 精华帖, literally meaning "essential posts." Usually, only posts that are good enough will have their titles highlighted in post listings.
6 San yisheng 散宜生, *Zha tu ji* 乍吐集, Bailu shuyuan 白鹿书院, 2015. Translator's note: the original link is defunct and is thus not given here.
7 Gu kou 古寇, *Lingwu "meishaonian"—tan Riben de "zhongxing zhimei" yu "danmei yawenhua"* 解悟"美少年"—谈日本的"中性之美"与"耽美亚文化,"Jinjiang luntan 晋江论坛, 2015.
Translator's note: *tanbi* in Japanese is equivalent to *Danmei* in Chinese. As a term, it literally means "the pursuit of beauty." Such a concept, however, is often used to refer to novels describing homosexual love, especially love between two good-looking men. The original post has been removed and the link is defunct.
8 Translator's note: *shudō* refers to love between men, literally meaning "the way of adolescent boys."
9 These articles were all published in the section "Academic Discussion in China" (Xueshu Zhongguo) on *Skyline Community* (Tianya shequ). See: http://bbs.tianya.cn/list-666-1.shtml.
10 Marshall McLuhan, *Understanding Media: The Extensions of Man* (Cambridge, MA: The MIT Press, 1994), 7.
11 Liu, Xia 刘夏, "Tengxun shengda lianyin, Wu Wenhui zhangduo 'wenxue diguo'" 腾讯盛大联姻, 吴文辉掌舵'文学帝国,'" *Xinjing bao* 新京报 (Beijing), Mar. 18, 2015.
Yuan, Suwen 苑苏文 and Ji, Shaoting 姬少亭, *Fensi jingji: Zhongguo wangluo xiaoshuo rebian yingshiju* 粉丝经济: 中国网络小说热编影视剧, Souhu搜狐, 2014. https://business.sohu.com/20140731/n402980285.shtml.
Chen, Muyi 陈木易, "Qicheng zhongxuesheng pian'ai wangluo xiaoshuo bu ai mingzhu 七成中学偏爱网络小说不爱名著," *Dongnan kuaibao* 东南快报 (Fuzhou), Dec. 10, 2013.
12 Zhou, Yafei 周亚飞, "Wangluo wenxue, menkan gaobugao? 网络文学, 门槛高不高?" *Renmin ribao* 人民日报 (Beijing), Feb. 24, 2014.
He, Liu 何流, "Wangluo wenxue: erfenqian zhishang de shangye dasha" 网络文学: 2分钱之上的商业大厦, *China Report* 中国报道 no. 7 (2009): 82–84.
Chen, Jie 陈杰, "Jiemi wangluo wenxue fensi jingji: dashang shouru po qianwan 揭秘网络文学粉丝经济: 打赏收入破千万," *Beijing shangbao* 北京商报 (Beijing), Aug. 16, 2013.
13 Shu, Jinyu 舒晋瑜, "Qiaoxiang wangluo xiaoyuan xiaoshuo de jingzhong 敲响网络校园小说的警钟," *Zhonghua dushu bao* 中华读书报 (Beijing), Jan. 21, 2004.
14 Shu, Jinyu 舒晋瑜, "Zhuixun qingchun wenxue de wangluo chushen追寻青春文学的网络出身," *Zhonghua dushu bao* 中华读书报 (Beijing), Feb. 23, 2005c.
15 Shu, Jinyu 舒晋瑜, "Chaochangpian qihuan xiaoshuo jiang da baofa 超长篇奇幻小说将大爆发," *Zhonghua dushu bao* 中华读书报 (Beijing), Apr. 20, 2005a.
16 Shu, Jinyu 舒晋瑜, "Youxi xiaoshuo huishi xiayizuo chuban jinkuang ma? 游戏小说会是下一座出版金矿吗？," *Zhonghua dushu bao* 中华读书报 (Beijing), Feb. 23, 2005b.
17 Xing, Yusen 邢育森, "Wangluo nüzuojia de mimi huayuan" 网络女作家的秘密花园, *The World of Information about the Internet* Internet信息世界 Feb. (2000): 72–74.

18 Mo, Yan 莫言, "Wangluo wenxue shige haoxianxiang 网络文学是个好现象," *Renmin ribao* 人民日报 (Beijing), Dec. 1, 2008.
19 Zhang, Kangkang 张抗抗, "Yougan wangluo wenxue" 有感网络文学, *Writer Magazine* 作家 May (2000): 10–11.
20 Xiao, Fuxing 肖复兴, "Yelai shuoshuo wangluo wenxue 也来说说网络文学," *Renmin ribao haiwaiban* 人民日报海外版 (Beijing), Jun. 18, 2009.
21 In 2006, Bai Ye posted an article, "The Current Status and Future of the Post-80s Generation" ("Baling hou" de xianzhuang yu weilai) "八零后"的现状与未来, in his blog, which caused a fierce debate between him and Han Han over the status of "the post-1980s writers" and their works.
22 In 2006, Tao Dongfeng posted an article, "Have We Entered into an Era When Chinese Literature Is Nothing but Gods and Ghosts?" (Zhongguo wenxue yijing jinru zhuangshennonggui shidai?) 中国文学已经进入装神弄鬼时代？, in his blog, to critique fantasy novels on the Internet, which received a pointed opposition from Xiao Ding, a cyberwriter famous for fantasy novels. Other scholars, including Zhang Yiwu and Zhang Ning, wrote articles to join the discussion.
23 Ye Kuangzheng, a critic, posted an article, "Literature Is Dead! A New Era of Interactive Text Has Come!" (Wenxue sile! yige hudong de wenben shidai laile!) 文学死了！一个互动的文本时代来了！, in his blog. Later, *Sina Blog* used the title "Ye Kuangzheng Has Dropped a Heavy Bomb on China's Literature in 2006: Literature Is Dead! Modern Chinese Literature Has Ceased to Exist since 2006" (Ye Kuangzheng touxia erlinglingliu Zhongguo wentan zhongbang zhadan: wenxue yisi! Zhongguo xiandai wenxue cong erlinglingliu nian yi bufucunzai) 叶匡政投下2006中国文坛重磅炸弹：文学已死！中国现代文学从2006年已不复存在 to initiate a public discussion, which attracted netizens, scholars, writers, and critics to have a series of debates on the current condition of literature.
24 In 2010, Wen Huajian published a story "Love in the Era of Microblog" (Weibo shiqi de aiqing) 围脖时期的爱情 on *Sina Weibo*, China's most popular microblogging platform, which made "microblog stories" popular among netizens.
25 In 2012, Mai Tian, a blog writer, published an article, "Han Han as a Fake Writer: A Farce about Him as a 'Citizen Who Cares about the Public Affairs'" (Renzao Han Han: yichang guanyu "gongmin" de naoju) 人造韩寒：一场关于"公民"的闹剧, in his blog. This is followed by a series of words by Fang Zhouzi on the microblogging platform *Sina Weibo* questioning whether Han Han's works were written by himself. Han Han and Fang Zhouzi then attacked each other on the Internet and further intensified the situation. In the end, Han filed a lawsuit against Fang.
26 Zhou, Wen 周文, "Wangluo wenxue yanjiu de kaituozhe—ji zhongnan daxue wenxueyuan Ouyang Youquan jiaoshou 网络文学研究的开拓者——记中南大学文学院欧阳友权教授," *Wenyi bao* 文艺报 (Beijing), Jan. 13, 2005.
27 Chen, Dingjia 陈定家, "Woguo wangluo wenxue de xueke kaichuang—ping Ouyang Youquan de wangluo wenxue yanjiu" 我国网络文学的学科开创——评欧阳友权的网络文学研究, *Creation and Criticism* 创作与评论 no. 8 (2016): 61.
28 Yang, Xinmin 杨新敏, "Wangluo wenxue chuyi" 网络文学刍议, *Literary Review* 文学评论 no. 5 (2000): 87–95.
29 Source: China Doctoral Dissertations Full-text Database & China Master's Theses Full-text Database, on China National Knowledge Infrastructure (CNKI), accessed December, 13, 2015.
30 Zhang, Yu 张雨, "Zhongwai wangluo wenxue bijiao fenxi" 中外网络文学比较分析 (master's thesis, Shaanxi Normal University 陕西师范大学, 2006.)

31 Meng, Xingyu 蒙星宇, "Beimei huawen wangluo wenxue ershinian yanjiu (yijiubaba-erlinglingba)" 北美华文网络文学二十年研究 (1988–2008) (PhD dissertation, Jinan University 暨南大学, 2010.)

32 Cui, Zairong 崔宰溶, "Zhongguo wangluo wenxue yanjiu de kunjing yu tupo" 中国网络文学研究的困境与突破 (PhD dissertation, Peking University 北京大学, 2011.)

33 Translator's note: according to Cui, "vernacular theory is the deep understanding and insight of [popular culture], possessed by the very natives of that particular culture," and "'networkedness' is the particular meaning or quality which some lexia, or some people's activity acquires when they exist in network. This concept helps us to overcome the limitation of former literary studies caused by traditional concepts such as 'work,' 'text,' and 'hypertext.'" See: Cui, Zairong 崔宰溶, "Zhongguo wangluo wenxue yanjiu de kunjing yu tupo" 中国网络文学研究的困境与突破, iii.

34 Translator's note: these terms are directly from the English abstract of Cui's dissertation, page iii. "Wakeng" literally means "to dig a hole." This vernacular expression refers to the condition that an author intentionally mentions characters and events at a certain point of the story, only to give fuller explanations and narrations much later. It can be understood as a narrative technique to create suspense and complicate the storyline.

Bibliography

Chen, Dingjia 陈定家. "Woguo wangluo wenxue de xueke kaichuang: ping Ouyang Youquan de wangluo wenxue yanjiu" 网络文学的学科开创——评欧阳友权的网络文学研究. *Creation and Criticism* 创作与评论 no. 8 (2016): 61–68.

Chen, Jie 陈杰. "Jiemi wangluo wenxue fensi jingji: 'dashang' shouru po qianwan 揭秘网络文学粉丝经济：'打赏' 收入破千万." *Beijing shangbao* 北京商报 (Beijing), Aug. 16, 2013.

Chen, Muyi 陈木易. "Qicheng zhongxuesheng pian'ai wangluo xiaoshuo bu ai mingzhu 七成中学生偏爱网络小说不爱名著." *Dongnan kuaibao* 东南快报 (Fuzhou), Dec. 10, 2013.

China Internet Network Information Center (CNNIC). "The 38th Statistical Report on Internet Development in China." *CNNIC*. Last modified November 14, 2016. www.cnnic.com.cn/IDR/ReportDownloads/201611/P020161114573409551742.pdf.

Cui, Zairong 崔宰溶. "Zhongguo wangluo wenxue yanjiu de kunjing yu tupo" 中国网络文学研究的困境与突破. PhD dissertation, Peking University 北京大学, 2011.

He, Liu 何流. "Wangluo wenxue: erfenqian zhishang de shangye dasha 网络文学：2分钱之上的商业大厦." *Zhongguo baodao* 中国报道 (Beijing) no. 7 (2009): 82–84.

Liu, Xia 刘夏. "Tengxun shengda lianyin, Wu Wenhui zhangduo 'wenxue diguo' 腾讯盛大联姻，吴文辉掌舵'文学帝国.'" *Xinjing bao* 新京报 (Beijing), Mar. 18, 2015.

McLuhan, Marshall. *Understanding Media: The Extensions of Man*. Cambridge, MA: The MIT Press, 1994.

Meng, Xingyu 蒙星宇. "Beimei huawen wangluo wenxue ershinian yanjiu (yijiubaba-erlinglingba)" 北美华文网络文学二十年研究（1988—2008）. PhD dissertation, Jinan University 暨南大学, 2010.

Mo, Yan 莫言. "Wangluo wenxue shige haoxianxiang 网络文学是个好现象." *Renmin ribao* 人民日报 (Beijing), Dec. 1, 2008.

Shu, Jinyu 舒晋瑜. "Qiaoxiang wangluo xiaoyuan xiaoshuo de jingzhong 敲响网络校园小说的警钟." *Zhonghua dushu bao* 中华读书报 (Beijing), Jan. 21, 2004.

Shu, Jinyu 舒晋瑜. "Chaochangpian qihuan xiaoshuo jiang da baofa 超长篇奇幻小说将大爆发." *Zhonghua dushu bao* 中华读书报 (Beijing), Ap. 20, 2005a.

Shu, Jinyu 舒晋瑜. "Youxi xiaoshuo huishi xiayizuo chuban jinkuang ma? 游戏小说会是下一座出版金矿吗？" *Zhonghua dushu bao* 中华读书报 (Beijing), Feb. 23, 2005b.

Shu, Jinyu 舒晋瑜. "Zhuixun qingchun wenxue de wangluo chushen 追寻青春文学的网络出身." *Zhonghua dushu bao* 中华读书报 (Beijing), Feb. 23, 2005c.

Xiao, Fuxing 肖复兴. "Yelai shuoshuo wangluo wenxue 也来说说网络文学." *Renmin ribao haiwaiban* 人民日报海外版 (Beijing), Jun. 18, 2009.

Xing, Yusen 邢育森. "Wangluo nüzuojia de mimi huayuan" 网络女作家的秘密花园. *The World of Information about the Internet* Internet信息世界 Feb. (2000): 72–74.

Yang, Xinmin 杨新敏. "Wangluo wenxue chuyi" 网络文学刍议. *Literary Review* 文学评论 no. 5 (2000): 87–95.

Yuan, Suwen 苑苏文 and Ji, Shaoting 姬少亭. *Fensi jingji: Zhongguo wangluo xiaoshuo rebian yingshiju* 粉丝经济：中国网络小说热编影视剧. Souhu 搜狐, 2014. https://business.sohu.com/20140731/n402980285.shtml.

Zhang, Kangkang 张抗抗. "Yougan wangluo wenxue" 有感网络文学. *Writer Magazine* 作家 May (2000): 10–11.

Zhang, Yu 张雨. "Zhongwai wangluo wenxue bijiao fenxi" 中外网络文学比较分析. Master's thesis, Shaanxi Normal University 陕西师范大学, 2006.

Zhou, Wen 周文. "Wangluo wenxue yanjiu de kaituozhe—ji zhongnan daxue wenxueyuan Ouyang Youquan jiaoshou 网络文学研究的开拓者——记中南大学文学院欧阳友权教授." *Wenyi bao* 文艺报 (Beijing), Jan. 13, 2005.

Zhou, Yafei 周亚飞. "Wangluo wenxue, menkan gaobugao? 网络文学，门槛高不高？" *Renmin ribao* 人民日报 (Beijing), Feb. 24, 2014.

3 Academic Achievements in Cyber Literary Studies

While cyber literary criticism as a *practice* directly influenced the writing of cyber literature in recent years, cyber literary criticism as *texts* was accumulated and stored in various media. Such texts, as embodiments of scholars' thoughts, today still function to guide the writing of cyber literature directly or indirectly.

Representative Achievements in Cyber Literary Studies

As cyber literary criticism is written by different groups of people on various media platforms, it can be divided into three types: 1. books and papers by scholars and professional critics; 2. articles in newspapers, magazines, and other print media that are short and meant to entertain readers; 3. ordinary netizens' thumbs-up, complaints, and discussions on websites and apps. While these *texts* are different in form, function, and significance, they all contribute to the development and flourishment of cyber literary criticism. Nevertheless, academic books and papers are based more on scholars' research and can best represent the achievements in cyber literary criticism.

Academic Books on Cyber Literature

Books are usually more academically crucial than other forms of cyber literary criticism. As they are longer than scholarly papers and netizens' comments, their discussions are more systematic and comprehensive. Moreover, they are rigorous in thinking, lucid in expressing, and meticulous in reasoning and analyzing. Of course, as it takes a long time to write and publish a book, compared with papers in academic journals and articles in newspapers and magazines, scholarly books cannot respond promptly to specific literary issues. Nevertheless, some books present deep thoughts and innovative theories—they are more influential in the field and receive more citations from other scholars.

Only a few academic monographs have titles containing the words "cyber literary criticism." They include *On Cyber Literary Criticism* (Wangluo wenxue pipinglun) by Tan Dejing and *Cyber Literary Criticism 100* (Wangluo wenxue pinglun yibai) by Ouyang Youquan.[1] Nevertheless, more than a hundred works

92 Part I

directly or indirectly related to cyber literary criticism have been published. According to statistics, from 1997—when books of the "Internet Culture Series" (Wangluo wenhua congshu) were published—to the end of 2003, a total of 83 academic books on cyber literature were published in China.[2] Between 2009 and 2013, 59 academic books were published, and ten publications received awards from the central government, the ministries of the central government, or provincial governments.[3] The following is a list of academic books on cyber literature, all published after 2000 and arranged in chronological order (see Table 3.1).

Among these books, only a few can be seen as pure literary criticism, but "criticism" and "theory" are often interrelated: they mesh without a clear boundary. Moreover, the books listed above all touch upon various issues related to literature in the Internet era, such as literature's transformation, social context, value and significance, and means of production. From different perspectives, these books all interpret and evaluate the newly rising cyber literature and contribute to the conceptualization and theorization of cyber literary criticism.

Academic Papers and Newspaper Articles

Compared with books, academic papers can give more pertinent responses to specific literary issues and timely evaluations of new literary works. In the Cyber Literary Research Archive (Wangluo wenxue wenxian shujuku), there are 907 academic journal articles, 1,035 newspaper articles, 229 master's theses and doctoral dissertations, and 143 conference papers.[4] Their entries are kept in *A Collection of Entries for Research Works on Cyber Literature* (Wangluo wenxue yanjiu chengguo jicheng). Overall, more pieces were published each year. An increasing number of scholars entered this field of research, and graduate students studied cyber literature for their master's theses and doctoral dissertations.[5] Their research was no longer limited to the basics of cyber literature but extended to cover a broader range of topics with more systematic and specific discussions.

For your reference, here we selected 50 journal articles and 50 newspaper articles as representative works from the Cyber Literary Research Archive, *A General Survey of Cyber Literature Across Five Years (2009–2013)*,[6] and China National Knowledge Infrastructure (CNKI). They are arranged in chronological order (see Tables 3.2 and 3.3).

Scholars' Viewpoints on Cyber Literature

Cyber literary criticism, with a short history, has not yet formed its own "norms." Nevertheless, as it is rapidly evolving and easily reshaped, we now have enough textual resources to create a historical account of its development. Meanwhile, cyber literary criticism is quite effective as practical feedback on the newest literary creations and thus has become an emerging power that guides and regulates the development of cyber literature. We select several

Table 3.1 Fifty representative books on cyber literature (2000–2016)

No.	Author/editor	Title	Publisher	Year
1	Huang Mingfen	Bits versus Muse: Network and Art (Bite tiaozhan miusi: wangluo yu yishu)	Xiamen University Press (Xiamen daxue chubanshe)	2000
2	Nan Fan	Double Visions: An Analysis of Contemporary Electronic Culture (Shuangchong shiyu—dangdai dianzi wenhua fenxi)	Jiangsu People's Publishing House (Jiangsu renmin chubanshe)	2001
3	Wang Qiang	The Possibilities of Internet Art: Revolutions in Modern Technology and Art (Wangluo yishu de keneng—xiandai keji geming yu yishu de bianqe)	Guangdong Education Press (Guangdong jiaoyu chubanshe)	2001
4	Ge Tao	Lu Xun on the Internet (Wangluo Lu Xun)	People's Literature Publishing House (Renmin wenxue chubanshe)	2001
5	Huang Mingfen	The Poetics of Hypertextuality (Chaowenben shixue)	Xiamen University Press	2001
6	Ouyang Youquan	An Outline for the Discussion on Cyber Literature (Wangluo wenxue lungang)	People's Literature Publishing House	2003
7	Ouyang Youquan	The Ontology of Cyber Literature (Wangluo wenxue bentilun)	CFLAC Publishing House (Zhongguo wenlian chubanshe)	2004
8	Tan Dejing	On Cyber Literary Criticism (Wangluo wenxue pipinglun)	CFLAC Publishing House	2004
9	He Xuewei and Lan Aiguo	A Review of Cyber Literature from the Perspective of Folk Culture (Wangluo wenxue de minjian shiye)	CFLAC Publishing House	2004
10	Xu Miaomiao	A Review of Cyber Literature from the Perspective of Gender Studies (Xingbie shiye zhong de wangluo wenxue)	Jiuzhou Press (Jiuzhou chubanshe)	2004
11	Ouyang Youquan	Studies of Literature and Art in the Context of Digitalization (Shuzihua yujing zhong de wenyixue)	China Social Sciences Press (Zhongguo shehui kexue chubanshe)	2005

(Continued)

Table 3.1 (Continued)

No.	Author/editor	Title	Publisher	Year
12	Zhang Deming	A Study of Web Poetry (Wangluo shige yanjiu)	China Literature and History Press (Zhongguo wenshi chubanshe)	2005
13	Su Xiaofang	On Web Novels (Wangluo xiaoshuo lun)	China Literature and History Press	2007
14	Yang Yu	On Web Poetry (Wangluo shige lun)	China Literature and History Press	2007
15	Lan Aiguo	Spoof Culture on the Internet (Wangluo egao wenhua)	China Literature and History Press	2007
16	Ouyang Wenfeng and Wang Xiaosheng	On Blog Literature (Boke wenxue lun)	China Literature and History Press	2007
17	Ouyang Youquan	An Academic Review of Cyber Literature (Wangluo wenxue de xueli xingtai)	Central Party Literature Press (Zhongyang wenxian chubanshe)	2007
18	Ma Ji	Writing in the Era When People Read on Screens: A Ten-Year History of Cyber Literature (Duping shidai de xiezuo: wangluo wenxue shinian shi)	China Workers Publishing House (Zhongguo gongren chubanshe)	2008
19	Shan Xiaoxi	Literature and Its Mode of Existence in Modern Media (Xiandai chuanmei yujing zhong de wenxue cunzai fangshi)	China Social Sciences Press	2008
20	Ouyang Youquan	Poetics in the World of Bits: A Discussion on Cyber Literature (Bite shijie de shixue: wangluo wenxue lungao)	Yuelu Publishing House (Yuelu shushe)	2009
21	Ma Ji	A Study and Record about Cyber Literature (Wangluo wenxue toushi yu beiwang)	China Social Sciences Press	2010
22	Jiang Shuzhuo and Li Fengliang	Literature and Its Mode of Existence in the Era of the Mass Media (Chuanmei shidai de wenxue cunzai fangshi)	Guangxi Normal University Press (Guangxi shifan daxue chubanshe)	2010
23	Yang Ke (editor)	A Review of Cyber Literature [a book series] (Wangluo wenxue pinglun)	Huacheng Publishing House (Huacheng chubanshe)	2011
24	Ouyang Youquan	The Transformation of Literature and Art in Digital Media (Shuzi meijie xia de wenyi zhuanxing)	China Social Sciences Press	2011
25	Zeng Fanting	On Cyber Writers (Wangluo xieshou lun)	China Social Sciences Press	2011

26	Ouyang Wenfeng	On Text-message Literature (Duanxin wenxue lun)	China Social Sciences Press	2011
27	Nie Qingpu	An Interpretation of Famous Web Stories (Wangluo xiaoshuo mingpian jiedu)	China Social Sciences Press	2011
28	Li Yuping	A General Discussion on Time-travel Stories on the Internet (Wangluo chuanyue xiaoshuo gailun)	Nankai University Press (Nankai daxue chubanshe)	2011
29	Chen Dingjia	The World of Bits: A Study of the Literary Production in the Internet Era (Bite zhijing: wangluo shidai de wenxue shengchan yanjiu)	China Social Sciences Press	2011
30	Meng Xingyu	Shao Jun: A Cyber Writer (Wangluo Shao Jun)	Jiuzhou Press	2011
31	Yang Jianlong, etc.	The Cultural Context and Cultural Phenomena in the Early 21st Century (Xinshiji chu de wenhua yujing yu wenxue xianxiang)	Central Compilation & Translation Press (Zhongyang bianyi chubanshe)	2012
32	Jiang Ying	The Value of Cyber Literature (Wangluo wenxue de jiazhi)	Bashu Publishing House (Bashu shushe)	2013
33	Ouyang Youquan	Cyber Literary Criticism 100 (Wangluo wenxue pinglun 100)	Central Compilation & Translation Press	2014
34	Zeng Fanting	Famous Cyber Literary Works 100 (Wangluo wenxue mingpian 100)	Central Compilation & Translation Press	2014
35	Yu Jianxiang	Key Words in Cyber Literature 100 (Wangluo wenxue guanjianci 100)	Central Compilation & Translation Press	2014
36	Ouyang Wenfeng	Big Events about Cyber Literature 100 (Wangluo wenxue dashijian 100)	Central Compilation & Translation Press	2014
37	Nie Mao	Famous Writers' Blogs 100 (Ming zuojia boke 100)	Central Compilation & Translation Press	2014
38	Nie Qingpu	Famous Cyber Writers 100 (Wangluo xieshou mingjia 100)	Central Compilation & Translation Press	2014
39	Ji Hailong	Literary Websites 100 (Wangluo wenxue wangzhan 100)	Central Compilation & Translation Press	2014
40	Creation and Research Department of China Writers Association (Zhongguo zuojia xiehui chuangyanbu)	Abstract and Concrete Issues Concerning the Evaluation System for Cyber Literature (Wangluo wenxue pingjia tixi xushitan)	Writers Publishing House (Zuojia chubanshe)	2014

(Continued)

Table 3.1 (Continued)

No.	Author/editor	Title	Publisher	Year
41	Huang Fayou	Media Studies Concerning Contemporary Chinese Literature (Zhongguo dangdai wenxue chuanmei yanjiu)	People's Literature Publishing House	2014
42	Li Shengtao	The Ecology of Cyber Literature (Wangluo xiaoshuo de shengtaixing wenxue tujing)	China Social Sciences Press	2014
43	Chen Dingjia	The Dance of Words: A Study of Cyber Literature and Intertextuality (Wen zhi wu: wangluo wenxue yu huwenxing yanjiu)	Social Sciences Literature Press	2014
44	He Zhijun and Qin Fengzhen	An Analysis of the Phenomena Concerning Aesthetic Appreciation in the Context of Digitalization in the New Century (Shuzhua yujing zhong xinshiji wenyi shenmei xianxiang jiexi)	People's Daily Press (Renmin ribao chubanshe)	2015
45	Zhou Zhixiong	The Development and Criticism of Cyber Literature (Wangluo wenxue de fazhan yu pingpan)	People's Publishing House (Renmin chubanshe)	2015
46	Shan Xiaoxi	Media and Literature: An Introduction to Media Studies Concerning Literature and Art (Meijie yu wenxue: meijie wenyixue yinlun)	The Commercial Press (Shangwu yinshuguan)	2015
47	Zhou Zhixiong	Portraits of Great Masters: Interviews with Cyber Writers (Dashen de xiaoxiang: wangluo zuojia fangtanlu)	Shandong People's Publishing House (Shandong renmin chubanshe)	2015
48	Ouyang Youquan	Collected Entries of Major Academic Publications on Cyber Literature (Wangluo wenxue yanjiu chengguo jicheng)	CFLAC Publishing House	2015
49	Tan Weiping	A Study of the Form of Literature in the Future (Weilai wenxue xingtai tanxi)	Hunan People's Publishing House (Hunan renmin chubanshe)	2015
50	Shao Yanjun	Interpreting Classics of Cyber Literature (Wangluo wenxue jingdian jiedu)	Peking University Press (Beijing daxue chubanshe)	2016

Academic Achievements in Cyber Literary Studies 97

Table 3.2 Fifty representative journal articles on cyber literature (2000–2016)

No.	Author	Title	Journal	Issue (Year)
1	Wang Yichuan	Literature in the Internet Era: What Is Indispensable? (Wangluo shidai de wenxue: shenme shi buneng shao de)	*Master* (Dajia)	no. 3 (2000)
2	Song Hui and Lai Daren	The "McDonaldization" and "Internetization" of Literary Production (Wenxue shengchan de maidanglao hua he wangluo hua)	*Literature and Art Criticism* (Wenyi pinglun)	no. 5 (2000)
3	Yang Xinmin	Legends in Cyberspace: On Cai Zhiheng's Novels (Wangluo chuanqi: Cai Zhiheng xiaoshuo lun)	*Forum for Chinese Literature of the World* (Shijie huawen wenxue luntan)	no. 1 (2001)
4	Jing Wendong	The Fate of the Writing of Classic Literature in the Internet Era (Wangluo shidai jingdian xiezuo de mingyun)	*Novel Review* (Xiaoshuo pinglun)	no. 3 (2001)
5	Cai Yan	A Utopia for Free Literary Creation: A Critique of the Aesthetics of Cyber Literature (Wenxue ziyou de wutuobang: dui wangluo wenxue de meixue piping)	*Journal of Qujing Normal University* (Qujing shifan xueyuan yuanbao)	no. 5 (2001)
6	Ouyang Youquan	The Landscape of Literature on the Internet: A Review and Trend Analysis of Cyber Literature in China (Hulianwang shang de wenxue fengjing—woguo wangluo wenxue xianzhuang diaocha yu zoushi fenxi)	*Journal of China Three Gorges University: The Humanities and Social Sciences Edition* (Sanxia daxue xuebao renwen shehui kexue ban)	no. 6 (2001)
7	Lin Huayu	A Heroic Tragedy and Classic Parody: Interpreting *The Story of Wukong* as a Web Novel (Yingxiong de beiju, xifang de jingdian—wangluo xiaoshuo *Wukong zhuan* de shendu jiedu)	*Masterpieces Review* (Mingzuo xinshang)	no. 4 (2002)
8	Huang Mingfen	My Opinions on Cyber Literature (Wangluo wenxue zhi wojian)	*Social Science Front* (Shehui kexue zhanxian)	no. 4 (2002)
9	Ouyang Youquan	The Spiritual Orientation of Cyber Literature (Lun wangluo wenxue de jingshen quxiang)	*Literature & Art Studies* (Wenyi yanjiu)	no. 5 (2002)

(*Continued*)

Table 3.2 (Continued)

No.	Author	Title	Journal	Issue (Year)
10	Tan Dejing	The Carnivalization of Literary Criticism: A Study of the "Public Square" in Cyber Literary Criticism (Piping de kuanghuan—wangluo piping guangchang bianxi)	Theory and Criticism of Literature and Art (Wenyi lilun yu piping)	no. 3 (2003)
11	Tan Dejing	Online Literary Criticism as a New Form (Zaixianxing dui wangluo piping xingshi de yingxiang)	Journal of Central South University: Social Sciences Edition (Zhongnan daxue xuebao shehui kexue ban)	no. 5 (2003)
12	Ouyang Youquan	A Brief Discussion on the Ontology of Cyber Literature (Wangluo wenxue bentilun gang)	Literary Review (Wenxue pinglun)	no. 6 (2004)
13	Wang Yuechuan	Cyber Literature: An Interpretation from an Academic's Perspective (Wangluo wenxue: lixing shiyu zhong de xueli chanshi)	Journal of Central South University: Social Sciences Edition (Zhongnan daxue xuebao shehui kexue ban)	no. 6 (2004)
14	Liu Lili and Li Yuping	Cyber Literature's Challenge to Literary Theories (Wangluo wenxue dui wenxue piping lilun de tiaozhan)	Journal of Lanzhou University (Lanzhou daxue xuebao)	no. 5 (2004)
15	Zhao Huiping	Issues of Literary Criticism in the Internet Era (Wangluo shidai de wenxue piping wenti)	Journal of Humanities (Renwen zazhi)	no. 2 (2005)
16	Tan Dejing	"Offence" and "Escape": An Analysis of the Spiritual Dimensions of Cyber Literary Critics (Maofan yu duobi—wangluo wenxue piping zhuti de jingshen xiangdu fenxi)	Literary and Artistic Contention (Wenyi zhengming)	no. 4 (2005)
17	Tao Dongfeng	Have We Entered into an Era When Chinese Literature Is Nothing but Gods and Ghosts? (Zhongguo wenxue yijing jinru zhuangshennonggui shidai?)	Contemporary Literary Criticism (Dangdai wentan)	no. 5 (2006)
18	Chen Dingjia	The Rise of Hypertexts and Literature in the Internet Era (Chaowenben de xingqi yu wangluo shidai de wenxue)	Social Sciences in China (Zhongguo shehui kexue)	no. 3 (2007)

Academic Achievements in Cyber Literary Studies 99

19	Zhan Shan	A Comparative Study of Online Cyber Literary Criticism and Offline Cyber Literary Criticism (Zaixian yu feizaixian wangluo wenxue piping zhi bijiao)	Fujian Tribune (Fujian luntan)	no. 10 (2007)
20	Fan Yugang	Cyber Literature: Between Literature and Technology (Wangluo wenxue: shengcheng yu wenxue yu jishu zhijian)	Literary Review	no. 2 (2008)
21	Lü Deqiang	A Brief Discussion on Cyber Literature (Wangluo wenxue piping jianlun)	Journal of Leshan Normal University (Leshan shifan xueyuan xuebao)	no. 2 (2008)
22	Li Yongyan	Professional Critics and Cyber Literary Criticism (Zhuanye pipingjia yu wangluo wenxue piping)	Journal of Yangtze Normal University (Changjiang shifan xueyuan xuebao)	no. 3 (2008)
23	Bai Ye	New Conditions and Challenges of Literary Criticism (Wenxue piping de xin jingyu yu xin tiaozhan)	Literature & Art Studies (Wenyi yanjiu)	no. 8 (2009)
24	Guo Chen and Cai Meijuan	A Review of the Functions of Contemporary Literary Criticism from the Perspective of Cyber Literature (Cong wangluo wenxue kan dangdai wenxue piping de gongneng)	Journal of Shandong University of Technology: Social Sciences Edition (Shandong ligong daxue xuebao shehui kexue ban)	no. 1 (2009)
25	Wang Ying	Ten Years of "Sword Fighting": Conditions and Problems of Cyber Literature in the New Century (Shinian lunjian: xinshiji wangluo wenxue xianzhuang yu wenti)	Journal of Tianjin Normal University: Social Sciences Edition (Tianjin shifan daxue xuebao shehui kexue ban)	no. 6 (2009)
26	Li Yuping	An Analysis of the Reasons for the Popularity of Time-Travel Stories on the Internet (Wangluo chuanyue xiaoshuo rechao yuanyin jiexi)	Literature in Contemporary Times (Shidai wenxue)	no. 12 (2009)
27	Chen Guoxiong	Digital Media and the Borders of Literary Criticism (Shuzi meijie yu wenxue piping de bianjie)	Academic Journal of Zhongzhou (Zhongzhou xuekan)	no. 2 (2010)

(Continued)

100 Part I

Table 3.2 (Continued)

No.	Author	Title	Journal	Issue (Year)
28	Zhou Zhixiong	The Current Condition and Problems of Cyber Literary Criticism (Wangluo wenxue piping de xianzhuang yu wenti)	Journal of Shandong Normal University: The Humanities and Social Sciences Edition (Shandong shifan daxue xuebao renwen shehuikexue ban)	no. 2 (2010)
29	Jiang Bing	The "Post-80s" Generation and the Cyberspace: Double Barriers of Literary Criticism (Baling hou yu wangluo: wenxue piping de shuangchong zuge)	Southern Cultural Forum (Nanfang wentan)	no. 4 (2010)
30	Wang Ying	From Intentional Absence to Forced Silence: How Should Traditional Literary Criticism Deal with Literature in the Internet Era (Cong zhudong quexi dao beidong shiyu?—chuantong piping ruhe yingdui wangluo shidai de wenxue)	Southern Cultural Forum	no. 4 (2010)
31	Bai Ye	Limitations and Possibilities: Traditional Literary Criticism and Cyber Literature (Youxianxing yu kenengxing—chuantong piping yu wangluo wenxue)	Southern Cultural Forum	no. 4 (2010)
32	Ouyang Youquan and Wu Yingwen	The Value and Limitations of Cyber Literary Criticism (Wangluo wenxue piping de jiazhi he juxian)	Exploration and Free Views (Tansuo yu zhengming)	no. 11 (2010)
33	Huang Mingfen	The Revolution in Internet Media and the Transformation of Cyber Literary Criticism (Wangluo chuanmei geming yu dianzi wenxue piping de shanbian)	Exploration and Free Views	no. 11 (2010)
34	Yu Jianxiang	Spatial Turn: Constructing a New Paradigm for Cyber Literary Criticism (Kongjian zhuanxiang: jiangou wangluo wenxue piping xin fanshi)	Exploration and Free Views	no. 11 (2010)

Academic Achievements in Cyber Literary Studies 101

35	Ma Ji	Online Writing in the Course of Discourse Transformation: A Review of Ten Outstanding Online Novels of the Past Decade (Huayu fangshi zhuanbian zhong de wangluo xiezuo—jianping wangluo xiaoshuo shinian shibu jiazuo)	Literary and Artistic Contention	no. 19 (2010)
36	Song Ting	The Current Condition of Criticism and Studies of Cyber Literature (Wangluo wenxue piping yanjiu xianzhuang)	Literatures (Wenxue jie)	no. 2 (2011)
37	Zeng Fanting	An Analysis of the "Freedom" in Cyber Literature (Wangluo wenxue zhi ziyou shuxing bianshi)	Literary Review	no. 1 (2012)
38	Zhang Chang	Literary Criticism in New Media (Chuanmei shidai xinmeiti wenxue piping)	Journal of Wenzhou Vocational and Technical College (Wenzhou zhiye jishu xueyuan xuebao)	no. 2 (2012)
39	Zhou Jing	The Difficulties in Cyber Literary Criticism and the Solutions (Wangluo wenxue piping de kunju yu xinlu)	Zhejiang Social Sciences (Zhejiang shehui kexue)	no. 7 (2012)
40	Shan Xiaoxi	From Cyber Literary Studies to Digital Literary Studies: A Paradigm Shift (Cong wangluo wenxue yanjiu dao shuzi wenxue yanjiu de fanshi zhuanhuan)	Study & Exploration (xuexi yu tansuo)	no. 12 (2012)
41	Li Jing and Shi Shaotao	Cyber Literary Criticism: The Construction of Its Criteria (Wangluo wenxue piping—jiangou shuyu zishen de biaozhun)	Journal of Beihua University (Beihua daxue xuebao)	no. 3 (2013)
42	Ouyang Ting and Ouyang Youquan	A Reflection on the Genealogy of Cyber Literature (Wangluo wenxue de tizhi puxixue fansi)	Theoretical Studies in Literature and Art (Wenyi lilun yanjiu)	no. 1 (2014)
43	Huang Mingfen	A New Outlook on Art Studies in the Era of New Media (Xinmeiti shidai yishu yanjiu xinshiye)	Journal of Xiamen University (Xiamen daxue xuebao)	no. 2 (2015)

(Continued)

Table 3.2 (Continued)

No.	Author	Title	Journal	Issue (Year)
44	Zhang Wendong	New Media and New Criticism: An Understanding of the Poetics in Cyber Literary Criticism (Xinmeiti yu xinpiping: wangluo wenxue piping de shixing lijie)	*Contemporary Literary Criticism*	no. 6 (2015)
45	Ouyang Youquan	The Way of Constructing a History of Cyber Literary Criticism (Wangluo wenxue pipingshi de jiangou luoji)	*Qiushi* (Qiushi xuekan)	no. 3 (2016)
46	Yu Jianxiang	The Multiple Dimensions of Criteria for the Evaluation of Cyber Literature (Wangluo wenxue piping biaozhun de duoweixing)	*Qiushi*	no. 3 (2016)
47	Ouyang Ting	A Review of Cyber Literary Criticism (Wangluo wenxue piping de xueshu shuli)	*Qiushi*	no. 3 (2016)
48	Zeng Fanting	The Changing Identities of Cyber Literary Critics (Wangluo wenxue piping zhuti de yanbian)	*Novel Review*	no. 5 (2016)
49	Wu Yingwen	The Rhetoric of Cyber Literary Criticism (Wangluo wenxue piping de xiucishu)	*Novel Review*	no. 5 (2016)
50	Ma Ji	Becoming the Mainstream: The New Conditions of Cyber Literature and Art (Wangluo wenyi de zhuliuhua yu xin geju)	*China Literary and Art Criticism* (Zhongguo wenyi pinglun)	no.6 (2016)

Table 3.3 Fifty representative newspaper articles on cyber literature (2000–2016)

No.	Author	Title	Newspaper	Date
1	Huang Mignfen	A Call for Studies of Computer Literature and Art with Theories of Literature and History (Diannao wenyi: dui lilun piping yu shixue de huhuan)	*Newspaper of Literature and Art* (Wenyi bao)	Nov. 11, 1997
2	Zhao Chenyu and Jiang Shuyuan	Does Cyber Literature Blow the Horn of a New Culture, or Is It Just "Old Wine in New Bottles"? (Wangluo wenxue: xin wenming de haojiao haishi xinping zhuang jiujiu)	*China Reading Weekly* (Zhonghua dushu bao)	Dec. 2, 1999
3	Zhang Kangkang	Random Thoughts about Cyber Literature (Wangluo wenxue zagan)	*China Reading Weekly*	Mar. 1, 2000
4	Ma Longqian	Cyber Literature: From Adaptation to Original Creation (Wangluo wenxue: cong zhuanhuan dao yuanchuang)	*China Reading Weekly*	Dec. 18, 2002
5	Ouyang Youquan	Where are the Weak Points of Cyber Literature? (Nali caishi wangluo wenxue de ruanlei)	*China Reading Weekly*	Jun. 18, 2003
6	Meng Fanhua	Cyber Literature: A Carnivalesque Game, or a Revolution? (Wangluo wenxue: youxi kuanghuan haishi geming)	*China Education Daily* (Zhongguo jiaoyu bao)	Nov. 4, 2004
7	Zhao Shuping	Three Key Words for the Value Judgement of Cyber Literature (Wangluo wenxue jiazhi pinggu de sange guanjianci)	*China Reading Weekly*	Nov. 10, 2004
8	Ma Xiangwu	The Cultural Significance of Text-message Literature (Duanxin wenxue de wenhua yiyi)	*Guangming Daily* (Guangming ribao)	Feb. 4, 2005
9	Ouyang Youquan	Ethical Questions Concerning Cyber Literature (Wangluo wenxue de lunlixue wenti)	*Newspaper of Literature and Art*	Apr. 12, 2005
10	Chen Qijia	Cyber Literature: A Power that Cannot Be Ignored (Wangluo wenxue: buke hushi de liliang)	*People's Daily* (Renmin ribao)	Jan. 5, 2007
11	Yuan Yuexing	Technology's Invasion of "Poetics" (Jishu dui shiyi de ruqin)	*Newspaper of Chinese Culture* (Zhongguo wenhuabao)	Jan. 16, 2007
12	Zeng Chunguang	Cold Reflection on the Heat of Cyberwriting (Wangluo xieshou re de leng sikao)	*Guangming Daily*	Apr. 8, 2007

(*Continued*)

104 Part I

Table 3.3 (Continued)

No.	Author	Title	Newspaper	Date
13	Yang Gu	We Shall Use Contemporary Masterpieces to Occupy the Battlefield of Cyber Literature (Yong shidai jingpin qiangzhan wangluo wenxue zhendi)	Guangming Daily	Aug. 19, 2007
14	Shu Jinyu	Ten Years of Cyber Literature (Ban wangluo wenxue zouguo shinian)	China Reading Weekly	Jul. 23, 2008
15	Ma Ji	The Significance of Cyber Literature to Social Reality (Wangluo wenxue de xianshi yiyi)	People's Daily	Apr. 16, 2009
16	Xu Miaomiao	Cyber Literature: Current Condition and Problems (Wangluo wenxue: xianzhuang ji wenti)	Newspaper of Literature and Art	Apr. 16, 2009
17	Chen Dingjia	The Crisis of Literature's Position in the Internet Era (Wangluo shidai wenxue shenfen de weiji)	Newspaper of Chinese Culture	Jul. 24, 2009
18	Hong Zhigang	Basic Ethical Principles and Aesthetic Tastes in Cyber Literature (Wangluo wenxue de jiben lunli yu shenmei quwei)	Newspaper of Literature and Art	Nov. 26, 2009
19	Chen Fumin	What Is Not "Cyber Literature"? (Shenme bushi wangluo wenxue)	Newspaper of Literature and Art	Dec. 26, 2009
20	Guo Guochang	A Call for Cyber Literary Criticism (Wangluo wenxue huhuan wenxue piping)	People's Daily	Feb. 5, 2010
21	Bai Ye	We Should Develop the Criticism of New Media Literature (Jiaqiang xinmeiti wenxue piping)	Guangming Daily	Nov. 20, 2010
22	Ma Ji	Cyber Literature: The Second Starting Point for Contemporary Chinese Literature (Wangluo wenxue: Zhongguo dangdai wenxue di'erci qihang)	People's Daily	Apr. 19, 2011
23	Ouyang Youquan	How Far Is Cyber Literature from Mao Dun Literature Prize? (Wangluo wenxue li Mao Dun wenxuejiang you duoyuan?)	Guangming Daily	Sep. 26, 2011
24	Suo Luo	An Overview of Cyber Literature from the Vantage Point of History (Zhanzai lishi de gaodu shenshi wangluo wenxue)	Newspaper of Literature and Art	Mar. 18, 2011
25	Ouyang Youquan	The Influence of Cyber Literature (Wangluo wenxue de yingxiang)	Newspaper of Literature and Art	May 16, 2011
26	Shan Xiaoxi	The New Space for the Development of Cyber Literature (Wangluo wenxue fazhan de xinkongjian)	People's Daily	Sep. 23, 2011

Academic Achievements in Cyber Literary Studies 105

27	Wang Guoping	A System of Evaluation Criteria for Cyber Literary Criticism Is in Urgent Need (Wangluo wenxue jidai queli piping zhibiao tixi)	*Guangming Daily*	Jul. 3, 2012
28	Shao Yanjun et al.	Cyber Literature: How Do We View and Study It? (Wangluo wenxue: ruhe dingwei yu yanjiu)	*People's Daily*	Jul. 7, 2012
29	Wu Yan	We Should Develop Online Literary Criticism (Jiaqiang wangluo wenxue de zaixian piping)	*Newspaper of Literature and Art*	Apr. 11, 2012
30	Wang Ying	A System of Evaluation for Cyber Literature Is in Urgent Need (Jixu jianli wangluo wenxue pingjia tixi)	*Newspaper of Literature and Art*	Aug. 13, 2012
31	Ge Hongbing	Literary Criticism: How Should It Change with the Times? (Piping: ruhe zhimian shidai xinbian)	*Literature Press* (Wenxue bao)	Sep. 20, 2012
32	He Jianming	To Establish a Healthy Environment for Cyber Literature (Jianli jiankang de wangluo wenxue huanjing)	*Guangming Daily*	Mar. 10, 2013
33	Yimeng	What Kind of Professional Criticism Does Cyber Literature Need? (Wangluo wenxue xuyao shenmeyang de zhuanye piping)	*China Art News* (Zhongguo yishu bao)	Jul. 15, 2013
34	Chen Qirong	A Call for the Establishment of an Evaluation System for Cyber Literature (Huyu jianli wangluo wenxue pingjia tixi)	*People's Daily*	Jul. 19, 2013
35	Tianxia guiyuan	The Entry Point into the Aesthetics of Cyber Literatutre (Wangluo wenxue de shenmei qierudian)	*Newspaper of Literature and Art*	Aug. 2, 2013
36	Kang Qiao	On the Evaluation Criteria for Cyber Literature (Wangluo wenxue piping biaozhun chuyi)	*Guangming Daily*	Sep. 3, 2013
37	Wu Changqing	A Tentative Discussion on the Difficulties in Cyber Literary Criticism (Shilun wangluo wenxue piping de kunjing)	*Guangming Daily*	Oct. 15, 2013
38	Zhang Ning	The Literariness and New Standards of Web Fiction (Wangluo xiaoshuo de wenxuexing he xinbiaozhun)	*Newspaper of Literature and Art*	Dec. 11, 2013
39	Chen Qijia	Cyber Literary Criticism Should Begin with an Examination of Cyber Literature as an Industry (Wangluo wenxue piping dang cong chanye jiaodu rushou)	*China Art News* (Zhongguo yishu bao)	Dec. 18, 2013
40	Ouyang Youquan	Social Responsibility and Positive Values: A Review of Cyber Literature (Yiyi zhixiang yu jiazhi chengzai—wangluo wenxue zai renshi)	*People's Daily*	Apr. 25, 2014
41	Li Jingze	Cyber Literature: Self-Awareness in Literary and Cultural Production (Wangluo wenxue: wenxue zijue yu wenhua zijue)	*People's Daily*	Jul. 25, 2014

(Continued)

Table 3.3 (Continued)

No.	Author	Title	Newspaper	Date
42	Li Chaoquan	The Establishment of an Objective and Impartial System for the Evaluation of Cyber Literature (Jianli keguan gongzheng de wangluo wenxue pingjia tixi)	Hebei Daily (Hebei ribao)	Dec. 5, 2014
43	Li Yongjie	The Establishment of New Criteria to Guide the Development of Cyber Literature (Queli yinling wangluo wenxue fazhan de xinbiaozhun)	Chinese Social Sciences Today (Zhongguo shehui kexue bao)	Dec. 23, 2014
44	Chen Long	We Should Establish an Evaluation System for Cyber Literature (Wangluo wenxue yao jianli pingjia tixi)	Southern Daily (Nanfang ribao)	May 12, 2015
45	Pan Kaixiong	How Should Cyber Literature Be Evaluated (Dui wangluo wenxue jiujing gai ruhe pingjia)	China Youth Daily (Zhongguo qingnian bao)	Jun. 19, 2015
46	Shi Shiping	The Confusion and Sobriety in Cyber Literary Critics' Minds (Wangluo wenxue: piping de mimang yu qingxing)	Chinese Social Sciences Today	Sep. 14, 2015
47	Shao Yanjun	To Study Cyber Literature Is to Study Contemporary Literature (Yanjiu wangluo wenxue jiushi yanjiu dangdai wenxue)	Literature Press	Mar. 2, 2016
48	Zeng Yiguo et al.	Interpreting the Phenomenon of "Dashang" [Sending Monetary Reward to Writers] (Wangluo dashang xianxiang jiedu)	China Youth Daily	Jul. 25, 2016
49	Zhuang Yong	Criticism of Cyber Literature and Art Should "Enter the Field" (Wangluo wenyi pinglun xu jinchang)	China Business News (Diyi caijing ribao)	Aug. 27, 216
50	Xia Lie	The Three Pillars in Cyber Literary Criticism (Wangluo wenyi piping de sange xueli zhizhu)	Guangming Daily	Sep. 3, 2016

scholars' critical viewpoints from existent publications to further illustrate this point.

A Call for Establishing an Evaluation System for Cyber Literature

Cyber literary studies aim at establishing a proper and practical evaluation system, which will significantly contribute to the development of cyber literature. Many scholars gave their opinions on this issue. Chen Qirong argued that we could use many criteria to evaluate cyber literature, but the most important ones should be the ideological connotation and aesthetic value of literary works. First of all, cyber literature should maintain positive values. It should be socially responsible and conform to laws and morals. Chen argued:

> Cyber literature should first and foremost serve the people. At the ideological level, it should actively shoulder the responsibility for the country and the nation. It should praise the true, the good, and the beautiful. It should criticize the false, the wicked, and the ugly. It should resist violence, expose deception, refuse to forget the past, unremittingly pursue the ultimate meaning of life, and untiringly explore the spiritual world of humanity.[7]

Second, cyber writers should have a refined aesthetic taste. They should have lofty ambitions for literary creation. Chen argued:

> Writers of cyber literature should actively pursue an aesthetic taste that is positive, healthy, optimistic, elegant, and refreshing. They should reject the negative, the decadent, the pessimistic, the vulgar, and the obscene. Such a pursuit and a rejection should be shown in various aspects of cyber literature, including the theme, plot, characterization, language use, and stylistic elements. Thus, to study this issue, we should give specific analyses to specific texts.[8]

Zhao Chenyu and Jiang Shuyuan discussed a question in their article: "What criteria should we use to evaluate cyber literature?"[9] They summarized scholars' different opinions as follows. 1. We should use the same criteria to evaluate all works, whether traditional literature or cyber literature. 2. Considering the current condition of cyber literature, we should lower the standards for cyber literature. 3. We should establish a new set of criteria for cyber literature. Such a discussion led to another question: does cyber literature need criticism at all? The authors then quoted Bai Ye's words to answer this question: "Cyber literature, in the current condition, needs literary criticism, and it is an urgent need." They also quoted Chen Cun's opinion: "Literature, first and foremost, should cater to readers, not critics. As cyber literature is already in existence, critics cannot ignore it simply because they do not like it."[10]

In an article, Kang Qiao pointed out: "When using some criteria to evaluate a particular cyber literary work, we should consider the author's promise to readers, the writing process, and readers' expectations. Often, the author promises reading pleasure, and readers also expect to enjoy reading."[11] Cyber literature is known for a number of excellent "fantasy novels" (xuanhuan xiaoshuo) and "travel-back-into-history novels" (chuanyue lishi xiaoshuo). Through representations of unrestrained fantasies, these novels fulfill the main characters' wishes and allow readers to experience pleasure through reading. As to "urban novels" (dushi xiaoshuo) and "novels about officialdom" (guanchang xiaoshuo), while they give more realistic depictions of people's daily life, they are still for readers' reading pleasure. The primary goal of cyber literature, in this sense, is not to faithfully reflect people's real life. Kang believed that reading pleasure and aesthetic experience are people's basic needs. Whether readers can feel intense pleasure and aesthetic experience through readers' identification with main characters is the key to a work's success. Thus, critics need to study how a work gives readers reading pleasure and aesthetic experience and how readers respond to the work.

Meanwhile, Li Chaoquan made such an argument in his article:

> Cyber literature combines literature with the Internet. To evaluate cyber literature, first of all, we need the set of criteria that are used for the evaluation of traditional literature, especially novels. These traditional criteria—the artistic, intellectual, and aesthetic values in literary works, the stylistic elements in language and narration, and the depths and colorfulness in the representation of human nature and culture—are still applicable to the evaluation of cyber literature. Meanwhile, there should be some other criteria to be used especially for cyber literature. This is because cyber literature has its distinct features and characteristics: it relies on the Internet in the process of creation, circulation, and reception; as a result, it is convenient, interactive, widely circulated, and easy to become profitable. As some scholars point out, cyber literature must follow a principle: it should give readers pleasure, which means that a work should make readers identify with the characters and feel the "dopamine" through reading. This principle is particularly useful for the evaluation of a cyber literary work.[12]

The Principles of Cyber Literary Criticism

Cyber literary criticism is different from traditional criticism in that it follows a different set of principles. This is due to its unique functions and characteristics. Liu Lili and Li Yuping, in an article, argued that the principles of cyber literary criticism should be determined by the functions of cyber literature.[13] A traditional literary work usually not only expresses the author's personal feelings but also allows the author to speak for the country and the nation. In contrast, cyber literature is more concerned about the personal than the social. It allows people to vent feelings and thoughts so that they can feel psychologically balanced; it does not intend to draw a panoramic picture of people's lives in society or give an in-depth analysis of the fate of a nation in history.

Therefore, cyber literary criticism should follow a new set of principles and criteria different from old ones. We should also consider that the hypertextuality of some cyber literary works may challenge the validity of traditional literary theories and evaluation criteria.

Huang Mingfen raised the issue that cyber literature should promote "positive spiritual energy and social values."[14] He argued that literature not only records the cultural history of a nation and a country but also contributes to the development of the nation, the country, and the society in a particular era. Cyber literature should follow this tradition and not abandon its aesthetic values and ideological significance. It should not simply meet the demands of commercial websites to make more profits and develop itself as an industry. If a work is not culturally significant and socially responsible, it will soon lose popularity and be forgotten by readers.

In an article, I stressed that cyber literature should retain humanistic values.[15] Compared with traditional literature, cyber literature is more based on the use of technology and focuses more on entertaining readers. Nevertheless, it is still an art through which people view and understand the world. It should still convey aesthetic and social values, especially the humanistic spirit. Although literature is now modified by computer technology, it should not simply celebrate instrumental rationality. Instead, it should use technology as a means to assert our value rationality: in cyberspace, it searches for a way people can "dwell poetically." Therefore, it should work to promote democracy in artistic creation, freedom in people's lives, and a belief in humanistic values.

The Characteristics and Methods of Cyber Literary Criticism

Tan Dejing's book *On Cyber Literary Criticism* mainly discusses netizens' comments on literary works.[16] He gave a concise explanation of the characteristics of such comments:

1. Such comments embody "the carnivalization of criticism": cyberspace is a "super-large square for literary criticism," which means that everyone can express their thoughts freely and equally, and people's voices are all mixed up. Meanwhile, some comments tend to be playful and even obscene.
2. Such comments are about people's subjective experience: they can reflect people's reading experiences, including their emotions and critical thoughts in response to the literary works.
3. Such comments signify "a revival of the ancient critical tradition, which focuses on the romantic charm in literature." Thus, writing such comments is a pleasure to netizens. It is an opportunity for them to express their thoughts and impressions of literary works with poetic words.

In an article, Tan analyzed how "being online" affects the writing and reading of literature and the form of literary criticism.[17] Tan believed that "being online" means that critics and readers are present on the site of literary criticism. Because of this, cyber literary criticism is usually short and close to people's daily life, and it pays attention to new forms and techniques in writing. In another article, he described the form of cyber literary criticism as "casual, short, and without a clearly defined central idea" and its language "colloquial and humorous."[18] According to Tan, such characteristics are determined by cyber critics' "spiritual dimensions." He thus proposed that an important entry point into the study of cyber literary criticism is to analyze the critics' "spiritual dimensions."[19]

Chen Dingjia analyzed the characteristics of "hypertext" in cyber literature. He proposed a way to understand hypertext and demanded we pay attention to its limits. In an article, he pointed out that hypertext quietly changes our thoughts and values about literature and aesthetics.[20] Critics thus must pay attention to the current conditions of cyber literature as follows:

1. As the Internet is all-inclusive and open to everything, hypertext has the spirit of inclusiveness that goes beyond people's imagination.
2. Hypertext allows literature to shake off the constraints of tradition and break the limits of language. It not only offers a new form of media for the creation, circulation, and consumption of literature but also gives artists/writers hope for unrestrained freedom of expression.
3. Hypertext transcends the boundary between images and words, fills the gap between writing and reading, and uses literary, artistic, and cultural elements to create a "carnival" of discourses—a symphony of texts with which readers can interact.

Chen made a further discussion based on such an idea of hypertexuality. All vivid images about the relation and interaction between people and everything in this world throughout human history are represented in cyberspace. In this sense, writers' dreams of a perfect spiritual world that is full of beauty can be turned into sounds and images that netizens can directly experience—in other words, a virtual reality that is even more real than the world in which we live. At this moment, we need to be especially vigilant about the damage caused to literature by the mechanical reproduction of literary texts. Such texts may be casual, irresponsible, false, boring, nonsensical, inelegant, and even full of obscenity and violence. We should be aware of the strengths and limitations of hypertextual literature so that our literary criticism can better reflect and critique the actual condition of such a type of literature.

In a newspaper article, Li Chaoquan made three points concerning the method of writing cyber literary criticism:[21]

1. Critics should maintain "zero degrees of feeling" toward cyber literary works. In other words, they should evaluate works with calmness, objectivity, fairness, and neutrality. They should neither be "obsessed" with cyber literature nor completely ignore it. An ideal critic should witness the production of cyber literature, be involved in it, experience it, and critique it.

2. Critics and writers should maintain an equal relationship as both opponents and friends. Critics should neither blindly praise writers nor simply repudiate them. Instead, they should be armed with a good sense of artistic appreciation and evaluation, as well as a talent for literary creation, so that they can better judge writers' works.
3. Critics should make efforts to pick excellent works and canonize them. It is a matter of time before critics include cyber literature in the history of contemporary literature. Critics and researchers must have a forward-looking vision and carefully select excellent works from the body of cyber literature. In this regard, critics must hold various activities to select and award cyber literary works because this is not only a way to set examples for other writers but also a process to canonize works in literary history and to establish an evaluation system that passes objective and fair judgment on cyber literary works.

Studies on Specific Works and Genres of Cyber Literature

Scholars also studied specific literary works and genres. There are three cases that particularly show the strength of their studies.

First, scholars published a series of critical articles in response to an activity called "Review of Cyber Literature in the Past Ten Years" (Wangluo wenxue shinian pandian) in 2009. This activity offered a chance for mainstream literary media and cyber writers to communicate. It also signified that scholars recognized cyber literature, still in its early days, as an indispensable part of Chinese literature. Scholars published articles to discuss the value and significance of this "review" activity and to analyze the works recognized as representatives of cyber literature during this "review." For example, in an article, Ma Ji reviewed ten web novels.[22] While reviewing *The Story of Wukong* (Wukong zhuan), he pointed out that the novel is "short and concise, with a high level of artistic value." He further argued: "This work is not just for fun. Its main purpose is to expose how material desires corrupt our society by representing Sun Wukong's changing thoughts and feelings. Only by representing such a special character can the novel be critical of reality while avoiding being attacked."[23] Ma then discussed *The Record of Heroes* (Yingxiong zhi): "[The novel] breaks away from the pattern of martial arts fiction as 'fairy tales for adults.' Instead, it portrays characters as ordinary people with worldly concerns and dreams. The characters must deal with troubles in their life. The novel thus embodies an in-depth realism and a spirit of humanism."[24]

Second, scholars published their reviews of cyber writers and their works. Such reviews usually attracted a lot of public attention. Representative books on cyber literary works include Nie Qingpu's *An Interpretation of Famous Web Stories* and Zeng Fanting's *Famous Cyber Literary Works 100*.[25] Various academic papers also discuss cyber literary works, such as Jiang Fei's review of *Chengdu, Please Forget Me Tonight* (Chengdu, jinye qing jiangwo yiwang) and Lin Huayu's review of *The Story of Wukong* (Wukong zhuan).[26]

Books on cyber writers include Zeng Fanting's *On Cyber Writers* (Wangluo xieshou lun), Nie Qingpu's *Famous Cyber Writers 100* (Wangluo xieshou mingjia yibai), and Nie Mao's *Famous Writers' Blogs 100* (Ming zuojia boke yibai).[27] There are also articles on cyber writers. For example, Zeng Fanting's article thoroughly examines the identity issue of cyber writers from various aspects.[28] It studies writers' "gold rush" in cyberspace as a new myth. It also analyzes the debate whether cyber writers' job requires more physical work or intellectual work and whether cyber writers are "artists of letters" or merely "artisans of letters." The conclusion is that we should "render unto Caesar the things that are Caesar's, and unto God the things that are God's": history will give answers to the debates.[29] Xu Miaomiao's article divides cyber writers into different kinds, including those who write as amateurs, those who write as intellectuals, and those who write as performers. It examines these writers' identities, purposes, and attitudes.[30] Lu Shanhua's article studies two writers—"Annie Baby" (Anni baobei) and "Ning, the God of Wealth" (Ning caishen)—and views them as opposite poles in cyber literature: it highlights the differences between the two writers in terms of their choice of topics, narrative method, aesthetic style, and view of life.[31]

Third, there are studies of genres in cyber literature. For example, Nie Qingpu explained why cyber writers tend to pad out their novels: "First, writers need more clicks from readers; second, writers want to have their works rank high on websites; third, writers have to meet readers' needs for longer works."[32] It is the commercialization of cyber literature that causes these problems. There are, nevertheless, some other factors that contribute to the padding out of stories: 1. Genre fiction as a form is easy to be padded out; 2. Writers follow some works as bad examples and have to pad their stories out like others; 3. Some writers do not have a clear plan for their stories—instead, they write quite casually and make stories unnecessarily long.

Many articles focus on genre fiction, which is the most popular form of cyber literature today. For example, in an article, I pointed out that genre fiction includes most web novels today—these works are the most promptly updated and receive the most attention from readers.[33] In other words, genre fiction has become the mainstream in cyberwriting. There are dozens of genres, including novels about "fantasy" (xuanhuan), "martial arts" (wuxia), "cultivation" (xiuzhen), "time travel" (chuanyue), "tomb robbery" (daomu), "mystery and suspense" (xuanyi), "urban life" (dushi), "romance" (yanqing), "workplace" (zhichang), and "officialdom" (guanchang). I argued that cyber writers need to readjust the narrative pattern, avoid repetitive plots across different works, and revitalize their imagination to develop genre fiction further. To do this, writers must learn from the literary tradition—successful genre fiction in Chinese and Western literary history. They also need to base their writings on a keen observation of reality, including people's daily life, their feelings and affections, and the culture of our society. There are various books examining web novels of popular genres as well. Yang Yu's *On Web Poetry* (Wangluo shige lun), Su Xiaofang's *On Web Fiction* (Wangluo xiaoshuo lun), and Lan Aiguo's *Spoof*

Culture on the Internet (Wangluo egao wenhua) are early works that study and evaluate the genres in cyber literature.[34] Xu Miaomiao's *A Review of Cyber Literature from the Perspective of Gender Studies* (Xingbie shiye zhong de wangluo wenxue) and Li Yuping's *A General Discussion on Time-travel Stories on the Internet* (Wangluo chuanyue xiaoshuo gailun) also touch upon the issue of genres.[35] There are also academic works interpreting and discussing literature in the era of we media—works in the form of text messages, blog posts, microblog posts, and WeChat articles.[36]

Research on the Problems and Limitations of Cyber Literature

There are several monographs on cyber literary criticism, including *The Transformation of Literature and Art in Digital Media* (Shuzi meijie xia de wenyi zhuanxing), *Key Words in Cyber Literature 100* (Wangluo wenxue guanjianci yibai), *Big Events about Cyber Literature 100* (Wangluo wenxue dashijian yibai), and *On the Industry of Cyber Literature* (Wangluo wenxue chanyelun).[37] These books expose, discuss, and analyze problems of cyber literature from different aspects. There are also papers of such kind, and here are two examples.

The first one is Tao Dongfeng's "Have We Entered into an Era When Chinese Literature Is Nothing but Gods and Ghosts?"[38] In this article, Tao bluntly criticized fantasy novels, or *xuanhuan xiaoshuo*, which were quite popular on the Internet. He used three examples in the article: they are the top three of "the best fantasy novels in 2005" selected by *Sina*, including *Attack of Heaven* (Zhu xian), *Legend of Little Soldiers* (Xiaobing chuanqi), and *How Are the Bad Buys Made* (Huaidan shi zenyang liancheng de). He criticized these stories for "being good at nothing but talking about gods and ghosts."[39] He pointed out:

> The so-called "fantasy worlds" are based on magic, witchcraft, and other crooked things, such as wands, rings, spells, and all kinds of strange and incredible monsters and beasts. They constantly change their forms and have boundless magical power... In traditional martial arts novels, the worldview remains stable. Evil cannot prevail over good, and crooked ways cannot eventually make a person successful. We may even say that only those who do not have real ability are keen to invoke gods and ghosts to deceive others. This concerns a more fundamental problem of fantasy literature: the worldview is disorderly and crooked.[40]

He then argued: "Talking about gods and ghosts to deceive people is a kind of abnormal display of the writer's imagination with cynicism and nihilism as the core. It is a kind of madness under the circumstances that people's creativity cannot properly work in reality and is not well guided by correct social values."[41] According to him, while the magical worlds described and shaped by fantasy novels are quite mystical and magnificent and the writers' imagination is quite amazing, fantasy literature is still lacking in literary value and significance.

Another article was written by Ouyang Ting and me, entitled "A Reflection on the Genealogy of Cyber Literature."[42] We argued:

> While the Internet media brought changes to literature, such changes are the manifestation of a more fundamental change in people's views of literature. There is a struggle between the literary tradition and the media technology, as both sides try to control and regulate literature. The digital technology, with its strong power, not only makes literature apparently "cyber," but also gives it some new features and unique qualities. It quietly changes literature's patterns and formats that have been a result of thousands of years of literary evolution.[43]

As ordinary netizens can now publish their writings online, they subvert the power of the cultural elite and thus reconstitute the ecology of literary production. This, however, also leads to the situation that today even those who are poor at writing can become writers.

As cyberspace allows people to write with a higher degree of freedom, they no longer need to follow the traditional rules and principles for writing literature. On the other hand, the media and the market allow cyber literature, with its massive volume of texts, to replace classic literature as what people read today. Cyber literary works can become successful suddenly and then quickly forgotten by the market. As cyber literary works must survive in the market, they have to be more commercialized than "literary." As a result, cyber writers do not make efforts to write excellent works and do not pay much attention to their social responsibilities. The Internet thus not only makes literary classics less read by people, but also undermines the mechanism of writing good literature.

Notes

1 See: Tan, Dejing 谭德晶, *Wangluo wenxue piping lun* 网络文学批评论 (Beijing: CFLAC Publishing House, 2004).
  Ouyang, Youquan 欧阳友权, *Wangluo wenxue pinglun yibai* 网络文学评论100 (Beijing: Central Compilation & Translation Press, 2014a).
2 Ouyang, Youquan 欧阳友权, *Wangluo wenxue yanjiu chengguo jicheng* 网络文学研究成果集成 (Beijing: CFLAC Publishing House, 2015b), 146–149.
3 Ouyang, Youquan 欧阳友权, *Wangluo wenxue wunian pucha (erlinglingjiu-erlingyisan)* 网络文学五年普查 (2009–2013) (Beijing: Central Compilation & Translation Press, 2014b), 102–111.
4 Translator's note: the link to the archive, which was provided in the Chinese edition of this book, is already defunct, and thus is not given here.
5 See: Ouyang, Youquan 欧阳友权, *Wangluo wenxue wunian pucha (erlinglingjiu-erlingyisan)* 网络文学五年普查 (2009–2013), 98.
6 Ouyang, Youquan 欧阳友权, *Wangluo wenxue wunian pucha (erlinglingjiu-erlingyisan)* 网络文学五年普查 (2009–2013).

7 Chen, Qirong 陈崎嵘, "Huyu jianli wangluo wenxue pingjia tixi 呼吁建立网络文学评价体系," *Renmin ribao* 人民日报 (Beijing), Jul. 19, 2013.
8 Chen, Qirong 陈崎嵘, "Huyu jianli wangluo wenxue pingjia tixi 呼吁建立网络文学评价体系."
9 Zhao, Chenyu 赵晨钰 and Jiang, Shuyuan 江舒远, "Wangluo wenxue: xinwenming de haojiao haishi xinping zhuang jiujiu? 网络文学：新文明的号角还是新瓶装旧酒？" *Zhonghua dushu bao* 中华读书报 (Beijing), Dec. 2, 1999.
10 Zhao, Chenyu 赵晨钰 and Jiang, Shuyuan 江舒远, "Wangluo wenxue: xinwenming de haojiao haishi xinping zhuang jiujiu? 网络文学：新文明的号角还是新瓶装旧酒？"
11 Kang, Qiao 康桥, "Wangluo wenxue piping biaozhun chuyi 网络文学批评标准刍议," *Guangming ribao* 光明日报 (Beijing), Sep. 3, 2013.
12 Li, Chaoquan 李朝全, "Jianli keguan gongzheng de wangluo wenxue pingjia tixi 建立客观公正的网络文学评价体系," *Hebei ribao* 河北日报 (Shijiazhuang), Dec. 5, 2014.
13 Liu, Lili 刘俐俐 and Li, Yuping 李玉平, "Wangluo wenxue dui wenxue piping lilun de tiaozhan" 网络文学对文学批评理论的挑战, *Journal of Lanzhou University: Social Sciences Edition* 兰州大学学报（社会科学版） no. 5 (2004): 1–8.
14 Huang, Mingfen 黄鸣奋, "Jingshen nengliang yu jiazhi hongyang 精神能量与价值弘扬," *Renmin ribao* 人民日报 (Beijing), Jun. 1, 2014.
15 Ouyang, Youquan 欧阳友权, "Wangluo wenxue de renwen dise yu jiazhi chengdan" 网络文学的人文底色与价值承担, *Qiushi* 求是学刊 no. 1 (2005): 94–97.
16 Tan, Dejing 谭德晶, *Wangluo wenxue piping lun* 网络文学批评论 (Beijing: CFLAC Publishing House, 2004), 112–183.
17 Tan, Dejing 谭德晶, "'Zaixianxing' dui wenxue piping xingshi de yingxiang" "在线性"对文学批评形式的影响, *Journal of Central South University: Social Sciences Edition* 中南大学学报（社会科学版） no. 5 (2003): 676–680.
18 Tan, Dejing 谭德晶, "'Maofan' yu 'duobi'—wenxue piping zhuti de jingshen xiangdu fenxi" "冒犯"与"躲避"——网络文学批评主体的精神向度分析, *Literary and Artistic Contention* 文艺争鸣 no. 4 (2005): 83–86.
19 Tan, Dejing 谭德晶, "'Maofan' yu 'duobi'—wenxue piping zhuti de jingshen xiangdu fenxi" "冒犯"与"躲避"——网络文学批评主体的精神向度分析, 84.
20 Chen, Dingjia 陈定家, "'Chaowenben' de xingqi yu wangluo shidai de wenxue" "超文本"的兴起与网络时代的文学, *Social Sciences in China* 中国社会科学 no. 3 (2007): 161–175.
21 Li, Chaoquan 李朝全, "Jianli keguan gongzheng de wangluo wenxue pingjia tixi 建立客观公正的网络文学评价体系."
22 Ma, Ji 马季, "Huayu fangshi zhuanbian zhong de wangluo xiezuo—jianping wangluo xiaoshuo shinian shibu jiazuo" 话语方式转变中的网络写作——兼评网络小说十年十部佳作, *Literary and Artistic Contention* 文艺争鸣 no. 19 (2010): 18–24.
23 Ma, Ji 马季, "Huayu fangshi zhuanbian zhong de wangluo xiezuo—jianping wangluo xiaoshuo shinian shibu jiazuo" 话语方式转变中的网络写作——兼评网络小说十年十部佳作, 20.
24 Ma, Ji 马季, "Huayu fangshi zhuanbian zhong de wangluo xiezuo—jianping wangluo xiaoshuo shinian shibu jiazuo" 话语方式转变中的网络写作——兼评网络小说十年十部佳作, 20.
25 See: Nie, Qingpu 聂庆璞, *Wangluo xiaoshuo mingpian jiedu* 网络小说名篇解读 (Beijing: China Social Sciences Press, 2011).
Zeng, Fanting 曾繁亭, *Wangluo wenxue mingpian yibai* 网络文学名篇100 (Beijing: Central Compilation & Translation Press, 2014).

26 See: Jiang, Fei 姜飞, "'Yiwang': xushi huayu he jiazhi taidu—ping Murong Xuecun de wangluo xiaoshuo *Chengdu, jinye qing jiangwo yiwang*" "遗忘"：叙事话语和价值态度——评慕容雪村的网络小说《成都，今夜请将我遗忘》, *Theory and Criticism of Literature and Art* 文艺理论批评 no. 2 (2003): 44–51.

Lin, Huayu 林华瑜, "Yingxiong de beiju, xifang de jingdian—wangluo xiaoshuo *Wukong zhuan* de shendu jiedu" 英雄的悲剧、戏仿的经典——网络小说《悟空传》的深度解读, *Masterpieces Review* 名作欣赏 no. 4 (2002): 105–109.

27 Zeng, Fanting 曾繁亭, *Wangluo xieshou lun* 网络写手论 (Beijing: China Social Sciences Press, 2011).

Nie, Qingpu 聂庆璞, *Wangluo xieshou mingjia yibai* 网络写手名家100 (Beijing: Central Compilation & Translation Press, 2014).

Nie, Mao 聂茂, *Ming zuojia boke yibai* 名作家博客100 (Beijing: Central Compilation & Translation Press, 2014).

28 Zeng, Fanting 曾繁亭, "Qianyue xieshou: aimei de shenxing yu ganga de shenfen" 签约写手：暧昧的身形与尴尬的身份, *Study & Exploration* 学习与探索 no. 2 (2010): 181–183.

29 Zeng, Fanting 曾繁亭, "Qianyue xieshou: aimei de shenxing yu ganga de shenfen" 签约写手：暧昧的身形与尴尬的身份, 183.

30 Xu, Miaomiao 许苗苗, "Wangluo wenxue de zuozhe (xieshou) leixing fenxi" 网络文学的作者（写手）类型分析, *Journal of Hainan Normal University: Social Sciences Edition* 海南师范学院学报（社会科学版）no. 1 (2003): 129–133.

31 Lu, Shanhua 陆山花, "Anni baobei yu Ning caishen—wangluo wenxue de yinyang liangji" 安妮宝贝与宁财神——网络文学的阴阳两极, *Journal of Guangxi Normal University for Nationalities* 广西民族师范学院学报 no. 1 (2011): 50–53.

32 Nie, Qingpu 聂庆璞, "Wangluo chaochangpian: shangyehua cuisheng de zhushui xiezuo" 网络超长篇：商业化催生的注水写作, *Study & Exploration* 学习与探索 no. 2 (2013): 133.

33 Ouyang, Youquan 欧阳友权, "Wangluo leixing xiaoshuo: jiyuan he kunju" 网络类型小说：机缘和困局, *Study & Exploration* 学习与探索 no.2 (2013): 122–125.

34 See: Yang, Yu 杨雨, *Wangluo shige lun* 网络诗歌论 (Beijing: CFLAC Publishing House, 2008).

Su, Xiaofang 苏晓芳, *Wangluo xiaoshuo lun* 网络小说论 (Beijing: China Literature and History Press, 2008).

Lan, Aiguo 蓝爱国, *Wangluo egao wenhua* 网络恶搞文化 (Beijing: China Literature and History Press, 2007).

35 See: Xu, Miaomiao 许苗苗, *Xingbie shiye zhong de wangluo wenxue* 性别视野中的网络文学 (Beijing: Jiuzhou Press, 2004).

Li, Yuping 李玉萍, *Wangluo chuanyue xiaoshuo gailun* 网络穿越小说概论 (Tianjin: Nankai University Press, 2011).

36 Such works include: Ouyang, Wenfeng 欧阳文风 and Wang, Xiaosheng 王晓生, *Boke wenxue lun* 博客文学论 (Beijing: China Literature and History Press, 2007).

Ouyang, Wenfeng 欧阳文风, *Duanxin wenxue lun* 短信文学论 (Beijing: China Social Sciences Press, 2011).

Yu, Wenxiu 于文秀, "Shouji wenxue xianxiang: wuhou chadian yu houwenxue jingguan 手机文学现象：午后茶点与后文学景观," *Wenyi bao* 文艺报 (Beijing), Apr. 25, 2009.

Ouyang, Youquan 欧阳友权 and Luo, Pengcheng 罗鹏程, "Boke wenxue de jiegou tishi yu chuangsheng xingtai" 博客文学的结构体式与创生形态, *Social Science Front* 社会科学战线 no. 8 (2010): 162–167.

Nie, Mao 聂茂 and Li, Jun 李君, "Lun mingren boke de jingshen tezhi jiqi yingxiang" 论名人博客的精神特质及其影响, *Journal of Central South University: Social Sciences Edition* 中南大学学报（社会科学版）no. 1 (2008): 116–122.

Li, Cun 李存, "Weibo wenxue de dingyi, fazhan, leixing ji tezheng" 微博文学的定义、发展、类型及特征, *Guizhou Social Sciences* 贵州社会科学 no. 10 (2010): 65–72.

Ouyang, Youquan 欧阳友权, "Weixin wenxue de cunzai fangshi yu gongneng quxiang" 微信文学的存在方式与功能取向, *Jianghai Academic Journal* 江海学刊 no. 1 (2015a): 192–200.

37 See: Ouyang, Youquan 欧阳友权, *Shuzi meijie xia de wenyi zhuanxing* 数字媒介下的文艺转型 (Beijing: China Social Sciences Press, 2011).

Yu, Jianxiang 禹建湘, *Wangluo wenxue guanjianci yibai* 网络文学关键词100 (Beijing: Central Compilation & Translation Press, 2014).

Ouyang, Wenfeng 欧阳文风, *Wangluo wenxue dashijian yibai* 网络文学大事件100 (Beijing: Central Compilation & Translation Press, 2014).

Yu, Jianxiang 禹建湘, *Wangluo wenxue chanyelun* 网络文学产业论 (Beijing: Central Compilation & Translation Press, 2011).

38 Tao, Dongfeng 陶东风, "Zhongguo wenxue yijing jinru zhuangshennonggui shidai?—you 'xuanhuan xiaoshuo' yinfa de yidian lianxiang" 中国文学已经进入装神弄鬼时代？——由"玄幻小说"引发的一点联想, *Contemporary Literary Criticism* 当代文坛 no. 5 (2006): 8–11.

39 Tao, Dongfeng 陶东风, "Zhongguo wenxue yijing jinru zhuangshennonggui shidai?—you 'xuanhuan xiaoshuo' yinfa de yidian lianxiang" 中国文学已经进入装神弄鬼时代？——由"玄幻小说"引发的一点联想, 8.

40 Tao, Dongfeng 陶东风, "Zhongguo wenxue yijing jinru zhuangshennonggui shidai?—you 'xuanhuan xiaoshuo' yinfa de yidian lianxiang" 中国文学已经进入装神弄鬼时代？——由"玄幻小说"引发的一点联想, 8–9.

41 Tao, Dongfeng 陶东风, "Zhongguo wenxue yijing jinru zhuangshennonggui shidai?—you 'xuanhuan xiaoshuo' yinfa de yidian lianxiang" 中国文学已经进入装神弄鬼时代？——由"玄幻小说"引发的一点联想, 11.

42 Ouyang, Ting 欧阳婷 and Ouyang Youquan 欧阳友权, "Wangluo wenxue de tizhi puxixue fansi" 网络文学的体制谱系学反思, *Theoretical Studies in Literature and Art* 文艺理论研究 no. 1 (2014): 90–98.

43 Ouyang, Ting 欧阳婷 and Ouyang Youquan 欧阳友权, "Wangluo wenxue de tizhi puxixue fansi" 网络文学的体制谱系学反思, 91.

Bibliography

Chen, Dingjia 陈定家. "Chaowenben de xingqi yu wangluo shidai de wenxue" "超文本"的兴起与网络时代的文学. *Social Sciences in China* 中国社会科学 no. 3 (2007): 161–175.

Chen, Qirong 陈崎嵘. "Huyu jianli wangluo wenxue pingjia tixi 呼吁建立网络文学评价体系." *Renmin ribao* 人民日报 (Beijing), Jul. 19, 2013.

Huang, Mingfen 黄鸣奋. "Jingshen nengliang yu jiazhi hongyang 精神能量与价值弘扬." *Renmin ribao* 人民日报 (Beijing), Jun. 1, 2014.

Jiang, Fei 姜飞. "'Yiwang': xushi huayu he jiazhi taidu—ping Murong Xuecun de wangluo xiaoshuo *Chengdu, jinye qing jiangwo yiwang*" "遗忘"：叙事话语和价值态度——评慕容雪村的网络小说《成都，今夜请将我遗忘》. *Theory and Criticism of Literature and Art* 文艺理论批评 no. 2 (2003): 44–51.

Kang, Qiao 康桥. "Wangluo wenxue piping biaozhun chuyi 网络文学批评标准刍议." *Guangming ribao*光明日报 (Beijing), Sep. 3, 2013.

Lan, Aiguo 蓝爱国. *Wangluo egao wenhua* 网络恶搞文化. Beijing: China Literature and History Press, 2007.

Li, Chaoquan 李朝全. "Jianli keguan gongzheng de wangluo wenxue pingjia tixi 建立客观公正的网络文学评价体系." *Hebei ribao*河北日报 (Shijiazhuang), Dec. 5, 2014.

Li, Cun 李存. "Weibo wenxue de dingyi fazhan leixing ji tezheng" 微博文学的定义、发展、类型及特征. *Guizhou Social Sciences* 贵州社会科学 no. 10 (2010): 65–72.

Li, Yuping 李玉萍. *Wangluo chuanyue xiaoshuo gailun* 网络穿越小说概论. Tianjin: Nankai University Press, 2011.

Lin, Huayu 林华瑜. "Yingxiong de beiju, xifang de jingdian—wangluo xiaoshuo *Wukong zhuan* de shendu jiedu" 英雄的悲剧、戏仿的经典——网络小说《悟空传》的深度解读. *Masterpieces Review* 名作欣赏 no. 4 (2002): 105–109.

Liu, Lili 刘俐俐 and Li, Yuping 李玉平. "Wangluo wenxue dui wenxue piping lilun de tiaozhan" 网络文学对文学批评理论的挑战. *Journal of Lanzhou University: Social Sciences Edition* 兰州大学学报（社会科学版）no. 5 (2004): 1–8.

Lu, Shanhua 陆山花. "Anni baobei yu Ning caishen—wangluo wenxue de yinyang liangji" 安妮宝贝与宁财神——网络文学的阴阳两极. *Journal of Guangxi Normal University for Nationalities* 广西民族师范学院学报 no. 1 (2011): 50–53.

Ma, Ji 马季. "Huayu fangshi zhuanbian zhong de wangluo xiezuo—jianping wangluo xiaoshuo shinian shibu jiazuo" 话语方式转变中的网络写作——兼评网络小说十年十部佳作. *Literary and Artistic Contention* 文艺争鸣 no. 19 (2010): 18–24.

Nie, Mao 聂茂 and Li, Jun 李君. "Lun mingren boke de jingshen tezhi jiqi yingxiang" 论名人博客的精神特质及其影响. *Journal of Central South University: Social Sciences Edition* 中南大学学报（社会科学版）no. 1 (2008): 116–122.

Nie, Mao 聂茂. *Ming zuojia boke yibai* 名作家博客100. Beijing: Central Compilation & Translation Press, 2014.

Nie, Qingpu 聂庆璞. *Wangluo xiaoshuo mingpian jiedu* 网络小说名篇解读. Beijing: China Social Sciences Press, 2011.

Nie, Qingpu 聂庆璞. "Wangluo chaochangpian: shangyehua cuisheng de zhushui xiezuo" 网络超长篇：商业化催生的注水写作. *Study & Exploration* 学习与探索 no. 2 (2013): 132–134.

Nie, Qingpu 聂庆璞. *Wangluo xieshou mingjia yibai* 网络写手名家100. Beijing: Central Compilation & Translation Press, 2014.

Ouyang, Ting 欧阳婷 and Ouyang Youquan 欧阳友权. "Wangluo wenxue de tizhi puxixue fansi" 网络文学的体制谱系学反思. *Theoretical Studies in Literature and Art* 文艺理论研究 no. 1 (2014): 90–98.

Ouyang, Wenfeng 欧阳文风. *Duanxin wenxue lun* 短信文学论. Beijing: China Social Sciences Press, 2011.

Ouyang, Wenfeng 欧阳文风. *Wangluo wenxue dashijian yibai* 网络文学大事件100. Beijing: Central Compilation & Translation Press, 2014.

Ouyang, Wenfeng 欧阳文风 and Wang, Xiaosheng 王晓生. *Boke wenxue lun* 博客文学论. Beijing: China Literature and History Press, 2007.

Ouyang, Youquan 欧阳友权. "Wangluo wenxue de renwen dise yu jiazhi chengdan" 网络文学的人文底色与价值承担. *Qiushi* 求是学刊 no. 1 (2005): 94–97.

Ouyang, Youquan 欧阳友权. *Shuzi meijie xia de wenyi zhuanxing* 数字媒介下的文艺转型. Beijing: China Social Sciences Press, 2011.

Ouyang, Youquan 欧阳友权. "Wangluo leixing xiaoshuo: jiyuan he kunju" 网络类型小说：机缘与困局. *Study & Exploration* 学习与探索 no.2 (2013): 122–125.

Ouyang, Youquan 欧阳友权. *Wangluo wenxue pinglun yibai* 网络文学评论100. Beijing: Central Compilation & Translation Press, 2014a.

Ouyang, Youquan 欧阳友权. *Wangluo wenxue wunian pucha (erlinglingjiu-erlingyisan)* 网络文学五年普查（2009–2013）. Beijing: Central Compilation & Translation Press, 2014b.

Ouyang, Youquan 欧阳友权. "Weixin wenxue de cunzai fangshi yu gongneng quxiang" 微信文学的存在方式与功能取向. *Jianghai Academic Journal* 江海学刊 no. 1 (2015a): 195–200.

Ouyang, Youquan 欧阳友权. *Wangluo wenxue yanjiu chengguo jicheng* 网络文学研究成果集成. Beijing: CFLAC Publishing House, 2015b.

Ouyang, Youquan 欧阳友权 and Luo, Pengcheng 罗鹏程. "Boke wenxue de jiegou tishi yu chuangsheng xingtai" 博客文学的结构体式与创生形态. *Social Science Front* 社会科学战线 no. 8 (2010): 162–167.

Su, Xiaofang 苏晓芳. *Wangluo xiaoshuo lun* 网络小说论. Beijing: China Literature and History Press, 2008.

Tan, Dejing 谭德晶. "'Zaixianxing' dui wenxue piping xingshi de yingxiang" "在线性"对文学批评形式的影响. *Journal of Central South University: Social Sciences Edition* 中南大学学报（社会科学版）no. 5 (2003): 676–680.

Tan, Dejing 谭德晶. *Wangluo wenxue piping lun* 网络文学批评论. Beijing: CFLAC Publishing House, 2004.

Tan, Dejing 谭德晶. "'Maofan' yu 'duobi'—wangluo wenxue piping zhuti de jingshen xiangdu fenxi" "冒犯"与"躲避"——网络文学批评主体的精神向度分析. *Literary and Artistic Contention* 文艺争鸣 no. 4 (2005): 83–86.

Tao, Dongfeng 陶东风. "Zhongguo wenxue yijing jinru zhuangshennonggui shidai?—you 'xuanhuan xiaoshuo' yinfa de yidian lianxiang" 中国文学已经进入装神弄鬼时代？——由"玄幻小说"引发的一点联想. *Contemporary Literary Criticism* 当代文坛 no. 5 (2006): 8–11.

Xu, Miaomiao 许苗苗. "Wangluo wenxue de zuozhe (xieshou) leixing fenxi" 网络文学的作者（写手）类型分析. *Journal of Hainan Normal University: Social Sciences Edition* 海南师范学院学报（社会科学版）no. 1 (2003): 129–133.

Xu, Miaomiao 许苗苗. *Xingbie shiye zhong de wangluo wenxue* 性别视野中的网络文学. Beijing: Jiuzhou Press, 2004.

Yang, Yu 杨雨. *Wangluo shigelun* 网络诗歌论. Beijing: CFLAC Publishing House, 2008.

Yu, Jianxiang 禹建湘. *Wangluo wenxue chanyelun* 网络文学产业论. Beijing: Central Compilation & Translation Press, 2011.

Yu, Jianxiang 禹建湘. *Wangluo wenxue guanjianci yibai* 网络文学关键词100. Beijing: Central Compilation & Translation Press, 2014.

Yu, Wenxiu 于文秀. "Shouji wenxue xianxiang: wuhou chadian yu houwenxue jingguan 手机文学现象：午后茶点与后文学景观." *Wenyi bao* 文艺报 (Beijing), Apr. 25, 2009.

Zeng, Fanting 曾繁亭. "Qianyue xieshou: aimei de shenxing yu ganga de shenfen" 签约写手：暧昧的身形与尴尬的身份. *Study & Exploration* 学习与探索 no. 2 (2010): 181–183.

Zeng, Fanting 曾繁亭. *Wangluo xieshou lun* 网络写手论. Beijing: China Social Sciences Press, 2011.

Zeng, Fanting 曾繁亭. *Wangluo wenxue mingpian yibai* 网络文学名篇100. Beijing: Central Compilation & Translation Press, 2014.

Zhao, Chenyu 赵晨钰 and Jiang, Shuyuan 江舒远. "Wangluo wenxue: xinwenming de haojiao haishi xinping zhuang jiujiu? 网络文学：新文明的号角还是新瓶装旧酒？" *Zhonghua dushu bao* 中华读书报 (Beijing), Dec. 2, 1999.

4 The Forms, Contents, and Rhetorical Expressions of Netizens' Critical Commentaries

Marshall McLuhan points out: "[T]he personal and social consequences of any medium—that is, of any extension of ourselves—result from the new scale that is introduced into our affairs by each extension of ourselves, or by any new technology."[1] The new media not only accelerates and facilitates the dissemination of information but also creates a new dimension for the acquisition and evaluation of such information. This is true for ordinary netizens' commentaries on literary works. The difference between such critical texts created under the new media technology and texts of traditional literary criticism lies in their forms, contents, and rhetorical expressions, as well as in their views of the way of practicing literary criticism using certain evaluation criteria. Here we will investigate the forms, contents, and rhetorical expressions of such a particular type of cyber literary criticism.

The Forms of Netizen's Critical Commentaries

Texts Being Fragmentary

"Fragmentation" refers to a state in which a thing falls apart. This concept was first proposed by Western scholars in the 1980s for their research on postmodernism. In the Internet era, as the wide use of digital technology allows individuals to access information based on their own preferences, the information becomes fragmented to suit individual needs. As a result, "fragmentation" has become an important trend in cyberculture.

The fragmentation in information production and dissemination in the era of new media allows people to receive various pieces of information within a short time. As a result, people become unwilling to think deeply. In fast-paced daily life, people's sense of time, which used to be a flow, is now split up into fragments by a wide variety of information. In consequence, reading long critical articles has almost become a luxury. People are unable to extricate themselves from the ocean of information fragments, and they are getting deeper and deeper into it. In this digital era, as people can experience intense pleasure by viewing visual images on screens, they begin to pursue more sensory stimuli

DOI: 10.4324/9781003428480-6

in cyberculture that can directly and instantly gratify them: the simpler, the better. The mainstream popular culture thus becomes shallow and lacking in good taste: in a sense, it becomes a thing just like fast food. In consequence, netizens' commentaries on literary works are concise, plain, and instantaneous, which suits people's desire to express themselves quickly and efficiently. With the evolution of media platforms—from BBSes to blogs, from microblogs to WeChat—the fragmentation of information makes it easier for ordinary people to read cyber literature and write critical commentaries based on their aesthetic experiences. Cyber literary criticism has a series of new characteristics: it is concise and straightforward in structure; people can write, publish, and read it instantly at any time and in any place. Because of this, it has become welcomed by consumers of the popular culture. Its greater significance lies in that it encourages more netizens to participate in the practice of literary criticism. Now people pay more attention to cyber literary works and phenomena. They develop new thoughts and values to nourish literary criticism.

From the perspective of cultural studies, we can view "fragmentation" as a kind of worldview held by postmodernists. It is a key concept by which postmodern theorists reject the ideas of modernity, such as wholeness and grand narrative. Postmodernists hold that the entire world, and even every text, is composed of fragments, and the fragments interact and interconnect to form a larger piece of fragment. Before the postmodern trend of thought, people pursued the unity of subjectivity and the unity of form in literature. Yet postmodernists believe that the so-called unities are our illusions: they do not exist at all, and the world is essentially made up of fragments.[2] In line with this view, the Internet brings people with different values and attitudes into one virtual space. The boundary between the media and ordinary people is becoming blurred, as their identities are now no longer fixed. The media loses its position and power over ordinary people. As the way of communication becomes decentered, fragmented, and unfixed, the meaning and purpose of communication are also deconstructed. This cultural phenomenon is a result of decentralization in the context of postmodernity. With the development and maturity of media technology, BBSes, webpages, blogs, microblogs, WeChat, and other Internet platforms are now becoming multimedia. This, together with the hypertextuality of the Internet, allows people to access, process, and circulate information in a diversity of ways. As a result, while writing commentaries on literary works, netizens are no longer obsessed with the idea that a text of literary criticism must have a complete structure.

Let us read some netizens' commentaries on Murong Xuecun's web novel *Forgive Me for Turning the World Upside Down* (Yuanliang wo hongchen diandao), posted on *Douban Reading* (Douban dushu).

"Iris the fifth day of October" (Iris shiyuechuwu) posted on October 30, 2015:

While I read the book, the character disgusted me with his foul personality. With so much difficulty, he walks out of his poor life in the countryside and no longer needs to bow and submit to others, yet he eventually chooses the wrong way of doing things and ruins his own life with one mistake after another. At the end of the novel, all this turns out to be nothing but a dream. The protagonist can wake up from his dream and make his life choices again. But in real life, we cannot retake the road we already missed, and we cannot wake up from a dream and start our life all over again. Of course, I know that while the novel highlights the conflicts, it is still based on people's real life, so I read this book to warn and encourage myself. The story is a bit confusing, so I had to skip some parts accordingly.

Zheng Shaojie posted on November 17, 2015:

It's worth reading. There is a lot of reality in it. Many parts of the novel are modeled on actual events and characters. But it exaggerates the conflicts too much and thus becomes overdramatized.

"Softnan" posted on November 24, 2015:

There is a taste of classical literature in the novel. It reminds me of *Romance of the Three Kingdoms* (Sanguo yanyi), *Outlaws of the Marsh* (Shuihu zhuan), and *Bizarre Happenings Eye-witnessed over Two Decades* (Ershinian mudu zhi guaixianzhuang). But the novel seems to be unable to get away from it.

"Eggs fried with everything" (Jidan chao yiqie) posted on December 1, 2015:

It is a very dark novel. The protagonist, immature as he initially enters society, later becomes quite sophisticated and cruel. His "teacher" is so powerful and influential as if he could reach heaven. But both of them are completely ruined and crushed by reality in the end.

Zouhuo posted on December 16, 2015:

Please let Wei Da die in the end. Otherwise, I won't have any courage to live in this society. The novel is lighthearted and full of humor, but it also fills me with a sense of frustration and doubt. The main characters are all pathetic people.

It can be seen that such commentaries are mostly to express netizens' instant feelings and experiences. They are outspoken, straightforward, concise, and flexible. The expressions are casual and unrestrained, not conforming to any established format. Yet, with just a few words, they can accurately hit the target and convey netizens' thoughts about specific issues. Nevertheless, as a product of the postmodern cultural condition, these commentaries tend to be lacking in depth, fragmented, and decentered. The absence of serious reasoning, thinking, and analyzing makes such critical commentaries not quite academically valuable.

This form of cyber literary criticism is an inevitable result of the new context of popular culture and aesthetic orientation. The fragmentation of these texts is correspondent to the postmodern culture, which itself is fragmented and lacking in depth. Under the influence of the postmodern culture, such texts are pastiches made of cuts and pastes.

Texts Being Interactive

While traditional literary criticism is written by an exclusive group of critics, who work independently without much communication with each other, today, writers and readers can interact and communicate dynamically. Thus, netizens' critical commentaries take on new forms that are significantly different from those of traditional literary criticism.

The topological structure of the Internet is based on a web of countless nodes of information that works without a center. Nodes can have two-way or multi-directional instantaneous communication with each other. Compared with traditional media, the Internet has a structure like a cobweb and can reach its tentacles to everyone. The hypertextuality of the Internet media turns literary creation, circulation, and appreciation into a very dynamic process. According to Lee Shuen-shing, in essence, it is the "interactive design" that makes hypertext appear drastically different from "print-based literature": "Products of interactive design, such as hyperlinks, can create multi-directional ways of reading. The media connected to hyperlinks can be texts, static or moving images, or a set of interactive games. Such an interactive design leads to the act of interactive reading."[3] Due to the instantaneity of digital communication, readers can post their feedback while writers are still writing. Writers can thus adjust their writing accordingly, while readers can also exchange ideas about their reading experience. Such a way of communication is un-traditional: writers no longer stand in a higher position to "preach" to readers; instead, they have dialogues with readers on an equal footing. In one of my books, I made a description of this condition:

> After a work is published online, it can immediately receive feedback from readers, not only in the form of click-through rate and its position in book rankings, but also in the form of readers' direct commentaries, which can be straightforward, blunt, and critical. While traditionally, a literary work serves the "implied readers," now there are netizens who can read on their screens and instantly let the writer know if the work meets their expectations or not.[4]

Thus, writers and readers can have multi-directional communication, which allows dialogues between an individual and another, between an individual and a group of people, and between different groups of people. As people can exchange their thoughts, it becomes possible for a work to have multiple interpretations. Yet because of such a multi-dimensional extension of the chain of critical discourses, the in-depthness seen in traditional literary criticism is no longer existent. As most web novels are published directly online in installments, during this process of publication, writers are still writing, and readers are reading. This allows writers and readers to instantaneously communicate and work together to create literary works and interpretations of the works. On websites, BBSes, blogging and microblogging platforms, and WeChat, interactive texts are the most common form of cyber literary criticism. For example, readers on the website *Reading with Beauty* (Hongxiu tianxiang) made the following commentaries on the novel *Romance Blessed by Heaven* (Tianjia liangyuan):

"136****9681" replied on January 27, 2016:

The male protagonist is a bastard. Jingyu's family is not good. Jingyu is good, but he is sacrificed, like cannon fodder. Those who love Jingyu can continue to love him. Those who love the bastard can continue to love him as well. It is just a novel. You don't need to be too serious about the plot. These days, many stories are about family feuds, acts of revenge, and so on, and the male protagonists are all perverts and bastards. The male supporting characters try to take care of the heroines, but their love is always unrequited. Well, at the end of the stories, it is always the bastards who marry the heroines, have babies, and live happy lives thereafter. It is as simple as that.

Nuhaohao replied on January 26, 2016:

I just want to say that when you marry, you should marry someone you truly love. Nian really loves Bo. There are two murderers in the Xu family. Muqin is a mistress, and her sister frames the victim. Xu's family is genetically evil. If you marry one of them, you are dancing with wolves, and you will be eaten sooner or later.

"lilingtao" replied on January 26, 2016:

I feel that the two of them are not completely suitable for each other! First, because Xu Jingyu has a crazy sister, he is destined not to have both. Secondly, Uncle Bo used to be a real jerk and is even more unpleasant because of his blind-hearted and bitchy grandmother.

But Xu is destined to be cannon fodder. I hope Uncle Bo will make everything clear and take revenge on Xu's evil dad and evil sister by killing them… As to the problem of the grandma, it depends on Su Nian's attitude. It's best to make a public apology and bow to Su Nian's family with sincerity. Then Su Nian should avoid Bo's grandma after that. Bo's grandma well embodies the so-called "women's short sight." She misguides the 8-year-old

Bo Yanbei and intends to recognize the Xu's family, who are supposed to be her foes, as in-laws! She is totally blind, and I cannot forgive her…

"Is65" replied on January 23, 2016:

What about our Jingyu?! Bo puts Su's father in prison, which causes his lung cancer. He also takes Su Nian's virginity by force and burns Su Nian's old house. He ignored Su Nian's love five years ago and repeatedly hurt her feelings. Bo is now punished, but he is not hurt and has no real loss at all, except that he is once shot and hospitalized! Oh, by the way, he is shot because he kidnaps Xu Jingyu and takes Su Nian away by force. Although Su Xiangnan causes something bad because of his violation of law, he is still Su Nian's father. This is not black and white to Su Nian, because she cannot overcome her feelings and choose not to help her own father! If Bo Yanbei had not taken Su Nian's virginity by force five years ago so that Xu Lixiao could have his chance, Su's father, with Jingyu's help, could have saved ten years in prison! Bo Yanbei's love is of no avail. Actually, everything he does hurts Su Nian directly or indirectly!

These are typical interactive commentaries posted on a literary website. There were about a thousand commentaries on the novel just over a month after it was published. With the update of the novel, netizens' commentaries were updated simultaneously. This kind of "salon-style" criticism is quite common in cyberspace. Authors and readers share thoughts and aesthetic experiences instantly. They not only write critical commentaries on particular works but also express their views about each other's commentaries.

This type of interactive text, as a form of cyber literary criticism, enjoys a high degree of plasticity. Kristeva once said: "Any text is constructed as a mosaic of quotations; any text is the absorption and transformation of another."[5] This refers to the relationship between texts, or "intertexuality." Such an idea of intertextuality is embodied in netizens' interactive commentaries: netizens can not only write posts to express their opinions of literary texts, but also reply to other people's critical commentaries, so that different posts can be interconnected. A reader can also build up a web of his/her own posts so that the originally separated critical commentaries can be connected to inspire more thoughts and ideas. Thus, these texts of criticism can create a benign circle and open up an unlimited space for literary interpretation.

Commentaries in the Form of Monologues

Criticism in the form of monologues mainly exists in we media. There is a huge volume of critical texts in the form of blog posts, microblog posts, text messages, and WeChat articles. We media have the advantage of integrating and connecting different digital terminals: after pens were replaced with computers, keyboards are now replaced with touchscreens. Smartphones and pads have become new terminals used widely among readers. Individuals now have more power to publish and express their opinions. The practice of cyber literary criticism thus becomes even more popular.

In we media, critics can use monologues to express their thoughts about specific literary texts. Such monologues are private, thus differing from traditional literary criticism, which is written for the reading public. Literary criticism in the form of monologues, therefore, returns to the private sphere, which was eclipsed by public discourses in the past. It can convey the most genuine and essential parts of individual thoughts, as well as the most personal attitudes toward and aesthetic experiences of literary artworks.

There is no restriction for people to access we media platforms, such as blogs, microblogs, WeChat, and QQ. The regulations are relatively loose. We media thus becomes a purely private virtual space that can ensure netizens to express their individual thoughts to the max. In comparison, traditional literary forums, restricted by their business positioning and censorship rules, and affected by click-through rates and readers' expectations, cannot become a space where netizens' expressions, thoughts, and value judgments are totally unrestrained. Instead, netizens have to make some efforts to organize their writing and be careful about their language use, just like what critics do for offline literary criticism.

In contrast, we-media literary criticism in the form of monologues allows netizens to have more freedom. As long as a person has a device that can access the Internet, he/she can read and comment on a literary work anytime and anywhere with no need to consider other people's thoughts. Writing literary criticism thus becomes as easy as a game, requiring just a few clicks, strokes, or presses. In this sense, criticism in the form of monologues means to tell the world "what I am reading and what I am thinking about." It liberates the "silent majority" and grants them a right to speak.

Here are some commentaries by "Bleak Building in Shanghai" (Shanghai xiaolou), posted on *Blog China* (Boke Zhongguo):[6]

> Title: Anna committed suicide on a railroad track posted on March 17, 2009
>
> After reading about Anna's suicide on the railroad, many readers were furious. They wrote to Leo Tolstoy, the author of *Anna Karenina*, asking him how he had the heart to let Anna die—how he could let her commit suicide, and it was suicide by train. Tolstoy replied that it was not he who asked Anna to commit suicide on a track. It was Anna herself who wanted to commit suicide on a track. It is said that Tolstoy burst into tears and couldn't help himself when he wrote about Anna's death. The character in the novel decides to kill herself. This sounds incredible. In fact, this is determined by the character's personality. Tolstoy said that if Anna didn't commit suicide, or if Anna took poison—like Madame Bovary—or hanged herself, it would not be his Anna anymore.

Title: Zhang Xianliang and *Das Kapital* posted on March 16, 2009

The Herdsman (Mumaren), a film adaptation of Zhang Xianliang's short story, became very popular after its screening. Zhang Xianliang's novel *Half of Man Is Woman* (Nanren de yiban shi nüren) also caused a sensation. Zhang's literary education was not based on his reading of literary masterpieces, nor was it based on his reading of textbooks on literature and literary theories. Zhang himself said that his knowledge of literature entirely came from Marx's *Das Kapital*.

In the best years of his life, Zhang Xianliang was in a labor camp. At that time, there were no books to read except *Das Kapital*, and some books were forbidden to read. Therefore, Zhang Xianliang read *Das Kapital* many times. Decades later, when Zhang Xianliang became a well-known writer, he said very emotionally that all his literary education came from *Das Kapital*, a book purely about political economy. This is unimaginable to many people.

Title: Sima Qian "gong gong" posted on March 16, 2009

I call Sima Qian "gong gong" here, but I absolutely do not mean to be disrespectful to him.[7] Among the greatest essayists in ancient times, Sima Qian, Han Yu, and Gui Youguang are my favorites.

Gongxing, also known as *fuxing*, is a great invention and creation of ancient Chinese emperors. It is a punishment that cuts off a man's genitals. After Sima Qian had *gongxing*, he said: "That is why my guts churn all day long. At home I am in a daze, as if I have lost something. Going out of the house, I forget where it is I am going. Every time I think of this shame, my back breaks out in a sweat that soaks my robe."[8]

The saddest thing is: "My family, being poor, had insufficient funds to purchase remission of my crime. None of my acquaintances offered to save me, and none of my close associates put in a single word on my behalf. A body is not made of wood or stone! With only the officers of the law for company, I was kept in confinement deep within the prison walls. To whom could I voice my grievances?"

Why does Sima Qian choose to live on with such shame? Sima Qian himself said that even a captive slave or a maidservant who received such a shameful punishment would commit suicide, but he still chose to live on. He explained why: "The reason I suffered in silence and lived on in disgrace, refusing to retreat even when mire in filth, was that I would have hated not to fully express what I held in my heart. I would have despised myself for dying before the glory of my writings could be displayed to later generations." In order to finish his masterpiece *Records of the Historian* (Shiji), he endured such great humiliation and lived on: "This being the case with me, this is something that can be discussed with wise men, but it is hard to speak of such things with vulgar people."

The netizen picks some details from these literary works and connects them to his/her own life experience and feelings. Meanwhile, we media plays a dual role both as a platform for the general public and as a platform for individuals: this allows personal discourses, previously blocked by other Internet media, to re-emerge; personal discourses are thus transformed into public discourses. A netizen posts thoughts and feelings in a relatively private space, while other netizens can still freely view these words and interact with the poster: if they like a piece of writing, they can bump the post or give it a thumbs-up; if they don't like it, they can complain about it. In this way, personal thoughts are conveyed anonymously, while a netizen can use critical commentaries to express himself or herself.

The Contents of Netizens' Commentaries

The contents of netizens' commentaries are eclectic and diverse, not following a uniform and fixed pattern. They often break the conventions and go "beyond paradigms." Judging from their contents, we can put such commentaries into the following categories.

Direct Experience of the Essence of Literature

In the chapter entitled "Tian Zi-fang" of *Zhuangzi*, there are such words: "Zhongni replied: 'As soon as my eyes lighted on that man, the Dao in him was apparent. The situation did not admit of a word being spoken.'"[9] This means that a smart person can instantly know another person's thoughts by looking at that person without having a conversation. People of later generations often used "witness to the existence of Tao" (muji daocun) to refer to the condition that one can directly and intuitively get to know the essence of things, or problems, by looking at them. In literary appreciation, it can mean the condition that a reader can instantaneously grasp the essence of a literary work and intuitively sympathize with it. While this happens in traditional literary criticism, intuition and epiphany play a more important role and can even become a common condition in netizens' critical commentaries.

Compared with the rigorous logical structure of a text of traditional literary criticism, a netizen's critical commentary is more of a fragmented expression of the netizen's personal thoughts and feelings as a response to a literary work. Usually, the text is short in length, free in structure, and straightforward in content. It is similar to the literary criticism in ancient times, which was based on personal reflections and impressions and focused on the romantic charm in literature. It is also consistent with the Taoist ideal that can be summarized as the phrase "witness to the existence of Tao."

Chinese literary criticism in ancient times paid much attention to personal thoughts and feelings. In "The Great Preface to *The Book of Poetry*" (Maoshi xu) there are words like this: "Poetry is where intent goes. In the heart, it is an intent; released through words, it is a poem."[10] Here the "intent" (zhi) means the expression of one's mind. Liu Xie, a prominent critic in the 5th century, used the word "mind" (xin) to entitle his work *The Literary Mind and the*

Carving of Dragons (Wenxin diaolong). He exclaimed: "Mind, it is beauty."[11] Zhong Rong, another critic in the 5th century, advocated that poems should "use depictions of scenery to move people's hearts" in his "Ranking Poetry" (Shipin); Sikong Tu, who lived in the 9th century, suggested that a poem should "use straightforward language without deep thoughts and calculations," but when you read it, "it is like meeting a quiet person, and you will see the Tao in his mind," in his "Twenty-four Categories of Poetry" (Ershisi shi pin).[12] Yan Yu, who lived in the 13th century, proposed in his *Canglang's Remarks on Poetry* (Canglang shihua) that "the way of poetry also lies in epiphany."[13] He argued that one should depend on an instinct, or epiphany, to experience the essence of poetry.

Many of netizens' critical commentaries clearly embody such a literary ideal by highlighting critics' thoughts and feelings. Although they are not as good as classical literary criticism in their appreciation of aesthetic values in literature, they follow the wisdom of ancient critics, as if they also bear "witness to the existence of Tao." See the following commentaries as examples.

> If you like a girl, you must like her to the point that you don't need to understand her too much, so that you will be accustomed to being "released like a pigeon" (stood up) by her once and again.[14] In the end, she will let you know that she has no bad intentions. You are just like a pigeon to her. She tries to release you so that you will be free. She means well. Of course, if you want, you can fly back brusquely to her as a carrier pigeon who has no mail to carry.
> (Commentary on "Love Is the Most Meaningless Cultivation" (Ai shi zui wuyiyi de yizhong xiuxing), a work by "Tree hole Zhou" (Shudong Zhou), from "Parrot Shi Hang" (Yingwu Shi Hang) on *Sina Weibo*)

> "To a lonely wanderer on a spiritual journey, poetry is the path to his loss." On the contrary, when I was in an undisturbed state these two days, I uttered this sentence: "I sing his elegance with a whimper of words, and remember a sad breeze among the olive trees."[15] These lines made me feel like I had found my true self. A good writer is like a shepherd. He leads us into the pasture. A bad writer is like a wolf. He chases us and makes us lose our way. Bei Dao is my shepherd.
> (Commentary on Bei Dao's *The Rose of Time* (Shijian de meigui) from "E" on *Douban*)

> I was wrong. I overestimated love and overvalued marriage. I thought love was powerful enough to fight the ruthlessness of time, and the fortress of marriage could protect one forever from homelessness. In fact, love and marriage are not unalterable and unquestionable. They do not necessarily last forever. What sounds so sweet is just a lover's prattle. Love is actually very short, as short as a fleeting meteor that quickly vanishes. Love is indeed

very light, as light as the unpredictable white clouds on the horizon that quickly changes their shapes.

(Commentary on Qian Zhongshu's Fortress Besieged
(Weicheng) from "Tears of Kikyo" (Jiegeng de yanlei) on
Skyline Community (Tianya shequ))

Such commentaries are not solidly based on theoretical or logical reasoning. Instead, they are more about critics' thoughts and feelings as responses to literary works. The first example above jokingly uses "the release of a pigeon" (fang gezi) as a metaphor to express the reader's understanding of unrequited love. The second example explains the critic's own aesthetic experience through reading poetry and how a good writer can guide a reader in life. The third example is just an expression of the critic's thoughts and feelings based on his/her own experience of love, and it reads more like a personal reading response. To some extent, although such commentaries are casual and personal, they do correspond with literary criticism in ancient times in terms of the way of aesthetic appreciation. They are of some value as they help us better understand literature as a form of art.

Casual and Unrestrained Discussions

Casual and unrestrained discussions are quite common in netizens' critical commentaries. Netizens use concise words to express thoughts and feelings about literary works directly, casually, and without much preparation or restriction. Such texts are distinctively fragmented.

Unlike a text of traditional literary criticism, a netizen's critical commentary does not need to have a complete structure and in-depth analysis. With an emphasis on personal thoughts and feelings, it takes the form of words scribbled casually and is posted online to be shared with the author of the literary work and other readers. While reviewing a work, a netizen sometimes will use flows of consciousness to shift the focus from one thing to another without much consideration of the logical connection in the discussion. A commentary thus can be like a montage, consisting of pieces of words that are incidentally related, without a predetermined topic, and not following a path of theoretical argumentation. It intends to draw other readers' attention and occupy a position quickly in the "square of criticism"—websites and forums—where people speak freely and their voices are all mixed. A large number of people then begin to post spam or use sensational or hyperbolic titles to attract readers. For example, a netizen named "Eternal Chaos Truth" (Yongheng hundun zhenli) on *Starting Points Chinese Website* posted a short commentary on the novel *The World in the Sky* (Tianyu cangqiong), entitled "This Short Review Is Not Important, But I Do Want to Sign in Here" (Xiaoping weifu, qiandao weizhu). It clearly indicates the netizen's intent to post spam.

> At first, I wanted to keep writing comments on the novel and build a long thread of posts, but in the end, I found it was too tiring, so it became a

thread where I could sign in every day. (an emoji of a crying face) The real reason for this is that I saw the requirements to receive the basic badges, and I felt like I was not about to get them. To get them, you have to write hundreds and thousands of posts. How ridiculous! I had no other way to do this, and I had to bite the bullet, so this thread was born! Thank you all in advance. I will have to do it anyways. If you have time, just write something random (post spam) here. Thank you! (a smiley)

In this type of commentary, netizens often rush to post their replies in a thread without making clear what the topic is: they scramble for the "sofa" (the first reply in a thread) and the "bench" (the second reply); they also work together to "construct a tall building" (which means piling up posts to make a long thread). Apart from this, netizens also post simple words, such as "bump (the post)"; they may also give thumbs-up or monetary rewards to a particular original poster. They do this to attract people's attention and do not care much about the content of the posts. Sometimes their replies are totally irrelevant to the thread starters. Tan Dejing, a scholar, included a netizen's explanation of such a condition in his book:

By checking the click-through rate, I can tell if my writing is liked by readers or not... I can directly post my writing online. People will decide if it is good or not. If only ten people read my writing, they won't be able to form a public opinion about it. But if there are a hundred of them, a strong public opinion will be formed. That will be more effective than a review by a famous critic. Literature will, in this sense, become more personal and get closer to readers.[16]

In an article, I also examined such commentaries and made my points as follows:

Netizens dislike abstract theories and logical reasoning. Occasionally, one or two of such posts [of theories and reasoning] appear, and they are often considered as too pretentious and ridiculed by others. Instead, posts are often concise, plain, and instantaneous. In this sense, these discussions are not to give a deep analysis of literary works in terms of their intellectual connotations and artistic styles. Consequently, they, as words of literary criticism, are depthless and casual. While traditionally literary criticism is an act to explore people's souls, now it has become a mere expression of the superficial things in literature just for fun and pleasure.[17]

Of course, casual and unrestrained commentaries are not necessarily without deep thoughts. On the whole, many of these texts are also insightful and enlightening. For example, here is a short essay by Ma Boyong, posted on *Sina Weibo*:

While reading "A Person Possessed by a Venomous Insect" (Rengu), a novella full of terrifying and supernatural elements, I felt a chill down my spine.

It is not a story that makes every effort to scare you. Instead, it goes unhurriedly and occasionally reveals a touch of details that suddenly surprise you. The whole story is very delicate, and its moral message is also very interesting. Although the narrative trick in the end is a little off, it is still a good work.

This short commentary is a little more than a hundred Chinese characters. It provides a personal discussion on the novella from different perspectives, including the reading experience, plot arrangement, artistic conception, ideological connotation, and narrative effect. Though very brief, it has a relatively complete structure as an essay and delivers a reasonable analysis of the literary work, which is reflective of the critic's own value orientation.

Subversive Commentaries that Break Rules and Traditions

Netizens' commentaries are not only fresh and lively: they are sometimes quite subversive. This reminds us of Bakhtin's argument that in carnivalesque activities, people play as clowns and behave blasphemously. In cyberspace, people embrace the grassroots spirit and reject hierarchical concepts. They view everyone as their equal and tend to be "blasphemous" to what seems sacred. In an article, I made the following argument concerning this condition:

> As netizens are protected by anonymity, their commentaries in the digital world can deconstruct the dichotomy between the rich and the poor, between the elegant and the vulgar, and between the high and the low. With words of grotesquery, mockery, ridicule, glibness, faked seriousness, and various elements from folk culture, they make people laugh out and subvert what is traditionally viewed as noble and elegant. In this way, it turns the traditional paradigms and values of literature upside down.[18]

The writing of literary commentaries online is an ongoing activity. Anonymous "grassroots" critics often deconstruct the sublime, ridicule the sacred, and mock the classic. In so doing, they embrace a value orientation that tends to view all people as equal and rebel against established hierarchies. Their commentaries thus become subversive. In terms of rhetorical device, these netizens often use parody, irony, intentional misinterpretation, and elements of grotesquerie; in terms of the way of expression, they often modify idioms and allusions, parody aphorisms, play with slang words, rewrite literary classics, confuse characters in stories, and borrow plots from films and TV series. They intend to use such ways to give personal reviews of literary texts while subverting the traditional way of literary criticism. As an example, here is a part of a long review entitled "An Absolutely Wry Review of *Journey to the West*" (*Xiyouji* zhi juedui waipi) by "A Depressed Windbreaker" (Xiaotiao de fengyi) on *SF Animation, Comics, and Games* (SF hudong chuanmei wang).

As we look back at history, we may wonder why *Journey to the West* was banned in the Ming Dynasty. But isn't it obvious? The Ming government worshipped Taoism, but the novel ridiculed Taoism so harshly, so why not ban it? Theoretically, the three parties—Buddhists, Taoists, and believers of the Jade Emperor—were still competing at that time.[19] *Journey to the West* was just a story about the conflict between Buddhism and Taoism. Whether important or not, the book signified a victory of Buddhism. So, it had to be banned.

A novel like this is the most interesting. Nowadays, web novels are abusing our imagination, as they all depict battles between several kingdoms and how characters become the strongest in the world through Taoist cultivation. Compared with these stories, is not *Journey to the West*, which uses intricate details to convey important messages, a more entertaining and meaningful story? Time is marching on, and our society is developing. But novels are going backward. This is especially true today as we have a boom in cyber literature.

There are countless critical commentaries in cyberspace that parody, ridicule, joke about, and deliberately misinterpret classics such as *Journey to the West*, *Romance of Three Kingdoms*, *Outlaws of the Marsh*, and poems by Li Bai and Du Fu. Among such commentaries, spoofs are the most representative and subversive. Examples of such spoofs include videos entitled *A Murder Caused by a Steamed Bun* (Yige mantou yinfa de xue'an), *Shining Red Stars: A Story of Pan Dongzi Participating in the Singers' Competition* (Shanshan de hongxing zhi Pan Dongzi cansaiji), and *Railway Guerrilla: A Mobilization for All-China National Young Singers' Television Competition* (Tiedao youjidui zhi qinggesai zongdongyuan). According to Professor Lan Aiguo, the ways of spoofing include "cuts and pastes of pictures," "edits of videos," "revisions to song lyrics," "lip-syncing performances," "imitations of writers' styles," "imitations of actors'/actress' acts," "modifications to video games," and "drawings of comic strips."[20] Spoofers express resistance to established rules and customs, thus embodying a spirit of playfulness and subversiveness in youth subcultures.

While spoofs can be comical and funny, the spirit of playfulness more essentially signifies a subversiveness to our tradition. Spoofers do not take traditional literary concepts as the norm. Instead, they are good at expressing their unique attitudes and thoughts in somewhat oblique manners, thus being critical of reality. Such critical commentaries give playful discourses to full play and allow all netizens to be entertained. Meanwhile, by playing with words and subverting the tradition, commentators can also experience a sense of fulfillment.

Critical Texts that Are Postmodern and Deconstructive

While the aforementioned subversive commentaries contain a postmodern spirit, there are commentaries of another kind that are more deconstructive and thus even more postmodern. Postmodernism is characterized by "depthlessness," "loss of historicity," "death of the subject," and "abolition of critical distance."²¹ Based on such a knowledge of postmodernism, Wang Yuechuan gave a discussion on art as follows:

> Art and aesthetics in the postmodern cultural context inevitably bear the hallmark of postmodernity. While people's perception of art becomes a fragmented process, the charm of art is lost. Art is no longer revolutionary and stylistically beautiful. It has become something no longer artistic or even something anti-artistic. Aesthetics—the appreciation of beauty—now has become the appreciation of the ugly. Art is no longer "transcendental." Instead, it has become a term that means concession and degradation. Art is now equivalent to people's real life, while life has become a checkerboard on which people in the postmodern context can play art just like chess.²²

Wang's idea applies to both cyber literature and cyber literary criticism. Netizens' critical commentaries inevitably contain postmodern discourses as they are subversive toward established knowledge and take the position on the margins of society.

Netizens' commentaries depart from traditional literary criticism in terms of content and form: they subvert mainstream discourses, deconstruct the long-established structure of writing, and reconstruct the norms for a new language used in cyberspace. They reject deep thoughts and decenter the meaning of language. As they are fragmented, they no longer pay much attention to the assertion of the values of society and the spirit of the times, which we see much in traditional literary criticism. The traditional criteria and discourse systems for evaluating literature are thus no longer as meaningful and valuable as before.

The postmodern stance of netizen-critics has two manifestations. First, these commentaries break with the traditional idea that literary criticism must chime in with mainstream values. The traditional view that literature must convey the truth and represent the interests of the people tends to be no longer valid. Instead, netizens' commentaries work to entertain readers and deconstruct established rules and customs. Second, the postmodern stance allows ordinary people—those on the margin of literature—to gain the right and the opportunity to express their opinions freely. Netizens' commentaries do not have to be reviewed by an editor before publication. As a result, these netizens can write whatever they want. A netizen wrote the following words to comment on this situation:

> Words of ordinary people finally have a chance to go together with words of nobility, obsolescence, pretension, verbosity, and fake elegance—words of people in a small circle who benefit from the aristocracy. At least in Internet media, the former is not less powerful than the latter. We can understand this now. Cyberspace is for the people; it at least provides people with equal rights and opportunities in front of literature.²³

As we are in the era of new media, each netizen now has the liberty to write and publish literary criticism. As a result, the value of literary artworks no longer lies in their being something to be worshipped, but in their being something to be exhibited. The culture of our society is controlled no longer by the elite but by the masses. Collage, parody, and spoof have become popular in netizens' critical commentaries. We-media platforms can powerfully and broadly circulate people's words, thus providing an ideal cultural context for cyber literature: in such a context, established discourses are deconstructed, a spirit of playfulness and depthlessness is highlighted, and the current condition is subverted.

Such deconstructive and postmodern commentaries are quite ordinary on the Internet. Here is a parody of Lu Xun's "Madman's Diary," written by "Wild Wheat" (Ye maizi) and entitled "Madman's Diary (the 2000 version)" (Kuangren riji erlinglingling ban), as an example.[24]

> This morning, there was no good moonlight.
>
> I hadn't seen myself for more than sixty years. Now, I saw myself, and I felt completely refreshed. Only today did I know that in the past sixty years or so, I was all dumb and blind.
>
> I had to be very careful. Otherwise, why would Wang Shuo's dog glare at me? The sun did not come out. The door was not open. I took two meals every day.
>
> I clamored for letting me get off the pedestal. They stopped me. They were very busy.
>
> They took out a flag with the words "National Spirit" on it. They planted the flag right at my front door.
>
> I took out my *Complete Works* and read carefully for a long time. I could see the words clearly without reading between the lines. The two words were written all over the book, and they were "curse people."[25]

The mockery of Lu Xun in this article is undoubtedly unacceptable to us, but it well represents many commentaries of this kind on the Internet. Together, they mean to be jocular and playful. Commentators do not intend to construct any ideas that are theoretically meaningful. Instead, they tend to deconstruct some well-established views in literature and literary research.

Such deconstructive commentaries tend to avoid deep thinking, subvert what is sublime and significant, and freely deconstruct classics. In so doing, they highlight a spirit of playfulness and embody the postmodern way of thinking, which can be summarized as being "blasphemous to what is deemed sacred." I explained this condition in an article:

> Cyber literature is a kind of literature that denies canonization and works to disenchant people. It is no longer a means for writers to earn a living and shoulder social responsibilities. Instead, it has become merely a way for people to entertain themselves and have carnivalesque celebrations of free personal expressions.[26]

Today, literature is no longer awe-inspiring. Netizens, as commentators and critics, have also lost their sense of social responsibility; their critical commentaries have thus become a game that allows them to share their thoughts on daily life and flaunt their wit and humor. This is the case for deconstructive commentaries, which are quite common in cyberspace.[27]

The Rhetoric of Free Writing

Texts in "Martian Language"

The term "Martian language" (huoxing wen) first appeared in a section called "kuso" on the famous Taiwanese video game website *Bahamut* (Bahamute). "Kuso" is originally a cuss word in Japanese, but it is now widely understood as "parody" and "spoof" on the Internet. People use "Martian language" for two reasons: they may intend to sound cute or to pretend to be mysterious. "Martian language" uses Mandarin phonetic symbols (zhuyin), Arabic numerals, English alphabets, and emoticons to replace Chinese characters in order to create a language atmosphere that is full of fun and joy. These characteristics incidentally correspond to young netizens' mentality that writing is to amuse people with the weird and the cute. In consequence, "Martian language" was soon adopted by some youth subcultures and became popular in cyberspace.

"Martian language" combines pictograms and words to make a new form of multimedia text. The word order can be untraditional, and the sentence structure can be based on a mixture of different languages. There are also many buzzwords and catchphrases. Thus, the texts in "Martian language" are unique, ingenious, and vivid, highlighting the writers' personalities as interesting and friendly.[28] Here are a few common types of words in "Martian language":

Emoticons. For example, & (ˆ _ _ ˆ) & for "smile"; ⊙__⊙ ‖ | for "embarrassed"; ~@ ˆ _ ˆ @~ for "cute."

Abbreviations in letters. For example, LZ for "laozi," literally meaning "I, your dad"; BT for "biantai," meaning "pervert"; CU for "see you."

Numerics. For example, 886 for "baibaile," meaning "bye-bye"; 9494 for "jiushi jiushi," meaning "yes, yes."

Combinations of Chinese and English. For example, "神马DD" for "shenma dongdong," meaning "what is that thing?"; "no zuo no die" for "you would not be in trouble had you not asked for it"; "大BOSS" for "da boss," meaning "big monster."

Words with changed meanings. For example, 坑爹, or "kengdie," literally means "you set a trap for your dad" and now is a joking expression that means "how dare you cheat me, your dad"; 打酱油, or "da jiangyou," literally means "to go out and buy soy sauce" and now means "to watch something happening as an onlooker."

Homophonic words. For example, 伊妹儿, or "yimei'er," means "email"; 瘟都死, or "wendousi," means "Windows"; 三克油, or "sankeyou," means "thank you."

Such words as "Martian language" can be seen everywhere in netizens' literary commentaries. For example, here is a post in the comment section for the novel *Massacre to the Edge of the Sky* (Tulu tianji) on *Starting Points Chinese Net*:

The version in "Martian Language"：情ㄗ夺渥の卟譜，爽嚱乜冇，雖嘫哎笔還稚嫩，但媞這嗰嘟岢苡逐渐改变。但媞俙望偂剘偝景妎紹崾呢，蒋幻尐說の偝景遰離現實社哙，卟妎紹清漤の話，呮哙讓亽①頭雾氺。
嗰亽嘿评，卟囍伤怪。

The version in Mandarin Chinese: 情节把握得不错，爽点也有，虽然文笔还稚嫩，但是这个都可以逐渐改变。但是希望前期背景介绍要足，科幻小说的背景远离现实社会，不介绍清楚的话，只会让人一头雾水。
个人点评，不喜勿怪。

English translation: The plot is well designed, and there are places that make you feel excited. Although the writing style is still immature, this can be improved gradually. But I hope that the background introduction should be sufficiently given in the beginning. The world in a sci-fi novel is quite different from our real world. If you don't explain it clearly, it will only make people confused.
This is just my personal comment, so don't blame me if you don't like it.[29]

Some of these creative expressions are directly based on words of "Martian language" that are used by many. Some others, however, are random creations of netizens, which fully demonstrate the free, flexible, and lively characteristics of cyber literary criticism. Under such a circumstance, the interpretation of literary works has become secondary, while the language game for fun has become the most important. Netizens are often immersed in such a game with endless combinations of words and symbols and find it difficult to extricate themselves. They enjoy the pleasure of expression with the utmost freedom and without any restraint.

The "Martian language" used in netizens' literary commentaries can take various forms and combine pictograms with characters and letters. It is vivid, lively, and quite expressive, giving readers a multimedia experience that may intensify their emotional responses. While the use of "Martian language" leads to a new form of literary criticism that is full of tensions and interactions between characters and symbols, it also blurs the boundary between texts of literary criticism and texts that no longer serve the function of literary criticism, thus reposing a series of fundamental questions to us, such as "what is literary criticism," "how shall we write literary criticism," and "what is the use of literary criticism."[30]

Colloquial and Vernacular Expressions

Netizens' commentaries, like ordinary communication in cyberspace, use colloquial and vernacular expressions. Compared with traditional literary criticism, they are simpler, more straightforward, easier to understand, and closer to daily life.

First, the use of colloquial language demonstrates a personal aesthetic standpoint. Many words and phrases used in netizens' commentaries are directly from our daily language, and they are suitable for readers who read fast. Meanwhile, some buzzwords and catchphrases people use in daily life have become popular. For example, a netizen on the website *Reading with Beauty* made a commentary on the novel *Garden of Beasts* (Yeshou huayuan).[31]

> It's a pity that the novel doesn't seem to have been made into a movie or TV series. There are all kinds of eye-catching elements: gangsters, fight and rage, revenge, conspiracy, politicians, heads of state, spies, charming killers, slutty women, assassinations, betrayals, loyalty, humanity, conscience... Also, the novel promotes the mainstream values embraced by all human societies to the utmost. If it is made into a blockbuster, movie theaters will be bursting with people.

In the original text in Chinese, words such as "seem to be" (maosi), "eye-catching" (xijing), "to the utmost" (ganggangde), and "burst with people" (baopeng), as well as the frequent use of commas in sentences, are all colloquial expressions. Apart from this, the humor in language also gives readers pleasure. For example, a netizen named "Transparent girl" (Touming shaonü) made such comments on Baudelaire's collection of poems *The Flowers of Evil*:

> How wonderful is this book! To praise the book, I can exhaust the whole dictionary of idioms, but it is still not enough. To those who have been chattering to me to prove that Baudelaire is a villain and pervert, I will simply quote the sentence at the end of an article on the post-90s generation by He Caitou—bite me!

In this paragraph, expressions such as "I can exhaust the whole dictionary of idioms, but this is still not enough" (yongjin zhengbu chengyu zidian dou xingrong bujin) and "bite me" (nimen yaowo a) are colloquial and with a sense of humor. Netizens, with such a spirit of playfulness, show off their good use of tricks in language to entertain both themselves and their readers. While the colloquial words are lively and artful, they also help inspire people with the distinctive wisdom of folk culture.

Second, expressions used in daily life can work to reshape people's ideas of aesthetics in literature. Currently, the Internet has successfully transformed our life by digitizing everything around us. While reshaping our way of life and our knowledge of society and culture, the Internet is also altering our way of thinking and speaking, thus further changing our notions concerning aesthetics. Today, non-linear narratives are replacing linear ones. Aesthetic experience through interaction is replacing that through one-way communication. Multimedia technology, which combines texts, images, and sounds, is replacing the traditional way of expression through mere written words. As a result, information in the mass media is no longer supposed to be classic, sacred, and rational. Instead, it has become playful and vernacular. Literature is thus more closely attached to daily life. While experience in daily life has become an important source of inspiration for literary creation, it has also influenced literary criticism. In cyberspace, most texts of literary criticism consist of everyday expressions. For example, here is an excerpt from "Lu Xun is a Mirror that Reveals the Monsters Among Us" (Lu Xun shi yiba zhaoyaojing) by Shen Jiake on *Sina Weibo*.[32]

> Lu Xun is like the best "zhaoyaojing"—mirror that can reveal images of monsters. His works show the evils in human nature. They demand that we should distinguish right from wrong. We should not be submissive to what is unfair. Nor should we be cheated by people who pretend to be kind and tolerant. These people often ask you to be generous and then take advantage of your generosity. They will rip you off and then tell you that you should not care about your loss, and if you do care, then you are just being narrow-minded. If you have such an experience, you will understand how true Lu Xun's articles are. We can never absolutely eliminate such evils in human nature, but we can choose to keep away from such people. On *Weibo*, we can blacklist those people that are self-righteous and hypocritical. In our daily life, we must keep away from them.

The above discussion on Lu Xun is based on the writer's own life experience. The expression seems random but still has some philosophical thoughts in it. It is worth noting that the aestheticization of daily life has blurred the boundary between life and art. Literary criticism, previously written by intellectuals as the elite in our society, now has to cater to ordinary people's aesthetic tastes in order to survive and develop itself. Meanwhile, the new aesthetics based on audio-visual media and cyber literature corresponds with the virtual reality created by digital technology: a new aesthetic space is thus created and plays an important role in people's daily life.

Third, the language used in netizens' critical commentaries tends to be vernacular. There are several cases worth mentioning here. First, the use of new modal particles to replace traditional ones in sentences can give a feeling of freshness and liveliness to readers. For example, "ma" (吗) can be replaced by "mie" (咩); "ne" (呢) can be replaced by "nie" (涅); and "shi de" (是的) can be replaced by "shi di" (是滴). Second, the use of slang words and phrases gives a feeling of familiarity and comfort to readers. For example, "cainiao" (literally "vegetable bird") refers to a newbie or a green hand without adequate knowledge and skill; "baobiao" is used for its literal meaning, which is "off the chart"; "gouxie" (literally "dog blood") means overdramatic, hackneyed, and contrived.[33] Replacing elegant and literary words with slang words and phrases used in daily life can create a quality of novelty and vividness. Third, the use of vulgar words makes the language more expressive. As commentaries are written freely by netizens and remain non-utilitarian, the language can be quite unrestrained. Though forbidden in traditional literary criticism, many vulgar words used in daily life are now used without much limitation and hesitation in netizens' critical writings. Netizens may deliberately use homophones or wrong words to create a sense of humor, such as "wocao" (卧槽) and "nima" (尼玛).[34] The use of vulgar words in netizens' commentaries facilitates communication and creates a feeling of closeness between commentators and readers. It is thus conducive to the construction of a new discourse system for literary criticism.

The Use of Vulgar Words

The use of vulgar words is a strategy that embodies the wisdom in folk culture. Netizens' literary commentaries use vulgar words to create expressions of ridicule, mockery, absurdity, faked seriousness, and glibness. Such an unconventional way of writing poses a challenge to the ways and aesthetic principles of traditional literary criticism. In this sense, literary criticism is no longer necessarily elegant and sacred. With unrestrained and unaffected expressions, netizens' commentaries can become a part of the folk culture—we may thus recognize it as a new type of literary criticism that is "folk" in nature. Dong Xuewen and Zhang Yougang made such an argument in their book:

> Reading literature allows readers to vent their emotions. It is an important way for them to transcend the difficulties in real life and spiritual restraints to reach a temporary psychological balance. Otherwise, they, while being repressed, would have to repress themselves as well. If they cannot find a way to vent their negative emotions, they will suffer a spiritual crisis or even a nervous breakdown.[35]

The use of vulgar words allows netizens to vent their negative emotions and assert their personal desires that are non-utilitarian. Thus, it can give people a feeling of satisfaction.

For example, a netizen named Wang Lu posted on the Chinese social networking site *Renren* the following article entitled "Du Fu's Poems Are So Good, But Did People of His Time Know It?" (Du Fu shi zheme hao, tongshidai de ren zhidao me):

> Everyone knew Li Bai's poems were good, not only because his poems were really good but also because He Zhizhang praised him. He Zhizhang, the big boss, said words like: "Li Taibai, are you a human? You are actually the Taibai Star [Venus] in the sky!"[36]
>
> As He, the bigwig, praised Li Bai in the first place, others could praise Li Bai too. There would be no problem at all, even if they lauded him to the skies.
>
> Similarly, another poet Bai Juyi came to the capital city Chang'an at a young age and was able to stand out quickly, all because of Gu Kuang's

recommendation. Gu Kuang just read Bai Juyi's lines—"Not even a prairie fire can destroy the grass. It grows again when the spring breeze blows." Then he told Bai Juyi that if Bai could write poems like this, he would be able to overwhelm all people in Chang'an.

The Tang Dynasty in its prime was good in this sense: as long as your poems are good, you don't need to give a damn about anyone; you don't even have to give a damn about the emperor.

Yet few people praised Du Fu. Didn't people know that Du's poems were great as well?

That would be tantamount to saying that all poets in the prime of the Tang Dynasty were blind. There were so many of them who made a living by writing poetry. Although we cannot say that all of them knew whose poems were good and whose were bad, at least some of them could see it very clearly. They knew, when Du Fu was still alive, that he would become a great poet, and that he would beat all other poets of his time and be on a par with Li Bai.

It is just that nobody said a word about it.

The use of vulgar language is clear both in the title and the main body of the article. The title uses a sentence patter that is popular on the Internet: "something is so ..., does someone know it?" ("... zenmeyang, ... zhidaoma?") The way of expression and tone of voice in the main body are even more casual. For example, the writer calls He Zhizhang, a famous poet, "He, the big boss" (He laoban) and "He, the bigwig" (He dalao), and uses sentences such as "you don't need to give a damn about anyone" (ni keyi shei dou buniao). Such casual and teasing words are purposefully used to denote an air of hooliganism. They are true and honest indicators of the commentator's attitude in life, psychological status, and values that are different from the mainstream ones.

Let's read an excerpt from the article "The Great Talented Girl's Whines: An Appreciative Analysis of Li Qingzhao's Work of Lyric Poetry 'Slow, Slow Tune'" (Dacainü de suisuinian rerenlian: Li Qingzhao ci Shengshengman shangxi), posted by "A Weirdo in the World of Letters" (Wentan guaitai) on *NetEase*.

If it were an ordinary illiterate woman who said the words "so dim, so dark/ so dense, so dull/ so damp, so dank/ so dead" (xunxunmimi lengleng qingqing qiqi cancan qiqi), I am sure that people would roll their eyes at her and swear: "What a sick, stupid, and whiny woman!"[37] It is not hard to imagine that such a pathetic woman would tirelessly keep babbling and talking nonsense like this. That would be so annoying.

Li Qingzhao is different. Everyone knows her. She is such a woman with talent. The thoughts of the talented woman are incredible. The talented women can turn stones into gold, turn trash into treasure, turn lines of nonsense into poetic masterpieces as if each word is a gem, and give the audience a good feeling of the brightness in rhythm and the beauty in rhyme.

This is just a prelude to what is even more beautiful.

Next, the talented woman Li Qingzhao will use a richer vocabulary to express her thoughts and feelings.

"The weather, now warm, now cold/ makes it harder/ than ever to keep fit." The capricious months at the end of the fall season or the beginning of spring usually blow hot and cold. Even people who are physically strong are easy to catch a cold during those days. The poet was almost half a century old—at the age of 45—at that time. As a person who was physically weak, she would find it difficult to keep fit and avoid catching a cold in such weather.

There is a saying: "If you try to dispel your sorrow by drinking alcohol, your sorrow will only become more intense." The poet knew it, so she did not dare to drink strong liquor, which would weaken her body. However, as we all know, alcohol can keep our bodies warm. What should the poet do then? Should she drink or not?

In such a dilemma, after consideration, she decided to drink some wine. However, even though it was just wine with little alcohol in it, the poet did not dare to drink too much. She could just take a few cups: "How can a few cups of thin wine/ bring warmth against/ the chilly winds of sunset?"

The use of such a "vulgar" style of language allows netizens' literary commentaries to highlight personal perspectives and experiences. However, we should also be aware that as such a style of language in netizens' writing becomes increasingly popular, if not properly checked and handled, it may become a mere expression of negative emotions that satisfies netizens' personal desires without helping to convey their unique opinions. In this sense, this language style may not always be conducive to the effect of literary criticism.

The Widespread Use of Internet Language

The Internet has given birth to a particular language characteristic of the times. With the awakening of netizens' awareness to make use of their right to speak and with the increase in netizens' enthusiasm for writing literary criticism, the distinctive Internet language has become a new phenomenon indicating the changes happening to literary criticism at the linguistic level. Lively, vivid, humorous, and full of personalities, such a language appears in netizens' commentaries to impress and even dazzle readers.

On the whole, the Internet language used by netizens can be defined from three aspects.

The first aspect is the style of the language. The Internet language includes various styles, and each style comes from a certain literary phenomenon. For example, "bosom friend style," or *zhiyin ti*, refers to a style of language originally used in the women's magazine *Bosom Friend* (Zhiyin). Articles in this style often use highly emotional titles and sensational words in the main body to attract readers and give them an intense "visual impact." Another style, "Qiong Yao style," or *Qiong Yao ti*, is modeled on the famous Taiwanese romance novelist Qiong Yao's works and especially dialogues in soap operas adapted from these works. Some netizens have summarized the characteristics of this style: the language has to be wordy, redundant, and repetitive, even though it is easy to make the language more concise; if it is possible to use complex sentences, will never use simple ones; if it is possible to let characters cry and shout the words, the author will never let them talk nicely. There is also the "pear flower style," or *lihua ti*, which is homophonic to the name of a female poet Zhao Lihua, whose poems are relatively untraditional and controversial on the Internet. Many netizens parody her poems to mock her and post their own "poems" in "pear flower style" on the Internet. Similar styles of this kind include "story for dummies" (xiaobai wen), "roaring style" (paoxiao ti), "popular styles on Xiaonei Network" (xiaonei ti), and "coquetry style" (mitang ti).

The second aspect of the Internet language concerns the evaluative, descriptive, and analytical expressions commonly used in cyber literary criticism. For example, "thumbs up" (dianzan) means to praise excellent works of cyber literature; "complain" (tucao) means to sharply criticize works for their shortcomings and deficiencies; "sprayer/shotgun" (penzi) means a person who unreasonably curses and attacks some phenomena and works of cyber literature; "headcanon" (naobu) means readers' personal associations and speculations based on literary works; "pleasure point" (shuangdian) means events and details in the plotline that make readers feel pleased and emotionally touched; "thunderbolt point" (leidian) means a part of the plot that surprises readers and render them speechless.[38] Ma Boyong's words on *Sina Weibo* are a good example here:

> There are so many fanfiction stories based on *Journey to the West* now. Almost all of them intend to shake off the influence of *Journey to the West* and give new representations of characters and stories to refresh readers' minds. What I am interested in is: what are the "thunderbolt points" in these stories? By "thunderbolt points," I mean these stories' adaptations of the original setting that make you decide to "abandon the pit" and even shout cusswords immediately after you see them.

Here, "thunderbolt points" and "abandon the pit" (qikeng) are typical Internet buzzwords.[39]

The third aspect of Internet language is about words referring to specific writing skills and rhetorical techniques. Many of such words are frequently used on the Internet. For example, "male pig's trotter" (nan zhujiao) and "female pig's trotter" (nü zhujiao), respectively, mean male and female protagonists in web novels. "Black belly" (fuhei) is a word to describe a character who appears as a gentle person but is evil and malicious inside. "I, an old monk" (laona) is how those who write spam posts in other people's threads would call themselves. "The head of the pear flower sect" (lihua jiaozhu) refers to Zhao Lihua. "The chrysanthemum yeast" (juhua jiaomu) refers to Guo Jingming, a "post-80s generation" writer. "To strike back" (nixi) is a word to describe how an unimportant person struggles against his/her fate and starts to be successful.[40]

In addition, there are many online buzzwords that have been introduced into online literary criticism, such as "go against Heaven" (nitian, meaning "powerful enough to turn the situation around"), "you are cheating me, your dad" (kengdie, often meaning "you must be kidding"), "give power" (geili, meaning "excellent"), "you know" (nidongde, meaning "I cannot say it, but you know what I mean"), "the gods and horses are all floating clouds" (shenma doushi fuyun, meaning "everything will be alright"), "hold on" (hold zhu), and "bump up your lung" (ding nige fei, meaning "I absolutely support you"), "Oh my God" (edige shenna), "what a mess in your social circle" (guiquan zhenluan), "the news is so exhilarating that we spread it all around" (xidapuben) and so on.

Internet language develops in the postmodern context as a form of folk language. While it twists our language and rebels against it by creating new meanings and forms, the use of the Internet language is also undoubtedly reasonable and can even be seen as a progress of our times, as this embodies how people use their wisdom to adapt our language to the new digital environment.

Notes

1 Marshall McLuhan, *Understanding Media: The Extensions of Man* (Cambridge, MA: The MIT Press, 1994), 7.
2 Ouyang, Youquan 欧阳友权, *Wangluo wenxue cidian* 网络文学词典 (Beijing: World Publishing Corporation, 2012), 36.
3 Lee, Shuen-shing 李顺兴, "Chaowenben wenxue xingshi meixue chutan" 超文本文学形式美学初探, *Intergrams* 2, no. 1 (February 2000). https://ir.lib.nchu.edu.tw/bitstream/11455/88236/1/87826-4.pdf.
4 Ouyang, Youquan 欧阳友权, *Wangluo wenxue gailun* 网络文学概论 (Beijing: Peking University Press, 2008), 114.
5 Julia Kristeva, "Word, Dialog and Novel," in *The Kristeva Reader*, ed. Toril Moi (New York: Columbia University Press, 1986), 37.
6 Translator's note: here is the link to these blog posts. https://xiatiandushu.blogchina.com/archive/201901_1.html.
7 Translator's note: in Chinese, the word "gong gong" literally means "old men" and is often used to refer to eunuchs.
8 Translator's note: Sima Qian's words here are from the translation collectively done by Stephen Durrant, Wai-Yee Li, Michael Nylan, and Hans Van Ess. See: Stephen Durrant et al., "The Letter to Ren An: English Translation," in *The Letter to Ren An & Sima Qian's Legacy* (Seattle: University of Washington Press, 2016), 22–29.
9 Translator's note: this is from James Legge's translation. See: Zhuang Zi 庄子, "Tian Zi-fang" 田子方, in *Zhuangzi* 庄子, trans. James Legge, Chinese Text Project 中国哲学书电子化计划, accessed August 22, 2022. https://ctext.org/zhuangzi/tian-zi-fang.

10 Translator's note: this is the translation done by Hyong Rhew. See: Hyong Rhew, "'The Great Preface' to *Shijing*, or *The Book of Poetry*," Reed College, accessed August 22, 2022, www.reed.edu/chinese/chin-hum/materials/shijing/gp.html.
11 Translator's note: this is the literal translation of the words *xin zai mei yi* in the introductory chapter (Xu zhi) of the work. Vicent Yu-Chung Shih translated this sentence as "What an excellent term indeed is 'mind!'" See: Liu, Hsieh (Liu Xie) 刘勰, *The Literary Mind and the Carving of Dragons*, trans. Vincent Yu-chung Shih (Hong Kong: The Chinese University of Hong Kong Press, 2015), 1.
12 He, Wenhuan 何文焕, *Lidai shihua* 历代诗话 (Shanghai: Zhonghua Book Company, 1981), 42.
13 He, Wenhuan 何文焕, *Lidai shihua* 历代诗话, 686.
14 Translator's note: "relase a pigeon" (fang gezi) is a phrase in Chinese, meaning "stand someone up."
15 Translator's note: These are lines from the poem "Lament for Ignacio Sanchez Mejias" by Federico García Lorca. They are translated by Pablo Medina from Spanish. See: Federico Garcia Lorca, "Lament for the Death of Ignacio Sánchez Mejías," trans. Pablo Medina, *The Literary Review*, accessed August 29, 2022. www.theliteraryreview.org/poetry-2/lament-for-the-death-of-ignacio-sanchez-mejias.
16 Tan, Dejing 谭德晶, *Wangluo wenxue pipinglun* 网络文学批评论 (Beijing: CFLAC Publishing House, 2004), 189.
17 Ouyang, Youquan 欧阳友权 and Wu Yingwen 吴英文, "Wangluo wenxue piping de jiazhi he juxian" 网络文学批评的价值和局限, *Exploration and Free Views* 探索与争鸣 no. 11 (2010): 64.
18 Ouyang, Youquan 欧阳友权, *Wangluo wenxue lungang* 网络文学论纲 (Beijing: People's Literature Publishing House, 2003b), 179.
19 Translator's note: Jade Emperor is a deity in Taoist theology, so the commentary is mistaken. It is likely that what the netizen-commentator wanted to refer to is "Confucians" rather than "believers of Jade Emperor."
20 Lan, Aiguo 蓝爱国, *Wangluo egao wenhua* 网络恶搞文化 (Beijing: China Literature and History Press, 2007), 22–25.
21 Translator's note: these characteristics are discussed and analyzed by Fredric Jameson. See: Fredric Jameson, "Postmodernism or the Cultural Logic of Late Capitalism," *New Left Review* no. 146 (1984): 53–92.
22 Wang, Yuechuan 王岳川, *Houxiandai zhuyi wenhua yanjiu* 后现代主义文化研究 (Beijing: Peking University Press, 1992), 244.
23 Ouyang, Youquan 欧阳友权, *Wangluo wenxue lungang* 网络文学论纲, 67–68.
24 Translator's note: the following passage mockingly imitates Lu Xun's style of writing and suggests that the narrative voice belongs to Lu Xun himself.
25 Huang, Jiwei 黄集伟, "Huangdan gaoxiao de wangluo weben" 荒诞搞笑的网络文本, *Dushi wenhua bao* 都市文化报 (Chengdu), Feb. 1, 2001.
26 Ouyang, Yuquan 欧阳友权. "Wangluo wenxue yanjiu shuping" 网络文学研究述评, *Theory and Criticism of Literature and Art* 文艺理论与批评 no. 5 (2003): 111.
27 Translator's note: this paragraph is significantly abridged in the translation.
28 Translator's note: this paragraph is significantly abridged and reorganized in the translation.
29 Translator's note: to show how the "Martian language" works, here we have the original text in "Martian language," the version in Mandarin Chinese, and the English translation.

30 Translator's note: the last two paragraphs are significantly abridged, reorganized, and corrected in the translation.
31 Translator's note: this is a novel originally written by Jeffery Deaver, an American mystery and crime writer.
32 Translator's note: Shen Jiake is not an ordinary netizen. He is a famous writer and critic who has published many books.
33 Translator's note: some corrections to the explanations of these three words were made during the process of translation.
34 Translator's note: "卧槽" is a substitute for "我操," meaning "fuck"; "尼玛" is used to replace "你妈," which means "your mother." The use of homophones also works to make the language less offensive.
35 Dong, Xuewen 董学文 and Zhang Yonggang 张勇刚, *Wangluo wenxue yuanli* 网络文学原理 (Beijing: Peking University Press, 2001), 249.
36 Translator's note: Taibai is Li Bai's "style name" (zi). It is also the name of the god of Venus in ancient Chinese mythology.
37 Translator's note: the translation of the poetic lines in this passage comes from Lin Yutang. See: Lin, Yutang 林语堂, trans. *Lin Yutang zhongying duizhao: Yangzhou shouma* 林语堂中英对照：扬州瘦马, ed. Li Ming 黎明 (Taipei: Cheng Chung Book, 2009), 41.
38 Translator's note: "thunderbolt point" literally means a point in a work where readers feel as if they are struck by a thunderbolt, mostly because they are surprised by how crudely the author arranges the storyline.
39 Translator's note: "abandon the pit" means to give up reading or following a story in the middle, usually because the story is no longer attractive.
40 Translator's note: "pig's trotter" (zhujiao) is homophonic to "protagonist" (zhujue, sometimes wrongly pronounced as zhujiao) in Chinese. "The pear flower sect" refers to people who write to spoof the poet Zhao Lihua's way of writing, which is called "pear flower style" (lihua ti) as it is homophonic to Zhao Lihua's name in Chinese. "The chrysanthemum yeast" (juhua jiaomu) is homophonic to "the godmother of the chrysanthemum sect" in Chinese. While "chrysanthemum" (juhua) is a euphemism for "anus" and is often used in a joking tone in Chinese, here it specifically implies that Guo Jingming lacks masculinity and is homosexual, which is untrue and abusive to the writer.

Bibliography

Dong, Xuewen 董学文 and Zhang, Yonggang 张勇刚. *Wangluo wenxue yuanli* 网络文学原理. Beijing: Peking University Press, 2001.
Durrant, Stephen et al. "The Letter to Ren An: English Translation." In *The Letter to Ren An & Sima Qian's Legacy*, 22–29. Seattle: University of Washington Press, 2016.
Garcia Lorca, Federico. "Lament for the Death of Ignacio Sánchez Mejías." Translated by Pablo Medina. *The Literary Review*. Accessed August 29, 2022. www.theliteraryreview.org/poetry-2/lament-for-the-death-of-ignacio-sanchez-mejias.
He, Wenhuan 何文焕. *Lidai shihua* 历代诗话. Shanghai: Zhonghua Book Company, 1981.
Huang, Jiwei 黄集伟. "Huangdan gaoxiao de wangluo weben 荒诞搞笑的网络文本." *Dushi wenhua bao* 都市文化报 (Chengdu), Feb. 1, 2001.
Jameson, Fredric. "Postmodernism or the Cultural Logic of Late Capitalism." *New Left Review* no. 146 (1984): 53–92.

Kristeva, Julia. "Word, Dialog and Novel." In *The Kristeva Reader*, 34–61. Edited by Toril Moi. New York: Columbia University Press, 1986.

Lan, Aiguo 蓝爱国. *Wangluo egao wenhua* 网络恶搞文化. Beijing: China Literature and History Press, 2007.

Lee, Shuen-shing 李顺兴. "Chaowenben wenxue xingshi meixue chutan" 超文本文学形式美学初探. *Intergrams* 2, no. 1 (February 2000). https://ir.lib.nchu.edu.tw/bitstream/11455/88236/1/87826-4.pdf.

Lin, Yutang 林语堂. trans. *Lin Yutang zhongying duizhao: Yangzhou shouma* 林语堂中英对照：扬州瘦马. Edited by Li, Ming 黎明. Taipei: Cheng Chung Book, 2009.

Liu, Hsieh (Liu Xie) 刘勰. *The Literary Mind and the Carving of Dragons*. Translated by Vincent Yu-chung Shih. Hong Kong: The Chinese University of Hong Kong Press, 2015.

McLuhan, Marshall. *Understanding Media: The Extensions of Man*. Cambridge, MA: The MIT Press, 1994.

Ouyang, Youquan 欧阳友权. "Wangluo wenxue yanjiu pingshu" 网络文学研究评述. *Theory and Criticism of Literature and Art* 文艺理论与批评 no. 5 (2003a): 107–114.

Ouyang, Youquan 欧阳友权. *Wangluo wenxue lungang* 网络文学论纲. Beijing: People's Literature Publishing House, 2003b.

Ouyang, Youquan 欧阳友权. *Wangluo wenxue gailun* 网络文学概论. Beijing: Peking University Press, 2008.

Ouyang, Youquan 欧阳友权. *Wangluo wenxue cidian* 网络文学词典. Beijing: World Publishing Corporation, 2012.

Ouyang, Youquan 欧阳友权 and Wu, Yingwen 吴英文. "Wangluo wenxue piping de jiazhi he juxian" 网络文学批评的价值和局限. *Exploration and Free Views* 探索与争鸣 no. 11 (2010): 63–66.

Rhew, Hyong. "'The Great Preface' to *Shijing*, or *The Book of Poetry*." *Reed College*. Accessed August 22, 2022. www.reed.edu/chinese/chin-hum/materials/shijing/gp.html.

Tan, Dejing 谭德晶. *Wangluo wenxue piping lun* 网络文学批评论. Beijing: CFLAC Publishing House, 2004.

Wang, Yuechuan 王岳川. *Houxiandai zhuyi wenhua yanjiu* 后现代主义文化研究. Beijing: Peking University Press, 1992.

Zhuang Zi 庄子. "Tian Zi-fang" 田子方. In *Zhuangzi* 庄子. Translated by James Legge. Chinese Text Project 中国哲学书电子化计划, accessed August 22, 2022. https://ctext.org/zhuangzi/tian-zi-fang.

5 Important Events in the History of Cyber Literary Criticism

While literary criticism is essentially about the expression of thoughts, it is the specific events that carry and disseminate these thoughts. A series of such events constitute the history of cyber literary criticism. If literary criticism is built on the interaction between literature and a series of other things—society, culture, art, and readers—then it is the crucial events of literary criticism that serve as the "nodes" to facilitate such interaction and to carry important ideas of literature. A review of some important events in the history of cyber literary criticism can thus help us see more clearly how critics on the Internet viewed contemporary literature and how they developed the concepts, criteria, and theories of cyber literary criticism step by step.

Important Events of Cyber Literary Criticism

Cyber literary criticism—both online and offline—has been quite active in China. Huang Mingfen made such a description on this point:

> Texts of online literary criticism mainly exist in BBSes, chat rooms, homepages, and blogs. Offline cyber literary criticism includes reviews and discussions in the form of articles, academic papers, edited collections, monographs, etc. In addition to the efforts of professional literary critics, researchers, and literature amateurs, the support and incentives from the government, the media, and the culture industry have played a vital role.[1]

These activities of literary criticism have left a positive impact on the writing of cyber literature and the conceptualization of cyber literature as a genre. Among them, a few hot issues attracted many people's attention.

Criticism of the "Mu Zimei Phenomenon"

The "Mu Zimei phenomenon" is a landmark event in the early years of cyber literary criticism in China. It is remarkable not only because people targeted Mu Zimei, a cyber writer, who posted journalistic descriptions of

DOI: 10.4324/9781003428480-7

her private life, but also because people's critical commentaries reflected their understanding of and judgment on cyberwriting as a highly free and personal activity. Particularly, it reflected people's views as to whether cyberwriting should be restricted by morals and ethics. Its impact thus went far beyond the domain of literature. Media outlets made a lot of commentaries on this issue, and scholars published many articles to discuss it as well.[2]

On June 19, 2003, a woman named Mu Zimei created an account on *Blog China* (Boke Zhongguo) and published her private diary there. In the diary, Mu Zimei described her sexual experiences with dozens of men and named the diary "The Last Love Letter" (Yiqingshu), which attracted much attention. As more people came to read the diary, Mu Zimei became popular. Netizens started a heated discussion over the diary. In August of the same year, Mu Zimei recounted in her diary many details about the "one-night stand" between her and a famous rock musician in Guangzhou and disclosed the musician's real name. This diary was quickly reposted on the forum *Xici hutong*, where the audiences were mostly media professionals. It caused a sensation and began to circulate widely in various forums. As a result, an even larger number of people read "Letter of Love." Mu Zimei is thus known as the first woman in Guangdong to "write about the female body." Compared with other female writers, such as Wei Hui, Mian Mian, and Jiu Dan, Mu Zimei was regarded as even bolder in her realistic depictions of sex.[3] In cyberspace, this was briefly referred to by some people as the "Mu Zimei phenomenon."

Few people criticized the "Mu Zimei phenomenon" from the perspective of literature. Most people who commented on it were concerned about netizens' ethics and rights in cyberspace. Yet still, as such commentaries were related to cyberwriting, they could be regarded as literary criticism in a broader sense. Some people said that Mu Zimei violated the rule about the prohibition on releasing pornographic materials online. As she disclosed on the Internet the names of people who had sex with her, she also infringed on people's right to privacy and reputation. Meanwhile, the sociologist Li Yinhe called her "Samantha of China" (Samantha is the beautiful mature woman who is unbridled in her pursuit of the joy of sex in the American TV series *Sex and the City*) and believed that the "Mu Zimei phenomenon" marked "a drastic change in people's mode of behavior in China's society, where traditional morals were deeply entrenched."[4] Li then called on people to be tolerant. Some netizens also pointed out that Mu Zimei should have the right to choose her way of life, and others had no right to denounce her.

Other netizens believed that Mu's lifestyle was pathetic and degenerate, and the publication of her diary would have a negative effect on young people. A mother of a 12-year-old child even said: "Is there no one who can stop this kind of shameless and immoral people?" More netizens believed that Mu Zimei's disclosure of her private life was meant to hype herself up and was more like a show for the public audience: Mu Zimei was a media professional, so she knew how to use the media to become famous.[5] According to them, Mu had three "weapons": she pretended to be an avant-garde; she flaunted her bad

150 *Part I*

petit-bourgeois taste; and she faked a sensitive personality. As a result, "these deceptive elements are mixed with the smell of cigarettes and gorgeous words, serving Mu's dazzling show."⁶ From the perspective of cyber literary criticism, we can argue that the significance of the "Mu Zimei phenomenon" lies in that, for the first time, it sharply raised the question of whether there should be a restriction on cyber (blog) writing, whether there should be an ethical line that cyberwriting does not cross, and whether cyberwriting should obey the moral order of our society. The raising of such questions can help people discern right from wrong and better understand a series of critical issues, including what cyber literature is, how to evaluate cyber literature, and how to construct a set of evaluation criteria that suit the characteristics of cyberculture as well as the way of literary production.

The Controversy over Zhao Lihua's Poems

In August 2006, a netizen set up a website under the name of the female poet Zhao Lihua and posted a few of Zhao's poems written before 2002, together with some poems falsely attributed to Zhao, such as "A Poem for Cucumbers" (Huanggua shi) and "Who Moved My Colorful Panties" (Shei dongle wode huaneiku). These poems were reposted in various other places, with descriptions of Zhao as "the judge for the Lu Xun Literature Prize" and "the national first-class female poet." Then, on September 13, 2006, a person with the username "Pear Flower Sect" (Lihua jiao) published a post in the entertainment and gossip section of *Skyline Community* entitled "Under the Wise Leadership of Zhao Lihua, the 'Pear Flower Sect' Is Grandly Established."⁷ In the following eight days, this account published a total of 28 posts related to Zhao Lihua and received countless replies. As a result, Zhao Lihua became popular on *Skyline Community* and was also known on other websites such as *Sina*. People began to be interested in her. In only three or four days, there came a grand spectacle: tens of thousands of people started to write in Zhao's style, or "pear flower style" (lihua ti), and created words of abuse, parody, and spoof. This, known as "the incident of Zhao Lihua's poetry" (Zhao Lihua shige shijian), was recognized by some media as the most significant event in poetry and popular culture after 1916, a year when Hu Shi and Guo Moruo launched the New Poetry Movement.

Zhao Lihua's poems are famous for their simplicity, plainness, and colloquialism. They are often not quite refined and poetic. The most widely circulated poem "I Came to Tennessee Alone" (Yigeren laidao Tiannaxi) is an example. The whole poem reads like a sentence broken into four lines: "There is no doubt/ The pie I made/ is the best/ in the world." As a sentence is split into a few lines, it becomes a poem. This triggered an upsurge in netizens' imitations of this style of writing. While such imitations were meant to be expressions of sarcasm and contempt, they helped "pear flower style" to become even more popular. Zhao Lihua, a "famous female poet" who was once the judge for Lu

Xun Literature Prize and received some literary awards, became famous overnight on the Internet and was referred to as "Sister Hibiscus in the field of poetry writing" (Shitan Furong jiejie).[8]

Mu Ye, a poet, commented on this incident: "It was not a bad thing. On the one hand, the public expressed their dissatisfaction, which is understandable; on the other hand, it also raised a serious question for poets to think about: what should the relationship between poetry and the public be like?"[9] Zhao Lihua responded in a blog post to this incident:

> Spoofing is a result of the development of the ideology of our society. It is a normal phenomenon in this era. The Internet happens to be able to provide free platforms for the rapid spread of this kind of spoofing. Whether it is the movie *The Promise* (Wuji), or *The Banquet* (Yeyan), or some oil paintings, or my poems, it is quite normal for works of art to be spoofed. The act of spoofing shows that there is not only one way to create an artwork. While your work is serious, I can create another version of it to ridicule yours; while your work is sublime, I can make a version that is based on it but is vulgar; while your work is grave, mine can be light-hearted... All these are understandable because we have quickly entered an era of deconstruction.[10]

Then, Zhao claimed: "If we ignore the damage to my personal dignity and reputation, we can regard this incident as an opportunity for modern Chinese poetry, which used to be a thing only for a small group of people, to receive more public attention."

In my opinion, the incident of Zhao Lihua's poetry is significant in the history of cyber literary criticism for two reasons.

First, the Internet is a space where people can freely express their thoughts; there is enough democracy and equality for people to discuss works of art. Acts of spoofing, based on the idea that ordinary people's voices should be heard and what is deemed sacred can be blasphemed, are characterized by people's indifference to the authoritative, subversion to the sublime, and appreciation of artworks without worshipping the artists. It shows that writing literary criticism is not a privilege for a few people but a right for every netizen to enjoy. In this sense, while there are various critical voices, no one is supposed to dominate over others. This is a major characteristic of cyber literary criticism.

Second, the criteria for evaluating cyber literature have begun to change. Cyber literary criticism is becoming the most dynamic and interactive way of literary criticism. Readers can speak straightforwardly about their views of literary texts, either positive or negative. They can be very critical without reservation. This well serves the function and purpose of literary criticism. As evaluation criteria are now pluralistic and democratic, people can better distinguish and understand different texts online, either as literature, quasi-literature, or non-literature.

The Debate between Han Han and Bai Ye

Han Han and Bai Ye, writers who belong to two different generations, had a dispute on the Internet. On February 24, 2006, Bai Ye posted an article, "The Current Status and Future of the Post-80s Generation" (Baling hou de xianzhuang yu weilai), in his blog. He believed that the "post-80s generation" writers could only be regarded as "literature amateurs" at best and that they had not yet entered the "literary world" because they seldom published their creative works in literary journals. As soon as the article came out, it immediately caused a strong reaction from the "post-80s generation" writer Han Han. He wrote a blog post entitled "The Literary World Is No More than a Fart, so No One Should Pose as More Important than Others" (Wentan shige pi, shui doubie zhuangbi) to vehemently criticize the current "literary world" and journals for their problems. This article was reposted on many websites and received much public attention.

Subsequently, Bai Ye published the article "My Statement: Responding to Han Han" (Wode shengming, huiying Han Han) in his blog to express his discontent, and Han Han immediately published "Some People Say Unpleasant Words to Tell the Truth, While Some Use Refined Words Only to Show How Unpleasant They Are" (Youxieren huacaolibucao, youxieren huabucao rencao) and "Farewell to the Old and Welcome the New" (Cijiu yingxin) to criticize Bai Ye further. The debate between the two attracted the attention of many scholars and fans and caused a lot of discussions. Bai Ye shut down his blog to avoid being attacked by a large number of Han Han's fans. Later, celebrities, such as Xie Xizhang, Lu Tianming, Lu Chuan, and Gao Xiaosong, joined the battle one after another. The debate escalated and became more intense, and there was even a threat to settle the debate in a law court. This controversy ended, however, as the two parties were reconciled. In such a highly entertaining way, this academically significant event faded out of people's sight.

Initially, it was just an academic debate about literature, the literary world, and literary journals. In the beginning, both sides put forward some original ideas. Unfortunately, as Han Han was still young, he was aggressive and used some foul language. As a result, the later debate deviated from its original academic topic and focused on whether Han Han used offensive words to attack Bai Ye personally. Ouyang Wenfeng commented on this event as such:

> This debate reflects how emerging writers born in the 80s and critics of the older generation had starkly different ways of thinking. It shows that young writers had no intention to commit themselves to literature as traditionally intellectuals had done and that they tried to deconstruct the meaning of words and treat literature as a game... The development of culture requires a healthy cultural ecology. An important factor in this ecology is the creation of an equal and healthy environment for discussion and contention. Uncontrolled and illogical verbal violence ultimately leads to irrationality

and disorder in cyberspace. This will also tarnish the public image of forums and blogs that are becoming public communication platforms and will eventually make people lose their hard-won right to speak.[11]

I would argue that the value of this debate lies not in itself as a hot issue on the Internet but in that it tells people a fundamental truth: people's freedom in cyberspace is a double-edged sword; if abused, it will not serve literary criticism but cause damage to it. This is a lesson about the stances we should take on cyber literature and the methods we should adopt for the writing of criticism.

The Debate over Cyber Literature in 2003

As cyber literature is a new thing, it is quite normal for people to have different opinions on the conceptualization and evaluation of it. However, fierce debates over how to conceptualize and evaluate cyber literature are still rare. The earliest debate of this kind happened in 2003 and touched upon some fundamental issues. Bai Ye's article, "A Review of the Debate Over Cyber Literature" (Zongshu: wangluo wenxue lunzheng), published in *People's Daily* (overseas edition) on February 9, 2014, introduced this event.

The debate started with my [Ouyang Youquan's] article published in *China Reading Weekly* (Zhonghua dushu bao) on February 19, 2003, entitled "Cyber Literature: Works of Technology or Works of Art?"[12] This article argues that there are more technological factors in cyber literature than in any other kind of literature in history. As a result, cyber literature may stress the importance of such technological factors and lose its literariness. In other words, it may deviate from the aesthetic principles that any literature should observe; it may also tolerate, or even encourage, the abuse of technologism and instrumental rationality, thus turning literature into a thing relying on technology rather than on artistic beauty. The specific manifestations of such a problem in cyber literature are as follows: 1. Serious aesthetic motivation gives way to an impulse to play with words merely as a game. 2. The traditional way of artistic creation yields to brilliant designs relying on the use of technology. 3. Value rationality is replaced by instrumental rationality. I thus wrote in the article:

> While studying cyber literature, we still need to firmly hold the position to treasure humanism and aesthetics. We shall not let technologism kill off our humanistic spirits and aesthetic principles. We shall not allow the overdose of instrumental rationality to smother our value rationality. We shall not permit technology to replace art and take over aesthetics.[13]

After this, Zhang Hui, a scholar, published an article entitled "Cyber Literature Is Not a Literary Game" in *China Reading Weekly*, which pointedly refuted my viewpoint.[14] First, he was "surprised [by Ouyang Youquan's idea] and felt that this argument was misleading." He believed that I, the author, "with an entrenched belief in literary tradition, had a strong bias against cyber literature …[and] did not seek truth from facts in his research." He then argued:

> While criticizing them [cyber writers] as "a marginal group in literary creation, or amateur writers," Professor Ouyang placed heavy demands on them by asking them to observe the principles of literary and artistic creation, only to embarrass them in the end. Well, it should be all right if they could objectively abide by such principles, but why criticize them for "not knowing the principles of literature and art"?

Then, Zhang Hui criticized: "the author has no interest in cyber literature at all, and I am sure that he has not read many works of cyber literature." He believed that although cyber literature lacked refinement and perfection, it was writers' sincere and free expression of themselves, demonstrating the idea "I write down what I truly want to say," thus not being hollow words with no thoughts: it was because of this that cyber literature was full of vitality.

After the publication of Zhang Hui's article, many scholars participated in the discussion. Among them, He Zhijun criticized Zhang Hui's view and supported my idea.[15] He believed that many works of cyber literature flaunted people's ways of living and thinking, their aesthetic tastes, and fashions in a society dominated by a culture of consumerism. The world depicted by cyber literature was full of desires, selfishness, vanity, and playacting: these elements were mass-produced and well packaged for mass consumption. Writers and readers of cyber literature were mostly white-collar workers or would-be white-collar workers living in cities. Cyber literature thus reflected and catered to these people's petit-bourgeois tastes and sentiments. It could not detach itself from the control of the largely homogenous consumer culture.

In an article, Zhu Chaohui argued that most people engaged in cyberwriting had their aesthetic ideals and dreamed of creating wonderful literary works. Still, a few people viewed cyberwriting just as a game and simply wrote to vent their negative emotions.[16] According to Zhu, we should not generalize about this situation without giving it adequate analysis. If we want to determine whether technology now dominates literature and art, we need to make clear whether the people who use technology to engage in creative activities can truly maintain and perfect the essence of art—aesthetics. While cyber literature is still in its early stages, it provides a valuable opportunity for us to deeply question instrumental rationality and reflect on the value and significance of our life in society.

Later, I published an article in response to Zhang Hui's criticism. The article said that our disagreement mainly lied in our different answers to the following questions: how should we evaluate cyber literature in the current condition? If it has a "soft underbelly," where is it? I held that cyber literature was currently not good enough for the following reason: cyber literature depended heavily on digital technology and served as the "new discourse of the masses," which was carnivalesque in nature, so it did not have enough aesthetic value; in other words, as cyber literature allowed technology to dominate and transform art, it became a means of entertainment for mass consumption and was devoid of artistic and aesthetic value. At the end of my article, I explained:

> The purpose of my humble article, which discusses how current cyber literature stresses the technological to obscure the artistic and how it becomes too playful and thus deviates from humanistic values, is to "expose the sickness and suffering so as to draw attention to it, in the hope that a cure might thereby be sought."[17] Thus, Mr. Zhang Hui did not need to "feel very surprised" and become so angry.[18]

The significance of this debate lies in that it emphatically raised a series of important questions, including how we should view cyber literature, how we should evaluate it, and how we should understand the relationship between cyber technology and the aesthetic appreciation of literature. This clash of starkly different opinions can be seen as an activity of cyber literary criticism, as it gave an in-depth scholarly discussion and helped clarify some critical notions of cyber literature.

Rankings and Other Activities for the Evaluation and Promotion of Cyber Literary Works

Cyber literature, as an emerging form of folk culture, needs a system of evaluation criteria. Efforts are also required to canonize the best works of this kind. This is not only for cyber literature to be recognized and valued by our society but also for the improvement of its quality. In an atmosphere promoting high-quality works, cyber writers will work to gain their confidence in literary creation and develop an awareness of the importance of artistic value. In recent years, novel rankings and other activities promoting cyber literature worked toward this goal. In such evaluative activities, a set of criteria were established and put into use. There are four major evaluative activities in the history of cyber literature, as follows.

The "Review of Cyber Literature in the Past Ten Years" (Wangluo Wenxue Shinian Pandian)

In October 2008, under the guidance of China Writers Association, the activity was jointly hosted by *17K Novels* (17K xiaoshuo wang)—a website run by *Chinese All Digital Publishing Group* (Zhongwen zaixian)—and the journal *Selected Novels* (Changpian xiaoshuo xuankan). It was the first time that scholars and organizations of mainstream literature made efforts to review and evaluate works of cyber literature. More than 20 literary journals, including *People's Literature* (Renmin wenxue) and *Chinese Writers* (Zhongguo zuojia), and more than 20 literary websites, including *Starting Points Chinese Net* (Qidian zhongwen wang) and *Book Union for Swordsmen's Legends* (Huanjian shumeng), participated in this activity. On June 25, 2009, after seven months of selection, recommendation, and online voting, more than 50 critics and senior editors selected the "top ten excellent works" from more than 1,700 works recommended by netizens. Netizens also voted their favorites for the list of "top ten popular works."

The "top ten excellent works" include: *There We Were* (Cijian de shaonian), *Chengdu, Please Forget Me Tonight* (Chengdu, jinye qing jiangwo yiwang), *A New History of the Song Dynasty* (Xin Song), *An Attempt to Overthrow the Great Ming* (Qie Ming), *Wei Shuaiwang's Adventures* (Wei Shuaiwang de jianghu), *Romance in the World of Mortals* (Chenyuan), *Homeland* (Jiayuan), *Zichuan* (Zichuan), *Homeless* (Wujia), and *Facial Makeups* (Lianpu). The "top ten popular works" include: *Romance in the World of Mortals, Zichuan, Wei Shuaiwang's Adventures, Blasphemy* (Xiedu), *The Legend of the Monster* (Dushi yao qitan), *Returning to the Ming Dynasty as the Prince* (Huidao Mingchao dang wangye), *Homeland, An Ode to Witchcraft* (Wusong), *The Story of Wukong* (Wukong zhuan), and *It's Lonely at the Top* (Gaoshou jimo).

The Novel Rankings by China Writers Association

In 2015, the quarterly and annual lists of the "Chinese Web Novel Rankings" (Zhongguo wangluo xiaoshuo paihangbang) were released, which marked the fact that cyber literature had been recognized, paid attention to, and valued by mainstream society. The rankings were based on a combination of online voting and offline review. Experts and scholars from the industry of cyber literature, universities, and China Writers Association were invited to work together as a group. They selected the best cyber literary works, including "new books" and "excellent books," and recommended them to the public. They made two ranking lists—the quarterly list and the annual list. The quarterly list included 30 "new books" and 30 "excellent books"; the annual list included 10 "new books" and 10 "excellent books": "new books" were books published in the year 2015, and "excellent books" were those finished and published within the past three years. Here we have the ranking lists of "excellent books" and "new books": the order of the books is based on the number of votes they received; if some books received the same number of votes, the order is then determined by their publication date (see Tables 5.1 and 5.2).[19]

The "Promotion and Recommendation of Excellent Creative Cyberwritings in 2015"
(Erlingyiwu Nian Youxiu Wangluo Wenxue Yuanchuang Zuopin Tuijie Huodong)

This activity was organized by the State Administration of Press, Publication, Radio, Film and Television (SAPPRFT) in October 2015. SAPPRFT gathered a team of authoritative critics, established a set of criteria, and worked out a clear mechanism for the selection and examination of literary works, so as to find and recommend to the public some excellent cyber literary works that embody "the pursuit of truth, goodness, and beauty, the spread of positive

Table 5.1 The Ranking List of China's Excellent Web Novels in 2015

No.	Titles	Authors	Recommenders
1	Throne of Magical Arcana (Aoshu shenzuo)	Cuttlefish That Loves Diving (Ai qianshui de wuzei)	Starting Points Chinese Net (Qidian zhongwen wang)
2	Return to the Past as a Cat (Huidao guoqu biancheng mao)	Clichéd Lyrics and Lazy Tunes (Chenci landiao)	Starting Points Chinese Net
3	The Woman Warrior, Mulan, Has No Brothers (Mulan wu zhangxiong)	Mr. Pray (Qidao jun)	Jinjiang Literature City (Jinjiang wenxuecheng)
4	An Ordinary Man's Surprising Success (Pifu de nixi)	Commander of the Valiant Cavalry (Xiaoji xiao)	Chinese All Digital Publishing Group (Zhongwen zaixian)
5	Once Upon a Time in Lingjian Mountain (Congqian youzuo Lingjian shan)	His Majesty the King (Guowang bixia)	Create the World Chinese Net (Chuangshi Zhongwen wang)
6	To Where the Beacon-fire and Its Smoke Is No Longer Seen (Fengyan jinchu)	Drinker (Jiutu)	Chinese All Digital Publishing Group
7	Phenix to the End of the Sky (Feng qing tianlan)	The Whole World Returns to Its Origin (Tianxia guiyuan)	Xiaoxiang Library (Xiaoxiang shuyuan)
8	A Brick in the Tang Dynasty (Tang zhuan)	Jie Yu 2	Starting Points Chinese Net
9	Ziyang	Fly Over Nine Autumn Seasons with Wind (Fengyu jiuqiu)	Chinese All Digital Publishing Group
10	A Household Where Woman is the Head (Nühu)	I Want to Eat Meat (Woxiang chirou)	Jinjiang Literature City

values, and the organic unity of intellectual, artistic, and aesthetic qualities." After strict evaluation, repeated discussion, and careful selection, from 323 works recommended by 13 provinces, municipalities, and autonomous regions, 21 works entered the final list and were officially recommended to the public.

SAPPRFT put forward some general requirements for this evaluative and promotional activity. Chen Qirong, director of the judging panel and vice chairman of China Writers Association, explained the requirements as follows: first, this should be a high-level cultural activity directly sponsored by the country; second, the governmental organization should hold a set of positive values and provide cultural guidance for the public; third, the selected

158 Part I

Table 5.2 The Ranking List of China's New Web Novels in 2015

No.	Titles	Authors	Recommenders
1	A Story of War in the Primitive Society (Yuanshi zhanji)	Clichéd Lyrics and Lazy Tunes	Starting Points Chinese Net
2	To Kill for Revenge (Zhu sha)	Xixing	Starting Points Chinese Net for Girls (Qidian nüsheng wang)
3	Forty Thousand Years of Taoist Cultivation (Xiuzhen siwannian)	"Crouching Bull," a Taoist Spiritual Master (Woniu zhenren)	Starting Points Chinese Net
4	Time Traveler (Chuanyue zhe)	Commander of the Valiant Cavalry	Chinese All Digital Publishing Group
5	The Star-shatters (Suixing wuyu)	Luo Sen	Chinese All Digital Publishing Group
6	As a Girl Cook, You Have to Be Strong (Chuniang dang ziqiang)	Thrive and Flourish (Xinxinxiangrong)	Jinjiang Literature City (Jinjiang wenxuecheng)
7	A Story of Witch Gods (Wu shen ji)	Blood Red (Xuehong)	Starting Points Chinese Net
8	Everlasting Immortal Firmament (Wanggu xianqiong)	Watching Chess Games (Guanqi)	Chinese All Digital Publishing Group
9	He Knows Where the Wind Blows From (Ta zhidao feng cong nage fangxiang lai)	Jiuyuexi	Jinjiang Literature City
10	The Gate to the End of the World (Mieshi zhimen)	Dark Lychee (Hei'an lizhi)	Starting Points Chinese Net

works should be those aesthetically appreciated by general readers; fourth, the selected works should exhibit some characteristics of cyber literature and be read widely online. Moreover, Chen also proposed some specific criteria for evaluating works, which concerned various aspects of literature, including the subject, the ideological and intellectual tendency, the aesthetic orientation, and the use of language.

There are other events for selecting and promoting works launched by literary societies and by the media. In recent years, two events organized by literary societies received much public attention. The first is the "Internet Literature Biennial Award" (Wangluo wenxue shuangnianjiang), co-hosted by the Cyber Writers Association in Zhejiang Province, the Federation of Literary and Art Circles in Ningbo City, and the Publicity Department of the CPC Committee in Cixi City. It was first launched in 2015, and ten web novels won gold, silver, and bronze awards.[20] The second is the "Recommendation Lists for

Web Literature in 2015" (Erlingyiwu niandu wangluo wenxue niandu zuopin tuijianbang), hosted by the Forum for Cyber Literary Research (Wangluo wenxue yanjiu luntan) at Peking University. In this event, ten "novels for male readers" and ten "novels for female readers" were recommended.[21]

The ranking lists made by the media generally put more emphasis on readers' responses, especially the "fandom" of works. Here we have two representative cases.[22] The first is the annual ranking list of web novels attached to the "Huadi Literary Awards" sponsored by *Yangcheng Evening News* (Yangcheng wanbao). The shortlist was released on March 27, 2016, with ten web novels. The second case is the "Ranking Lists of the Most Successful Creative Writings in China" (Zhongguo yuanchuang wenxue fengyunbang), sponsored by Forbes and first released in 2015, with ten works for young male readers and ten for young female readers: Er Gen's *I Desire to Rise to the Top of the World* (Woyu fengtian) and Su Xiaonuan's *The Demonic King Who Chases His Wife* (Xiewang zhuiqi) were, respectively, on top of the two lists. Except for this, Forbes also sponsored some other awards, including those for "Most Popular Writers," "Popular New Writers," "Original Works that Had Most Successful Adaptations," and "Works with the Most Potential for Adaptation," all for the year 2015. Apart from this, there are annual ranking lists of cyber literary works in "The Report on China's Cyber Literature" (Zhongguo wangluo wenxue baogao), released by Sootoo Research Institute (Sutu yanjiuyuan), and "The Report on the Industry of Cyber Literature in China" (Zhongguo wangluo wenxue hangye yanjiu baogao), released by iResearch.

Seminars and Discussions on Cyber Literature

We need to pay attention to seminars and discussions on cyber literature, as they are the most direct practice of literary criticism. There are many of them, among which the most representative are seminars organized by China Writers Association, by the Writers Associations of various provinces and cities, and by some related academic societies. Here are a few examples:

(1) On June 28, 2012, China Writers Association held the first seminar on cyber literature in Beijing. The seminar focused on five web novels, namely *Smoke Signals of War Everywhere* (Biandi langyan), *Empress Fuyao* (Fuyao huanghou), *Chaos in the Sui Dynasty* (Sui luan, originally entitled *Homeland*, or Jiayuan), *A New History of the Song Dynasty* (Xin Song), and *Ning Mu Yan*.[23] During the seminar, two critics commented on each novel, and writers talked about their experiences and feelings about writing. Critics not only analyzed the strengths and characteristics of these works but also directly pointed out the shortcomings and places where improvements were needed. They also expressed their hope for the authors' future literary creations.

(2) On May 18, 2013, China Writers Association and Guangdong Provincial Writers Association jointly hosted the Guangdong Cyber Literature

Seminar (Guangdong wangluo wenxue yantaohui) in Beijing. Twelve critics, including Bai Ye, Ouyang Youquan, Wang Xiang, Ma Ji, Chen Dingjia, Yang Zao, Yue Wen, Yu Aicheng, Zhuang Yong, Wu Changqing, Suo Luo, and Liu Ying, discussed six cyber literary works, including *A Story Recorded in The Classic of Mountains and Seas* (*Shanhaijing mima*), *Stories of the Spring and Autumn Period* (Shuo *Chunqiu*), *To Kill a Dream* (Shameng), *She Turns Out to Be a Beautiful Fox* (Yuanlai shi meihu a), *Poisonous Rouge* (Du yanzhi), and *A Male Phoenix Seeks His Mate* (Fengqiuhuang).[24] During the seminar, critics discussed these works' characteristics, pointed out their merits and shortcomings, and gave pertinent suggestions to writers.

(3) On July 5, 2013, the Seminar on the Current Condition and the Future of Literature in Popular Genres (Leixing wenxue de xianzhuang yu qianjing yantaohui) was held in Beijing.[25] Nearly 30 critics and scholars participated in the seminar. They discussed the rise, origin, and development of cyber literature in popular genres and analyzed the underlying reasons. They also discussed a series of other issues, such as the characteristics of popular genres, the way of conducting in-depth research on popular genres, and some problems in writing literature in popular genres. They also suggested how cyber literature in popular genres should be guided to serve mainstream social values.

(4) On July 11 and 12, 2014, the National Seminar on Theories of Cyber Literature (Quanguo wangluo wenxue lilun yantaohui) was held. It was jointly organized by China Writers Association, *People's Daily*, and *Guangming Daily*. More than 70 officials and scholars from various organizations participated in the seminar and clearly articulated the need to establish a system of theories for evaluating and interpreting cyber literature. As participants raised many new and insightful ideas, this seminar is quite significant in the history of China's cyber literature.[26]

(5) On September 25, 2015, the First China's Cyber Literature Forum (Zhongguo wangluo wenxue luntan) was launched in Shanghai. The forum was co-hosted by China Writers Association and regional Writers Associations in Shanghai, Guangdong, Zhejiang, and Jiangsu.[27] These regions are not only where the earliest cyber writers emerged but also have the largest number of cyber writers and literary websites today. Nearly 100 cyber writers, critics, and scholars joined the forum to discuss how China's cyber literature should be further developed. The forum consists of three subforums, respectively, for the exchange of work experience between regional Writers Associations, for the theoretical discussion on cyber literature, and for the critical review of cyber literary works. In the third subforum, critics such as He Xiangyang, Ouyang Youquan, Wang Xiang, Zhou Zhixiong, Suo Luo, Wu Changqing, Wulan Qimuge, Xiang Jing, and An Yi discussed a series of works, including *Giving Birth to a Baby While Being Poor* (Luosheng), *Mecha Storm* (Jidong fengbao), *The*

Toughest Soldier in Special Forces (Zuiqiang tezhongbing), *The Legend of Mi Yue* (Mi Yue zhuan), and *The Order of Evil* (Emo faze).
(6) From September 25 to 27, 2016, the Second China's Cyber Literature Forum was held in Guangdong. The heads of more than 50 literary websites, such as *Starting Points Chinese Net*, *Jinjiang Literature City*, and *Under the Banyan Tree* (Rongshuxia), many famous Internet writers, such as "The Third Young Master of the Tang Sect" (Tangjia sanshao), "Blood Red" (Xuehong), "Wolf in a Jungle" (Conglinlang), "Monster Night" (Yaoye), "Dreaming into Prehistory" (Mengru honghuang), and a group of critics, gathered in Nanhai District, Foshan City. Officials from the Publicity Department of the Central Committee of the Party, the National Radio and Television Administration, and China Writers Association made their speeches. The forum, with more than 200 participants, consisted of three subforums, respectively, on "guidance and management of cyber literature," "news of the industry," and "theory and criticism." In the forum, 13 famous literary critics were hired as consultants for the academic journal *Internet Literature Review* (Wangluo wenxue pinglun). The Base for Cyber Literary Creation in Guangdong Province (Guangdong wangluo wenxue chuangzuo jidi) was established to develop an industrial chain that connected cyber literary creation with television/film adaptation and production. Fourteen literary websites signed the agreement to cooperate and build up China's first exhibition platform for cyber literature.

In addition to the hot issues reviewed above, there are some other important events in the history of cyber literary criticism. Here are a few examples. 1. *The First Intimate Contact* (Diyici de qinmi jiechu) was hotly discussed after its publication. 2. The "Review of Cyber Literature in the Past Ten Years" caused a rising tide of literary criticism by ordinary readers. 3. The first short story to be read on cellphones, *Outside the City* (Chengwai), was published. 4. Some web novels were considered for the Mao Dun Literature Prize, which became controversial. 5. Some cyber writers filed lawsuits to protect their rights. These incidents are also historically important and deserve our attention.

Scholars' Critical Thoughts on Cyber Literary Criticism

While cyber literary criticism is still in its early stage, there have already been many important events related to it. This is partly because of cyber literature's unique characteristics and partly because of the cultural ecology in this particular age. The development of digital media technology makes literary criticism distinctively "cyber" and provides it with new approaches and forms.

The Changes in the Conceptualization of Literature

Cyber literature not only influences and changes the media platforms but also fundamentally reshapes the logic, concept, and value of literature. Cyber literary criticism, both as theoretical discussion and literary practice, serves to express such historical changes. In cyber literary criticism, we can see how such changes are described and studied.

First, cyber literary criticism gives new answers to the question, "what is literature?" Scholars still do not have a consensus on this issue and often debate with each other, and writers usually do not even pay attention to it. Nevertheless, in both China and the West, scholars did give us various definitions and descriptions of literature, such as "poetry is where intent goes" (shi yan zhi), "poetry is an expression of emotions" (shi yuan qing), "the description of nature can make readers spiritually touched and morally educated" (chang shen bi de), "literature should convey the truth" (wen yi zai dao), "literature should teach readers while entertaining them" (yu jiao yu le), "literature should reflect people's life in their society" (shehui shenghuo de fanying), and "literature should strike a balance between aesthetics and ideology" (shenmei yishi xingtai).

It should be said that literature plays an important role and shoulders a moral responsibility in our society and culture. This is an honor to literature. However, in the era of new media, with the development of cyber literature, we are faced with a series of questions. Has our conceptualization of literature changed? If yes, what kind of changes are there? Should we totally abandon our traditional ideas of literature? These questions are thus discussed and re-examined by literary scholars.

For example, I once studied the difference between cyber literature and traditional literature, focusing on the fact that they depend on different media platforms. Then, I found that what makes cyber literature essentially different from conventional literature is that it embodies a spirit of freedom.[28] Cyber literature is essentially a free representation of a virtual world. The Internet, as a space where people can enjoy freedom and equality and where resources are shared across different terminals, fully liberates artistic creation so that artists can enjoy a higher degree of freedom as they build up a spiritual homeland for us. However, it should be noted that the freedom of art in digital media is not simply equivalent to the freedom of art in the ontological sense. The latter aims to develop a correct knowledge of history and reality: through aesthetic appreciation of reality, the artist has the freedom to represent the laws of our objective world. The freedom of art in digital media, however, is based on the nature of the *virtual world*: it is about free expression *in* cyberspace rather than a free representation *of* the laws of our objective world. Thus, the freedom of art in digital media has its unique connotation and does not mean a reaffirmation of the freedom of art in the ontological sense.[29]

Wang Yichuan, a scholar, once gave his answer to the question, "what is essential to cyber literature?" He said:

> Literature in the Internet age may bring new and revolutionary changes to our conceptualization of literature. For example, as already mentioned, cyber literature can break the author's hegemony and allow readers to enjoy

a higher degree of freedom. It emphasizes people's quotidian experience more than their spiritual conditions. It provides a massive number of texts and shares them with readers. These changes are apparent to us. But the problem is that these so-called "revolutionary" changes happen merely at the level of media technology, not at the level of the meaning of literature itself.[30]

According to Wang, it is the writer's experience, imagination, talent, and what is based on all of these—creativity—that are the quintessential factors that make cyber literature "literary."

Zhang Kangkang, a writer, discussed the question "what is literature?" based on dialectics between what is changed and what is unchanged as literature goes online:

> Cyber literature can bring changes as it uses new media and novel means of communication. It can change readers' reading habits, writers' perspectives, mentalities, and ways of thinking and writing. But to what extent can cyber literature change literature itself—the components of literature, such as emotion, imagination, moral sense, and language?[31]

Second, cyber literary criticism gives new answers to the question, "what does a writer write about?" Traditionally, we believe that literature is a representation of human nature, as well as people's experiences, emotions, and dreams in particular historical periods, based on our ideas of literature, such as "literature is about humanity" and "literature reflects people's lives in society." This is the ontological basis on which we establish our theories of literature. Yet, in reality, cyber literature, with its variety of possibilities, makes this idea not to be taken for granted. Huang Mingfen discussed this issue:

> Traditionally, scholars studying theories of literature view literature as written by people, about people, and for people. Although acknowledging the validity of this idea in a certain historical period, the theory of cyber literature and art does not take it for granted. Instead, we argue that we must widen our scope and study the activities of literary creation done by people equipped with computers and by artificial intelligence. Currently, there are at least the following questions that have been brought up: as computers are now used as a tool for literary creation, does this have any impact on people's way of thinking and on writers' and critics' way of creating and reviewing literary works? How shall we evaluate "works" that are generated, either randomly or purposefully, by computer programs or robots? How shall we view works that depict the psychological movements of robots (such as Isaac Asimov's *I, Robot*)? How shall we critically think about the relationship between humans and other species from the perspective of ecological ethics? How shall we understand the aesthetic experiences in human psychology, explore the mysteries of inspiration and epiphany in people's minds, and teach artificial intelligence about all this? How shall we use

artificial intelligence to develop a system that can help us evaluate works of art and literature?[32]

As artificial intelligence can create literary works, the works it produces must be different from works of traditional literature. In an article, I pointed out that the narratives written by ordinary people in the digital era manifest a subtle change in our conceptualization of literature:

> In terms of the content, literary works in digital media are mostly representations of young urbanites' new life in the digital era, including their fashions, desires for consumption, and emotional choices. Yet, such things, though depicted in digital media works, can also be represented in traditional literature and art.[33]

My article then proceeded to argue that the true uniqueness of cyber literature lies in two things:

First, cyber literature is particularly good at representing people's lives in virtual reality. It is written by netizens, about netizens, and for netizens. They are composed of various texts on websites and forums in the form of a series of web pages and posts dedicated to particular topics. Without Internet media, they would not exist at all.

If works such as *Chengdu, Please Forget Me Tonight* (Chengdu, jinye qing jiangwo yiwang) and *To the Left is Heaven, to the Right is Shenzhen* (Tiantang xiangzuo, Shenzhen xiangyou) can be published either on the Internet or in the form of printed books, then some other works, such as *Roses Shiver in the Wind* (Meigui zai fengzhong chandou), *My Love Slowly Drifts Across Your Web* (Wode'ai manman piaoguo nidewang), *I Must Find You* (Wo yiding yao zhaodao ni), and *The First Intimate Contact* (Diyici de qinmi jiechu), have to be published on the Internet: as works representing people's experience in cyberspace, they have to be read online by a large number of netizens so that they can sate netizens' appetite and resonate with them. This is further supported by the fact that currently, the most popular genres of cyber literature, such as "mystery and fantasy novels" (xuanhuan), "magic and fantasy novels" (mohuan), "travel-back-into-history novels" (chuanyue), and "novels of alternate history" (jiakong), are all based on fantasy. In this sense, cyber literature is particularly good at representing virtual reality.

Second, cyber literature, as an art of narration, reflects the perspectives and mentalities of ordinary people. As the virtual space constructed by digital technology is open to the public, non-professional writers, including those who are at the bottom of our society, can have an opportunity to realize their dreams of artistic creation and self-expression. Ordinary people's works can be shared across digital platforms.

Cyber literary criticism also changes people's ideas about "how to write literature." Chinese scholars discussed this question at two different levels. Some of them focused on the form of literature and argued that cyber literature is unique in the following ways: it replaces pens with computers so that a writer does not write on paper but on a screen; it breaks the limitation of language and is transformed from an art of language into an art of digital symbols, as it conveniently uses multiple media, such as videos and sounds, to help the expression of meanings and emotions; it is dependent no longer on the physical but on the digital, which means that now words are based on bytes in a virtual space and do not have to be printed on physical books. Moreover, in cyber literature, genres become more diversified and blurred, so we see the merge between the fictional and the journalistic and between the literary and the non-literary. Now cyberwriting takes on various new forms: we have texts in the form of "chats" (liaotian ti), "threads of posts" (jielong ti), "text messages" (duanxin ti), "hyperlinks" (lianjie ti), "pastiche" (pintie ti), "role-play dialogues" (banyan ti), and "nonsensical words" (feihua ti). This turns cyberwriting into an experiment on narrative techniques.[34]

Meanwhile, some other scholars discussed the values and meanings in literary texts. For example, Jing Wendong argued in his article as follows:

> The Internet provides an open space that allows literary creation to completely depart from its tradition. It breaks the boundary of time and space in an incredible way. In such a virtual space, at least theoretically speaking, an infinitely large number of writers can simultaneously participate in the writing of a single work. Every writer can, to a certain degree, alter, determine, and readjust the direction in which the story progresses.[35]

Song Hui and Lai Daren regarded cyberwriting as an embodiment of the "McDonaldization" and "Internetization" of literature. They pointed out:

> As the content in the modern media can be easily duplicated, the mass production of literary works becomes technically possible. As the media can raise controversial questions to be widely discussed, it is significantly powerful in the hyping up of certain topics, the packaging and popularizing of writers, and the promotion of literary works. It is the mass media that has turned reading into a fashionable act and brought people into popular culture—a domain created and manipulated by the mass media. As the mass media is so powerful, popular culture can spread widely. As a result, people's personal feelings about art and literature are dulled, and people's thoughts tend to become uniform. A large batch of readers, who have the same taste and are satisfied with standardized cultural commodities as a result of the "McDonaldization" of literature, are thus produced.[36]

In an article, I proposed that cyberwriting is an act of "spreading personal feelings with a computer instead of a pen":

> Cyberwriting, based on the use of digital media, is about the input of codes using computer programs. If literary creation in the traditional sense is

to physically write down words on paper, then cyberwriting is more like a dance of the writer's fingers on a keyboard. Now, artistic creation has become a mechanical, automatic, and unrestrained action of typing and copying. With the means of production reconstituted by digital technology, literature and art in new media are destined to be digitalized.[37]

As I argued, what is significant here is the replacement of a pen with a computer and the use of mechanical reproduction. This can subvert the authoritativeness of literary text in its physical form. As a writer "types" rather than "writes," the writer thinks in "words" rather than "characters" and no longer has the real experience of using a pen to physically create vivid language. The writer thus cannot feel the pleasure of writing Chinese that is calligraphically beautiful. We can even argue that the tradition is lost in this process, as the writer now no longer feels the moral obligation that "literature should be historically significant" and no longer has a mentality to seriously and persistently perfect the work, which writers used to have, back in the days before cyber literature. The sense of history one can feel as old pages turn yellow is also no longer felt. Thus, I argued:

> Now what writers feel is just a pleasure of expressing their personal feelings. Cyberwriting often depicts mundane affairs from ordinary people's perspectives. In this way, writers express the banality of their life with a sense of self-pity. The vulgar now coexists with the elegant; the ordinary is together with the extraordinary; the sacred and the sublime are now replaced by the lowly and the commonplace. Everything that used to be metaphysically above us has now moved downward. As the creation of a virtual world does not threaten to disrupt our reality, cyber writers can release their desires and passions as much as they like and thus convey their true feelings about their life.[38]

Cyber literary criticism also gives new answers to the question, "what should literature do?" This question involves the function, role, and value of literature. Traditional literature is supposed to have various functions as established by conventions. There are generally three aspects to the functions of literature. First, literature should be spiritually elevating to readers. It should enrich readers' spiritual world, cultivate their sense of humanity, and purify their souls. It should be emotionally comforting and intellectually edifying. Second, literature should contain an idealism about the ultimate meaning of life. It should use its artistic ingenuity to express writers' yearning for, as well as inquiry and pursuit of, a spirituality that transcends the mundane reality. It should uphold a faith that we can find what is ideally true and good to build a spiritual homeland for all humans. Third, literature should be concerned about social reality. It should spread the truth in the service of the country. It should speak for the people and represent how difficult their life is. It should light up our civilization and pass down our culture. It should use excellent works to motivate the people.

Traditionally, literary theories in China and the West give their clear answers to the question "what should literature do?" based on the abovementioned ideas. For example, Confucius proposed that poetry should "give aesthetic pleasure, reflect social conditions, bring people together to facilitate their communications, and criticize social ills" (xing guan qun yuan). Aristotle proposed the idea of catharsis. Horace raised the idea that literature should educate readers while entertaining them. In cyberwriting, these thoughts are still valid. Yan Zhen discussed this issue as follows:

> Cyber literature is not only about technology. It is also about social values. While it is a product of technological advancement, such technological advancement has an impact on social values. As a result, cyber literature embodies a distinctively new conceptualization of literature and a unique value system. In this sense, we should view it not merely as a matter of technology but also as a matter of culture and philosophy.[39]

Yet at the same time, the function of literature has subtly changed in cyberwriting: writers now write to entertain both themselves and their readers, and their works have become cultural commodities to be consumed.

Cyberwriting does not aim to help people and make the world a better place. It does not care about grand motifs or the ultimate philosophical questions that can guide and comfort people. Instead, it pays more attention to the free expression of personal thoughts and feelings. Under such a circumstance, both writers and readers are willing to view literature as a means of entertainment. If traditionally, we base our judgment of literary works more on their social values than on individual issues, then cyber literature is supposed to pay more attention to the individual experiences—the feeling of joy, relaxation, and happiness through reading. Thus, cyber literature is like "electronic noodles": while it is not meant to match expensive dishes, it still well sates people's appetites. There is no need for it to be acknowledged by the authoritative powers. To netizens who read cyber literature, what is important is to have fun. They seldom examine the deep meaning or the aesthetic values of what they read. In contrast, people who read literary classics are expected to peruse slowly, think deeply, and find the real meaning buried in words.

Meanwhile, cyber literature is inevitably incorporated into the modern consumer culture. The "new folk culture" in the context of digital media has indeed become a culture of mass consumption. Therefore, in an article collaborated by Ouyang Ting and me, we pointed out:

> To survive in the market, works of cyber literature are encouraged to become more commercialized and less serious and ambitious… As digital technology allows writers to write on computers rather than on paper, literary creation, which used to be deemed an act of sacredness, has now become a means of entertainment consumed in cyberspace. The old principle that literature must be socially responsible and useful has been replaced with

the idea that literature is merely a game for fun to both writers and readers and embodies a pursuit of commercial success. This subverts the traditional conceptualization of the function of literature at the very bottom.[40]

Important Questions Concerning Cyber Literary Criticism

The Cultural Dimension of Cyber Literary Criticism

In China, cultural studies had already been quite popular when the Internet and cyber literature appeared. Cyber literary criticism thus can be viewed as a kind of cultural studies. Xia Lie pointed out:

> Cyber literature is first and foremost an issue of culture... If cyber literature is still in its youth today and not quite well developed, the culture it reflects and carries should not be regarded as unsophisticated. In other words, today's cyberwriting is more of a cultural issue than a literary issue. It is important and receives a lot of attention mainly because of its cultural values.[41]

He believes that the writing, reading, publishing, and consuming of cyber literature today denote the success of a culture shaped both by technology and ordinary people. The consumer culture and culture industry powerfully commercialize and popularize cyber literature. Meanwhile, the traditional culture and the public knowledge of our history and reality provide cyberwriting with a rich cultural background. Moreover, cyber literature epitomizes writers' psychological reactions to the cultural condition in this era. Xia thus made such a conclusion:

> Therefore, cyber literature has a vast cultural dimension. It embodies the hybridity of various complex forces and trends in today's culture. The study of cyber literature can help us better understand contemporary times and the cultural essence of the times. In other words, cyber literature is still in the process of transformation and is still in need of our guidance. Its future development will signify how successfully we influence and change the culture of our nation and the culture of the world based on our understanding of, reflection on, and communication about the current social condition.[42]

As cyber literature in many ways departs from our cultural tradition, the criticism of cyber literature also challenges and changes the existing ideas of literature and culture. We are thus faced with an increasing number of questions because of this new phenomenon. Song Binghui pointed out: "The cyberculture has a great impact on literature, and such an impact is still getting stronger. This, to different extents, influences the creation, circulation, acceptance, and criticism of literature."[43] He envisions several obvious consequences of this situation. First, printed books of literature will significantly decrease in numbers or even disappear in the end. Second, correspondingly, there will be more and more writers and readers in cyberspace, and the writing and reading of literature happen mostly in such a virtual space. Third, the socio-cultural system that has formed on the basis of written languages since thousands of years ago will be fundamentally changed.

Chen Fumin, a literary critic, points out that cyberwriting has the power to "shatter" our cultural traditions. He argued: "In the Internet era, the strict cultural hierarchy in the past is shattered, and all those who write in cyberspace and claim that they and their acts are authoritative, truthful, and morally superior will look suspicious and ridiculous to us."[44] Meanwhile, he viewed cyber literature as "a symptom, a carrier, and a result of the postmodern culture": "The most conspicuous difference between cyber literature and traditional literature is that the former does not expect to produce anything meaningful. As a heretical force in the time of cultural changes, cyber literature is 'fragmented and broken.'"[45]

In an article, I gave an analysis of cyber literature from the perspective of postmodern culture: "In order to understand the cultural significance of cyber literature, we need to make clear how cyber literature uses our culture as a background and builds itself on it—in this way, we follow the logic of the postmodern cultural poetics. The Internet and its culture are firmly associated with a postmodern spirit."[46] Cyber literature exemplifies the idea of disenchantment, which is postmodern as an intellectual tendency. Cyber literature tends to deconstruct mainstream discourses, which corresponds with postmodernists' critical stance toward the center and the periphery. Moreover, cyber literature refuses to embed deep meaning in the texts, thus demonstrating a postmodern cultural logic known as "the lack of depth."

The characteristics of cyber literature thus reflect writers' intellectual attitudes in the context of postmodern culture. Postmodernists deconstruct myths, oppose essentialism and fundamentalism, and advocate cultural relativism, pluralism, difference, and uncertainty. In so doing, they aim to deconstruct the culture of modernity based on binary oppositions. This intellectual attitude corresponds to the cultural logic of Internet communication and the ensuing spirit of disenchantment in cyberspace. For example, the deconstruction of mainstream discourses can work in two ways in cyber literature. First, as ordinary people can speak freely with different voices, they break the tradition that writers must chime in with mainstream values. Second, as cyber literature is no longer constrained by printed media and can freely circulate in cyberspace, those who are socially marginalized now have more freedom to speak for themselves and write their own literature. The mechanism of writing and publishing that allows writers to enjoy a high degree of freedom naturally tends to deconstruct mainstream discourses and reinforce the postmodern spirit that values the margin over the center.

Meanwhile, the postmodern culture also has a negative influence on cyber literature. For example, the playfulness in writers' creative motives may harm the works' artistic exquisiteness, refinement, and creativity. While writers have more freedom, they tend to lose a sense of social responsibility. This may block their works from becoming intellectually and philosophically meaningful. It may deprive these works of their grandness, sublimity, depths, and profundity, negating the premise that these works can attain poetic excellence. Based on the cultural logic of postmodernism, cyberwriting may tend to deconstruct grand narratives and the aesthetic tradition as an embodiment of logos-centrism, thus putting an end to people's belief in poetics in the context of new technologies.

The Competition Between Different Critical Voices

As the Internet is structured in the shape of a web and does not have a center, it subverts the traditional hierarchy of discursive power. In the past, literary criticism was the profession of academics and not a business of outsiders. It was not until the emergence of the Internet and the popularity of cyber literature that this situation changed. The Internet's characteristics, such as freedom, equality, compatibility, and sharedness, technically determine that the right of speaking and writing, which used to belong to the privileged few, now should be shared among ordinary netizens. As a result, readers and writers can have real-time interaction and communication on a cyber media platform with no restraint. This means that every ordinary netizen now has the right and freedom to write and publish literary criticism. Consequently, how people construct their own identities and struggle to express their views through activities of criticism (both in print media and online) becomes an important issue.

While ordinary people can make their voices heard, different voices compete fiercely in the field of cyber literary criticism. The debate between Han Han and Bai Ye, as mentioned earlier, is an apt example of this condition. Ouyang Wenfeng commented on this issue in his article:

> Unlike traditional media, where only a selected few can show up and make remarks, blogging platforms—a new space for public opinions based on the Internet—allow everyone to express themselves freely and equally. Han Han was discontented with the situation that older writers had established themselves and enjoyed absolute control over China's literature. He then decided to stand up against these authoritative writers by writing blog posts.[47]

Han Han and Bai Ye belong to two generations. Their debate is not only personal. It is also representative of a disagreement between two groups of writers. As is pointed out in a newspaper article, before China's reform and opening-up, there was a clear boundary between writers and non-writers. If a person was officially recognized as a writer, it meant that he/she had a professional ability to do this job. The article explains:

After the reform and opening-up, the boundary between writers and non-writers gradually became blurred: while some writers are directly hired by the government, some writers work independently; while some writers are professionals, others are amateurs. These groups of writers also overlap in one way or another. All of them struggle to solidify their identities as writers. While Bai Ye's identity as a writer was granted by the governmental system, Han Han established his position as a writer because of his popularity in the market.[48]

Although the debate may benefit young writers' freedom of speech as they struggle to make their own voices heard, if they do not restrain their verbal violence and if they abandon logical thinking, they will make the cyberspace full of chaos and disorder, and eventually make literature amateurs lose their right to speak—a thing that they have made a lot of efforts to obtain.

The Exploration and Adjustment of Evaluation Criteria

The important events of cyber literary criticism in recent years mentioned earlier in this chapter, including people's criticism of the "Mu Zimei phenomenon," the controversy over Zhao Lihua's poems, the debate between Han Han and Bai Ye, the debate over cyber literature in 2003, and rankings and other activities for the evaluation and promotion of cyber literary works, are all based on people's use of certain evaluation criteria, whether conscious or unconscious.

As people organized activities to evaluate and promote cyber literary works, they all needed to set up their scales and models. In this sense, they, as pathfinders, made a lot of effort to construct a system of evaluation criteria. As mentioned, the State Administration of Press, Publication, Radio, Film and Television (SAPPRFT) initiated an activity to promote and introduce excellent cyber literary works. As mentioned earlier, in this activity, some general requirements were put forward. Moreover, there were specific criteria for the selection of books:

> First, works should represent positive motifs, thoughts, and values: they should meet the basic requirements of the core socialist values; they should embody correct ideas about the country, the nation, the history, the culture, and the ethics; they should exemplify how we weigh justice over self-interest, and distinguish the beautiful from the ugly; they should carry the excellent cultural genes and spiritual core of the Chinese nation; they should shoulder social responsibilities, conform to legal norms, and maintain basic ethical principles. Second, works should demonstrate positive aesthetic tastes: they should represent real life and important motifs, creatively develop popular genres, and strive to be positive, healthy, optimistic, elegant, refreshing, and beautiful. Third, works should meet requirements in terms of textual features and language use: they should be

first published, circulated, and read online; they should not be products of plagiarism or be highly similar to other works; they should not be simple adaptations from video games or cartoons; their language should be plain, elegant, pure, and tasteful; we oppose those works that are intentionally padded out.[49]

Apart from this, in such activities dedicated to the evaluation and promotion of cyber literary works, critical commentaries and reviews were presented to judge the selected works for their literary excellence. All these commentaries and reviews embody certain criteria and values, thus paving the way for establishing a system for evaluating cyber literature. In other words, as sediments of ideas, they will eventually become "the granules of truth" in the history of cyber literary criticism.

Generally speaking, the works selected and recommended in the rankings can be regarded as masterpieces of cyber literature. They are highly iconic and serve as good examples for others to follow. The inclusion of them in the rankings and the subsequent evaluation of them can effectively guide common readers and help them quickly find the best from an ocean of cyber literary works, in a way like panning for gold out of gravel. Usually, to cyber writers, the works in the rankings can serve as good examples not only for them to imitate but also for them to surpass. Thus, the making of ranking lists can guide cyberwriting. It is an effort to turn cyberwriting, which is done by ordinary netizens and inconsistent in quality, into a kind of literature that is well regulated, better in quality, and with richer literariness. The making of ranking lists, as Suo Luo pointed out, is "an important act to explore how a system of evaluation should be established for cyber literature."[50]

The reflection on and construction of the evaluation criteria of cyber literature received the most critical ideas. In an article, Guo Guochang gave his analysis.[51] According to him, we still have not yet formed a real theoretical framework through the writing of cyber literary criticism. As words of cyber literary criticism are casually posted online for entertaining readers and hyping up certain works and topics, they are not theoretically meaningful enough and thus cannot effectively guide cyberwriting. Meanwhile, traditional literary criticism does not quite fit cyberwriting either. As a result, the immaturity of cyber literary criticism and the inapplicability of traditional literary criticism put cyberwriting in a state of confusion and disorientation. Guo then put forward the following suggestions: first, we should integrate traditional literary criticism and cyber literary criticism to form a new universal theory that can be applied to cyber literature; second, we should renew the traditional literary criticism and develop a variety of approaches to literary criticism; third, we should make cyber literary criticism more theoretically meaningful while paying attention to the unique characteristics of cyber literature.

Constructive Reflections on the Value and Limitations of Cyber Literary Criticism

According to Hong Zhigang, the overload of information about consumption in the information age has led to the expansion of our perception and the decline of our rationality. However, literary criticism requires us to reason, analyze, and compare. It is a highly rational and professional artistic practice, thus unable to meet the needs of the mass media. What the mass media needs is to make quick judgments on works: even though an explanation is needed, it should be no longer than just a few words. As a result, many critical words of cyber literature are too simplistic, arbitrary, and judgmental: while attracting people's attention, they do not inspire any thoughts and cannot convince readers. Hong thus argued that in the Internet age, we should "bring literary criticism back on track by making it more rational and academic."[52] He then asserted: "[Literary criticism] should be an intellectual confrontation between critics and literary works. It is communication between professional readers. There is no need to hang shoulders with the media all day long or even embrace and kiss it."

In order to develop a set of ideas to guide our practice of cyber literary criticism, we need to think critically about the characteristics, advantages, and limitations of cyber literary criticism in the first place. Critics have already had many valuable and critical thoughts in this regard. For example, Zhou Zhixiong, in his article, pointed out that cyber literary criticism in China had not yet become as in-depth and professional as traditional literary criticism.[53] Yet he also argued:

> Cyber literary criticism is valuable. In such a period, when literature has lost its popularity and literary criticism itself is repeatedly criticized by academics, cyber literary criticism gained vitality, as it vividly manifests the spirit of the times, allows ordinary people to participate, and provides them with a feeling of real participation. It thus well supplements traditional literary criticism nowadays.[54]

Meanwhile, Zhou also discussed the weakness of cyber literary criticism:

> While people have more freedom in cyberspace, some of their critical articles are overly emotional. Many simply want to appear "cool" and attract readers with their grandstanding. Rather than giving deep thoughts and analyses, they merely discuss literary works based on quick impressions. While this can yield some insightful ideas, these critical articles are, after all, fragmentary, casual, and unsystematic. Their evaluations of literary works are often unfair.[55]

In an article, I made the following argument. I put it here as a conclusion to our discussion in this section:

> The Internet has changed the mechanism and scope of literary criticism. While writing literary criticism used to be a privilege for a selected

few, now it has become a practice of ordinary people. Critical voices thus have become equal and shared across the Internet. However, as cyber literary criticism can be casually written just for fun and sometimes spoof other works to subvert their seriousness, it lacks the power of intellectual reasoning and indepthness to some extent. It may even cause the "violence of public opinion" and lead to mistaken evaluations. This deserves our serious consideration.[56]

Notes

1 Huang, Mingfen 黄鸣奋, "Wangluo chuanmei geming yu dianzi wenxue piping de shanbian" 网络传媒革命与电子文学批评的嬗变. *Exploration and Free Views* 探索与争鸣 no. 11 (2010): 61.
2 There are many discussions on the "Mu Zimei phenomenon." I used "Mu Zimei" as the keyword to search on CNKI database for journal articles and found 319 of them, on April 1, 2016.
3 Translator's note: these female writers are contemporaries and they are all known for the writing of sex scenes.
4 Wan, Xingya 万兴亚, "'Mu Zimei' riji wangshang chixu fashao '木子美'日记网上持续发烧," *China Youth Daily* 中国青年报 (Beijing), Nov. 16, 2003.
5 Ri, Jing 日京, "Wangshang wangxia jiaofeng 'Mu Zimei' xianxiang 网上网下交锋'木子美'现象," *Yangcheng wanbao* 羊城晚报 (Guangzhou), Nov. 17, 2003.
6 Translator's note: this is a blogpost by a netizen named "I am not free" (Wo bu ziyou), entitled "Mu Zimei, This Chinese Blogger Is Indeed Too Astounding to All of Us" (Mu Zimei, zhege Zhongguo boke shizaishi tai jingshihaisu le) 木子美，这个中国博客实在是太惊世骇俗了. The link, however, is already defunct and is thus not provided here.
7 Translator's note: in Chinese, "pear flower" (lihua) is homophonic to Zhao Lihua's name.
8 Translator's note: "Sister Hibiscus" (Furong jiejie) originally refers to another Internet celebrity known for her unreasonable narcissism and boldness.
9 Translator's note: see *"Shitan Furong" yinfa fangxiechao, cheng bei egao yin dezui quanneiren* "诗坛芙蓉"引发仿写潮，称被恶搞因得罪圈内人, Souhu 搜狐, 2006. http://news.sina.com.cn/s/2006-09-30/090210146175s.shtml.
10 Translator's note: this is from Zhao Lihua's blog post, entitled "Words I Want to Say" (Wo yao shuo de hua) 我要说的话, on *Sina*. However, Sina has suspended its blogging service and all previous blog posts are now no longer available.
11 Ouyang, Wenfeng 欧阳文风, *Wangluo wenxue dashijian yibai* 网络文学大事件100 (Beijing: Central Compilation & Translation Press, 2014), 262.
12 Ouyang, Youquan 欧阳友权, "Wangluo wenxue: jishuhu? yishuhu? 网络文学：技术乎？艺术乎？," *Zhonghua dushu bao* 中华读书报 (Beijing), Feb. 19, 2003c.
13 Ouyang, Youquan 欧阳友权, "Wangluo wenxue: jishuhu? yishuhu? 网络文学：技术乎？艺术乎？."
14 Zhang, Hui 张晖, "Wangluo wenxue bushi youxi wenxue 网络文学不是游戏文学," *Zhonghua dushu bao* 中华读书报 (Beijing), Apr. 23, 2003.
15 He, Zhijun 何志钧, "Wangluo wenxue: wufa hulue de 'wuzhi jiyin' 网络文学：无法忽略的'物质基因,'" *Zhonghua dushu bao* 中华读书报 (Beijing), May 21, 2003.

16 Zhu, Chaohui 朱朝晖, "Youxi chongdong yu wenxue de jishu yilai 游戏冲动与文学的技术依赖," *Zhonghua dushu bao* 中华读书报 (Beijing), May 21, 2003.
17 Translator's note: the words in the single quotation marks are originally written by Lu Xun in his article "How I Came to Write Fiction?" (Wo zenme zuoqi xiaoshuo lai?) 我怎么做起小说来？. The English translation is from von Kowallis's article. See: Jon Eugene von Kowallis, "On Translating Lu Xun's Fiction," *Studia Orientalia Slovaca II* no. 2 (2012): 211.
18 Ouyang, Youquan 欧阳友权, "Nali caishi wangluo wenxue de ruanlei? 哪里才是网络文学的'软肋'？," *Zhonghua dushu bao* 中华读书报 (Beijing), Jun. 18, 2003a.
19 For the lists, see: *Erlingyiwu niandu Zhongguo wangluo xiaoshuo paihangbang bangdan* 2015年度中国网络小说排行榜榜单, Zhongguo zuojiawang 中国作家网, 2016. www.chinawriter.com.cn/bk/2016-02-03/85802.html.
20 Translator's note: the link provided in the original Chinese edition of this book is already defunct and thus is not given here. For more information, including the works awarded, see: Chen, Chong 陈冲, *Shoujie wangluo wenxue shuangnianjiang banjiang dianli juxing, xiaoshuo Jiangye huo jinjiang* 首届网络文学双年奖颁奖典礼举行，小说《将夜》获金奖, Renmin wang 人民网, 2015. http://culture.people.com.cn/n/2015/1103/c87423-27771302.html.
21 Translator's note: the link provided in the original Chinese edition of this book is already defunct and thus is not given here.
22 Translator's note: the links provided in the original Chinese edition of this book is already defunct and thus are not given here. For the sake of concision, the titles of the works on these lists are no longer kept in this translation.
23 Translator's note: the link provided in the original Chinese edition of this book is already defunct and thus is not given here.
24 *Zhuanjia yantao Guangdong wangluo wenxue* 专家研讨广东网络文学, Zhongguo zuojia wang 中国作家网, 2013. www.chinawriter.com.cn/bk/2013-05-20/69642.html.
25 *Qingnian chuangzuo xilie yantao leixing wenxue de xianzhuang yu qianjing yantaohui zai jing juxing* 青年创作系列研讨·类型文学的现状与前景研讨会在京举行, Zhongguo zuojia wang 中国作家网, 2013. www.chinawriter.com.cn/news/2013/2013-07-05/166485.html.
26 *Quanguo wangluo wenxue lilun yantaohui* 全国网络文学理论研讨会, Zhongguo zuojia wang 中国作家网, 2016. www.chinawriter.com.cn/z/wlwxllyth/index.shtml.
27 Translator's note: the link provided in the original Chinese edition of this book is already defunct and thus is not given here. But the article can be found here: Sun, Liping 孙丽萍, *Shoujie Zhongguo wangluo wenxue luntan zai Shanghai juxing* 首届中国网络文学论坛在上海举行, Shanghai zuojia wang 上海作家网, 2015. www.shzuojia.cn/plus/view.php?aid=1336.
28 Ouyang, Youquan 欧阳友权 et al., *Wangluo wenxue lungang* 网络文学论纲 (Beijing: People's Literature Press, 2003), 147.
29 Translator's note: a significant reorganization of the original text is done in the translation of this paragraph, in order to make this paragraph clearer and more concise.
30 Wang, Yichuan 王一川, "Wangluo shidai de wenxue: shenme shi buneng shao de?" 网络时代的文学：什么是不能少的?, *Master* 大家 no. 3 (2000): 202.
31 Zhang, Kangkang 张抗抗, "Wangluo wenxue zagan 网络文学杂感," *Zhonghua dushu bao* 中华读书报 (Beijing), Mar. 1, 2000.

32 Huang, Mingfen 黄鸣奋, "Nüwa, weinasi, yihuo mogui zhongjiezhe?—diannao, diannaowenyi yu diannao wenyixue" 女娲、维纳斯，抑或魔鬼终结者?——电脑、电脑文艺与电脑文艺学, *Literary Review* 文艺评论 no. 5 (2000): 84.
33 Ouyang, Youquan 欧阳友权, "Wenyi bianjie tuozhan yu wenlun yuandian weiyi" 文艺边界拓展与文论原点位移, *Journal of Langfang Normal University: Social Sciences Edition* 廊坊师范学院学报（社会科学版）23, no. 4 (2007b): 1–2.
34 There are several articles discussing this issue. See: Chen, Dingjia 陈定家, "Chaowenben de xingqi yu wangluo shidai de wenxue" 超文本的兴起与网络时代的文学, *Social Sciences in China* 中国社会科学 no.3 (2007): 161–175.
Wu, Xiaoming 吴晓明, "Wangluo wenxue chuangzuo shulun" 网络文学创作述论, *Journal of Zhanjiang Normal College* 湛江师范学院学报 21, no. 4 (2000): 58–65.
Huang, Yanni 黄燕妮, "Lun wangluo wenxue dui chuantong wenxue zhixu de xin jiangou" 论网络文学对传统文学秩序的新建构, *Contemporary Literary Criticism* 当代文坛 no. 4 (2002): 94–95.
Huang, Chunling 黄春玲, "Xin xiezuo shidai xia de wangluo xiezuo" 新写作时代下的网络写作, *Contemporary Literary Criticism* 当代文坛 no. 6 (2008): 70–73.
He, Zhijun 何志钧, "Wangluo wenxue leixinghua xiezuo guankui" 网络文学类型化写作管窥, *Study & Exploration* 学习与探索 no. 2 (2010): 188–190.
Ouyang, Youquan 欧阳友权, "Shuzi meijie yu Zhongguo wenxue de zhuanxing" 数字媒介与中国文学的转型, *Social Sciences in China* 中国社会科学 no. 1 (2007a): 143–156+208.
35 Jing, Wendong 敬文东, "Wangluo shidai jingdian xiezuo de mingyun" 网络时代经典写作的命运, *Novel Review* 小说评论 no. 3 (2001): 42.
36 Song, Hui 宋晖 and Lai, Daren 赖大任, "Wenxue shengchan de maidanglao hua he wangluo hua" 文学生产的麦当劳化和网络化, *Literature and Art Criticism* 文艺评论 no. 5 (2000): 28.
37 Ouyang, Youquan 欧阳友权, "Wenyi bianjie tuozhan yu wenlun yuandian weiyi" 文艺边界拓展与文论原点位移, 3.
38 Ouyang, Youquan 欧阳友权, "Wenyi bianjie tuozhan yu wenlun yuandian weiyi" 文艺边界拓展与文论原点位移, 3.
39 Yan, Zhen 阎真, "Wangluo wenxue jiazhilun xingsi" 网络文学价值论省思, *Literature and Art Contention* 文艺争鸣 no. 4 (2005): 77.
40 Ouyang, Ting 欧阳婷 and Ouyang, Youquan 欧阳友权, "Wangluo wenxue de tizhi puxixue fansi" 网络文学的体制谱系学反思, *Theoretical Studies in Literature and Art* 文艺理论研究 no. 1 (2014): 96.
41 Xia, Lie 夏烈, "Wangluo wenxue shouxian shige wenhua wenti 网络文学首先是个文化问题," *Zhonghua dushu bao* 中华读书报 (Beijing), Sep. 30, 2009.
42 Xia, Lie 夏烈, "Wangluo wenxue shouxian shige wenhua wenti 网络文学首先是个文化问题."
43 Translator's note: the original link to this article "The Rise of Cyber Culture and Its Challenge to Literature" (Wangluo wenhua de boxing jiqi dui wenxue de tiaozhan), provided in the Chinese edition of this book, is defunct. For an article with a slightly different title, see: Song Binghui 宋炳辉, "Wangluo boxing dui wenxue de tiaozhan" 网络勃兴对文学的挑战, in *Fangfa yu shijian: zhongwai wenxue guanxi yanjiu* 方法与实践：中外文学关系研究, 291-301 (Shanghai: Fudan University Press, 2004).
44 Chen, Fumin 陈福民, "Wenhua bianqian shidai yu wangluo wenxue 文化变迁时代与网络文学," *Xuexi shibao* 学习时报 (Beijing), Apr. 8, 2002.

45 Chen, Fumin 陈福民, "Wenhua bianqian shidai yu wangluo wenxue 文化变迁时代与网络文学."
46 Ouyang, Youquan 欧阳友权, "Wangluo wenxue de houxiandai wenhua qingjie" 网络文学的后现代文化情结. *Theory and Criticism of Literature and Art* 文艺理论与批评 no. 2 (2003b): 38.
47 Ouyang, Wenfeng 欧阳文风, *Wangluo wenxue dashijian yibai* 网络文学大事件100 (Beijing: Central Compilation & Translation Press, 2014): 262–263.
48 *Ruhe kaidai Han Bai zhizheng* 如何看待韩白之争, Souhu 搜狐, 2006. http://news.sohu.com/20060407/n242686697.shtml.
49 Yin, Kun 尹琨, "Rang tuijiehuodong fahui 'zhishideng' xiaoying—fang 'erlingyiwu nian youxiu wangluo wenxue yuanchuang zuopin tuijie huodong' pingweihui zhuren, Zhongguo zuoxie fuzhuxi Chen Qirong 让推介活动发挥'指示灯'效应——访'2015年优秀网络文学原创作品推介活动'评委会主任、中国作协副主席陈崎嵘," *Zhongguo xinwen chuban guangdian bao* 中国新闻出版广电报 (Beijing), Mar. 28, 2016.
50 Suo, Luo 桫椤, *Zhangxian wenxue lichang, tuijie wangluo jingpin: erlingyiwu niandu Zhongguo wangluo xiaoshuo paihangbang zongshu* 彰显文学立场，推介网络精品: 2015 年度中国网络小说排行榜综述, Zhongguo zuojia wang 中国作家网, 2016. www.chinawriter.com.cn/zs/2016/2016-02-26/266183.html.
51 Guo, Guochang 郭国昌, "Wangluo wenxue huhuan wenxue piping 网络文学呼唤文学批评," *Renmin ribao* 人民日报 (Beijing), Feb. 5, 2010.
52 Hong, Zhigang 洪治纲, "Xinxi shidai piping hewei? 信息时代，批评何为？" *Wenxue bao* 文学报 (Shanghai), Aug. 15, 2013.
53 Zhou, Zhixiong 周志雄, "Wangluo wenxue piping de xianzhuang yu wenti" 网络文学批评的现状与问题, *Journal of Shandong Normal University: The Humanities and Social Sciences Edition* 山东师范大学学报（人文社会科学版） 55, no. 11 (2010): 44.
54 Zhou, Zhixiong 周志雄, "Wangluo wenxue piping de xianzhuang yu wenti" 网络文学批评的现状与问题, 41.
55 Zhou, Zhixiong 周志雄, "Wangluo wenxue piping de xianzhuang yu wenti" 网络文学批评的现状与问题, 44.
56 Ouyang, Youquan 欧阳友权 and Wu, Yingwen 吴英文, "Wangluo wenxue piping de jiazhi he juxian" 网络文学批评的价值和局限, *Exploration and Free Views* 探索与争鸣 no. 11 (2010): 66.

Bibliography

Chen, Chong 陈冲. *Shoujie wangluo wenxue shuangnianjiang banjiang dianli juxing, xiaoshuo Jiangye huo jinjiang* 首届网络文学双年奖颁奖典礼举行，小说《将夜》获金奖. Renmin wang 人民网, 2015. http://culture.people.com.cn/n/2015/1103/c87423-27771302.html.
Chen, Dingjia 陈定家. "'Chaowenben' de xingqi yu wangluo shidai de wenxue" "超文本"的兴起与网络时代的文学. *Social Sciences in China* 中国社会科学 no. 3 (2007): 161–175.
Chen, Fumin 陈福民. "Wenhua bianqian shidai yu wangluo wenxue 文化变迁时代与网络文学." *Xuexi shibao* 学习时报 (Beijing), Apr. 8, 2002.

Erlingyiwu niandu Zhongguo wangluo xiaoshuo paihangbang bangdan 2015 年度中国网络小说排行榜榜单. Zhongguo zuojia wang 中国作家网, 2016. www.chinawriter.com.cn/bk/2016-02-03/85802.html.

Guo, Guochang 郭国昌. "Wangluo wenxue huhuan wenxue piping 网络文学呼唤文学批评." *Renmin ribao* 人民日报 (Beijing), Feb. 5, 2010.

He, Zhijun 何志钧. "Wangluo wenxue: wufa hulue de 'wuzhi jiyin' 网络文学：无法忽略的'物质基因.'" *Zhonghua dushu bao* 中华读书报 (Beijing), May. 21, 2003.

He, Zhijun 何志钧. "Wangluo wenxue leixinghua xiezuo guankui" 网络文学类型化写作管窥. *Study & Exploration* 学习与探索 no. 2 (2010): 188–190.

Hong, Zhigang 洪治纲. "Xinxi shidai piping hewei? 信息时代，批评何为？" *Wenxue bao* 文学报 (Shanghai), Aug. 15, 2013.

Huang, Chunling 黄春玲. "Xin xiezuo shidai xia de wangluo xiezuo" 新写作时代下的网络写作. *Contemporary Literary Criticism* 当代文坛 no. 6 (2008): 70–73.

Huang, Mingfen 黄鸣奋. "Nüwa, weinasi, yihuo mogui zhongjiezhe?—diannao, diannaowenyi yu diannao wenyixue" 女娲、维纳斯，抑或魔鬼终结者?——电脑、电脑文艺与电脑文艺学. *Literary Review* 文艺评论 no. 5 (2000): 77–86.

Huang, Mingfen 黄鸣奋. "Wangluo chuanmei geming yu dianzi wenxue piping de shanbian" 网络传媒革命与电子文学批评的嬗变. *Exploration and Free Views* 探索与争鸣 no. 11 (2010): 58–62.

Huang, Yanni 黄燕妮. "Lun wangluo wenxue dui chuantong wenxue zhixu de xin jiangou" 论网络文学对传统文学秩序的新建构. *Contemporary Literary Criticism* 当代文坛 no. 4 (2002): 94–95.

Jing, Wendong 敬文东. "Wangluo shidai jingdian xiezuo de mingyun" 网络时代经典写作的命运. *Novel Review* 小说评论 no. 3 (2001): 38–45.

Ouyang, Ting 欧阳婷 and Ouyang, Youquan 欧阳友权. "Wangluo wenxue de tizhi puxixue fansi" 网络文学的体制谱系学反思. *Theoretical Studies in Literature and Art* 文艺理论研究 no. 1 (2014): 90–98.

Ouyang, Youquan 欧阳友权 et al. *Wangluo wenxue lungang* 网络文学论纲. Beijing: People's Literature, 2003.

Ouyang, Youquan 欧阳友权. "Nali caishi wangluo wenxue de 'ruanlei'? 哪里才是网络文学的'软肋'？," *Zhonghua dushu bao* 中华读书报 (Beijing), Jun. 18, 2003a.

Ouyang, Youquan 欧阳友权. "Wangluo wenxue de houxiandai wenhua qingjie" 网络文学的后现代文化情结. *Theory and Criticism of Literature and Art* 文艺理论与批评 no. 2 (2003b): 38–43.

Ouyang, Youquan 欧阳友权. "Wangluo wenxue: jishuhu? yishuhu? 网络文学：技术乎？艺术乎？," *Zhonghua dushu bao* 中华读书报 (Beijing), Feb. 19, 2003c.

Ouyang, Youquan 欧阳友权. "Shuzi meijie yu Zhongguo wenxue de zhuanxing" 数字媒介与中国文学的转型. *Social Sciences in China* 中国社会科学 no. 1 (2007a): 143–156+208.

Ouyang, Youquan 欧阳友权. "Wenyi bianjie tuozhan yu wenlun yuandian weiyi" 文艺边界拓展与文论原点位移. *Journal of Langfang Normal University: Social Sciences Edition* 廊坊师范学院学报（社会科学版）23, no. 4 (2007b): 1–4.

Ouyang, Youquan 欧阳友权 and Wu, Yingwen 吴英文. "Wangluo wenxue piping de jiazhi he juxian" 网络文学批评的价值和局限. *Exploration and Free Views* 探索与争鸣 no. 11 (2010): 63–66.

Ouyang, Wenfeng 欧阳文风. *Wangluo wenxue dashijian yibai* 网络文学大事件100. Beijing: Central Compilation & Translation Press, 2014.

Qingnian chuangzuo xilie yantao leixing wenxue de xianzhuang yu qianjing yantaohui zai jing juxing 青年创作系列研讨・类型文学的现状与前景研讨会在京举行. *Zhongguo zuojia wang* 中国作家网, 2013. www.chinawriter.com.cn/news/2013/2013-07-05/166485.html.

Quanguo wangluo wenxue lilun yantaohui 全国网络文学理论研讨会. *Zhongguo zuojia wang* 中国作家网, 2016. www.chinawriter.com.cn/z/wlwxllyth/index.shtml.

Ri, Jing 日京. "Wangshang wangxia jiaofeng 'Mu Zimei' xianxiang 网上网下交锋'木子美'现象." *Yangcheng wanbao* 羊城晚报 (Guangzhou), Nov. 17, 2003.

Ruhe kaidai Han Bai zhizheng 如何看待韩白之争. Souhu 搜狐, 2006. http://news.sohu.com/20060407/n242686697.shtml.

"Shitan Furong" yinfa fangxiechao, cheng bei egao yin dezui quanneiren "诗坛芙蓉"引发仿写潮，称被恶搞因得罪圈内人. Souhu 搜狐, 2006. http://news.sina.com.cn/s/2006-09-30/090210146175s.shtml.

Song, Binghui 宋炳辉. "Wangluo boxing dui wenxue de tiaozhan" 网络勃兴对文学的挑战. In *Fangfa yu shijian: zhongwai wenxue guanxi yanjiu* 方法与实践：中外文学关系研究, 291–301. Shanghai: Fudan University Press, 2004.

Song, Hui 宋晖 and Lai, Daren 赖大任. "Wenxue shengchan de maidanglao hua he wangluo hua" 文学生产的麦当劳化和网络化. *Literature and Art Criticism* 文艺评论 no. 5 (2000): 26–32.

Sun, Liping 孙丽萍, *Shoujie Zhongguo wangluo wenxue luntan zai Shanghai juxing* 首届中国网络文学论坛在上海举行. *Shanghai zuojia wang* 上海作家网, 2015. www.shzuojia.cn/plus/view.php?aid=1336.

Suo, Luo 桫椤, *Zhangxian wenxue lichang, tuijie wangluo jingpin: erlingyiwu niandu Zhongguo wangluo xiaoshuo paihangbang zongshu* 彰显文学立场，推介网络精品：2015年度中国网络小说排行榜综述. *Zhongguo zuojia wang* 中国作家网, 2016. www.chinawriter.com.cn/zs/2016/2016-02-26/266183.html.

von Kowallis, Jon Eugene. "On Translating Lu Xun's Fiction." *Studia Orientalia Slovaca II* no. 2 (2012): 193–213.

Wan, Xingya 万兴亚. "'Mu Zimei' riji wangshang chixu fashao '木子美'日记网上持续发烧." *Zhongguo qingnian bao* 中国青年报 (Beijing), Nov. 16, 2003.

Wang, Yichuan 王一川. "Wangluo shidai de wenxue: shenme shi buneng shao de?" 网络时代的文学：什么是不能少的?, *Master* 大家 no. 3 (2000): 200–202.

Wu, Xiaoming 吴晓明. "Wangluo wenxue chuangzuo shulun" 网络文学创作述论. *Journal of Zhanjiang Normal College* 湛江师范学院学报 21, no. 4 (2000): 58–65.

Xia, Lie 夏烈. "Wangluo wenxue shouxian shige wenhua wenti 网络文学首先是个文化问题." *Zhonghua dushu bao* 中华读书报 (Beijing), Sep. 30, 2009.

Yan, Zhen 阎真. "Wangluo wenxue jiazhilun xingsi" 网络文学价值论省思. *Literature and Art Contention* 文艺争鸣 no. 4 (2005): 77–80.

Yin, Kun 尹琨. "Rang tuijiehuodong 'fahui zhishideng' xiaoying—fang 'erlingyiwu nian youxiu wangluo wenxue yuanchuang zuopin tuijie huodong' pingweihui zhuren, Zhongguo zuoxie fuzhuxi Chen Qirong 让推介活动发挥'指示灯'效应——访'2015年优秀网络文学原创作品推介活动'评委会主任、中国作协副主席陈崎嵘." *Zhongguo xinwen chuban guangdian bao* 中国新闻出版广电报 (Beijing), Mar. 28, 2016.

Zhang, Hui 张晖. "Wangluo wenxue bushi youxi wenxue 网络文学不是游戏文学." *Zhonghua dushu bao* 中华读书报 (Beijing), Apr. 23, 2003.

Zhang, Kangkang 张抗抗. "Wangluo wenxue zagan 网络文学杂感." *Zhonghua dushu bao* 中华读书报 (Beijing), Mar. 1, 2000.

Zhou, Zhixiong 周志雄. "Wangluo wenxue piping de xianzhuang yu wenti" 网络文学批评的现状与问题. *Journal of Shandong Normal University: The Humanities and Social Sciences Edition* 山东师范大学学报（人文社会科学版） 55, no. 11 (2010): 41–46.

Zhu, Chaohui 朱朝晖. "Youxi chongdong yu wenxue de jishu yilai 游戏冲动与文学的技术依赖." *Zhonghua dushu bao* 中华读书报 (Beijing), May. 21, 2003.

Zhuanjia yantao Guangdong wangluo wenxue 专家研讨广东网络文学. Zhongguo zuojia wang 中国作家网, 2013. www.chinawriter.com.cn/bk/2013-05-20/69642.html.

Part II

6 The Conceptual Transformation in Literary Criticism of the Internet Era

As we study the history of cyber literary criticism, we need to clarify a series of related issues. We should study the conceptual transformation in cyber literary criticism, the context and domain of such a transformation, and the relationship between what has been transformed and what has been maintained.

The Changing Ideas of Literature and Its Criticism

Literary criticism must adapt to the development of literature. To examine the changing ideas of literary criticism, we should first review the changes in the conceptualization of literature. Particularly, we should look into the question, "what is literature?" Such a question plays the role of a "gatekeeper" guarding the palace of literature: if we properly answer this question, we can well distinguish literature from non-literature. In other words, it is the foundation on which people develop ideas to define literature and evaluate literary works.

In ancient China, literature was initially defined by the famous argument that "poetry is where intent goes" (shi yan zhi). Later, scholars proposed other ideas such as "poetry can give aesthetic pleasure, reflect social conditions, bring people together to facilitate their communications, and criticize social ills" (xing guan qun yuan) and "literature should convey the truth" (wen yi zai dao). Such ideas correspond to the Confucian idealism that a man should "improve himself, manage his family, help govern the state, and bring justice and virtue to the world" (xiushen, qijia, zhiguo, pingtianxia). Later, during the May Fourth Period, influenced by the New Culture Movement, intellectuals proposed other ideas of literature: "art for art's sake" was quickly replaced by the idea that literature should be "cogs and nails on the machine of the working class," and should "serve workers, farmers, and soldiers" as "weapons for class struggle." All these ideas tended to be highly pragmatic, as they recognized literature as valuable not in itself but in its socio-political aspects. After the Cultural Revolution, intellectuals had discussions on the "aesthetics of literature" (wenxue shenmeixing) and on the idea that "literature should be the study of humanity" (wenxue shi renxue). This allowed them to refocus on literature itself, examine its essence, and propose diverse thoughts of literature.

DOI: 10.4324/9781003428480-9

Traditional concepts of literature are based on metaphysical ideas. According to Plato, art is an imitation of reality, while reality is an imitation of the world of ideas: art is thus a shadow of a shadow. According to Hegel, art is the practice of philosophical ideas, and beauty is the "sensuous appearing of the Idea."[1] He regards grand narrative and social responsibility as the basics of literature. Through careful reading of a text, readers find the essence and the truth embedded by the writer in images.

Cyber literature, characterized by its vagueness in meaning, fragmentation in imagery-representation, interactivity in narration, visual and auditory immersive-ness, freedom from restraints, and a high degree of commercialization, departs from the values of traditional literature: while the latter pursues "grand narratives," "truth," and "essence," the former tends to negate such a pursuit. As everyone can write and publish online, elaborate literary creations are replaced by casual expressions that go without many restraints. In this sense, the boundary between literature and non-literature becomes blurred.

While traditional literature attaches great importance to writers, cyber literature strives to erase the traces of authors and regards readers as the center of literary activities. It has been catering to the market since the beginning: without the demand from the audience, it could not sustain itself. This is what theorists of "reception aesthetics" expect literature to be.

Moreover, writers of cyber literature have introduced computer programs for their literary creation. Particularly, hypertextual literature is a result of the collaboration between human writers and computers. Some programs can even automatically generate literary pieces.

With the help of digital technology, literature has transformed itself: it is no longer in a material form but has become a type of pure information. Traditionally, the original copies are undoubtedly precious and irreplaceable; now, what is important in cyber literature is not the carrier of information but the information itself. The difference between the "original" and its copies thus disappears. While traditional literature seeks to fix its words on pages, cyber literature is composed of strings of bits and thus can be revised at any time. While the creation, circulation, and appreciation of works of traditional literature rely on these works' relative unchangeability, cyber literature provides readers with works that are fluid and dynamic. As a result, the traditional mechanism of literary canonization is no longer valid: if works of cyber literature can be canonized, they have to be canonized in a new context with a set of new evaluation criteria.

With the rapid development of cyber literature, the call for establishing a system to guide cyber literary criticism has become stronger. Yet, how to construct such a system and change our concepts of cyber literature remains a difficult problem for literary theorists. In essence, cyber literature is still a type of literature. It neither goes beyond the domain of literature nor has the ability to split from and rival traditional literature. Therefore, we should base our views of cyber literary criticism on our traditional ideas of literary criticism. We shall not completely break with the old paradigm, which results from people's practice of literary criticism over the past thousands of years. Instead, we should continue the explanatory activity while acknowledging cyber literature as a new object of study. However, cyber literature was born in a context where people embraced their technological rationality for a better use of the Internet. It is, therefore, different from traditional literature in the ideas of creation and the use of technologies. Moreover, as it has to cater to the market and serve as cultural commodities for mass consumption, cyber literature has to become "anti-literary" in some sense. Traditional literary criticism is already incapable of well explaining such a new type of literature, so we shall establish a new system and a new paradigm.

The Cultural Context of the Changing Ideas

As mentioned above, we need to base our ideas of cyber literary criticism both on our literary heritage and on the social and cultural context of the Internet age. Only by doing this can we avoid misjudging cyber literature and allow literary criticism to perform its basic functions well.

The Aesthetic Turn

In the context of globalization, the aesthetic turn has become an indisputable intellectual trend. Richard Shusterman, an American scholar, and Wolfgang Welsch, a German scholar, pay special attention to the phenomenon that people's daily life has been filled with aesthetic experiences. Thus, these scholars argue that we should not be limited by the narrow view of aesthetics that pays no attention to people's daily life and only considers art in the traditional sense. As Shusterman argues, our study of aesthetics should not be limited to the study of the art of beauty. Instead, it should be expanded to people's perceptual experience in life, especially to the realm of human body and physical experience, which was neglected by scholars who studied aesthetics in the past. In this regard, Shusterman proposed to establish the concept of "somaesthetics"—an aesthetics of the human body that has senses and perceptions. He believes that the study of philosophy should be regarded not purely as an academic pursuit of knowledge but as a kind of practical wisdom and art of life.

Wolfgang Welsch also recognizes that the world is now going through a process in which everything becomes aesthetically meaningful. The related areas range from physical decorations, entertainment industry, and marketing strategies, to the structure of things changed by the use of new materials, people's sense of reality virtualized by the mass media, and the tendency for people to learn about science and epistemology from an aesthetic perspective. Society as a whole—from the inside to the outside, and from cultural aspects to physical aspects—has been transformed, so that it gives people aesthetic experiences. Aesthetics is no longer a field of study reserved for a small group of intellectuals but has become a way of life commonly adopted by the general public. Therefore, it is necessary for us to renew our understanding of the relationship between aesthetics and daily life and liberate aesthetics from the narrow focus on the art of beauty.[2]

On the other hand, the use of the Internet both as a form of media and as a technology profoundly influences literature in terms of aesthetics. The Internet has thoroughly changed people's way of viewing, thinking, behaving, and understanding. Today, the print media are under pressure from a multimedia culture based on artificial intelligence and data processing. The Internet also brings new topics, ideas, forms, and means of expression to literary creation, thus opening up areas writers were previously unable to reach and allowing them to seek new inspiration. This enhances their ability to think in an artistic way so that their creative ideas become bolder and broader.

As we are going through such an aesthetic turn and witnessing the development of Internet technology, we should not overlook the new context and the new problems of literary criticism. We should not merely adhere to traditional ideas of literary criticism, which have existed for thousands of years. Instead, we should embrace the aesthetic turn: we should make the criteria and means of literary criticism fit into the age of Internet media, when people's daily life is filled with aesthetic experiences; we should let literary criticism get off its pedestal and come closer to social reality, to people's real life, and to the actual writing of cyber literature, so as to construct a new idea of literary criticism suitable for the age of Internet media.

Postmodernism

Postmodernism and cyber literature are inherently consistent and interconnected. In an article, I discussed their relationship as follows:

> Computer networks are developed in the context of "post-modernization" in Western society. Cyber literature has been imprinted with marks of postmodern culture as well. Thus, while making cultural interpretations of cyber literature, we need to clarify the relationship between the literary landscape and its cultural context—in other words, the logic of postmodern cultural poetics. The typical characteristics of postmodernism are "depthlessness," "loss of historicity," "death of the subject," and "abolition of critical distance." It is in this sense that the Internet and cyber literature contain cultural elements that are inevitably postmodern. The postmodern attitude to knowledge, the identification with the "margin," and the deconstruction of the hierarchy have influenced the spirit in cyber literature.[3]

In postmodern society, cyber literature has moved from the margin to the center and has gradually become one of the main forms of literature. While postmodernism is the philosophical, ideological, and theoretical basis of cyber literature, cyber literature is an expression and representation of postmodernism. The major postmodern traits of cyber literature are as follows:

Depthlessness. An important feature of traditional art is the pursuit of "depth," "profundity," or "comprehensiveness," with the goal of fully representing people's life in society. Postmodernism tends to deconstruct all this, and what is left is nothing but texts without depth in meaning. Cyber literature no longer pursues depth or comprehensiveness. A work of such a kind is just a body of words and images, which no longer have deep meanings. It is a game of language. Readers do not need to explain it. They just feel and experience it.

Simulacrumization. Cyber literature, following the postmodern cultural logic, creates "simulacra." A simulacrum leads to, or expresses, not a certain meaning, but just itself: in other words, a simulacrum is nothing but itself. As we see in web novels of popular genres, the simulacra have already lost the intellectual and emotional connotations that reside in works of traditional literature. Instead, they have become mere products for consumption and entertainment. Cyber literature thus tends to elongate narratives without limit and create a high volume of simulacra. As both urban space and cyberspace are full of such simulacra, people are losing their sense of reality.

Cybermedia as the Context

As a new type of media, the Internet exhibits new aesthetic characteristics in its language styles, textual structures, and linguistic activities.

The first issue to be discussed here is the carnivalesque language style. Communication in cyberspace is based on an integration of words, sounds, graphics, videos, and animated pictures. It is highly comprehensive and creates a new aesthetic space. In cyber literature and criticism, we see a large number of texts that combine words with graphics, symbols, sounds, and animated pictures. Some words from daily vocabulary are deliberately misused, modified, extended, or abbreviated, while others are invented for online communications. All kinds of symbols flood cyberspace and create an effect of cacophony, thus greatly enhancing the expressiveness of the cyber language. This type of language allows the media in cyberspace to provide texts that are concise, clear, vivid, lively, fluent, relaxing, and playful. Cyber language, with a revolutionary posture, freely deconstructs existing language norms, thus embodying the postmodern cultural spirit that challenges what is regarded as "central" and "authoritative."

The second issue is the ironic and playful language style, which is distinctive in a type of text called "big talk" (dahua) and "playful talk" (xishuo). This is also a manifestation of the postmodern cultural tendency that turns many things into mere games for entertainment. Cyberspace, which relies on high technologies, is ruled by capital: it is a place where companies make huge investments and seek profits. Cyberculture, consequently, in its process of commercialization, no longer pays much attention to humanistic values. It no longer shoulders a sense of duty for the reconstruction of people's spiritual homeland. Instead, it turns into a means of entertainment for mass consumption.

Everything that used to be classic and sacred can now be ridiculed and revised as long as it satisfies the public need to entertain, amuse, and consume.

According to Terry Eagleton, compared with modernism, postmodernism is more willing to cater to a market where the culture is popular, commercial, democratic, and consumerist; the typical style of the postmodern culture is marked by its playfulness, self-parody, hybridity, comprehensiveness, and use of irony.[4] As an example, the web novel *The Story of Wukong* (Wukong zhuan) playfully revises the classic *Journey to the West* (Xiyouji). It challenges what is celebrated as righteous and just by our traditional culture. In addition to parodying classic works, cyber literature sometimes changes the meaning of some words to create an effect of irony: for example, "idol" (ouxiang) can become "the person who makes me feel like vomiting" (outu de duixiang); "genius" (tiancai) can mean "born stupid" (tiansheng de chuncai); "protein" (danbaizhi) can refer to a person who is "stupid, idiotic, and neurotic" (bendan, baichi, shenjingzhi).

Hypertext

In 1965, the concept of hypertext was proposed by the American scholar Theodor Holm Nelson. Hypertext was originally meant to be "non-sequential writing": "text that branches and allows choices to the reader, best read at an interactive screen."[5] In 1989, Tim Berners-Lee, who was working at European High Energy Physics Laboratory, developed the Hypertext Markup Language, which led to the birth of the World Wide Web and created unprecedented opportunities for the sharing of artworks across the globe.

In the early 1990s, the rapid popularization of the Internet and the widespread use of hypertext technology created the technical conditions for the birth of hypertext literature. Some American writers began to use hypertexts and hyperlinks to write experimental works of fiction. In 1986, Michael Joyce released his hypertext work *afternoon, a story* with a link button at the bottom of each page, which enabled readers to freely navigate different pathways of the story. It is recognized as the first work of hypertext fiction. Stuart Moulthrop's *Victory Garden* (1991) is also recognized as a masterpiece of hypertext fiction. In China, Lin Yan's "The White-haired Girl in 1971" (Baimaonü zai yijiuqiyi), published in the literary journal *Dajia* (the first issue in 2002), is deemed a masterpiece of hypertext literature.

Hypertext has a nonlinear, web-like structure. Through hyperlinks, hypertexts are connected and extended without an end. Such a structure brings great opportunities for, and challenges to, writers' creation of aesthetic experience and readers' appreciation of it. Readers can freely choose and browse through such a type of literature to meet their expectations to the utmost. Hypertext literature breaks authors' monopoly on narratives and thus gives readers the power of narration to the greatest extent. As readers can determine the direction of stories, hypertext literature truly realizes the ideal of reception aesthetics. Of course, hypertext is also a double-edged sword: while it brings a massive flood of information, it also causes us to be lost in it; while it enriches our language, it also takes us to a conflict of different discourses; while it makes literary texts more open to readers, such texts are becoming more fragmented; while it creates a plurality of meanings, it also leads us to the dissolution of such meanings. Therefore, how to maximize the strengths of hypertext literature and avoid its weaknesses remains a fundamental question to scholars.

Ten Notions in Cyber Literary Criticism

Intersubjectivity

Intersubjectivity refers to the notion of interpersonal relationships embedded in people's consciousness, language, and culture. It is not about the objective cognition of the external world but is a kind of activity that allows subjects to have dialogues, communications, and mutual understandings. Digital media, represented by the Internet, has greatly strengthened people's intersubjectivity.

The interactivity of the Internet dismisses a unidirectional subject-object relationship and demands dialogue between subjects. In an article, I described such a condition as follows:

> [In the process of cyberwriting] the communicative relationship between the subject and others is not one between a speaker and listeners, but an encounter and interaction between subjects, who have communications and dialogues on an equal footing and coexist in a harmonious way. While cyber literature can be instantaneously shared among readers, readers also need to open web pages to read. This mechanism further regulates and enhances the condition of intersubjectivity. Intertextuality and intersubjectivity, which have a reciprocal causal relationship, work together to shape the condition for the aesthetics of cyberwriting.[6]

In cyberspace, where people enjoy freedom, equality, and openness and share their resources, writing and its criticism effectively overcome the shortcomings of traditional media. Literary criticism is thus based on an interaction between different subjects: critics, writers, and readers are all equal, and their identities are interchangeable.

Worship of the Mediocre

The Internet provides a space of democracy, equality, freedom, and virtual interaction for literary activities. As our society is going through industrialization and is increasingly reliant on information technology and mass consumption, such a social context nourishes postmodern values and modes of thinking. Under such a cultural influence, writers and critics of cyber literature pay much attention to ordinary people's experiences, especially the trivialities in daily life. Such a tendency is manifested in various aspects of cyber literature, including its theme, technique, and language use.

Cyber literary criticism tends to acknowledge the merits in the writing of the quotidian and the mediocre. The mediocre is not only what writers love to write about but has also become a quality that critics highly value. More specifically, it refers to a critical view that goes against ideas such as "center," "power," "hierarchy," "authority," "heroism," "sublimity," and "sacredness." Instead, it identifies with the mundane and the commonplace. Most of those who have such a "worship of the mediocre" are young netizens. While reading literature, they neither aim to accept the values of the predominant ideology nor to appreciate how writers find something meaningful in their life. Instead, they only intend to amuse themselves through reading. In this sense, they develop a worship of the mediocre and refuse to admire what is high above them. These ordinary netizens who have such a mentality jokingly call themselves "losers" (diaosi).[7] As I pointed out in an article, in cyber literature and its criticism, such worship of the mediocre has the following manifestations:

> First, people generally favor amateur writers, particularly those amateurs who can write well. Second, they appreciate the writing of ordinary people's mundane life instead of images of heroes and acts of heroism. Third, they admire the use of plain words and the expression of true feelings instead of superb writing techniques. They do not, therefore, care much about the use of ornate language and rhetorical devices or a rich meaning embedded in a text.[8]

A Blasphemous Tendency

The so-called "blasphemous tendency" refers to a mode of thinking and writing that subverts the sublime and the sacred and rebels against the authoritative and the classic. It is a manifestation of anti-essentialism in a postmodern context. In cyberspace, people are disenchanted and no longer worship the authoritative and the sublime. They can write at a low cost, interact with others equally, and enjoy a high degree of freedom in expressing themselves without revealing their real identities. As a result, cyberwriting has become a good means for people to be "blasphemous." The sacredness of literature is no longer there: the writing of individuals' real experiences in mundane life has dismissed the sense of awe toward literature, and writers also tend to rebel against traditional values. Literature has gotten off the pedestal and come back to ordinary people. Kitsch becomes a fad, and grand narratives—the sublime and sacred—are now playfully ridiculed.

For example, *The Story of Wukong* (Wukong zhuan) by Jin Hezai is a revision to the classic *Journey to the West* (Xiyouji): while the characters are kept, the grand motif is no longer there; the respect for the Buddhist master Tang Seng, together with the sense of justice and sacredness, as he is on a journey to the

West with his three students in search of Buddhist scriptures, is all lost in the new narrative. Now, the Monkey King is no longer a great hero who wholeheartedly protects the master Tang Seng on the journey. He is, instead, an ordinary man who suffers from a troubled relationship with his lover. He wants more freedom in his life and is unwilling to go for scriptures and become a Buddha.

Another example is *A Spicy Version of Outlaws of the Marsh* (Mala shuihu), an adaptation of the classic *Outlaws of the Marsh* (Shuihu zhuan). Now, the slogan of the outlaws in the original novel, which is "to enforce justice on behalf of heaven" (titianxingdao), becomes "to enforce justice on behalf of money" (ticaixingdao). Liangshan, the mountainous region where outlaws gather together to rebel against the government, becomes "Liangshan Outlaws Company," where the famous 108 outlaws use their unique ways to make money for themselves. As such works subvert traditional values, they caused widespread controversy both on the Internet and in other media.

This way of thinking is similar to Bakhtin's idea of "degradation": "that is, the lowering of all that is high, spiritual, ideal, abstract; it is a transfer to the material level, to the sphere of earth and body in their indissoluble unity."[9] In an article, I described this "blasphemous tendency" as such:

> The vulgar now coexists with the elegant; the ordinary is together with the extraordinary; the sacred and the sublime are now replaced by the lowly and the commonplace. Everything that used to be metaphysically above us has now moved downward. Boundaries are broken, and privileges are abolished. The center cannot hold, and grand narratives are debunked. Literature, together with the idea of freedom and equality, is dragged off from the pedestal and returned to the common people.[10]

Parody of Classics

A parody is an imitation of another work with a sense of ridicule, mockery, and playfulness. Works that are parodied are mostly well-known classics. The use of parody can affect aspects such as the storyline, narrative perspective, characterization, and motif. A parody can either revolve around the original text (both affirming and negating its meaning), depart from it (so that the new text becomes not directly related to the original text), or go against it. Most works of parody on the Internet belong to the third type. For example, Lao Gu's "I Fall in Love with a Woman Who Is Not Disturbed by Men" (Wo aishang nage zuohuaibuluan zhong de nüzi) is a modern love story that parodies the ancient Chinese tale of Liuxia Hui.[11] Such a parody tends to ridicule and degrade the historical figure Liuxia Hui, a man with eminent virtue.

Parody is also an act of literary criticism: as writers ironically imitate or exaggerate the plots, scenes, images, and dialogues in classic works, they express their critical views of these classics. Such a "defamiliarization" of well-known works offers alternative meanings and values to replace what has been taken for granted. This also demonstrates the sense of humor and wit of the writers of such parodies. Therefore, works of parody are as meaningful and effective as other texts of cyber literary criticism. See netizens' posts that parody Lu Xun as examples:

> To intimidate and insult is by no means a proper way of fighting. Sadly, someone has become a lackey of his master and has his soul corrupted. He doesn't know that yet. He thinks he is still a good fighter, but what he can do is only spit out some trash-talk.
> (From "Lu Xun's Running Dog" (Lu Xun de zougou) by Ximen Saoxue)

> In recent years, I began to feel increasingly sad. The world's dust effectively covers my shame every day and makes me forget about my vulgarity. Suddenly, I found that I couldn't face my teacher anymore.
> (From "Pathetic Lu Xun" (Bei'ai de Lu Xun) by "cure")[12]

While the two writers borrow Lu Xun's words and his language style to express their own views toward life and society, such use of parody can also be seen as an expression of the writers' critical view of Lu Xun's classics. In this way, it fits the cyberculture and extends our concept of literary criticism.

The Use of Vulgar Words

The use of vulgar words as a strategy to convey feelings was originally a kind of folk wisdom, but now it is widely used in cyberwriting. Opposing ideas such as "elegance" and "solemnity," the use of vulgar and colloquial words helps express writers' and critics' mockery of the classic and worship of the mediocre. I discussed this issue in an article: "The use of vulgar words as a narrative strategy has become an important aesthetic characteristic of cyber literature. It is a carnivalesque act that 'dethrones' what is in power and expresses a mockery of the sublime, an appreciation of the mundane, and a blasphemy of the sacred."[13]

While writers write vulgar words in their narratives, critics in cyberspace also write casually and freely instead of giving serious judgments on cyber literature, and sometimes they also write vulgar words, thus turning their criticism into a unique show of folk culture. Many critical articles no longer follow the traditional way of literary criticism: instead, they dismiss the sacredness of such a tradition and abandon ideas and values that demand critics to be elegant and honorable. I once argued: "Critics in cyberspace do not aim to create classics in literary criticism; instead, they simply want to express themselves through communication. They show off their wit and humor by skillfully making jokes and giving funny gimmicks. This often attracts more readers to their critical texts."[14] However, whether such a type of criticism is still scientific and effective in its interpretation of cyber literature and in its guidance on literary creation is quite debatable.

Spread of Feelings

Without rational thinking and under no restraint, cyberwriters can freely write about their feelings and spread them. Cyberwriters are often anonymous, so they do not have many checks on their feelings; instead, they spread such feelings so that readers can share, identify with, and comment on them. Writers and readers can thus work together to compose a symphony of feelings in a carnivalesque way. In addition, the use of hypertext and multimedia allows people to combine texts with symbols, pictures, sounds, and videos, thus providing a multi-dimensional virtual space that people never experienced in the past. Such a fully developed environment helps writers' creation and readers' appreciation of literary works: they can be totally immersed in such a virtual world and enjoy their aesthetic experience, which is highly comprehensive and cannot be matched by the reading and writing of traditional literature.

Cyber literary criticism also participates in such a spread of feelings. In cyberspace, critics pass judgment on literary works and phenomena without giving them careful and rational thoughts. Instead, they simply follow their feelings and say whatever comes to mind. Their casual and fragmentary words are then spread over the Internet, especially on forums and media platforms. Many fans post critical comments on popular web novels. While these comments may not be quite systematic and sophisticated, they are straightforward and effective in communication with authors. In this sense, they play an important role in increasing the influence of cyber literature and creating a good atmosphere for cyber literary criticism.

Spoofing

Spoofing is the use of absurd, parodistic, and irrational words and deeds to create a work that has a prank-like and ironic effect. It is also a popular cultural phenomenon on the Internet: texts, sounds, and images are used to negate the original values of a particular object. In 2006, Hu Ge put together scenes from a popular movie, *The Promise* (Wuji), dialogues from reports on the "Society and Law" Channel of China Central Television, and some strange commercials to create an absurd and laughable spoof video entitled *A Murder Caused by a Steamed Bun* (Yige mantou yinfa de xue'an). As it soon spread across the Internet, people started to see what spoof was.

Spoofing is a phenomenon of youth subculture, reflecting young people's subversive attitude toward the current order and condition as they stand on the margins of society. It is also a unique way of literary criticism: by using parodies, exaggerations, pastiches, jokes, and self-mockeries, and by departing from the norm, pretending to be serious, and talking nonsense, spoofers intend to subvert literary classics, despise the hierarchy, negate the authority, or vent a feeling of dissatisfaction and an attitude of subversiveness. Sometimes, they try to stimulate and refresh those who are already tired of seeing beautiful things by presenting them with something ugly. Some language styles in cyber literature, such as "pear flower style" (lihua ti), "bosom friend style" (zhiyin ti), "Zhen Huan style" (Zhen Huan ti), and "grumbling woman style" (yuanfu ti), are representative of such a way of spoofing. Spoofing can be seen as a unique way of literary criticism. If used properly, it can have effects that conventional methods of criticism cannot achieve.

Disenchantment

According to Tao Dongfeng, disenchantment in literature means "the disintegration of the authoritative and sacred that used to be unified and highly hegemonic in its rule over literary activities." It particularly refers to "the disintegration of the authoritative and sacred in the system of literature that upholds the idea that only the intellectual elite can and should decide the future of literature."[15] Cyber literature completely ends the elite's monopolistic control of the resources concerning literature, especially that of the media. As writing and publishing online have become easy, inexpensive, interactive, and efficient, ordinary people can now have a sense of equality and celebrate their victory over the elite. Literature thus goes through a process of disenchantment and loses its mysteriousness.

Literary Criticism Posted on "Bulletin Boards"

BBS refers to the "Bulletin Board System," a system that allows users to interact with each other and exchange a high volume of information. Popular BBSes include *Beida weiming BBS*, *Baidu Post Bar* (Baidu tieba), *Skyline Community* (Tianya shequ), *Xici hutong*, *Shuimu shequ*, and *Kaidi shequ*. There are many posts on these BBSes to discuss works, writers, and other topics of cyber literature, which can be viewed as a common type of online criticism. They can become a powerful voice on the Internet and greatly influence the public. As communications on BBSes are convenient and frequent, the creation, circulation, and evaluation of literary works are dynamic. While writing, writers need to consider readers' critical comments and adjust their narratives accordingly. Readers who post critical comments on literary works should bear in mind that other readers can also post comments. Thus, an individual's act of reading literature and writing literary criticism can become a component of a larger process of interaction.

For example, Jiang Zidan's novel *Everlasting Days in Prison* (Qiujie wubian) was first published in installments as posts in a section named "juggling with words" (wuwen nongmo) on *Skyline Community*, with the author's nickname being "Thus Spoke the Old Cat" (Laomao rushishuo). Readers then posted their comments on the novel to discuss with the author. Such a process of writing, reading, and posting lasted more than seven months. During this period of time, many readers, while waiting for the author's new posts, made their guesses at how the story would develop and end. The novel thus became quite popular online. After its publication as a book, it was even nominated for the Ninth Mao Dun Literature Prize. See the following two posts on *Skyline Community* as commentaries on this novel.

> The richness of this work is immeasurable. It offers readers the newest concepts and the oldest magic spells. It depicts the most advanced technology and the most primitive techniques. It shows us hypocritical words about human rights but also represents savage acts that turn out to be friendly and warm. It portrays characters who are petty-mined and relates experiences that are intense and soul-stirring. It tells both stories of conspiracy and stories of head-on confrontation... All of this is accompanied by the characters' extremely complex and contradictory inner movements. The novel is thus quite fascinating and thought-provoking.
>
> ("A quiet boy 2010" (Anjing nanhai 2010))

> In the novel, there is such a fantastic description of the female prisoners growing garlic sprouts in prison. By describing how the female prisoners grow garlic sprouts, the story shows how much they desire freedom, love, happiness, etc. This can touch many readers. But when the writer wrote this part, she seemed to be in a hurry. Obviously, she gave up deep thinking to catch up with the writing progress.
>
> (Du Hongbo)

The author Jiang Zidan later talked about her thoughts on the writing experience:

> The novel was finished. I can now count myself as an amateur player who made a performance on a virtual stage... I used to think that writers on the Internet enjoyed a high degree of freedom and were not restricted by rigorous standards or taboos. As I dabbled in cyberwriting, I realized that there were indeed many taboos. One thing that impressed me the most was that readers on the Internet did not accept literature as exclusive and professional. For example, I, the "old cat," initially planned to take a break after writing each paragraph and discuss issues in my writing, but readers strongly opposed that.[16]

Thus, we can see that the critical comments posted on BBSes can be especially effective, as they can have a powerful influence on a writer's creation.

Virtual Persona

"Virtual persona" refers to one's persona shown consciously or unconsciously in cyberspace, which differs from real life. This, as a phenomenon related to people's psychological and ethical conditions, is a consequence of the development of the Internet. As people interact while remaining anonymous, they can show their unique personalities, which have been repressed and hidden in real life. As a result, in virtual communication and interaction, a set of behavior patterns different from those in real life can be at work: one can create his or her own identity, or even have multiple identities, and then act based on this without restraints.[17] Such a virtual persona can have a positive effect, as one can use it to release stress and restore a mental balance. However, the virtual personal can also be negative, as one who loses all restrictions may indulge himself or herself in malicious behaviors. There are two types of virtual personae: those repressed in daily life and those admired and respected in daily life.[18] As the Internet becomes more user-friendly, convenient, intelligent, portable, and wearable, people's personae carry more cultural and philosophical significance.

Cyber literature is the art form that allows people to work with their virtual personae most easily. It is a stage on which writers actively perform. Accordingly, writing literary criticism on the Internet also becomes an important means for critics to perform their own virtual personae. Just like cyber literature, cyber literary criticism allows commentators to get rid of their anxieties and burdens caused by their real identities and to use their personae to express what they cannot and dare not express in real life—their true ideas about works, about writers, and about phenomena of cyber literature. In this sense, the virtual persona actually reflects one's true self, which is unrestrained and undisguised. Literary criticism under such a virtual persona may not be in-depth, objective, or systematic enough, but it is honest and straightforward; it may be unreasonable, but it may also be right on target and reveal what is essential. Netizens' personae can be seen in various kinds of acts: they can give thumbs-up and even monetary rewards to authors; they can drop smart and harsh comments or write spam posts; they can choose to respond to others' posts or simply remain silent.

What Has Been Transformed and What Has Been Maintained

From "Literariness" to "Networkedness"

People have a disagreement over what literature and literary criticism should be. In China, such a disagreement originates from people's different interpretations of the traditional idea that "poetry is where intent goes" (shi yan zhi). In ancient times, while some intellectuals argued that literature should "express one's emotions" (yan qing), others claimed that "literature should convey the truth" (wen yi zai dao). In cyber literature, fictional narrative, especially the novel as a genre, occupies a crucial position. Here we will take fictional narrative as a subject and discuss traditional and new ideas about it.

In ancient China, intellectuals had different views on whether the literary genre *xiaoshuo*, or fictional narrative, should reflect social reality or remain totally fictional.[19] According to "Treatise on Literature" (Yiwenzhi) of *Book of Han* (Hanshu), "most writers of fictional narratives are lowly bureaucrats;

they got hearsay from streets and alleys to make up stories of their own."[20] In the Tang Dynasty, the emergence of short stories in classical Chinese known as "transmissions of the strange" (chuanqi) marked writers' intentional creation of fictional narratives. In the Song Dynasty, there was a form of fictional narrative called "story scripts" (huaben). From then on, *xiaoshuo* started to have its fixed characteristics as "fictional" and "narrative." Yet still, as a narrative was easily related to a particular social and historical condition, fictional narrative, like poetry, was regarded as responsible for helping intellectuals realize their ideal that one should "improve himself, manage his family, help govern the state, and bring justice and virtue to the world" (xiushen, qijia, zhiguo, ping tianxia).

In the West, literature is regarded as what can represent writers' subjective experience through mimesis. Nevertheless, the novel as a genre was recognized as lowly and excluded from the literary canon for a long time. It was not until the 18th and 19th centuries that people viewed novels as valuable social and historical documents. Realism was thus regarded as a basic principle for the writing of novels. After World War II, scholars in the West, while still studying the realistic aspects of literature, developed various other ideas that went beyond the issue of realism.

The discussion above can help us draw basic trajectories for the changing concept of the fictional narrative in literary criticism. In both the East and the West, people oscillated between the idea that fictional narratives should be truthful representations of reality and the idea that fictional narratives should be essentially fictional. Nevertheless, they seemed to agree that fictional narratives concern social and individual conditions and used such an idea as a basis to measure against the fictionality of works. Before the mid-20th century, no matter how drastic social changes could be, critics still regarded literature as a representation of our physical reality.

However, the information age with digital technologies at its core differs fundamentally from all previous social stages. Cyberspace has become a dimension of reality that earlier societies did not have. For example, it blurs the philosophical boundary between the "primary quality" and the "secondary quality" so that the physical/objective and the spiritual/subjective can be related in a new way. In such an information age, literature and its "literariness" in the traditional sense cannot satisfy people's needs. The core concept of literature has been completely revised, and "literariness" has been gradually replaced by "networkedness." Accordingly, literary criticism in the information age must go through a process of transformation, though it still continues the tradition to some extent.

At the same time, as technology develops, our ways of information acquisition become more diversified and efficient. In the past, painters needed many years of study to master their painting skills. Today, children at elementary schools or even kindergartens can produce pictures instantly with the help of digital cameras and computers. In the past, people would make a lot of effort and spend a lot of time to access some documents, but today we can do that online in an instant. Similarly, in the past, only a handful of talented and diligent people could become artists, but today everyone can create works of art. In the past, most writers were those who had much experience in living and writing, but today most cyber writers are young people with little experience. In the past, literary criticism was a professional and academic practice, but today it has become amateurish, casual, and fragmentary, as ordinary netizens can do it. Netizens' general knowledge, intellectual tendencies, emotional experiences, aesthetic tastes, preferred styles, value orientations, and narrative strategies are all quite different from those of professional writers and critics. Their ideas of literature and literary criticism thus differ from traditional ones.

As mentioned above, in both China and the West, as the concept of the fictional narrative and its criticism evolved, people reached a consensus that an important characteristic of such a genre is its "fictionality" (xugou). As we are in the Information Age, "fictionality" (xugou) is further transformed by the use of digital technologies into a quality that we can call "simulativeness" (xuni). While "fictionality" and "simulativeness" have commonalities, they are also quite different. "Fictionality" is purely about people's imagination: while reading a traditional fictional narrative, readers can only passively understand and experience it, with a notion that there is a clear boundary between the fictional and the real. Images portrayed in such a fictional narrative is related to our real life in all kinds of ways or even directly based on what we have in reality. In contrast, images that are "simulated" with the help of digital technologies can be completely irrelevant to reality and make people feel as if such images "objectively" exist. In other words, the boundary between the simulated and the real is blurred.

Cyber literature thus carries important features of traditional literature but also significantly departs from it. Cyber literature still mainly uses language to create images and express thoughts and feelings. However, with the support of digital technologies, cyber literature also uses other media (such as video and sound) and hypertext to create a virtual reality so that readers can be better immersed in and experience it. In this sense, "networkedness," which is marked by readers' immersion and interaction, is at work.

Traditional Chinese literature pays particular attention to vivid and realistic representations of images, sounds, characters, and scenes to make readers feel as if they could directly see, hear, or even feel them. Unfortunately, as literature in the past was restricted by print media, such a literary effect can only work through readers' imagination. Now, as we have a virtual reality system based on digital technologies, we can directly and effortlessly fulfill the dream of ancient writers. To our surprise, while people made efforts to realize their literary dream, once it came true, they started to feel upset because they now had no dream anymore: they even criticized such a dream for its lack of depth and tension. This may be a paradox, but things often develop with contradictions.

In short, as society is developing and the concept of literature is changing, our literary criticism must also keep pace with the times. Critical concepts, such as "poetry can give aesthetic pleasure, reflect social conditions, bring people together to facilitate their communications, and criticize social ills" (xing guan qun yuan) and "literature should convey the truth" (wen yi zai dao), also need to change. Since the 20th century, literary criticism has gone from modernism to postmodernism and has given us a flood of theories and concepts that can make us feel dazzled and disoriented. Nevertheless, these theories and concepts are restricted as they are about literature in print media, which is two-dimensional and unidirectional. After the emergence of digital media, traditional literary criticism can no longer fit the practice of cyberwriting. The ecology of literature and the way of literary criticism thus change in such a new context.

Transformation of Literary Criticism and Retention of Its Traditional Values

In human history, new technologies exert their influence on literature and literary criticism through the use of the media. If we ignore the fact that we are already living in an information age and stick to the traditional ideas of literature, if we ignore cyber literature's "networkedness" and only focus on the so-called "literariness," we will definitely be left behind by the literary practice of our time.

While we are trying to transform and renew our literary criticism, we should neither be complacent about the current situation and adhere only to traditional ideas of literature, nor refuse to view the literary aspects of cyber literature and only value its technological aspects. I agree with Li Jingze's idea that we should "establish a comprehensive view of literature based on our new experience." He argued in a newspaper article:

> While we all feel the need to strengthen cyber literary criticism, we also find it very difficult to do it. In the face of the sea of literary texts, critics may feel as if they were, in a Chinese idiom, "tigers who want to eat the sky but cannot put their teeth on it." More importantly, cyber literature has a mechanism of production and consumption that greatly differs from that of traditional literature. Critics cannot find their positions in such a mechanism. The effect of their criticism of particular works is quite limited. Therefore, we need to recognize the unique characteristics of cyber literature and then explore effective mechanisms and ways [for cyber literary criticism].[21]

I also agree with Chen Qirong, who claimed that we should "establish a system of theories and discourse with Chinese characteristics step by step for evaluating cyber literature" and that critics should "[clarify] the aesthetic elements of cyber literature and put forward a set of evaluation criteria that fits both the nature of literature and the characteristics of cyber literature, so that we can lay a basis for the evaluation of cyber literature in the future."[22]

Therefore, we need a "foothold" for our efforts to transform literary criticism while keeping its traditional values in the context of new media technologies. In my view, to establish such a foothold, we need to follow a set of principles.

First, we need to establish the logical basis of cyber literary criticism: as a type of literary criticism, cyber literary criticism needs to inherit the values and resources from the tradition. While we are to establish a system of values and criteria for cyber literary criticism, we are not starting from scratch. Instead, we shall learn the thoughts and theories of literature both in the past and in the present, both in China and in the West. All valuable ideas of literature, such as "literature should convey the truth" (wen yi zai dao) in ancient China and "literature should teach readers while entertaining them" (yu jiao yu le) in the West, and all classics on literary theories, such as Liu Xie's *The Literary Mind and the Carving of Dragons* (Wenxin diaolong) and Aristotle's *Poetics*, should be studied and absorbed.

Second, we should plant cyber literary criticism in the context of new media technologies. Without proper consideration of the new media technologies and the Internet, we cannot really understand cyber literature, let alone give an adequate evaluation of it, because cyber literature is a combination of "literariness" and "networkedness." Cyberspace offers ordinary people an opportunity to interact freely with each other. This can have a direct impact on various aspects of literature. Scholars in China have had a lot of discussions on this issue. For example, in an article, Liu Qiong made the following argument:

> Cyber literature, which developed with the support of the Internet and mobile applications, has distinctive "networkedness." It reaches all people without discrimination, limitation, or disruption at a fast speed. It allows people to access a high volume of texts and to interact with each other conveniently. This, from various aspects, distinguishes cyber literature from traditional literature.[23]

Consequently, we shall not simply use traditional modes and criteria to evaluate cyber literature. Otherwise, we would be unable to recognize its unique characteristics and values reasonably, and our study and criticism would be ineffective or irrelevant.

Third, the foothold of criticism needs to be established on the basis of the aesthetic characteristics of cyber literature. There are many studies on this issue. For example, Ma Ji made his argument in an article: "Simply put, [we need to] pay attention to various aspects of literature, including the way it develops, its contemporariness, its social significance, and its unique means of communication, to locate its aesthetic position."[24]

In a journal article, I argued that we should understand the aesthetic characteristics of cyber literature by considering the relationship between art and reality: cyber literature represents our lifeworld that has been transformed by the Internet or even a world of virtual reality that is independent of and drastically different from reality.[25] In this sense, cyber literature readjusts our aesthetic focus, as we no longer recognize the relation between art and reality—a relation that has long been assumed as "realistic." Instead, our aesthetic relation with reality has been replaced by our interactive relation with cyberspace. Cyber literature either represents a world of virtual reality or a world of the human psyche that our aesthetic and ideological values have not yet modulated. It is thus no longer reliant on mimesis of reality. On the other hand, as cyber literature can be easily reproduced and pastiche is widely used as a narrative technique, the aura of literature has disappeared. As texts of cyber literature are unstable and subject to change, writers and critics no longer use the traditional way to write their works. Instead, they must create new genres, styles, and forms for their writings. This leads to a new paradigm called the "postaesthetic."

Another scholar, Kang Qiao, summarized cyber literature's three important characteristics based on a review of its aesthetic effects.[26] First, cyber literature rewards readers with pleasure and attracts them with aesthetic experience; as cyber literature must survive and develop in the market, it provides readers with pleasure they cannot have in real life and unique emotional experience. Second, cyber literature aims to lure readers into an identification with the main character so that readers can experience what the character experiences; in this way, cyber literature brings the writer, the main character, and readers into the same position so that they can share their dreams and emotions. Third, the primary purpose of cyberwriting is not to represent physical or social reality but to actualize people's dreams through creating a virtual world that is both fantastic and realistic. Kang then argued that we should not establish the evaluation criteria for cyber literature and the related ideas of literary criticism without giving due consideration to these characteristics.

Fourth, cyber literary criticism's most important goal is to let literature reshape our social values. Li Jingze made a discussion on this issue:

> [While we are writing cyber literary criticism,] we should pay attention to the matter of social values. Cyber literature, as a type of popular literature, is not unrelated to this matter; instead, it highlights such a matter. Cyber literature is about consumption, entertainment, and people's daily life. When you read a web novel, you immerse yourself in it and may follow the story for a whole year before finishing it. This is how cyber literature can truly change a person unconsciously. It thus profoundly influences an individual's outlook both on the world and on his/her life.[27]

In an article, I also pointed out that whether we view cyberwriting as cultural commodities or as literary works, as long as it is still "literature," it should demonstrate a positive and healthy spirit and spread correct social values.[28] This is because cyberwriting, after all, is a subjective expression and a cultural construction: authors thus have the agency to endow their works with social values and meanings. By the same token, cyber literary criticism should stick to correct values too, and it needs correct values even more than cyber literature does. This is because it not only interprets cyberwriting but also guides it. It should set criteria and the bottom line for cyber literature. Therefore, cyber literary criticism needs to establish social values that fit social development and people's needs.

In an article, Chen Qirong also discussed the issue of value orientation. He argued:

> [Cyber literary criticism should] orient cyberwriting toward positive social values. It should clarify cyber literature's relationship with the people, the times, and the core values of socialism. Based on how cyber literary works follow the way of art and the principles of aesthetics and on their popularity among readers, cyber literary criticism should interpret and evaluate these works in terms of their intellectual connotations, artistic presentations, and aesthetic styles. Cyber literary criticism should then elucidate how such works fulfill their cognitive, educational, aesthetic, and entertainment functions. Through an analysis of the different genres, styles, schools, and texts of cyber literature, cyber literary criticism should make clear how various ways of writing, such as realism, romanticism, and modernism, are shown in cyber literature and find something universally truthful from this.[29]

In all, scholars have made specific discussions and published various academic works on how cyber literature should embody positive social values.[30]

Notes

1 See: Lydia L. Moland, *Hegel's Aesthetics* (New York: Oxford University Press, 2019), 23–51.
2 See: Du, Shuying 杜书瀛, "Quanqiuhua yujingxia de shenmei, yishu, meixue xinzhuanxiang" 全球化语境下的审美、艺术、美学新转向, *Hebei Academic Journal* 河北学刊 no. 6 (2003): 137–140.
3 Ouyang, Youquan 欧阳友权, "Wangluo wenxue de houxiandai wenhua qingjie" 网络文学的后现代文化情结, *Theory and Criticism of Literature and Art* 文艺理论与批评 no. 2 (2003): 38.
  Translator's note: for the typical characteristics of postmodernism, see: Fredric Jameson, "Postmodernism or the Cultural Logic of Late Capitalism," *New Left Review* no. 146 (1984): 53–92.
4 Terry Eagleton, "Zhi Zhongguo duzhe" 致中国读者, in *Houxiandai zhuyi de huanxiang* 后现代主义的幻象, trans. Hua Ming 华明 (Beijing: Commercial Press, 2000), 1.
  Translator's note: this short essay, entitled "To Chinese Readers," is only included in the Chinese edition of Eagleton's book *The Illusions of Postmodernism*; the original English version is not provided.
5 Theodor Holm Nelson, *Literary Machines: edition 87.1* (Published by the author, 1987), 0/2.
6 Ouyang, Youquan 欧阳友权, "Wangluo xiezuo de zhuti jianxing" 网络写作的主体间性, *Theoretical Studies in Literature and Art* 文艺理论研究 no. 7 (2006): 95–96.
7 Translator's note: while "diaosi" is now widely used and means "loser," its literal translation is "pubic hair."

8 Ouyang, Youquan 欧阳友权, *Wangluo wenxue cidian* 网络文学词典 (Beijing: World Publishing Corporation, 2012), 27–28.
9 Mikhail Bakhtin, *Rabelais and His World*, trans. Helene Iswolsky (Bloomington: Indiana University Press, 1984), 19–20.
10 Ouyang, Youquan 欧阳友权, "Lun wangluo wenxue de cukouxiu xushi" 论网络文学的粗口秀叙事, *Journal of Qujing Normal University* 曲靖师范学院学报 no. 4 (2004): 2.
11 Translator's note: Liuxia Hui is known for the story that once he held a woman in his lap to warm her up as she was nearly frozen in winter, without the slightest intention of taking advantage of her sextually.
12 Ge, Tao 葛涛, ed. *Wangluo Lu Xun* 网络鲁迅 (Beijing: People's Literature Press, 2001), 8, 21.
13 Ouyang, Youquan 欧阳友权, *Wangluo wenxue cidian* 网络文学词典, 32.
14 Ouyang, Youquan 欧阳友权 and Wu, Yingwen 吴英文, "Wangluo wenxue piping de jiazhi he juxian" 网络文学批评的价值和局限, *Exploration and Free Views* 探索与争鸣 no. 11 (2010): 66.
15 Tao, Dongfeng 陶东风, "Wenxue de qumei" 文学的祛魅, *Literary and Artistic Contention* 文艺争鸣 no.1 (2006): 6.
16 Jiang, Zidan 蒋子丹, "Wangshang jianghu" 网上江湖, in *Qiujie wubian* 囚界无边, 444, 447 (Beijing: People's Literature Press, 2012).
17 Li, Li 李莉, "Lun xuni renge zai wangluo zhong de chuanbo" 论虚拟人格在网络中的传播 (master's thesis, Jilin University 吉林大学, 2008).
18 Deng, Zeqiu 邓泽球 and Zhang, Guiqun 张桂群, "Lun wangluo xuni renge" 论网络虚拟人格, *Journal of Changde Normal University: Social Sciences Edition* 常德师范学院学报（社会科学版） no. 3 (2002): 33–35.
19 Liu, Xianglan 刘湘兰, "Cong gudai muluxue kan Zhongguo wenyan xiaoshuo guannian de yanbian" 从古代目录学看中国文言小说观念的演变, *Jiang-huai Tribune* 江淮论坛 no. 2 (2006): 136–142.
20 Translator's note: for the Chinese text, see Ban, Gu 班固, "Yiwen zhi" 艺文志, in *Hanshu* 汉书, Chinese Notes, accessed July 30, 2022. http://chinesenotes.com/hanshu/hanshu039.html.
21 Li, Jingze 李敬泽, "Wangluo wenxue: wenxue zijue yu wenhua zijue 网络文学：文学自觉与文化自觉," *Renmin ribao* 人民日报 (Beijing), Jul. 25, 2014.
22 Chen, Qirong 陈崎嵘, "Zhubu jianli Zhongguo tese de wangluo wenxue lilun tixi, pingjia tixi he huayu tixi" 逐步建立中国特色的网络文学理论体系、评价体系和话语体系, in *Wangluo wenxue pingjia tixi xushitan* 网络文学评价体系虚实谈, ed. Creation and Research Department of China Writers Association 中国作家协会创研部 (Beijing: Writers Publishing House, 2014), 9.
23 Liu, Qiong 刘琼, "Wangluo dui 'wenxue' de gaibian 网络对'文学'的改变," *Wenxue bao* 文学报 (Shanghai), Aug. 14, 2014.
24 Ma, Ji 马季, "Wangluo wenxue shenmei tezheng 网络文学审美特征," *Guangming ribao* 光明日报 (Beijing), Oct. 29, 2013.
25 Ouyang, Youquan 欧阳友权, "Yong wangluo dazao wenxue shiyi" 用网络打造文学诗意, *Literary Review* 文学评论 no. 1 (2006): 193–196.
26 Kang, Qiao 康桥, "Wangluo wenxue de jiben yuanli" 网络文学的基本原理, in *Wangluo wenxue pingjia tixi xushitan* 网络文学评价体系虚实谈, ed. Creation and Research Department of China Writers Association 中国作家协会创研部 (Beijing: Writers Publishing House, 2014), 55–57.

27 Li, Jingze 李敬泽, "Wangluo wenxue: wenxue zijue yu wenhua zijue 网络文学：文学自觉与文化自觉."
28 Ouyang, Youquan 欧阳友权, "Yiyi zhixiang yu jiazhi chengzai—wangluo wenxue zai renshi 意义指向与价值承载——网络文学再认识," *Renmin ribao* 人民日报 (Beijing), Apr. 25, 2014.
29 Chen, Qirong 陈崎嵘, "Zhubu jianli Zhongguo tese de wangluo wenxue lilun tixi pingjia tixi he huayu tixi" 逐步建立中国特色的网络文学理论体系、评价体系和话语体系.
30 Academic papers focusing on the social values of cyber literature include: Liang, Hongying 梁鸿鹰, "Wangluo wenxue de jiazhi chuanda" 网络文学的价值传达.
Huang, Mingfen 黄鸣奋, "Jingshen nengliang yu jiazhi hongyang" 精神能量与价值弘扬.
Peng, Yun 彭云, "Wangluo wenxue hongyang hexin jiazhiguan de jidian sikao" 网络文学弘扬核心价值观的几点思考.
Dong, Yang 董阳, "Wangluo wenxue yu hexin jiazhiguan" 网络文学与核心价值观.
Li, Hongwei 李宏伟, "Wangluo wenxue ying hongyang shehuizhuyi hexin jiazhiguan" 网络文学应弘扬社会主义核心价值观.
He, Hong 何弘, "Wangluo wenxue de moshi zhuanbian he jingshen dandang" 网络文学的模式转变和精神担当.
These articles are all collected in *Wangluo wenxue pingjia tixi xushitan* 网络文学评价体系虚实谈, ed. Creation and Research Department of China Writers Association 中国作家协会创研部 (Beijing: Writers Publishing House, 2014).

Bibliography

Bakhtin, Mikhail. *Rabelais and His World*. Translated by Helene Iswolsky. Bloomington: Indiana University Press, 1984.

Chen, Qirong 陈崎嵘. "Zhubu jianli Zhongguo tese de wangluo wenxue lilun tixi pingjia tixi he huayu tixi" 逐步建立中国特色的网络文学理论体系、评价体系和话语体系. In *Wangluo wenxue pingjia tixi xushitan* 网络文学评价体系虚实谈, edited by Creation and Research Department of China Writers Association 中国作家协会创研部, 5–11. Beijing: Writers Publishing House, 2014.

Deng, Zeqiu 邓泽球 and Zhang, Guiqun 张桂群. "Lun wangluo xuni renge" 论网络虚拟人格. *Journal of Changde Normal University: Social Sciences Edition* 常德师范学院学报（社会科学版） no. 3 (2002): 33–35.

Du, Shuying 杜书瀛. "Quanqiuhua yujingxia de shenmei yishu meixue xinzhuanxiang" 全球化语境下的审美、艺术、美学新转向. *Hebei Academic Journal* 河北学刊 no. 6 (2003): 137–140.

Eagleton, Terry. "Zhi Zhongguo duzhe" 致中国读者. In *Houxiandai zhuyi de huanxiang* 后现代主义的幻象, translated by Hua Ming 华明, 1–3. Beijing: The Commercial Press, 2000.

Ge, Tao 葛涛, ed. *Wangluo Lu Xun* 网络鲁迅. Beijing: People's Literature Press, 2001.

Jameson, Fredric. "Postmodernism or the Cultural Logic of Late Capitalism." *New Left Review* no. 146 (1984): 53–92.

Jiang, Zidan 蒋子丹. "Wangshang Jianghu" 网上江湖. In *Qiujie wubian* 囚界无边, 444–450. Beijing: People's Literature Press, 2012.

Kang, Qiao 康桥. "Wangluo wenxue de jiben yuanli" 网络文学的基本原理. In *Wangluo wenxue pingjia tixi xushitan* 网络文学评价体系虚实谈, edited by Creation and

Research Department of China Writers Association 中国作家协会创研部, 55–65. Beijing: Writers Publishing House, 2014.

Li, Jingze 李敬泽. "Wangluo wenxue: wenxue zijue yu wenhua zijue 网络文学：文学自觉与文化自觉." *Renmin ribao* 人民日报 (Beijing), Jul. 25, 2014.

Li, Li 李莉. "Lun xuni renge zai wangluo zhong de chuanbo" 论虚拟人格在网络中的传播. Master's thesis, Jilin University 吉林大学, 2008.

Liu, Qiong 刘琼. "Wangluo dui 'wenxue' de gaibian 网络对'文学'的改变." *Wenxuebao* 文学报 (Shanghai), Aug. 14, 2014.

Liu, Xianglan 刘湘兰. "Cong gudai muluxue kan Zhongguo wenyan xiaoshuo guannian de yanbian" 从古代目录学看中国文言小说观念的演变. *Jiang-huai Tribune* 江淮论坛 no. 2 (2006): 136–142.

Ma, Ji 马季. "Wangluo wenxue shenmei tezheng 网络文学审美特征." *Guangming ribao* 光明日报 (Beijing), Oct. 29, 2013.

Moland, Lydia L. *Hegel's Aesthetics*. New York: Oxford University Press, 2019.

Nelson, Theodor Holm. *Literary Machines: edition 87.1*. Published by the author, 1987.

Ouyang, Youquan 欧阳友权. "Wangluo wenxue de houxiandai wenhua qingjie" 网络文学的后现代文化情结. *Theory and Criticism of Literature and Art* 文艺理论与批评 no. 2 (2003): 38–43.

Ouyang, Youquan 欧阳友权. "Lun wangluo wenxue de cukouxiu xushi" 论网络文学的粗口秀叙事. *Journal of Qujing Normal University* 曲靖师范学报 no. 4 (2004): 1–6.

Ouyang, Youquan 欧阳友权. "Wangluo xiezuo de zhuti jianxing" 网络写作的主体间性. *Theoretical Studies in Literature and Art* 文艺理论研究 no. 7 (2006): 93–99.

Ouyang, Youquan 欧阳友权. "Yong wangluo dazao wenxue shiyi" 用网络打造文学诗意. *Literary Review* 文学评论 no. 1 (2006): 193–196.

Ouyang, Youquan 欧阳友权 and Wu, Yingwen 吴英文. "Wangluo wenxue piping de jiazhi he juxian" 网络文学批评的价值和局限. *Exploration and Free Views* 探索与争鸣 no. 11 (2010): 63–66.

Ouyang, Youquan 欧阳友权. *Wangluo wenxue cidian* 网络文学词典. Beijing: World Publishing Corporation, 2012.

Ouyang, Youquan 欧阳友权. "Yiyi zhixiang yu jiazhi chengzai—wangluo wenxue zai renshi 意义指向与价值承载——网络文学再认识." *Renmin ribao* 人民日报 (Beijing), Apr. 25, 2014.

Tao, Dongfeng 陶东风. "Wenxue de qumei" 文学的祛魅. *Literary and Artistic Contention* 文艺争鸣 no.1 (2006): 6–22.

Wangluo wenxue pingjia tixi xushitan 网络文学评价体系虚实谈. Edited by Creation and Research Department of China Writers Association 中国作家协会创研部. Beijing: Writers Publishing House, 2014.

7 The Establishment of Evaluation Criteria for Cyber Literature

Cyber literature in China, especially web novels, can be called a unique literary wonder of the world as it has a vast volume and variety of texts. What corresponds to this is a large amount of cyber literary criticism. Huang Mingfen searched for books on cyber literary criticism at the Library of Congress of the US, the Harvard Library, and the National Library of China. He found that China had the largest number of printed publications of cyber literary criticism compared with Western countries.[1] If we count netizens' posts and thumbs-up, as well as websites' book rankings, as unique types of literary criticism, then China undoubtedly has the largest volume of cyber literary criticism in the world.

However, such a large volume does not mean that cyber literary criticism has become the center of literary criticism in general. The paradigm of cyber literary criticism has not yet been completely established. We feel unsure about the evaluation criteria and are still trying to figure them out in our practice. As literary criticism has become popular in modern media, we must establish a paradigm of cyber literary criticism that is academically and scientifically meaningful. In response to the current condition that cyber literary criticism is mostly casually written by netizens, two scholars, Liu Lili and Li Yuping, in their 2004 article, proposed to establish principles and criteria for evaluating cyber literature.[2] Before they were aware of this issue, many scholars had already tried to use new criteria to review cyber literature. In recent years, with many publications of cyber literary criticism, the evaluation criteria gradually took shape and improved further.

The Multiple Dimensions in the Evaluation Criteria

The Positive and Negative Views of Cyber Literature

Cyber literary criticism came into existence together with cyber literature. Since March 1998, when Cai Zhiheng, a writer based in Taiwan, China, published his web novel *The First Intimate Contact* (Diyici de qinmi jiechu), an increasing number of cyber literary works have been written and read. This

DOI: 10.4324/9781003428480-10

"fever of cyber literature" eventually broke the silence of critics. While they had been unfamiliar with cyber literature and felt unsure about its importance, they now started to view and examine it with a more serious attitude. Some of them focused on specific works, while others explored cyber literature's general development. Many critics and writers, with insight into contemporary literature, expressed their opinions on cyber literature. The earliest group of critics include Huang Mingfen, Ouyang Youquan, Bai Ye, Ge Hongbing, Yang Xinmin, Wang Meng, Mo Yan, Zhang Kangkang, Cai Zhiheng, Li Xunhuan, and Wu Guo. They discussed cyber literature from different perspectives and with different criteria. Their focuses were thus not the same. With limited resources but strong determination, they had a timely exploration of this new field. Thanks to their efforts, cyber literary criticism could develop alongside cyber literature, and a set of evaluation criteria could take form.

The boom in China's cyber literary criticism came after 2000. At that time, major literary websites were being established, and a large group of early cyber writers, such as Xing Yusen, Li Xunhuan, "Ning, the God of Wealth" (Ning caishen), and "Annie Baby" (Anni baobei), started to gain fame. As their works became popular quickly on the Internet, professional literary critics paid attention to them, and more common netizens also participated in writing literary criticism. Under such a circumstance, cyber literary criticism was no longer limited to the practice of traditional literary theories and concepts but became a highly personal activity.

Around the year 2004, the industry of cyber literature significantly developed: the commercial operations of literary websites further matured, and cyber literary criticism became connected with pay-per-view content. After 2005, major portal websites offered blogging services, so many literary critics started using their blogs to comment on cyber literature. Meanwhile, various literary websites opened sections for the review of literary works, which made it quite convenient for netizens to post their thoughts timely after reading. In this sense, the number of critics was further enlarged. Modern media thus directly helped the development of cyber literature and allowed netizens to replace professionals as the mainstay. As businesses and modern media work together, it becomes harder for us to determine what criteria we should have for evaluating cyber literature.

Although cyber literature inevitably became an important part of China's contemporary literature, some people still stuck to the old ideas and viewed cyber literature negatively. For example, Qiu Huadong, a famous writer, said that cyber literature was mostly just trash: its topics and themes, including "martial arts" (wuxia), "time travel" (chuanyue), "humor" (gaoxiao), "romantic love" (yuanyang hudie), "horror" (kongbu), "shady dealings" (heimu), and "crime and detective" (zhenpo), were opposed by Lu Xun and Chen Duxiu, two prominent intellectuals during the May Fourth period, thus being very low in quality. He also argued that literature was not so much related to media: whether words are carved on stones, brushed on silk, written on paper, or stored in computers, they are the same—either as literature or as non-literature—because there is just one criterion to decide if they are literature or not and this has nothing to do with media. According to him, most "literature" on the Internet is not real literature but just trashy words. Furthermore, Qiu thought very poorly of *The First Intimate Contact*, which was ranked as the "greatest" web novel in the past ten years. He said cynically: "I cannot believe such a thing is called the 'greatest'—this shows how poor cyber literature is."[3]

As we know, cyber literature is not only about the new form of publication. The changes to the ideas and motifs of literature brought by new media and digital technologies are conspicuous and revolutionary. If we ignore the changes, we will not be able to review the fundamental transformation in contemporary Chinese literature correctly. Some works of cyber literature are poor in quality, but some pieces can become classics. If we judge cyber literature simply by its motifs and themes, our views will be blocked, and our evaluation criteria will be inflexible and outdated.

Meanwhile, more critics came closer to the "site" of literary production and consumption—cyberspace—and examined cyber literature more carefully. In an article published in 2010, Ma Ji commented on ten important web novels published in the past ten years.[4] He argued that there was a common feature in these novels: they do not follow the old way but demonstrate a spirit of creativity. According to him, such a spirit is a result of the social changes of our times: traditional writers do not experience such changes, and it is natural for some of them to fall behind the times. Thus, cyber literature's importance in this new century will gradually become more evident as time goes on.

Ma then pointed out that as we encourage writers to write in creative ways, we should be tolerant toward web novels and forgive them if they are not doing well. He added that we should also have this attitude toward non-cyber literature today. While arguing that we should pay attention to creativeness as the most valuable quality of cyber literature, Ma also expressed deep concern about the phenomenon that too much commercialization was forcing cyber writers to follow fixed themes and patterns, which killed off the spirit of creativity. He then advocated that we should pay more attention to and better support the few works that are highly creative.

Many young scholars also indirectly expressed their views of the evaluation criteria for cyber literature in their critical words. For example, Zhang Xuan, a student from Hebei Normal University, wrote her master's thesis to examine the changes in literature brought by the use of new media technologies.[5] She analyzed different aspects of romance novels for female readers on the Internet, including their development, features, and forms. She concluded that such a type of literature has general postmodern traits. She employed feminist theories often used in traditional literary criticism to examine how this new type of literature carried and transformed the female consciousness. She also observed the predicament of romance novels: the excessive commercialization discouraged writers from writing works of high quality, and the market was also disorderly.

Young critics studied specific texts as cases. They knew the difference between cyber literature and traditional literature and consciously used critical methods to study cyber literature. However, they also had their limitations: they were unsure what evaluation criteria they should stick to and thus were inconsistent. On the one hand, they recognized the unique artistic characteristics of cyber literature; on the other hand, they still used the ideas of traditional literary criticism to review cyber literature so that they could find the "deficiencies" in cyber literature. Such an inconsistency made their criticism possibly lacking in depth, superficial, and trite.

If cyber literature was initially just free expressions of individuals and later published as printed books, now it has already become a commodity primarily sold online in its electronic form. In such a context, no matter what criteria people use to evaluate cyber literature, cyber literary criticism plays an important role in the promotion of works, in the recommendation of writers, and in the increase of cyber literature's circulation and social influence in general. Cyber literary criticism thus has become an effective means for the Internet media to organize, arrange, and guide the production of cyber literature. While traditional critics pay no adequate attention to cyber literature and remain largely silent, cyber literary criticism comes to the foreground, offering valuable critical resources for our study of cyber literature. Meanwhile, among such a wide variety of critical discourses, the evaluation criteria for cyber literature start to take shape and draw scholars' attention.

The Traditional and New Ideas

As cyber literature represents a brand-new literary paradigm, critics realized that a set of new criteria should be established to evaluate cyber literature. However, they had a debate over what these criteria should be exactly. Some scholars argued that the criteria should remain consistent, whether we study traditional or cyber literature. Other scholars, with a misconception about cyber literature, even argued that we should not maintain the old criteria but lower our standards a little when we study cyber literature. Still others, however, held that cyber literature had gone beyond the paradigm of traditional literature, and thus we should establish a new set of evaluation criteria for it. Until now, such a disagreement has not been solved, and scholars have not yet established the evaluation criteria that are reasonable and appropriate.

When cyber literature was still in its early stage of development, researchers had already raised some new criteria for evaluating cyber literature. They thought that if we simply view the Internet as a new media platform, then our study of literature on the Internet is just a matter of communication studies and textual criticism. However, as I argued in an article, the real uniqueness of cyber literature lies in its spirit of creativity: the most fundamental difference between cyber literature and traditional literature is that the former includes works that incorporate multi-media elements, such as videos, sounds, and hyperlinks.[6] Cyber literary criticism thus should focus particularly on such a quality of creativity.

In 2002, critics proposed that we should consider how cyber literary works convey "humanistic spirits." They recognized that cyber literature was characterized by its straightforward and even journalistic expressions of true feelings and was marked by the representations of the quotidian, the individual, and the emotional. As I argued in an article, cyber literature signified a rebellion against the traditional Confucian moral principles, which demanded people to restrain themselves and follow rules of etiquette; meanwhile, Chinese literati in ancient times tended to be either excessively sentimental or too reserved, but cyber literature departed from such ways of expressing emotions.[7] The discussion on the emotional aspects marks scholars' recognition of the "humanistic spirits" as cyber literature's core value and principle. Based on this, scholars evaluated cyber literary works to see whether they affirmed and celebrated people's vitality and whether they cared about and asserted people's personalities and desires to decide whether these works had positive humanistic spirits.

Still in 2002, Huang Mingfen proposed that cyber literary criticism should be based on the use of hypertext.[8] According to him, traditional literary criticism is based on the linear text: both literature and criticism are linear. As a result of this linearity, traditional literary criticism is unidirectional, straightforward, and static. In contrast, cyber literary criticism, to embody the idea of hypertextuality, should be interactive, hyperlinked, and dynamic. Yet Huang also looked back to the past in search of valuable intellectual resources to nourish cyber literary criticism. In 2004, Huang proposed that critics of cyber literature should not only find inspiration from the postmodern culture but also seek valuable intellectual resources from our traditional culture.[9] In other words, while we can use concepts of postmodernism and poststructuralism to interpret cyber literature, we can also connect cyber literary criticism with classic literary criticism in the hope of using the latter to improve our modern theories.

As scholars deepened their discussion on the evaluation criteria for cyber literature, in 2011, Wang Yan developed her ideas through a review of the studies of cyber literature in the West.[10] According to Wang, the earliest scholars of cyber literature in the West include Jay David Bolter and George Landow. Yet, they only viewed cyber literature as an extension and supplement to traditional literature instead of an independent literary type. Thus, they still used the traditional way to review cyber literature. Wang further mentioned that the real starting point of research on cyber literature is *Cybertext: Explorations of Ergodic Literature* by Espen Aarseth, published in 1997. In this book, Aarseth proposed a theory of cybertext and applied methods of literary criticism to study hypertext fiction, computer-generated poetry, and even computer games and other complex applications. In so doing, he could develop an entirely new perspective on the phenomena of cyber literature that earlier critics could not explain. His book thus has a long-lasting influence on cyber literary studies.

The Establishment of Evaluation Criteria for Cyber Literature 211

According to Wang Yan, after the publication of Aarseth's work, more research methods were developed in the West: critics, inspired by theories of semiotics, phenomenology, hermeneutics, sociology, and reception aesthetics, used different perspectives to analyze and interpret cyber literature, which led to the rapid development of cyber literary studies. Despite such a development, as Wang observed, scholars in the West have not yet formed a complete system of theories and methods, which is similar to the condition in China.

The Roles of Market and Technology in Cyber Literary Criticism

As cyber literature is based on new technology and has to cater to the market, its evaluation criteria are inevitably associated with these two factors. In 2013, Chen Jiaqi proposed that cyber literary criticism itself was going through a transformation because critics were now working with the mass media to serve the market.[11] In such a context, critics' identities changed. While they used to focus on literary and aesthetic values, now they needed to consider the commercial importance of cyber literature, and cyber literary criticism itself also became commercially significant. Chen argued: "No matter if this is for the making of regular TV series or cartoon series, critics need to discover, evaluate, and make use of the elements in cyber literature that can have commercial value."[12] As a result of the commercialization of cyber literature, the most important criterion for critics to evaluate texts is how the media can make use of such texts to make profits. In this sense, critics become businessmen, and literary criticism becomes more diversified and complex.

As critics of cyber literature pay much attention to the market, their critical words become increasingly reliant on the media. Some cyber literary critics consciously work to increase certain websites' click-through rates or promote certain literary works. They can do various things for this purpose: traditionally, they can publish book reports and book reviews through the mass media; now, they also work with the mass media to launch events and activities. Literary criticism, in this way, can further modernize itself. Meanwhile, cyber literary criticism is no longer limited to a single form: instead, it incorporates texts, sounds, pictures, and videos. Besides, ordinary people can now participate in the practice of literary criticism: their postings of thoughts and discussions based on personal experiences in new media can be taken as activities of cyber literary criticism as well.

In addition to the impact from the market, cyber literary criticism is also under the strong influence of new technologies. Huang Mingfen, in a 2010 article, discussed the transformation of cyber literary criticism against the backdrop of the revolution in digital technology. He pointed out:

"Critics should not avoid discussing how literature is influenced by operating systems, network protocols, and applications (including their cultural aspects). They should not avoid talking about the roles of microblogging, mobile live streaming, Wikipedia, RSS (Really Simple Syndication), and other new network services with the advent of Web 3.0. We must elucidate how cyber literary criticism inherits and deviates from traditional literary criticism. Particularly, we should pay attention to the analysis of the literariness of specific literary works."[13]

According to Huang, while studying cyber literature's ontological and typological features, we shall also clarify how cyber literature is related to video games, music videos, and traditional literature. With enough attention paid to the condition that literature in cyberspace has become anonymous, virtualized, and interactive, we shall study many aspects of literature, including how it exactly meets people's needs in certain environments and with certain renewal mechanisms, how it is created, appreciated, and circulated, how it is regulated and restrained by ethnics, laws, and policies, and how various literary phenomena are caused by the fact that literature is industrialized, monopolized, and globalized. Huang proposed his thoughts in response to various questions and problems which cyber literary criticism faces.

As cyber literature is closely associated with market and technology, how should critics decide its value? Ma Ji, in a 2015 article, argued that there are three variables in cyber literature—the aesthetics, the method of expression, and the audience.[14] According to him, critics should pay attention to how cyber literature provides readers with new aesthetic experiences. Cyber literature differs greatly from traditional literature in terms of its way of production: as it is written online in installments and as it allows writers and readers to interact, it is aesthetically suitable for ordinary readers rather than intellectuals. Other marketing strategies, such as the sale of monthly passes, the activities to help a work hit the charts, and the encouragement to readers to pay monetary rewards to writers, to a certain extent, all have impacts on the aesthetic orientation of cyber literature. A writer's daily update on a story and readers' daily reading of the story can "work together" to shape the work. While traditional literature represents the "possibilities" of life, cyber literature is about the "impossibilities": for example, there are unnatural narrative elements in fantasy novels, such as daydreams, superpowers, alternative histories, time travels, rebirths after death, and space explorations. Such narratives have become a way for young readers to understand society and the world in general. As critics, we should pay attention to such vivid and straightforward narratives.

While cyber literary criticism considers multiple aspects of literature, it lacks a coherent core. In an article, I discussed cyber literary criticism's problems. First, it focuses on technology rather than aesthetics. Second, it focuses on the media that carry literature rather than the value of literature. Third, it focuses on the commonalities and differences between cyber literature and traditional literature, rather than treating cyber literature as an independent art form. Fourth, it focuses on the changes in popular culture rather than the ontological significance of this new type of literature.[15] As critics, we should study the changes in literature as a result of people's changing relationship with cyberspace. We should pay more attention to the changes and developments of literary criticism due to the collaboration between the market and the new technology. We should do more research on how cyber literature influences people's way of communication and way of life. Only by considering all such factors can we establish a set of evaluation criteria for cyber literature that can be right to the point and scientific.

The Necessity and Possibility for the Evaluation Criteria

Critics' Anxiety about the Lack of Evaluation Criteria

Critics feel embarrassed in the 21st century. They can no longer adequately lead the trend in literature. Nor can they well represent the development of cyber literature. Jiang Bing, in a 2010 article, described such a predicament.[16] According to him, in the 1980s, critics, as prophets and models, worked together with writers to lead the cultural and spiritual enlightenment of the country. In the 2000s, when cyber literature flooded in, these critics, who worked in academia and were already in their middle age, still loved literary classics and held on to traditional values. While cherishing the memories of their radiant past, they found themselves in an embarrassing position, as they were already one step behind the times. With the transformation of traditional literature and the rise of cyber literature, critics are confused and disoriented. It is difficult for them to find a new way out. Should they stick to the cultural tradition and make efforts to maintain the old critical ideas, or blaze a trail and lead the way in the field of cyber literary criticism? This is a tough question, as they are not clear on how to develop a set of criteria for evaluating cyber literature.

Guo Chen and Cai Meijuan analyzed the reason for such a problem.[17] Traditionally, critics occupy a high position to guide literary writing and appreciate literary works. They embody the mainstream ideas of literature and are responsible for enlightening the masses. However, cyber literature disrupts the traditional order in literature by producing new literary forms that never existed before. As a result, critics feel embarrassed as they lack the theoretical resources to explain such new literary phenomena adequately. They also tend to dismiss cyber literature from their minds, regarding it as non-mainstream and thus not quite valuable. Even though some critics write on cyber literature, they still use traditional criteria to evaluate new works, making their criticism look quite uncoordinated. Meanwhile, ordinary netizens write more literary commentaries spontaneously but lack specific criteria and theoretical guidance. Most of these commentaries are thus based on personal thoughts and are not well formulated or organized: as literary criticism, they are rather effective.

We thus need a set of evaluation criteria to help cyber literature develop healthily. Although ancient Chinese scholars' literary commentaries on classics can also serve as a model, they are too casual and have their own problems. Si Ningda analyzed the causes of the lack of evaluation criteria. As he argues, many critics today simply pay attention to theoretical discussions and do not give specific commentaries on cyber writers and their works. As a result, the evaluation criteria have become a question that is "suspended" and ignored.[18] Si thus reminds critics that we should come closer to the "site" of cyber literature's production and base our discussions on specific literary works.

Nevertheless, to work out a set of evaluation criteria, we still need to grasp the issue at a macroscopic level. Only through induction and abstraction can we succeed in theorizing about the universal laws at work in the reading and writing of cyber literature as a highly complex cultural phenomenon. Only through this can we better understand cyber writers' and readers' psychological conditions, general knowledge, intellectual tendencies, and aesthetic tastes. Only through this can we effectively study a series of issues, including the interaction between literary criticism and literary creation, the interaction between literary criticism and readers' reading, and how literary criticism functions to impact cyber writing and reading.

In 2011, Shao Yanjun presented her idea of how scholars should view and write cyber literary criticism. She believed that there were several problems concerning cyber literary criticism:

> First, scholars blindly admire the West and borrow theories of "hypertext" from the West, which are too abstract and idealized to suit the actual condition of cyber literature in China. Second, they regard themselves as the cultural elite and demand cyber literature to have the essentialized quality of "literariness." This makes them wrongly conclude that cyber literature now lacks artistic and spiritual value.[19]

Shao proceeded to criticize scholars as they tended to study the external factors of cyber literature instead of focusing on the literature itself. She pointed out that scholars mechanically employed theories of popular culture and mass consumption to explain cyber literature as a cultural phenomenon. They simply followed the Frankfurt school's standpoint to critique cyber literature as a means of entertainment that allowed readers to escape from the harsh reality. Shao's critique is valid in a sense: such a way of criticism indeed signifies scholars' condescending attitude and does not truly touch upon the essence of cyber literature. Only through a critical review of the current evaluation criteria, which are based on a notion of elitism, can we better understand cyber literature and establish adequate criteria for it.

Cyber Literature's Demands for Evaluation Criteria

In a 2007 article, I clearly proposed that we should study the transformation of literary criticism in the context of digital media.[20] New media now influences literature and art in all aspects, causing drastic changes to their creation, circulation, appreciation, and evaluation. As cyber literature takes on new forms, our study of literature should also change in terms of its boundary and content. In other words, because cyber literature has changed the aesthetic relationship between people and the external world and combines "the literary" with "the technological," old rules and ideas used for literary criticism should be critically reviewed. While netizens write commentaries in a carnivalesque manner to deconstruct such old rules and ideas, new evaluation criteria have not yet been established to effectively guide cyber literary criticism.

The lack of evaluation criteria has led to a disconnection between cyber literary criticism and cyberwriting. In an article discussing the basis and context of cyber literary studies, I made my point as follows:

> Facing the condition that literature is irreversibly becoming incorporated into digital media, critics of cyber literature will have to fundamentally reform their criticism in terms of the use of theory and choose new effective methodologies. This does not only concern our academic standpoint that we need to respond to social realities and changes but also concerns how we should use certain ideas to guide the study of literature and art in China on the whole.[21]

The problem that cyber literary criticism and cyberwriting are disconnected has to be redressed. In a 2010 article, Guo Guochang pointed out:

> Cyber literary criticism, which has come into existence together with cyber literature, has not yet created its real critical theory. As literary commentaries are casually posted online for entertaining readers and hyping up certain works and topics, they are not theoretically meaningful enough and thus cannot effectively guide cyberwriting.[22]

Since cyber literary criticism impacts the development of cyber literature and people's understanding of cyber literature, its importance is self-evident.

In an article, Guo Chen and Cai Meijuan pointed out that the reason for the disconnection between cyber literary criticism and cyberwriting is that scholars stuck to traditional evaluation criteria.[23] Scholars form a society of their own and base their research heavily on literary theories. Thus, they maintain a certain set of criteria that make them ignore or even look down upon phenomena and activities of cyber literature. As cyber literature differs fundamentally from traditional literature in aesthetic qualities, it does not manifest the values of traditional literature. Consequently, some scholars view cyber literature as "heretical" and simply exclude it from their field of study. Meanwhile, traditional literary criticism uses obscure and difficult words that differ much from the language used in cyber literature, which is vivid, conversational, and expressive. This also makes scholars alienated from cyber writers. As scholars' criticism misses the target, it deepens the gap between cyber writers and scholars. The narrow field of vision and the outdated evaluation criteria make scholars unable to write adequately on cyber literature.

While traditional literary criticism is unsuitable for cyber literature, some critics changed their strategy. They abandoned the system of literary theories used by scholars in the past and adopted a new language—that used in cyberspace—to help their practice of literary criticism. They also lowered their standards while examining cyber literature. In an article written by Wu Yingwen and me, we had our reflection on such a condition:

> The Internet has changed the mechanism and scope of literary criticism. While writing literary criticism used to be a privilege for a selected few, now it has become a practice of ordinary people. Critical voices thus have become equal and shared across the Internet. However, as netizens can write literary commentaries casually and just for fun, and as they sometimes write such words to spoof other works to subvert their seriousness, their words lack the power of intellectual reasoning and profundity to some extent. It may even cause the "violence of public opinion" and lead to mistaken evaluations.[24]

Therefore, it is a hard job to establish a set of evaluation criteria. On the one hand, we should use theories to give in-depth analyses of literary works; on the other hand, we should use simple language to convey the messages. How to strike a balance between the two is already a big problem. To study the huge significance and value of cyber literature is even more difficult.

In response to such a problem, Luo Yong, a scholar, made a speech at the National Conference on Literary Theory, Criticism, and Creation (Quanguo wenxue lilun piping ji chuangyan gongzuo huiyi) held in Beidaihe District of Qinhuangdao City, Hebei Province in 2012. He stressed that as people of every new generation have their own ways of writing literature, literary criticism should also be updated accordingly, so there is a need to train and promote a group of young critics. Critics of cyber literature should come to the site of literary practices to find new objects of study and develop new ways of writing and publishing their critical articles. They should provide theoretical resources to guide the canonization of literary works and the writing of a literary history in a scientific way. They should practice new theories, test their validity, and improve them further. Meanwhile, they should use a set of evaluation criteria to guide their study of cyber literature so that they can not only develop effective interpretations and insightful ideas concerning the works, writers, issues, and ideological trends of cyber literature, but also express their thoughts about social reality and truly participate in the shaping of the public culture for people's spiritual wellbeing.

In 2015, Ma Ji pointed out that the evaluation criteria for cyber literature have been firmly controlled by the market, as it is the market that has the strongest power to decide whether a cyber literary work is good or not.[25] According to Ma, the "writing, marketing, and consuming" of cyber literature are interactive and interdependent. Cyberculture and the market have been playing a dominant role in the success of cyber literary works. If critics only care about people's "carnivalesque" writing and reading of cyber literature at a superficial level and remain ignorant of how business and market work as a strong undercurrent, then their criticism will be ineffective, and their conclusions will not reflect the real condition. Ma then pointed out that while works of traditional literature can become popular after long years of obscurity, it is impossible for works of cyber literature to do so: if they are "undervalued," it means that they are not popular on the market; as a result, no matter how valuable they are as works of literature, it is almost impossible for them to survive in cyberspace. For works of cyber literature, their economic value is more important than their literary value. Our traditional critical criteria can only be used to evaluate the literary works that have already been well received by the market. Yet, an excellent work may be ignored by the market in the first place and then disappears before it can receive any critical attention. In this sense, critics of cyber literature should take a much heavier responsibility nowadays: they have to use a set of evaluation criteria that works well with the market to help excellent works avoid being ignored and forgotten.

Critics' Attempts to Construct Evaluation Criteria

In a 2013 article, I further explored the ways of constructing a set of evaluation criteria for cyber literature.[26] I argued that cyber literature has two kinds of values. The first is cyber literature's literary value in the traditional sense. Yet, most cyber writers write to express themselves rather than create literary masterpieces, so they rarely follow the traditional way to make their works valuable as good literature. It would not be quite effective if we use "literary value in the traditional sense" as a criterion to evaluate cyber literature. Instead, we should use new criteria to evaluate cyber literature, focusing on its value in the untraditional sense. As the Internet has become the media platform that carries literature, it has become easier for readers to communicate with each other and with writers. The traditional unidirectional relationship between writers and readers as "subjects" and "objects" is deconstructed, and the way of writing literature has thus gone through fundamental changes. Meanwhile, literary works have become cheaper and more accessible. We should consider this as we are constructing the evaluation criteria.

While the aforementioned two kinds of values are different, they are also interrelated. I thus argued in the article:

> These huge differences do not mean that cyber literature and traditional literature have nothing in common regarding their value. In fact, the cultural values in cyber literature—freedom, equality, democracy, inclusiveness, and the idea of sharing—correspond with the humanistic spirit we traditionally expect literature to carry. For example, cyber literature gives individuals, including those on the margins of society, an opportunity to make their voices heard. This undoubtedly signifies a tendency to deconstruct the discursive power of mainstream culture. Meanwhile, it acknowledges, respects, and celebrates the individuality of writers. As ordinary people can participate in literary creation, readers are on an equal footing with the literary works they read. As a result, literature loses its "sacredness," and people can enjoy equal rights to writing and reading literature. All this denotes that

218   Part II

literature has now returned to the people: it highlights a spirit of humanism, celebrates human nature, and asserts the value of life and morality.[27]

Meanwhile, it is gratifying to see that young scholars were courageous enough to break through the barriers of traditional literary theories and explore how we should establish evaluation criteria for cyber literature. A few master's students wrote their graduation theses on this issue.[28] Among them, Liu Xiangning wrote a chapter to discuss the necessity and possibility of establishing evaluation criteria for cyber literature.[29] According to Liu's thesis, it is a misconception that cyber literature is not fundamentally different from traditional literature except that it is on the Internet and it is also wrong to assume that we can simply use existing criteria to evaluate cyber literature. Liu explicitly argued that critics of cyber literature should have enough courage to break the tradition and establish new criteria.

Li Jing and Shi Shaotao also called for new criteria. In an article, they argued that using the traditional critical criteria to study cyber literature would be neither viable nor reasonable.[30] There should be a set of new criteria based on the specific socio-cultural conditions to guide cyber literary criticism to perform its unique functions.

Kang Qiao, a critic, proposed that we need to consider three particular issues when constructing the criteria. First, we must consider that cyber literature follows "the way of providing pleasure and aesthetic experience" for readers. As cyberwriting has to survive and thrive on the market, it must provide such a pleasure and emotional experience. Second, we need to pay attention to the fact that cyber literature encourages readers to identify with the main characters and experience their stories, thus sharing their wishes and emotions. Third, we need to realize that cyberwriting intends to allow readers to have fantasies rather than simply represent the physical and social realities—in other words, "cyber literature pursues the unities of the fantastic and the realistic."[31] According to Kang, as we establish a set of evaluation criteria for cyber literature, we should consider such literature's unique characteristics and functions.

What Criteria We Need for Cyber Literature

The Poetic and the Commercial

Critics generally believe that although cyber literature signifies a fundamental paradigm shift in literary creation, it still has its "poeticity," and such "poeticity" should be held as a criterion for evaluating cyber literature.

In an article published in 2004, I pointed out that there were two problems for cyber literary criticism.[32] First, we still do not have a theoretical framework that can guide our study of literary texts. Second, the object of study is still in its early stage of development, and we do not know what it will be like in the future. In response to such a new and unique condition, I argued that we should avoid judging works as simply good or bad; we should not merely study the technical aspects of cyber literature. Instead, we should study specific works based on an evaluation of their poeticity.

In an article published in 2004, Liu Yu and Li Yuping also proposed that the evaluation criteria for cyber literature should be constructed in a way similar to those for traditional literature.[33] Critics thus should stick to "poeticity" as a criterion and thoroughly analyze such a quality in cyber literature.

On the other hand, as cyber literature is based on digital technology and is ruled by the market, it embodies values significantly different from those of traditional literature. Cyber literary criticism thus also has to adapt to the new situation. Huang Mingfen pointed out:

> By comparing different cultures, media, and disciplines, we may be able to find a way to interpret cyber literature appropriately. We may be able to integrate Western literary theories with their Chinese counterparts, amalgamate contemporary literary theories with ancient ones, and combine theories of literature with theories of art so as to develop our literary theories further.[34]

Cyber literary criticism is inherently cross-cultural, so we need to develop new theories and evaluation criteria.

With the further development of cyber literature as an industry, Ma Ji argued that currently, cyber literature is no longer reliant on writers' personal creations: "Whether a work is good or not is not only decided by readers' responses on the Internet but is also decided by how broad the work's impact can be."[35] To make more profits, literary websites have already established a set of criteria to evaluate cyber literature. Usually, these websites judge literary works and guide cyberwriting by focusing on whether these works can serve the whole chain of the culture industry— in other words, whether these works can be effectively adapted into other forms of culture commodities, such as video games, films, TV series, books, and cartoons. Such a criterion brings new questions and challenges to our study of cyber literature.

In 2013, *Baidu, Tencent,* and other Internet giants entered the market of cyber literature to compete with *Shanda Group*, which used to be the only giant that dominated this market. In the face of this new change, Ma Ji pointed out: "The establishment of a system of evaluation criteria for cyber literature may be dependent on the change in our idea about what is good literature in general."[36] While fully acknowledging that the business operations of literary websites were bringing changes to our evaluation criteria for literature, Ma still held that literariness should still be a criterion for cyber literature. What he stressed was that while literariness was the key criterion for serious literature in the 20th century, now it should not be the only criterion for our study of cyber literature.

The Values and Dimensions of Cyber Literature

As cyber literary criticism has a relatively short history, critics still tend to use traditional ways to analyze this new type of literature. As a result, the evaluation criteria for cyber literature are still in their formative stage: they are not yet clear, as critics have different ideas. Nevertheless, thanks to critics' explorations, some criteria are coming into existence and developing over time. They can be constructive and inspiring to our study of the values and dimensions of cyber literature.

In an article published in *People's Daily* in 2013, Chen advocated that we needed to "establish a system for the evaluation of cyber literature" and argued that although there might be various criteria, two of them were the most important: they were "the ideological value and the aesthetic value" of cyber literature. As to the ideological value, he pointed out:

> Cyber literature should maintain the correct ideological principles. The national values of "prosperity," "democracy," "civility," and "harmony," the social values of "freedom," "equality," "justice," and "the rule of law," and the individual values of "patriotism," "dedication," "integrity," and "friendship," should also be advocated in cyber literature.[37] Cyber literature should first and foremost serve the people. At the ideological level, it should actively shoulder the responsibility for the country and the nation. It should praise the true, the good, and the beautiful. It should criticize the false, the wicked, and the ugly. It should resist violence, expose deception, refuse to forget the past, unremittingly pursue the ultimate meaning of life, and untiringly explore the spiritual world of mankind.[38]

As to the aesthetic value of cyber literature, Chen proposed:

> Cyber writers should have an elegant and fine aesthetic taste. They should have a feeling of awe toward literature and an ambition to create excellent works in cyberspace. Writers of cyber literature should actively pursue an aesthetic taste that is positive, healthy, optimistic, elegant, and refreshing. They should reject the negative, the decadent, the pessimistic, the vulgar, and the obscene. Such a pursuit and a rejection should be shown in various aspects of cyber literature, including the theme, plot, characterization, language use, and stylistic elements. Thus, to study this issue, we should give specific analyses to specific texts.[39]

Chen's argument of the two kinds of value has set the general principles to guide and regulate the writing of cyber literature while acknowledging the unique characteristics of cyber literature. This is by far the most explicit expression of the evaluation criteria for cyber literature.[40]

Meanwhile, based on relevant ideas in China's cyber literary studies, I proposed that we should consider three dimensions in our construction of the evaluation criteria. We know that compared with traditional literature, cyber literature is more closely connected with technology and market. Thus, we can consider the aesthetic, technological, and commercial dimensions in our study of cyber literature.

The first dimension is aesthetics. Cyber literature, in nature, is still literature. It is necessary to evaluate its intellectual and aesthetic aspects, just as what we do for the study of traditional literature. However, cyber literature does not simply share the aesthetic values with traditional literature. While its aesthetic values are still manifested in the texts—styles, forms, and genres—cyber literature is fundamentally new. It stresses the communication between readers and writers and intends to create virtual realities rather than simply representing our real life. Besides, cyber literature tends to turn everything into what is aesthetically appreciable. Thus, the aesthetic experience of writing and reading cyber literature can be in many ways different from the experience of writing and reading traditional literature. The traditional criteria to evaluate the aesthetic value of literature are thus no longer quite effective. We shall consider the novelty in the means and functions of cyber literature's aesthetics, thus expanding the definition of "aesthetics" in cyber literary studies.

The second dimension is technology. Cyber literature does not simply mean that people now use computers instead of pens and paper: the changes technology brings to literature, in terms of writing, publishing, and reading, are much more revolutionary and comprehensive. The Internet not only changes the traditional mode of existence of literary works and creates new forms of literature such as hypertexts. As the Internet allows people to communicate across time and space through different media, it also signifies a fundamental change in writers' ways of thinking. It allows writers to enjoy more freedom in artistic creation. Critics must effectively predict and evaluate such effects on the writing of cyber literature and discuss the technological aspects of literary texts. For example, critics should assess the new media that carry literature and consider whether technology plays a vital role in the appearance or disappearance of "aura" in cyber literature.

The third dimension is business. Traditionally, we believe that if a literary work is commercialized, its literary value will inevitably be harmed. In other words, we usually have unfavorable views on commercialization. However, our view of commercialization should be more scientific when it comes to the study of cyber literature because a literary work's importance in cyberspace is directly related to its commercial value. To become a success, a cyber literary work must be put on the market and well received by readers. As cyber literature became a business in recent years, most writers started to write for commercial purposes. This brought some changes to literary activities: for example, it takes less time for writers to write their works, and it has become common for websites to charge readers for their access to literary works. More importantly, the commercialization of literature has brought great changes to the form of literature: on the one hand, as cyber writers follow the trend to write what is popular on the market, other forms and topics of literature that are not so popular on the market may hardly survive; on the other hand, the commercialization of literature paradoxically helps the creation of a variety of themes and genres, as well as new styles and narrative methods. As new themes and topics are developed, the idea of genre becomes less important, and the boundaries between different genres are blurred. Critics must be aware of such changes and rationally analyze them. This demands us to develop relevant criteria to evaluate the pros and cons of the commercialization of cyber literature.

Notes

1 Huang, Mingfen 黄鸣奋, "Wangluo chuanmei geming yu dianzi wenxue piping de shanbian" 网络传媒革命与电子文学批评的嬗变, *Exploration and Free Views* 探索与争鸣 no.11 (2010): 58–62.
2 Liu, Lili 刘俐俐 and Li, Yuping 李玉平, "Wangluo wenxue dui wenxue piping lilun de tiaozhan" 网络文学对文学批评理论的挑战, *Journal of Lanzhou University: Social Sciences Edition* 兰州大学学报（社会科学版）no. 5 (2004): 1–8.
3 Shu, Jinyu 舒晋瑜, "Qiu Huadong tan suowei wangluo wenxue: juedabufen shi wenzi laji 邱华栋谈所谓网络文学：绝大部分是文字垃圾," *Zhonghua dushu bao* 中华读书报 (Beijing), Dec. 7, 2011.
4 Ma, Ji 马季, "Huayu fangshi zhuanbian zhong de wangluo xiezuo—jianping wangluo xiaoshuo shinian shibu jiazuo" 话语方式转变中的网络写作——兼评网络小说十年十部佳作, *Literary and Artistic Contention* 文艺争鸣 no. 19 (2010): 18–24.
5 Translator's note: the original English title of the master's thesis is "The Preliminary Study of Network Female Romantic Novel," but it may be better translated as "A Preliminary Study of Romance Web Novels for Female Readers." See: Zhang, Xuan 张萱, "Wangluo nüxing yanqing xiaoshuo chutan" 网络女性言情小说初探 (master's thesis, Hebei Normal University 河北师范大学, 2012). For another case, see: Li, Juejun 李珏君, "Wangluo nüxing yuanchuang xiezuo yanjiu—yi shengda gongsi 'hongxiu tianxiang' wang weili" 网络女性原创写作研究——以盛大公司"红袖添香"网为例 (master's thesis, Shaanxi Normal University 陕西师范大学, 2012).
6 Ouyang, Youquan 欧阳友权, "Hulianwang shang de wenxue fengjing—woguo wangluo wenxue xianzhuang diaocha yu zoushi fenxi" 互联网上的文学风景——我国网络文学现状调查与走势分析, *Journal of China Three Gorges University: The Humanities and Social Sciences Edition* 三峡大学学报（人文社会科学版）no. 6 (2001): 5–9.
7 Ouyang, Youquan 欧阳友权, "Lun wangluo wenxue de jingshen quxiang" 论网络文学的精神取向, *Literature & Art Studies* 文艺研究 no. 5 (2002): 74–82.
8 Huang, Mingfen 黄鸣奋, "Wangluo wenxue zhi wojian" 网络文学之我见, *Social Science Front* 社会科学战线 no. 4 (2002): 93–98.
9 Huang, Mingfen 黄鸣奋, "Bijiao wenxue shiye zhong de wangluo wenxue yanjiu" 比较文学视野中的网络文学研究, *Social Science Journal* 社会科学辑刊 no. 5 (2004): 140–143.
10 Wang, Yan 王艳, "Wangluo wenxue yanjiu zai xifang" 网络文学研究在西方, *Journal of Beijing International Studies University* 北京第二外国语学院学报 no. 12 (2011): 42–48.
11 Chen, Qijia 陈奇佳, "Wangluo wenxue piping dang cong chanye jiaodu rushou 网络文学批评当从产业角度入手," *Zhongguo yishu bao* 中国艺术报 (Beijing), Dec. 18, 2013.

12 Chen, Qijia 陈奇佳, "Wangluo wenxue piping dang cong chanye jiaodu rushou 网络文学批评当从产业角度入手."
13 Huang, Mingfen 黄鸣奋, "Wangluo chuanmei geming yu dianzi wenxue piping de shanbian" 网络传媒革命与电子文学批评的嬗变, *Exploration and Free Views* 探索与争鸣 no. 11 (2010): 62.
14 Ma, Ji 马季, "Shichang jizhi xia de wangluo wenxue shenmei shiyu—wangluo wenxue zhiyu Zhongguo dangdai wenxue de sange bianliang" 市场机制下的网络文学审美视域——网络文学之于中国当代文学的三个变量, *Creation and Criticism* 创作与评论 no. 4 (2015): 54–60.
15 Ouyang, Youquan 欧阳友权, "Wangluo wenxue yanjiu de qianyan wenti 网络文学研究的前沿问题," *Newspaper of Literature and Art* 文艺报 (Beijing), Sept. 30, 2004.
16 Jiang, Bing 江冰, "'Baling hou' yu wangluo: wenxue piping de shuangchong zuge" "80后"与网络：文学批评的双重阻隔, *Southern Cultural Forum* 南方文坛 no. 4 (2010): 26–28.
17 Guo, Chen 郭晨 and Cai, Meijuan 蔡梅娟, "Cong wangluo wenxue kan dangdai wenxue piping de gongneng" 从网络文学看当代文学批评的功能, *Journal of Shandong University of Technology: Social Sciences Edition* 山东理工大学学报（社会科学版）no. 1 (2009): 77–79.
18 Si, Ningda 司宁达, "Miwang yu qingxing—wangluo wenxue piping chutan" 迷惘与清醒——网络文学批评初探, *Journal of Nanyang Normal University: Social Sciences Edition* 南阳师范大学学报（社会科学版）no. 11 (2005): 70–73.
19 Shao, Yanjun 邵燕君, "Miandui wangluo wenxue: xueyuanpai de taidu he fangfa" 面对网络文学：学院派的态度和方法, *Southern Cultural Forum* 南方文坛 no. 6 (2011): 16.
20 Ouyang, Youquan 欧阳友权, "Shuzi meijie xia wenlun zhuanxing de sange weidu" 数字媒介下文论转型的三个维度, *Hebei Academic Journal* 河北学刊 no. 2 (2007): 119–122+131.
21 Ouyang, Youquan 欧阳友权, "Zhongguo wangluo wenxue yanjiu jidian jiqi yujing xuanze" 中国网络文学研究基点及其语境选择, *Hebei Academic Journal* 河北学刊 no. 4 (2015): 96.
22 Guo, Guochang 郭国昌, "Wangluo wenxue huhuan wenxue piping 网络文学呼唤文学批评," *Renmin ribao* 人民日报 (Beijing), Feb. 5, 2010.
23 Guo, Chen 郭晨 and Cai, Meijuan 蔡梅娟, "Cong wangluo wenxue kan dangdai wenxue piping de gongneng" 从网络文学看当代文学批评的功能, *Journal of Shandong University of Technology: Social Sciences Edition* 山东理工大学学报（社会科学版）no. 1 (2009): 77–79.
24 Ouyang, Youquan 欧阳友权 and Wu, Yingwen 吴英文, "Wangluo wenxue piping de jiazhi he juxian" 网络文学批评的价值和局限, *Exploration and Free Views* 探索与争鸣 no. 11 (2010): 64.
25 Ma, Ji 马季, "Shichang jizhi xia de wangluo wenxue shenmei shiyu—wangluo wenxue zhiyu Zhongguo dangdai wenxue de sange bianliang" 市场机制下的网络文学审美视域——网络文学之于中国当代文学的三个变量, *Creation and Criticism* 创作与评论 no. 4 (2015): 54–60.
26 Ouyang, Youquan 欧阳友权, "Chongxie wenxueshi yu wangluo wenxue 'rushi' wenti" 重写文学史与网络文学"入史"问题, *Hebei Academic Journal* 河北学刊 no. 5 (2013): 8–12.
27 Ouyang, Youquan 欧阳友权, "Chongxie wenxueshi yu wangluo wenxue 'rushi' wenti" 重写文学史与网络文学"入史"问题, 9.

28 Zhang, Jing 张晶, "Wangluo wenxue piping zhi yanjiu" 网络文学批评之研究 (master's thesis, Tianjin Normal University 天津师范大学, 2005).
Liang, Ya 梁娅, "Jiangouzhong de wangluo wenxue pingpan jizhi" 建构中的网络文学评判机制 (master's thesis, Central China Normal University 华中师范大学, 2006).
Si, Ningda 司宁达, "Lun wangluo wenxue fazhan yu wangluo wenxue piping he lilun de hudong guanxi" 论网络文学的发展与网络文学批评和理论的互动关系 (master's thesis, Shandong University 山东大学, 2007).
Zhou, Qiuhong 周秋红, "Wangluo wenxue piping: xianzhuang jiqi zouxiang" 网络文学批评：现状及其走向 (master's thesis, Jiangxi Normal University 江西师范大学, 2007).
Liu, Ying 柳颖, "Saibo kongjian zhong de zhongsheng xuanhua—wangluo wenxue piping texing yanjiu" 赛博空间中的众声喧哗——网络文学批评特性研究 (master's thesis, Hebei University 河北大学, 2012).
Wang, Long 王龙, "Lun Zhongguo wangluo wenxue piping de tezheng yu fazhan qushi" 论中国网络文学批评的特征与发展趋势 (master's thesis, Inner Mongolia University 内蒙古大学, 2013).
29 Liu, Xiangning 刘湘宁, "Woguo wangluo wenxue piping cunzai de wenti yu duice yanjiu" 我国网络文学批评存在的问题与对策研究 (master's thesis, Central South University 中南大学, 2013).
30 Li, Jing 李静 and Shi, Shaotao 石少涛, "Wangluo wenxue piping—jiangou shuyu zishen de biaozhun" 网络文学批评——建构属于自身的标准, *Journal of Beihua University: Social Sciences Edition* 北华大学学报（社会科学版） no. 3 (2013): 92–94.
31 Kang, Qiao 康桥, "Wangluo wenxue de jiben yuanli" 网络文学的基本原理, in *Wangluo wenxue pingjia tixi xushitan* 网络文学评价体系虚实谈, ed. Creation and Research Department of China Writers Association 中国作家协会创作研究部 (Beijing: Writers Publishing House, 2014), 55–64.
32 Ouyang, Youquan 欧阳友权, "Wangluo wenxue yanjiu de qianyan wenti 网络文学研究的前沿问题," *Wenyibao* 文艺报 (Beijing), Sep. 30, 2004.
33 Liu, Lili 刘俐俐 and Li, Yuping 李玉平, "Wangluo wenxue dui wenxue piping lilun de tiaozhan" 网络文学对文学批评理论的挑战, 1–8.
34 Huang, Mingfen 黄鸣奋, "Bijiao wenxue shiye zhong de wangluo wenxue yanjiu" 比较文学视野中的网络文学研究, *Social Science Journal* 社会科学辑刊 no. 5 (2004): 143.
35 Ma, Ji 马季, "Guimo chixu zengzhang, qidai yuanchuang fali—erlingyi'er nian wangluo wenxue zongshu" 规模持续增长，期待原创发力——2012年网络文学综述, *Literary and Artistic Contention* 文艺争鸣 no. 2 (2013): 35.
36 He, Jing 何晶, "Wangluo wenxue pinglun biaozhun tixi ruhe jianli? 网络文学评论标准体系如何建立？," *Wenxue bao* 文学报 (Shanghai), May 29, 2014.
37 Translator's note: these are called "core socialist values," promoted at the 18th National Congress of the Communist Party of China in 2012.
38 Chen, Qirong 陈崎嵘, "Huyu jianli wangluo wenxue pingjia tixi 呼吁建立网络文学评价体系," *Renmin ribao* 人民日报 (Beijing), Jul. 19, 2013.
39 Chen, Qirong 陈崎嵘, "Huyu jianli wangluo wenxue pingjia tixi 呼吁建立网络文学评价体系."
40 In this article, Chen also proposed some specific criteria concerning the aesthetics of cyber literature. As to the theme of literary works, he argued:

We do not believe that the theme can determine the value of a certain work, but we do not agree that all themes are equally good. Cyber writers should consciously record the social reality of our times and faithfully represent people's life today, instead of simply writing about ghosts and gods, or about people who lived in ancient times.

As to the popular genres of cyber literature, he pointed out:

We need to pay full respect to people's choice of genres and encourage writers to make full use of these genres; we expect writers to create excellent works, or even masterpieces, of popular genres, some of which may even be passed down to later generations. Meanwhile, we should be aware that works that lack artistic creativity will die out eventually, so artistic creativity is the key to the success of cyber literature. While writing works of popular genres, writers should be creative; they should not simply follow the crowd and imitate others; they should not let their works follow a fixed pattern and become similar to each other.

As to the writing of plots, Chen pointed out:

Cyber writers should make full use of their imagination and avoid letting their plots be structurally monotonous and superficial; yet as they try to write stories that are full of mysteries and suspense, as they try to create twists and turns, they should not simply indulge in sensual pleasures and use inappropriate ways just to attract readers. Cyber literature should provide readers with a feeling of novelty, but not a feeling of grotesqueness. It should represent something fantastic, but not something eccentric.

As to the use of literary expressions, Chen argued:

We appreciate the use of the vernacular, which makes cyber literature uniquely refreshing; meanwhile, we hope that the language can be simple, pure, and refined, instead of being crude, casual, vulgar, and in a way like the "Martian language." It is okay to be self-mocking, but it is not right to be self-abasing. It is good to be creative, but it is not good to carelessly make up stories that do not make sense. It is all right to use popular elements to attract readers, but it is wrong to use unhealthy materials to contaminate readers' minds.

References

Chen, Qijia 陈奇佳. "Wangluo wenxue piping dang cong chanye jiaodu rushou 网络文学批评当从产业角度入手." *Zhongguo yishu bao* 中国艺术报 (Beijing), Dec. 18, 2013.

Chen, Qirong 陈崎嵘. "Huyu jianli wangluo wenxue pingjia tixi 呼吁建立网络文学评价体系." *Renmin ribao* 人民日报 (Beijing), Jul. 19, 2013.

Guo, Chen 郭晨 and Cai, Meijuan 蔡梅娟. "Cong wangluo wenxue kan dangdai wenxue piping de gongneng" 从网络文学看当代文学批评的功能. *Journal of Shandong University of Technology: Social Sciences Edition* 山东理工大学学报（社会科学版） no. 1 (2009): 77–79.

Guo, Guochang 郭国昌. "Wangluo wenxue huhuan wenxue piping 网络文学呼唤文学批评." *Renmin ribao* 人民日报 (Beijing), Feb. 5, 2010.

He, Jing 何晶. "Wangluo wenxue pinglun biaozhun tixi ruhe jianli? 网络文学评论标准体系如何建立？" *Wenxue bao* 文学报 (Shanghai), May 29, 2014.

Huang, Mingfen 黄鸣奋. "Wangluo wenxue zhi wojian" 网络文学之我见. *Social Science Front* 社会科学战线 no. 4 (2002): 93–98.

Huang, Mingfen 黄鸣奋. "Bijiao wenxue shiye zhong de wangluo wenxue yanjiu" 比较文学视野中的网络文学研究. *Social Science Journal* 社会科学辑刊 no. 5 (2004): 140–143.

Huang, Mingfen 黄鸣奋. "Wangluo chuanmei geming yu dianzi wenxue piping de shanbian" 网络传媒革命与电子文学批评的嬗变. *Exploration and Free Views* 探索与争鸣 no.11 (2010): 58–62.

Jiang, Bing 江冰. "'Baling hou' yu wangluo: wenxue piping de shuangchong zuge" "80后"与网络:文学批评的双重阻隔. *Southern Cultural Forum* 南方文坛 no. 4 (2010): 26–28.

Kang, Qiao 康桥. "Wangluo wenxue de jiben yuanli" 网络文学的基本原理. In *Wangluo wenxue pingjia tixi xushitan* 网络文学评价体系虚实谈, edited by Creation and Research Department of China Writers Association 中国作家协会创研部, 55–65. Beijing: Writers Publishing House, 2014.

Li, Jing 李静 and Shi, Shaotao 石少涛. "Wangluo wenxue piping—jiangou shuyu zishen de biaozhun" 网络文学批评——建构属于自身的标准. *Journal of Beihua University* 北华大学学报（社会科学版）no. 3 (2013): 92–94.

Li, Juejun 李珏君. "Wangluo nüxing yuanchuang shuxie yanjiu—yi shengda gongsi 'hongxiu tianxiang' wang weili" 网络女性原创写作研究——以盛大公司"红袖添香"网为例. Master's thesis, Shaanxi Normal University 陕西师范大学, 2012.

Liang, Ya 梁娅. "Jiangouzhong de wangluo wenxue pingpan jizhi" 建构中的网络文学评判机制. Master's thesis, Central China Normal University 华中师范大学, 2006.

Liu, Lili 刘俐俐 and Li, Yuping 李玉平. "Wangluo wenxue dui wenxue piping lilun de tiaozhan" 网络文学对文学批评理论的挑战. *Journal of Lanzhou University: Social Sciences Edition* 兰州大学学报（社会科学版）no. 5 (2004): 1–8.

Liu, Xiangning 刘湘宁. "Woguo wangluo wenxue piping cunzai de wenti yu duice yanjiu" 我国网络文学批评存在的问题与对策研究. Master's thesis, Central South University 中南大学, 2013.

Liu, Ying 柳颖. "Saibo kongjian zhong de zhongsheng xuanhua—wangluo wenxue piping texing yanjiu" 赛博空间中的众声喧哗——网络文学批评特性研究. Master's thesis, Hebei University 河北大学, 2012.

Ma, Ji 马季. "Huayu fangshi zhuanbian zhong de wangluo xiezuo—jianping wangluo xiaoshuo shinian shibu jiazuo" 话语方式转变中的网络写作——兼评网络小说十年十部佳作. *Literary and Artistic Contention* 文艺争鸣 no. 19 (2010): 18–24.

Ma, Ji 马季. "Guimo chixu zengzhang, qidai yuanchuang fali—erlingyi'er nian wangluo wenxue zongshu" 规模持续增长，期待原创发力——2012年网络文学综述. *Literary and Artistic Contention* 文艺争鸣 no. 2 (2013): 34–42.

Ma, Ji 马季. "Shichang jizhi xia de wangluo wenxue shenmei shiyu—wangluo wenxue zhiyu zhongguo dangdai wenxue de sange bianliang" 市场机制下的网络文学审美视域——网络文学之于中国当代文学的三个变量. *Creation and Criticism* 创作与评论 no. 4 (2015): 54–60.

Ouyang, Youquan 欧阳友权. "Hulianwang shang de wenxue fengjing—woguo wangluo wenxue xianzhuang diaocha yu zoushi fenxi" 互联网上的文学风景——我国网络文学现状调查与走势分析. *Journal of China Three Gorges University: The Humanities and Social Sciences Edition* 三峡大学学报（人文社会科学版）no. 6 (2001): 5–9.

Ouyang, Youquan 欧阳友权. "Lun wangluo wenxue de jingshen quxiang" 论网络文学的精神取向. *Literature & Art Studies* 文艺研究 no. 5 (2002): 74–82.

Ouyang, Youquan 欧阳友权. "Wangluo wenxue yanjiu de qianyan wenti 网络文学研究的前沿问题." *Wenyi bao* 文艺报 (Beijing), Sep. 30, 2004.

Ouyang, Youquan 欧阳友权. "Shuzi meijie xia wenlun zhuanxing de sange weidu" 数字媒介下文论转型的三个维度. *Hebei Academic Journal* 河北学刊 no. 2 (2007): 119–122+131.

Ouyang, Youquan 欧阳友权. "Chongxie wenxueshi yu wangluo wenxue 'rushi' wenti" 重写文学史与网络文学"入史"问题. *Hebei Academic Journal* 河北学刊 no. 5 (2013): 8–12.

Ouyang, Youquan 欧阳友权. "Zhongguo wangluo wenxue yanjiu jidian jiqi yujing xuanze" 中国网络文学研究基点及其语境选择. *Hebei Academic Journal* 河北学刊 no. 4 (2015): 96–99.

Ouyang, Youquan 欧阳友权 and Wu, Yingwen 吴英文. "Wangluo wenxue piping de jiazhi he juxian" 网络文学批评的价值和局限. *Exploration and Free Views* 探索与争鸣 no. 11 (2010): 63–66.

Shao, Yanjun 邵燕君. "Miandui wangluo wenxue: xueyuanpai de taidu he fangfa" 面对网络文学：学院派的态度和方法. *Southern Cultural Forum* 南方文坛 no. 6 (2011): 12–18.

Shu, Jinyu 舒晋瑜. "Qiu Huadong tan suowei wangluo wenxue: juedabufen shi wenzi laji 邱华栋谈所谓网络文学：绝大部分是文字垃圾." *Zhonghua dushu bao* 中华读书报 (Beijing), Dec. 7, 2011.

Si, Ningda 司宁达. "Miwang yu qingxing—wangluo wenxue piping chutan" 迷惘与清醒——网络文学批评初探. *Journal of Nanyang Normal University: Social Sciences Edition* 南阳师范大学学报（社会科学版）no. 11 (2005): 70–73.

Si, Ningda 司宁达. "Lun wangluo wenxue fazhan yu wangluo wenxue piping he lilun de hudong guanxi" 论网络文学的发展与网络文学批评和理论的互动关系. Master's thesis, Shandong University 山东大学, 2007.

Wang, Long 王龙. "Lun Zhongguo wangluo wenxue piping de tezheng yu fazhan qushi" 论中国网络文学批评的特征与发展趋势. Master's thesis, Inner Mongolia University 内蒙古大学, 2013.

Wang, Yan 王艳. "Wangluo wenxue yanjiu zai xifang" 网络文学研究在西方. *Journal of Beijing International Studies University* 北京第二外国语学院学报 no. 12 (2011): 42–48.

Zhang, Jing 张晶. "Wangluo wenxue piping zhi yanjiu" 网络文学批评之研究. Master's thesis, Tianjin Normal University 天津师范大学, 2005.

Zhang, Xuan 张萱. "Wangluo nüxing yanqing xiaoshuo chutan" 网络女性言情小说初探. Master's thesis, Hebei Normal University 河北师范大学, 2012.

Zhou, Qiuhong 周秋红. "Wangluo wenxue piping: xianzhuang jiqi zouxiang" 网络文学批评：现状及其走向. Master's thesis, Jiangxi Normal University 江西师范大学, 2007.

8 Changes in the Function of Cyber Literary Criticism

Since the end of the 20th century, the old ecological structure of literary criticism has been under a subversive impact from the rise of cyber literature and its criticism. In just a few decades, legions of netizens broke into the holy temple of literary criticism and claimed its territories. The virtual space, which is home to nearly 380 million literary netizens, has become the base for cyber literary criticism.

As it became the norm for netizens to write commentaries after reading online, cyber literary criticism became the first choice through which many young people met literature and literary criticism. Over time, this new form of popular literary criticism grew out of its original chaos and became more orderly, organized, and personalized. Cyber critics congregated, while the textual form, media platform, and criteria for cyber literary criticism also took shape. This has not only given rise to a group of professional websites dedicated to literary criticism but also attracted many online literary critics, who are familiar with the ecology of cyber literature and well-armed with online communication skills and fair theoretical literacy. Thus, the critical writings generated in cyberspace now serve to guide the creation and reading of cyber literature, a sign that cyber literary criticism is becoming increasingly influential and its unique value increasingly apparent.

What different functions, then, has cyber literary criticism served, compared to its traditional counterpart? Originating on the Internet and flourishing among the masses, what kind of changes has it undergone? This chapter will trace the development of China's cyber literary criticism over the past 20 years to present a history of transformations: first, cyber literary criticism subverted the condition of traditional literary criticism and shared with the masses the right to write their own literary criticism; then, an online criticism ecology with postmodern characteristics was created; finally, there was a convergence of netizens' commentaries and scholars' articles, which gave rise to many innovations in theoretical discussions.

DOI: 10.4324/9781003428480-11

Sharing the Right to Literary Criticism through Subversion

For a long time, the discursive power of literary criticism was seized by an elite group consisting mainly of scholars and was wielded by literary and art practitioners and critics who had received higher education and undergone professional training. As a result, literary criticism followed the classic criteria recognized by the academic circle to represent a universal standard. Articles of criticism were written in a systematic and rational way with the assistance of critical theories and reviewed by editors before they were published. However, since the birth of cyber literary criticism, everything has been indisputably subverted. The anti-traditional "devils" released by the Pandora's Box of the Internet, in the form of ordinary netizens, broke all rules of literary criticism and initiated a redistribution of the right to literary criticism. A new phase of literary criticism was introduced by the Internet era.

Breaking the Monopoly of Elite Criticism: The Rise of the Grassroots

Premodern Chinese literary criticism followed the tradition of "essays by sagacious Confucian scholars," reserving the right to talk about literature and criticism to the erudite. It was a time when not many could read and write. Only the elite could cultivate a sense of literary criticism and leave behind thoughts, essays, and monographs, whereas the general public could only expect to be occasionally guided and enlightened. As time passed, people came to see literary criticism as a highbrow and exclusive activity, unrelated to ordinary literature lovers, let alone people who knew little about literature.

Things are very different with cyber literary criticism. The advent of the Internet and new technology brought literature online. A global village was formed, and the World Wide Web, with its vast open cyberspace and the equality, immediacy, interactivity, low cost, personalization, easy transmission, and easy storage enabled by new media platforms, for the first time conferred the right to literary criticism to anyone with the basic Internet operation skills. The tradition of literary criticism was subverted and the monopoly of elite criticism was broken. Everyone who can type has the equal right to publish literary reviews on the Internet. The scarcity of "communication capital" is no longer a stumbling block that hinders ordinary people from participating in literary criticism. Editors and reviewers—the traditional goalkeepers of literary criticism—are bypassed, and the podium previously reserved for a few experienced speakers is now open to all. This innovative and immensely popular platform for speech and publishing has attracted an overwhelming number of literary netizens. By leaving comments on portal websites, (micro) blogging platforms, WeChat, forums, and other social network media, they participate in online literary criticism. Each day brings out a large number of new critics hailing from all professions and fields of training. As someone famously puts it on the Internet, "Online criticism works at any time for everyone without restraint. In the internet era, we are all literary critics."

It is against this background that a group of early literary netizens, intentionally or not, joined the camp of cyber literary criticism. Beginning with a few words and phrases to express their feelings after reading an online article, the readers gradually gathered toward websites that were dedicated to literary criticism and published longer commentaries with strong opinions, prospering cyberspace with a wide variety of ideas.

As one example, *Dragon's Sky* (Long de tiankong), a platform for original web fiction and criticism, is home to a large group of cyber literary critics who have taken part in the rise of China's cyber literature. Even before 2006, the website had already registered more than 10,000 critics, and over 3,000 original reviews can still be viewed today. Many early participants were not professional critics but readers who liked cyber literature or wrote fiction online. They joined the camp of cyber literary criticism and left behind many well-known reviews. Li Xunhuan, one of the first-generation cyber writers in mainland China, commented on this tide of cyber literary criticism: "I can judge by the market and see how many times my article was downloaded and clicked ... No trend could be formed if only ten people looked at my stuff, but when a hundred people have read it, the impact will be stronger than that of the review by a famous critic."[1] His view is very representative, calling attention to the influence of public participation in the field of criticism. Tie Ning, chairman of China Writers Association, also remarked, "The Internet is a space for numerous ideas to clash and flourish. In no other era have literature and literary criticism prospered without restraint like this."[2]

The Entrance of Netspeak

Cyber literary criticism set off a linguistic revolution. Born out of the marriage of literary criticism and the Internet, cyber literary criticism speaks a down-to-earth language that can be understood by ordinary people. It has broken through the "siege" of traditional literary criticism with an overwhelming momentum, subverting the professional model of discourse with simple, straightforward, and popular narratives.

To begin with, cyber literary criticism undercuts the seriousness of academic literary criticism with colloquialism, using a crisp and lively netspeak that is easy to understand and close to the language used in daily communication. Cyberwriting happens online, and so does the majority of its criticism, which takes place instantly and interactively. The communication between critics and readers via the Internet is more like a conversation over the phone and very different from epistolary correspondence or the reading of books and newspapers. The communicating parties seek to quickly understand each other and strike up a conversation, exchanging short pieces of writing with lively and relaxed expressions, in contrast to the analytical language employed by traditional literary criticism. In some cases, the criticism reads just like blabber. Take, for example, the following comment on a web novel, *The Strongest Rebirth System* (Zuiqiang chongsheng xitong).

It's the old story of a mature guy dating a juvenile girl, plus scoring a career and kicking some ass. But unlike the previous books in the series, this one doesn't impress me much, and there are several reasons. First, the heroine's inclination for arrogance and jealousy is truly unlovable, and second, the guy, when dating the heroine, also flirts with the girl next door, and this shady relationship is glossed over by the name of "taking care of a little sister." Is that how you take care of your little sister? I'd feel better if you simply say you want to be two-timing. What's more, he is also taken with the heroine's mother and admired by his cousin (a distant one, maybe). Oh, what a mess.[3]

Comments like this use a slangy and straightforward language to critique cyber literature and express opinions, aiming not at any serious academic inquiry but to ridicule and poke fun.

Moreover, cyber literary criticism dissolves the academic nature of criticism with a lowbrow character that is manifested in three aspects. First, cyber literary criticism seldom employs technical terms or applies critical theories; instead, it targets specific issues in the text and focuses on the object of criticism without resorting to abstract concepts or contexts. Second, it foregrounds the critic's reading experience, supplementing it with a comparison with other cyberwritings, and downplays logical reasoning and analytical arguments. Third, it fosters a closer relationship with authors, readers, and other critics in cyberspace, treating the authors with an equal or sincere attitude instead of being condescending. For example, a netizen who used the nickname "Big Fathead Fish" (Da pangtouyu) wrote in a post entitled "A Few Casual Words on *Solo Dancer in Troubled Times*" (Guanyu *Luanshi de duwu zhe*, suibian liao shang jiju) in 2004:

As a fellow writer who also writes this kind of long fictional pieces and who has been walking a long way down this path with much stumbling, I'd like to share these words with latecomers...

The portrayal of the characters makes one feel a bit like reading a purified version of *Rivers and Mountains* (Jiangshan ruci duo jiao) in a military setting,[4] not only because both use the first-person perspective but also because the characters are very similar—they're either exceptionally smart or extremely skilled in martial arts. In short, no one is an ordinary person. The gathering of so many extraordinary characters forms a typical scene in Wen Rui'an's work—nine out of ten people selling cabbage on that street are first-rate masters, and the remaining one a one-time master.[5] Is there only one selling tofu? Oh, that's the master of masters...

Regarding the portrayal of the protagonist: the author seems to have intended the protagonist as a bystander character but is unwilling to exclude him from experiencing the real thing, so there is some contradiction in the protagonist's depiction... It's like, when the author invites us to watch the protagonist play cards with the others, he wants us to enjoy the thrills but is unwilling to take the risk of losing. So the author repeatedly tells us that the protagonist has a trump card in his hand—"he is one of the demons' clan and he will never lose"—that kind of thing, ha ha.[6]

The reviewer is also a web fiction writer, so his review is based on his experience of writing long fictional works. He adopts a simple and frivolous style to convey his feelings without quoting any theories, which is typical of online reviews.

Last, cyber literary criticism "disenchants" the sacredness of literary criticism with a casual and impromptu style. "Disenchantment" is a term used by Max Weber to describe people's doubt about and devaluation of the sublime, elegant, and grand narrative of science, culture, and knowledge. I once said in an article: "Internet technology, which makes anything imaginable possible, not only helps people visualize their imagination and realize their dreams, but also brings the 'authoritative discourse' down from its pedestal. It strips away the mysticism of the classic, the noble, the magnificent, and the sacred and hands over the tool of 'disenchantment' to the ordinary people."[7] Online critics do not regard literary criticism as a sacred matter but treat it as a doodle board for scribbling and entertaining themselves and others. They tap a few lines on the keyboard on a whim, producing a few words, a long article, or just a few simple emoticons. With such impromptu writing, the literary criticism of former times has been desacralized by technology.

Take, for example, the following review on *A Record of a Mortal's Journey to Immortality* (Fanren xiuxian zhuan), a novel regarded as the acme of fantasies about attaining immortality.

> He keeps gulping down medicine and growing herbs. He keeps participating in the exchange meetings. He keeps going into instance dungeons. He keeps looking for stupid fellows to team up with, and his teammates are fairies, pretty women, old men, strapping guys, and youngsters... The instance dungeons he enters always look simple, but accidents always happen. His teammates are always killed by accidents, and he reaps the profit. His opponents generally seem to come from higher levels than he, but... they don't run as fast as him... Then he goes on to brew his medicine. Now let's change the names and do it again![8] But you will never get tired of it! Because there're so many names and they are awesome! The Yuanhe Mountain of Five Levels! The Supreme Spirit-Slaughtering Sword! The Sky-Scraping Creation Dew! The Tripod of Empty Heaven! The Formula of Grand Evolution! The Glazed Bells of Five Wonders! The Supreme Blade of Wish! The Blood Crystal Maha Sword! (OMG, how is one to write the next book if they forget the names) whatever[9]... Han Li pinches his fingers with his thumb as he chants the formula and, turning into a flash of light, sweeps away![10]

This reviewer incisively mocks the inconsistency in the protagonist's image and repeated patterns in the plot but also acknowledges the novel's creation of magical weapons and a magical world. Despite its impromptu style and mixed use of Chinese and English, this review strikes a chord with many netizens, receiving more than a thousand "likes."

Building the Paradigm of Cyber Literary Criticism

With new works springing up in large numbers every day, cyber literature poses a challenge to criticism. Netizens' freedom needs to be guaranteed, but literary criticism as a science requires that certain standards and principles must be followed. Traditional critics may be indifferent to cyber literature, or they may want to learn about and understand cyber literature but have no clue how to choose from the sea of works or are unfamiliar with Internet technology. Still others, after their critical views went online, were caught by vengeful netizens and, unable to stand the pressure, have chosen to be mere bystanders in order to stay away from trouble. Meanwhile, ordinary netizens now enjoy an environment that allows them to be anonymous and free, where they are motivated to grab the attention of others. With the casual and community-based online atmosphere, they have the impulse to express themselves, and many become active literary critics.

Unlike traditional literary criticism, which has established a set of evaluation criteria, online criticism does not have a unified evaluation rubric or a fixed procedure to follow, and there is no specified format for the text to be evaluated. However, some netizens also try to propose criteria for cyber literary criticism. For example, netizen Ailu'en proposed six criteria to judge the quality of a review and the competence of the reviewer:

1) [Strength] Lucid expression. Strength is related to the most basic melee damage output. An article with a low strength level will fail to convey meaning and instead cause confusion.
2) [Dexterity] Clear structure. Dexterity means two things. The first is speed, which is reflected by the rate at which words are produced. The second is the coordination of movements, which refers to how arguments are organized in a review.
3) [Physical constitution] Rigorous logic. The logic of a review is founded on rigorous reasoning supported by accurate evidence. In addition, the perseverance in writing reviews is also an indicator of one's physical constitution.
4) [Intelligence] Solid theory. If a reviewer scores high on the above three attributes, they can write reviews that are well organized and thoroughly reasoned. But reviews of this kind can still vary in quality. To a review, its strength in each attribute determines its value.
5) [Perception] Keen observation. As long as your attribute points of perception are high, you can give a powerful roasting even if your other attributes are weak.
6) [Charm] Graceful style. This is easy to understand: the style of a review should be charming. If the review and the novel it reviews are close in style, the review may be able to achieve the best effect.[11]

Similar ideas about the criteria for judging texts of literature and their criticism are often seen on the Internet. Although the validity and appropriateness of such critical texts remain disputable, they demonstrate an awareness of the need to establish criteria and paradigms for cyber literary criticism and an innovative endeavor to achieve that goal.

In fact, most online literary reviews base their evaluations on reviewers' subjective opinions. Under the Matthew effect of accumulated advantage and the psychological mechanism of the "spiral of silence," the numerous netizens' opinions inevitably work together to exclude dissenting views and form a dominant view that influences the opinion of others. Such an evaluation system and opinion environment are like a double-edged sword, bringing both opportunities and challenges to the construction of the criteria for cyber literary criticism.

On the one hand, with the minority yielding to the majority and pleasure and fun taking precedence, cyber literary criticism lays the cornerstone for the establishment of values that are free from the monopoly of academia. Cyber literature that withstands the test of time and is popular among netizens not only makes a name for itself, but also impels scholarly critics to see readers' reception and satisfaction as an important criterion for literary criticism. This system urges elite literature to "come from the masses and go to the masses." On the other hand, with its spontaneity, disorder, and lack of a standard, cyber literary criticism dissolves the values of traditional criticism to the extent that "the criteria that have been considered to be ideal are repressed and greatly invalidated."[12] The power to judge is completely placed in the hands of online critics. As a result, the humanist and aesthetic value of literary criticism is compromised, leading to overgeneralization and diminution of the evaluation criteria, as well as shallow interpretations or misreadings of texts.

Postmodern Characteristics of Cyber Literary Criticism

Cyber literary criticism in China took root in a culture that rejected centralized and authoritative discourses and promoted cultural diversity. Emerging in the era of Reform and Opening-up, when new ideas rushed in thanks to China's ideological emancipation, cyber literary criticism, as well as cyber literature, is nurtured by postmodernism and plays a role that bespeaks its postmodern upbringing.

Promoting Openness, Interaction, and Competition in Criticism

Cyber literary criticism occupies an open space on the Internet, where the competition between cyber literary criticism and traditional criticism is intensified. Literary criticism before the Internet era saw competitions only among individuals within the elite group or between different schools of scholars. Such competitions rigidly revolved around literature despite the contesting methodologies. Cyber literary criticism broke the monopoly by handing over the right to criticism to the general public, creating an open space that encompasses opposing viewpoints and diverse methods.

The formation of this new public sphere encourages competition and interaction between traditional literary criticism and cyber literary criticism and opens up new vistas. This is not only because the latter establishes itself by challenging the authority of the former, but also because each functions both as the target of criticism and the object of reference for the other, working toward their mutual improvement through competition. Take, for example, a representative web novel, *The Story of Wukong* (Wukong zhuan) by "Where Has All This Gone" (Jin hezai), which has attracted the attention of scholars as well as netizens. Both sides have published many review articles, but the titles, perspectives, and contents of those reviews show a distinct difference. Whereas scholarly reviews generally focus on a novel's characterization, its representation of characters' psychological movements, its stylistic and cultural elements, and the postmodern spirit, netizens tend to concentrate on their reading experience as well as the novel's textual features and techniques. In an open and competitive environment, the two groups complement and learn from each other to bring readers a fuller understanding of the literary text. Table 8.1 compares the two types of review articles on *The Story of Wukong*:

Table 8.1 Representative reviews on *The Story of Wukong* written by scholars and ordinary netizens

Scholars' reviews		Netizens' reviews	
Article title	A Heroic Tragedy and Classic Parody: Interpreting *The Story of Wukong* as a Web Novel (Yingxiong de beiju, xifang de jingdian— wangluo xiaoshuo *Wukong zhuan* de shendu jiedu)	Article title	A Great Book (Henhao de yibu shu)
Author	Lin Huayu	Author	Xiaoxiaosheng
Source	*Masterpieces Review* (Mingzuo xinshang)	Source	*Douban*
Date	August 15, 2002	Date	July 1, 2005
Article title	Can the World be Without a "Circlet"? (Shijie mei "gu" xingma?)	Article title	One of the Books that Influenced My College Life: *The Story of Wukong* (Daxue shidai yingxiang wode shu zhi *Wukong zhuan*)

(*Continued*)

Table 8.1 (Continued)

Scholars' reviews		Netizens' reviews	
Author	You Xin	Author	"Nine P.M." (Wuhou Jiushi)
Source	*China Press Publication Radio Film and Television Journal* (Zhongguo xinwen chuban guangdian bao)	Source	*Douban*
Date	March 25, 2003	Date	March 23, 2006
Article title	Nobler than All the Gods: A Way of Reading Jin Hezai's *The Story of Wukong* (Benxing bi suoyou de shenming dou gaogui Jin Hezai *Wukong zhuan* de yizhong jiedu)	Article title	A Sad Look in Mute Pain (Teng de fabuchu sheng lai de bei'ai yanshen)
Author	Yang Xinmin	Author	"Bigheaded Lollipop" (Datou Lollipop)
Source	*Journal of Nanjing University of Posts and Telecommunications* (Nanjing youdian xueyuan xuebao)	Source	*Douban*
Date	June 30, 2005	Date	September 19, 2007
Article title	A Preliminary Study of the Writing Style of *The Story of Wukong* (*Wukong zhuan* de yuyan tese chutan)	Article title	A Reflection on the Chinese People's Character (Guoren jingshen de fansi)
Author	Zhao Chan	Author	Youba
Source	*Journal of Hubei University of Broadcasting and Television* (Hubei guangbo dianshi daxue bao)	Source	*Douban*
Date	July 20, 2008	Date	April 12, 2008
Article title	An Analysis of the Psychological Structure in *The Story of Wukong* (*Wukong zhuan* xinlijiegou weidu de fenxi)	Article title	The Gist is Love: She is Not Vulgar at All (Zhuzhi shi ai: ta yidian ye busu)
Author	Tian Lin	Author	Wuxi
Source	*Xiandai Yuwen* (Modern Chinese)	Source	*Douban*
Date	April 5, 2009	Date	May 30, 2009

Table 8.1 (Continued)

Scholars' reviews		Netizens' reviews	
Article title	*The Story of Wukong*: Deconstructing the Sacred through Parody (*Wukong zhuan*: zai xifang zhong jiegou shensheng)	Article title	He Who Cannot Forget His Dream (Wangbuliao mengxiang de ren)
Author	Gong Fanmin	Author	Renjian Jiangliu
Source	*Journal of Kaili University* (Kaili xueyuan xuebao)	Source	*Douban*
Date	August 25, 2010	Date	June 2, 2009
Article title	A Preliminary Study of the Postmodern Spirit of the Characters of *The Story of Wukong* (Qianxi Wukong zhuan zhong renwu de houxiandai zhuyi jingshen)	Article title	Sun Wukong and the Illusory Nature of the World: On *The Story of Wukong* (Sun Wukong he sidajiekong: du *Wukong zhuan*)
Author	Shao Min	Author	shark-bones
Source	*Journal of Mudanjiang University* (Mudanjiang daxue xuebao)	Source	*Douban*
Date	August 25, 2012	Date	October 28, 2009
Scholarly reviews	Online reviews		
Article title	Reading *Journey to the West* through the Lenses of *A Chinese Odyssey* and *The Story of Wukong* (*Dahua xiyou* yu *Wukong zhuan* shijiao xia de *Xiyou ji*)	Article title	Gibberish on *The Story of Wukong* (Luhui luantan zhi *Wukong zhuan*)
Author	Jia Ningbo	Author	Beiyuan
Source	*Culture and Education* (Wenjiao ziliao)	Source	*Good Books Net* (Youshu wang)
Date	November 25, 2012	Date	November 5, 2010
Article title	On the Rebellious Spirit in *The Story of Wukong*, An Old Story Retold (Lun gushi xinbian xiaoshuo *Wukong zhuan* zhong de panni jingshen)	Article title	About Youth and Existence: *The Story of Wukong* in My Memory (Guanyu qingchun guanyu cunzai: wo jiyizhong de *Wukong zhuan*)
Author	Jia Yingni and Liu Ziyu	Author	Zhaoyang

(*Continued*)

Table 8.1 (Continued)

Scholars' reviews		Netizens' reviews	
Source	*Masterpieces Review* (Mingzuo xinshang)	Source	*Douban*
Date	May 1, 2013	Date	September 1, 2011
Article title	*The Story of Wukong* through a Postmodernist Lens (Houxiandai zhuyi guanzhao xia de *Wukong zhuan*)	Article title	The Classic of all Time in My Heart—*The Story of Wukong* (Jinian xinzhong yongheng de jingdian—*Wukong zhuan*)
Author	Zhao Rubing	Author	Ruqianwojiao'ao
Source	*Journal of Yichun College* (Yichun xueyuan xuebao)	Source	*Good Books Net*
Date	July 25, 2013	Date	May 28, 2012
Article title	Not Dying, Not Vanishing: Reflections on *The Story of Wukong* (Busibumie—du *Wukong zhuan* yougan)	Article title	*The Story of Wukong*, I Read It But Didn't Quite Get It (*Wukong zhuan*, kanle bushi hendong)
Author	Xu Minglü	Author	Yingye
Source	*Fine Writing* (Meiwen)	Source	*Good Books Net*
Date	November 15, 2013	Date	May 9, 2013
Article title	Modernist Writing in a Postmodern Disguise (Houxiandai pixiang xia de xiandaizhuyi xiezuo)	Article title	I Read *The Story of Wukong* and It Really Is a Knockout! (Kanle *Wukong zhuan*, bukui wei zhongkouxiangchuan de shenzuo)
Author	Jiang Zhenyu	Author	Huimou Yixiao
Source	*Newspaper of Literature and Art* (Wenyi bao)	Source	*Good Books Net*
Date	July 21, 2014	Date	June 3, 2013
Article title	A Classical Hero's Sortie Against the World: The Evolution of the Theme of *Journey to the West* Seen through the Lenses of *A Chinese Odyssey* and *The Story of Wukong* (Gudian yingxiong de shisu tuwei—cong *Dahua xiyou*, *Wukong zhuan* kan xiyou zhuti de bianqian)	Article title	The Masterpiece in My Heart (Xinzhong de shenzuo)

Table 8.1 (Continued)

Scholars' reviews		Netizens' reviews	
Source	*Culture and History Vision* (Wenshi bolan)	Source	*Good Books Net*
Date	September 28, 2014	Date	October 9, 2015

(Source: data collected by the author)

As can be seen from the titles of the articles, scholarly reviews are dignified and elegant, while netizens' reviews are simple and straightforward; the former are more rational and emphasize textual interpretation, while the latter are more perceptual, focusing on individual experience and intuition. The two types of reviews were published on different platforms, and the difference in their style and content demonstrates their distinct characteristics. Cyber literary criticism thrives through the complementary co-existence of the two types. This decentered heteroglossia is one of the postmodern characteristics of cyber literary criticism.

Recent years have witnessed a shift in cyber literary criticism: it is no longer wordy and lacks solid reasoning but has become more professional with the advent of some websites dedicated to literary criticism. Critical articles are collected and published from time to time, and new critics like Wang Shuo and Han Han made their names. Traditional scholars, buffeted by a loss of audience and impact, are also working hard to make their reviews of cyber literature more readable. Scholars like Bai Ye and Ma Ji now participate in the review of cyber literary works. Criticism of cyber literature will prosper as scholars and ordinary netizens compete and complement each other in their writings.

Respecting Netizens' Personal Experience and Different Styles

Another postmodern characteristic of cyber literary criticism is its respect for personal experience, support for the liberation of individuality, and promotion of freedom and diversity.

After an early period of unchecked growth, cyber literary criticism has become the choice of many literary netizens. When they participate in online literary criticism, the netizens do not seek to understand and study literary theories or methodologies but simply transcribe whatever they think or feel into words. They share their reading experience as to whether they were captivated by the story and enjoyed reading it, whether they get to read a new installment every day, whether they can sympathize with the world described and the protagonist's experience, and so on. In cyber literary criticism, one is allowed to describe a unique mindset, vocalize some unconventional views, deviate from accepted formats, and write a tit-for-tat response to another critic. There is room for sentimental improvisation, comic hyperbole, and slapstick humor, but obscure jargon and unoriginal views will incur ridicule. In order to attract attention, online critics do not hesitate to use extreme expressions to stir up strong emotions as much as possible, and the sensational is constantly in the spotlight. All this has certainly contributed to the pursuit of novelty and the rise of verbal violence on the Internet and hindered the rationalization and maturity of cyber literary criticism, but it has also played an irreplaceable role in promoting equal participation and free expression of individual netizens.

In the book review section of literary websites, apart from the functional "sign-in" and "like" posts, a majority consists of simple comments of one or two sentences. These comments may be fragmentary and informal, but they arouse the enthusiasm of others to respond and post longer reviews. The opinion of one person is inevitably one-sided, but the confluence of opinions can assist the comprehensive evaluation of a work.

The longer reviews also show diversity in styles and techniques. For example, a reader writes in a review of the cyber writer "Annie Baby" (Anni baobei):

> When my brainpower sags, I read the IKEA pamphlets, short pieces by Haruki Murakami, and Annie Baby ... It seems to me she used to be inexperienced and vain, and it makes me snigger to reread many of the sentences in *Farewell to Vivian* (Gaobie Wei'an). With the invariable scene of black lace lingerie and the long-haired woman on top, she didn't seem to be very experienced with sex. And the luxuries she so smugly flaunted—Esprit, Kenzo—are merely midrange stuff. She also had a small vocabulary and had to use one image again and again, not to mention her repetition of the adjectives. After *The Era of Awakening* (Qingxing ji), however, she seems to have reconciled with herself and settled down. Her writing becomes relaxed and sumptuous, and she demonstrates much richer experience. It is just like the change of an actress of humble origin, who, after marrying into a rich and influential family, washes off her heavy makeup to keep a low profile.[13]

This review combines an evaluation of the writer with the experience and imagination of the reviewer. It is precisely because the reviewer's subjective expression has captured some of the typical features of Annie Baby's works that it strikes a chord with many other readers and is widely circulated.

For another example, someone wrote about the famous web novel *Stories of the Ming Dynasty* (Mingchao naxie shi'er) on *Douban* as follows:

> The *Stories of the Ming Dynasty* hit the Internet with great success, and it did so with nothing other than gossip and entertainment. We have not treated the word "gossip" with fairness. What is gossip? It's to pry into and dig out something unknown to most people ... Just like the popular Super

Girls, the *Stories of the Ming Dynasty* satisfies the need of us, the so-called "grassroots," to gossip about history.[14]

While many critics write about the plot, characterization, and style of *Stories of the Ming Dynasty*, this reviewer's interpretation of readers' psychology provides a new perspective. Online reviews like this not only liberate netizens' power to speak but also change the ecology of literary criticism, thus being conducive to perfecting the paradigm of literary criticism.

Promoting Diversity in Aesthetic Trends

In literary criticism, an aesthetic trend is the values—the aesthetic, social, historical, humanistic, and cultural values—that criticism is based on. The Internet, with its multiple centers and nodes, its web-like structure, and a space that tolerates free and equal speech, renders cyber literary criticism "decentralized." It promotes diverse cultural values by subscribing to postmodernism's defiance of centralized discourses.

First, cyber literary criticism jettisons literary criticism's tendency toward a unitary standard and turns criticism from a "center" into a "node." The monolithic constitution of critics, who belong to the same class and have similar tastes, gives way to a multi-center and multi-node tree structure on the Internet. Among the diverse literary ideals, traditional values of literary criticism no longer remain at the center, and the value system of literary criticism is changed as a result.

Second, since cyber literary criticism connects with the masses and the market, it enables popular literary tastes and values of the culture industry to become important parts of literary criticism. Some fiction genres, such as martial arts, romance, and thriller, are excluded from the mainstream and often overlooked by traditional literary criticism. But with cyber literary criticism, a work is valued for its click-through rate (CTR) and the ratio of the positive reviews it receives, no matter what genre it belongs to. The clear data and short comments become the advertisement of online publications, among which martial arts stories, romances, fantasies, and thrillers tend to receive more attention. As a result, works in those popular subgenres are mass-produced: we can see this on the cyber literature rating website, *Good Books Net* (Youshu wang).[15]

In addition, with the development of the culture industry, cyber literature acquires an economic value as it is now put on the market. The economic value thus becomes a new dimension for the evaluation of cyber literature, apart from its value as serious literature and its value as popular literature.

The diversity in cyber literary criticism makes it possible for critics to more effectively guide specific cyberwritings and make them more valuable. Cyber literature boasts a vast diversity, and its fictional subgenres alone number in the dozens, ranging from fantasy and martial arts novels to city and workplace fiction, and from historical and military accounts to time-traveling and gaming stories. Each subgenre hosts a great variety of subject matters, writing styles, and artistic tastes, which inevitably affects the evaluation criteria, making it possible to replace the traditional monistic model of criticism with the pluralism endorsed by postmodernism.

Old and the New Roles of Literary Criticism

The Perpetual Humanist Concern of Literary Criticism

Literary criticism aims to "decode" a work's literariness and aesthetic value, a role that originated from the importance we attach to literature. If the functional value given to literature has any stability and consistency, then any kind of literature should have the same stability and consistency in its functional value as such. I call it literature's "burden of significance and value."[16] Cyber literature has its own burden of significance and value and must carry on the literary tradition. Cyber literary criticism thus needs to identify and evaluate such a burden in cyber literature. No matter if it is regarded as a work of intellectual significance, a product of popular culture, or simply a literary work, a work of cyber literature should always focus on its value, meaning, aesthetics, and other ideological functions, while its criticism focuses on these "foci" in turn.

Cyber literature, as a product of mass culture, should convey positive cultural values, and its criticism also has the responsibility to evaluate and relay that message. People's freedom in cyberspace and the lack of a threshold for online publication have fundamentally changed literature and its criticism: the rapid popularization of digital "we media," such as blogs, microblogs, and WeChat, has made the dream that "everyone can be a writer" come true; as a result, literary creation is rendered less elitist and more approachable, to the extent of being like the production of fast food at McDonald's, and literature is valued less as something to be worshipped than for entertainment. Driven by profit and under the pressure to release new installments, cyber writers bang out works with little regard for quality and content. Shoddy products flood the Internet as there are now no editors serving as "gatekeepers." The boundaries between literary creation and the mass production of cultural commodities, as well as the boundaries between literature and non-literature, are blurred. It has become more difficult to separate good works from bad ones.

An overtly commercialized media environment that prioritizes entertainment may dampen writers' sense of responsibility, leading to a lack of loftiness in cyber literature and alienating literature from its duty to represent the "conscience of the times" and speak for the people. The result is collusion between Internet media and popular culture: what they produce is not the positive energy that society needs, but expressions solely aimed at amusing themselves and the masses—in other words, cultural fast food that caters to the market—and even noises in the public sphere. To rectify such a deviation, we must first correct the values that went astray, and that is exactly the duty of cyber literary criticism: to bring the erroneous values back to the path of cultural and aesthetic correctness.

Furthermore, cyber literature, as a kind of literature, must be endowed with a humanistic aesthetics, which should be supported by cyber literary criticism, as it has the function of evaluating and guiding cyberwriting and is capable of leading public opinion. Most literary writing and reading, in print or online, should be an act of artistic appreciation that carries a humanistic spirit, expresses or satisfies people's wishes, offers pleasure, and represents the relationship between humanity and the world. Therefore, cyber literature, instead of being a mere technical operation, should be a purposeful activity that engages literary netizens and carries humanistic values. If literature is the torch of the national spirit, cyber literature should fuel it and make it brighter; if literature is the "light that guides the nation on its spiritual path to the future" (Lu Xun's words), cyber literature has the responsibility to safeguard it and make sure it continues to guide us in the age of the Internet. In other words, cyberwriting should assume the responsibility of carefully handling literature's relationship with history, morality, social justice, and positive cultural values. It must engage society to boost positive energy and tell "China stories" well, which is also the invariable responsibility of cyber literary criticism.

Of course, compared with traditional literature, cyber literature has more freedom and fewer restrictions. It values readers' choices and the recognition by the market over conventions. From this point of view, it may seem unreasonable to ask cyber literature to be a carrier of positive social values, to ask literary netizens to contribute to the promotion of such values, or to ask cyber literary criticism to adhere to an "orthodox" just as traditional criticism does. However, we do have such an expectation for literature and literary criticism through all times, from poems in the Tang and the Song dynasties to fiction in the Ming and the Qing, and throughout the literary tradition since the May Fourth. Even Western modernist writers known for their nonconformity and rebellious spirits, such as Baudelaire, Kafka, Ionesco, and Faulkner, all wrote about the conflicts and spiritual needs of their times, proving literature to be the reflection of social values. Sartre once wrote, "it is meaning alone which can give words their verbal unity. Without it they are frittered away into sounds and strokes of the pen."[17] The purpose of literary criticism, as well as the immutable function of cyber literary criticism, is exactly that: to seek meaning, without which literature and its criticism cannot exist.

The Change and Extension of Cyber Literary Criticism's Functions

Cyber literary criticism must also be attentive to the unique structure of the Internet, which not only determines the media that carries literary criticism but also affects the functions of literary criticism. As Liu Xie (ca. 465–522) once put it, "literary changes are affected by the ways of the world, and a literary style's rise and decline in popularity are caused by the changes of the time."[18] Each generation has its own literature and literary criticism. In the age of the Internet, the functions of cyber literary criticism also reflect changes of the time.

To begin with, works of literary criticism that are open and frank can provide guidance for readers' reading choices. If a critic cannot maintain an open attitude and insist on telling the truth, literary criticism will be deprived of its soul, and its value and meaning cannot be redeemed even with rigorous logic, fabulous rhetoric, or lively metaphors. In traditional literary criticism, the influence of the elite circle, nepotism, and pecuniary connections can make some critics hesitate and lose their frankness. But cyber literary criticism encourages critics to show their "true selves" and can better circumvent these shortcomings.

This is first because the anonymity and remote personal connection on the Internet eliminate critics' "interpersonal anxiety." Hiding behind an alias, one can roam unimpeded across the major literary websites, forums, and social platforms. Distance does not block any virtual communication, and years of "cohabitation" or many rounds of heated exchanges with netizens in the same forum do not necessarily result in acquaintance in real life. This invisibility emboldens netizens to put aside qualms about fame and interests and let their true selves speak out freely and candidly about literary works, voicing outlandish ideas and ill-timed opinions. New ideas and diverse views are therefore fostered on the Internet, whereas reviews that try to present the reviewers' positive images and unreasonably praise writers as reviewers' friends are relatively rare.

Moreover, as cyber literary criticism is mainly written by amateurs, it brings less psychological burden. As these amateur critics are not public figures and lack social influence, they feel less pressure when expressing their opinions as long as they respect public order, customs, and morality. Unlike professional critics, they are usually untrained and more likely to open themselves on the Internet.

A third reason for the openness of cyber literary criticism is that it is a participatory "aggregate criticism." Hundreds and thousands of short comments on one work gather together to become a group of netizens' collective review of that work. This "big data" makes "readers' satisfaction" a reference guiding public reading.

For those reasons, the language of cyber literary criticism is dislocated from social intercourse. The identities of the interlocutors are just imagined. Without the physical presence of the critics, the communication between them has to become purely spiritual. As interlocutors do not have to wear masks to present themselves in a positive light, such communication restores the essential attributes of "conversation."[19] The "true opinions" help readers identify reads of their interest more quickly among a sea of works.

Cyber literary criticism's "sharpness" also helps authors improve their writing. Pushkin once called criticism a science "uncovering the beauties and shortcomings in works of art and literature."[20] This is now more fully reflected in cyber literary criticism, which rejects condescending advice and tortuous word games and favors quick remarks and straightforward expressions. Such criticism can "hit people's hearts" and inspire authors to better understand the beauties and shortcomings in their works and improve their writing. For example, a netizen named Su Shanshan comments on the web novel *Ghost Blows Out the Light* (Guichuideng) as follows:

> It's interesting in the beginning. But the plot is repetitive, and the whole thing eventually becomes like a "beat'em up" game: when the background, equipment, and players are ready, the adventure kicks off in search of the thrilling and bloody. There are only a dozen dead bodies in Jingjue City, but at the Tomb of Prince Xian, fish are feeding off hundreds of drifting corpses. In Tibet, even a minor scene involves over one thousand frozen corpses with their faces down in the ice. It's as if the ancient population had nowhere else to go and no other productive labor than swarming to build tombs. This is disgusting.
>
> At last, probably the author himself can't carry on like this any longer, so he hurries to end the story with many things unexplained.[21]

Instead of flaunting a knowledge of literary theories, the reviewer simply seizes upon the loophole in the plot to point out the flaw of the novel. Quick and sharp reviews like this help readers see the shortcomings of a work at a glance.

For another example, a reviewer writes about the web novel, *The Chessboard under Heaven* (Tianxia qipan), as follows:

> The writing style is passable, but the author has a poor grasp of how to write "feel-good novels" (shuangwen), or commercial novels on *Starting Points Chinese Net* (Qidian zhongwen wang). He must have read too few of those. In my opinion, this book makes too many mistakes—and I don't care how the author views this book; I'm only judging it by the criteria for "feel-good novels." First, why do those transcultural fantasy novels emphasize time travel? Advantage No. 1: it's for the pure sake of letting readers identify with the characters. Advantage No. 2: it advocates the prestige of our nation though in a rather tasteless way. *The Chessboard under Heaven* has no time travel, and that can be seen as one of the failures. Since you're writing a commercial novel, you should naturally try to please the majority of your readers. Second, the beginning of a novel should never present the protagonist as unusual or negative. Don't No. 1: you may describe the protagonist as being materially poor, or physically weak, but don't give us a hero with an inferior spiritual state. Or else, who can the reader fantasize about? Don't No. 2: many newbie authors think that if they write about women, they will satisfy the readers. But because they don't really know how to portray women, they often end up making the women disagreeable, causing readers to abandon the novel. If you're not good at representing women, then don't write about them. Wait until your reader grows to like

your novel, and then you can add as many pretty faces as you like. Don't No. 3: don't let your protagonist leave the reader's sight, especially in the most critical beginning …[22]

Based on his/her rich experience of reading "feel-good novels,"[23] this reviewer is able to identify some major drawbacks in the novel and has received many likes from other readers. Even the author of *Chessboard* replied to this review post. Thanking the reviewer, the author admitted that all the tips were "right on target." He called himself not good enough at writing and promised to rewrite the novel, asking the reviewer to offer more suggestions.[24]

On some literary criticism websites, such as *Dragon's Sky* and *Douban Reading*, critical reviews like these abound. They not only analyze the works, but also point out drawbacks and offer suggestions for revision. This has some positive influence on the writers. Take *Dragon's Sky* for example. The forum is taken up by highly targeted reviews that contain as many as thousands or even tens of thousands of Chinese characters, and "anyone who messes around with literature online or is messed up by literature likes to hang out there."[25] *Dragon's Sky* is particularly famous because it is where a lot of "vipers" gather—"vipers refer to those sharp-tongued critics, who are not only able to identify a loophole that has slipped the author's inspection, but are also able to detect a foreshadowing that skips most readers' attention, and are even able to dig out the author's hidden theme."[26] Here, "many experienced writers write reviews for other novels or comment on others' reviews, and they often respond to comments on their own works."[27] Good communication between writers and reviewers is well maintained.

Furthermore, the frequent exchanges between writers and critics make a great difference. From the perspective of criticism, the critic (i.e., reader) is put in touch with unfinished works and engages in the writing process through dialogues with the writer. He/she thus becomes the "second author" and acquires a twofold capacity as a writer-critic. From the perspective of literary creation, as the author writes for a specific group of readers, he/she will inevitably think about the prospective readers' (and critics') interests, habits, and tastes, so as to meet their requirements. He/she becomes his/her own critic, thus also assuming a dual capacity. On the other hand, as the critic turns into a "second author," the original author also becomes a "second critic," initiating a "second criticism" by incorporating the feedback of the readers. In a word, the interaction between author and critic dissolves the boundary between creation and criticism and makes their positions interchangeable. Many writers have noted the importance of such an interaction to their literary creations. The famous cyber writer, Xing Yusen, wrote: "The encouragement and praise from a group of enthusiastic readers at Beijing University of Posts and Telecommunications (BUPT) helped us acquire maturity and self-consciousness. That is why I say that the BBS of BUPT made a writer out of me."[28] "Bright and Wavy Purple" (Liulianzi), the author of the popular novel, *The Legend of Zhen Huan* (Zhen Huan zhuan), said in an interview,

A very important thing for writing and publishing on the Internet is the participation of readers in the creation of a work. Readers and editors, based on their understanding and knowledge, can help identify the author's factual errors or logical fallacies. Their timely feedback greatly helps the perfection of a work. *The Legend of Zhen Huan* benefited greatly from this.[29]

What is more, novels serialized on BBSes, such as *Rose in the Wind* (Fengzhong meigui), and works created in relays, such as *The Blue Skies of Dreams* (Mengxiang de tiankong fenwai lan) and *The Legend of Wenfeng Heroes* (Wenfeng qunxia zhuan), are indisputably the products of the interaction between authors and critics.

The dialogue between authors and critics is very much in line with the theory of "reception aesthetics." The unprecedented closeness between authors, readers, and critics makes criticism more effective and plays an irreplaceable role in the popularization of cyber literature.

Notes

1 Zhang, Ying 张英, *Wangshang Xunhuan* 网上寻欢 (Changchun: Times Literature and Art Publishing House, 2002), 54.
2 Zhao, Limei 赵李梅 and Fu, Zonghong 傅宗洪, "Chuantong wenxue piping ruhe yingdui wangluo wenxue de tiaozhan" 传统文学批评如何应对网络文学的挑战, *Journal of Mianyang Teachers' College* 绵阳师范学院学报 no. 7 (2010): 69.
3 Taxue feihong 踏雪飞鸿, *Cong chuzhong kandao shuoshi biye gongzuo, shiduonian lao shuchong zhengli jiyi de tuishudan* 从初中看到硕士毕业工作，十多年老书虫整理记忆的推书单, Youshu wang 优书网, 2015. www.yousuu.com/booklist/567e58393dbf228b483c67bb.
4 Translator's note: *Rivers and Mountains* is a pornographic martial arts (wuxia) novel first published in 2004.
5 Translator's note: Wen Rui'an is a writer of martial arts novels.
6 Da pangtouyu 大胖头鱼, *Guanyu Luanshi de duwu zhe, suibian liao shang jiju* 关于《乱世的独舞者》，随便聊上几句, Long de tiankong 龙的天空, 2015.
Translator's note: the website has been closed.
7 Ouyang, Youquan 欧阳友权, "Wangluo wenxue de houxiandai wenhua qingjie" 网络文学的后现代化情结, *Theory and Criticism of Literature and Art* 文艺理论与批评 no. 2 (2003): 39.
8 Translator's note: this perhaps is referring to the repetition of themes and plots.
9 Translator's note: the "whatever" is written in English.
10 Translator's note: this review was posted on *Good Books Net* (Youshu wang), but the link provided in the original Chinese edition of this book is already defunct and thus is not given here.
11 Ailu'en 艾露恩, *Tixian pinglunzhe nengli de liuxiang shuju* 体现评论者能力的六项数据, Long de tiankong 龙的天空, 2015.
Translator's note: the website the website has been closed.
12 Zhao, Huiping 赵慧平, "Wangluo shidai de wenxue piping wenti" 网络时代的文学批评问题, *The Journal of Humanities* 人文杂志 no. 2 (2005): 104.

13 Li ge 黎戈, *Xianhua Anni baobei* 闲话安妮宝贝, Wangyi boke 网易博客, 2015. Translator's note: the link is already defunct and is thus not provided here.
14 Da shuini 大水牛, *Lishi de bagua* 历史的八卦, Douban 豆瓣, 2009. http://book.douban.com/review/2093915.
15 *Good Books Net* (Youshu wang) is a popular website that combines searching, reading, rating, and recommendation of web fiction, with daily updates on the top charts on various web fiction websites, such as *Dragon's Sky* (Long de tiankong) and *Starting Points Chinese Net* (Qidian zhongwen wang). It has a great influence on readers' choice and rating of cyber literature.
16 Ouyang, Youquan 欧阳友权, "Yiyi zhixiang yu jiazhi chengzai 意义指向与价值承载," *Renmin ribao* 人民日报 (Beijing), Apr. 25, 2014.
17 Jean-Paul Sartre, *What Is Literature and Other Essays* (Cambridge, Mass.: Harvard University Press, 1988), 29–30.
18 Translator's note: to make the translation more suitable for this specific context, here I do not follow Vincent Yu-chung Shih's translation. For Shih's translation, see: Liu, Hsieh (Liu Xie) 刘勰, *The Literary Mind and the Carving of Dragons*, trans. Vincent Yu-chung Shih (Hong Kong: The Chinese University of Hong Kong, 2015), 316.
19 Li, Yangquan 黎杨全, "Shuzi meijie yu wenxue piping de zhuanxing" 数字媒介与文学批评的转型 (PhD dissertation, Central China Normal University 华中师范大学, 2012).
20 Alexander Pushkin, "On Criticism," in *The Critical Prose of Alexander Pushkin, with Critical Essays by Four Russian Romantic Poets*, ed. and trans. Carl A. Proffer (Bloomington: Indiana University Press, 1969), 75.
21 Su, Shanshan 苏珊珊, *Rongyi pilao* 容易疲劳, Douban 豆瓣, 2006. http://book.douban.com/review/1089896.
22 Bu geili 不给力, *Tianxia qipan, Xie shuangwen buyinggai fan de cuowu jian tan weishenme yao chuanyue* 《天下棋盘》,写爽文不应该犯的错误兼谈为什么要穿越, Long de tiankong 龙的天空, 2015.
Translator's note: the website has been closed.
23 *Shuangwen*, or "feel-good novels," was a word coined on *Starting Points Chinese Net* (Qidian zhongwen wang) to refer to the kind of novel that makes the reader feel "shuang" (refreshed or satisfied) through fantasies that fulfill common wishes and desires.
24 Bu geili 不给力, *Tianxia qipan, Xie shuangwen buyinggai fan de cuowu jian tan weishenme yao chuanyue* 《天下棋盘》,写爽文不应该犯的错误兼谈为什么要穿越.
25 Kong, Lingqi 孔令旗, "Long Kong dang: ma zi gongren de 'jizhongying' 龙空党: 码字工人的 '集中营'," *Jianghuai chenbao* 江淮晨报 (Hefei), Jan. 22, 2010.
26 Kong, Lingqi 孔令旗, "Long Kong dang: ma zi gongren de 'jizhongying' 龙空党: 码字工人的 '集中营'."
27 Kong, Lingqi 孔令旗, "Long Kong dang: ma zi gongren de 'jizhongying' 龙空党: 码字工人的 '集中营'."
28 Zhang, Ying 张英, *Wangshang Xunhuan* 网上寻欢 (Changchun: Times Literature and Art Publishing House, 2002), 61.
29 Yimeng 怡梦, "Wangluo wenxue xuyao shenmeyang de zhuanye piping? 网络文学需要什么样的专业批评?," *Zhongguo yishu bao* 中国艺术报, Jul. 15, 2013.

Bibliography

Ailu'en 艾露恩. *Tixian pinglunzhe nengli de liuxiang shuju* 体现评论者能力的六项数据. Long de tiankong 龙的天空, 2015. (link defunct)

Bu geili 不给力. *Tianxia Qipan*: Xie shuangwen buyinggai fan de cuowu jian tan weishenme yao chuanyue 《天下棋盘》,写爽文不应该犯的错误兼谈为什么要穿越. Long de tiankong 龙的天空, 2015. (link defunct)

Da pangtouyu 大胖头鱼. *Guanyu Luanshi de duwu zhe, suibian liao shang jiju* 关于《乱世的独舞》, 随便聊上几句. Long de luntan, 龙的天空, 2015. (defunct)

Da shuiniu 大水牛. *Lishi de bagua* 历史的八卦. Douban 豆瓣, 2015. http://book.douban.com/review/2093915.

Kong, Lingqi 孔令旗. "Long Kong dang: ma zi gongren de 'jizhongying' 龙空党: 码字工人的'集中营'." *Jianghuai chenbao* 江淮晨报 (Hefei), Jan. 22, 2010.

Li ge 黎戈. *Xianhua Anni baobei* 闲话安妮宝贝. Wangyi boke 网易博客, 2015. (link defunct)

Li, Yangquan 黎杨全. "Shuzi meijie yu wenxue piping de zhuanxing" 数字媒介与文学批评的转型. PhD dissertation, Central China Norman University 华中师范大学 2012.

Liu, Hsieh (Liu Xie) 刘勰. *The Literary Mind and the Carving of Dragons*. Translated by Vincent Yu-chung Shih. Hong Kong: The Chinese University of Hong Kong, 2015.

Ouyang, Youquan 欧阳友权. "Wangluo wenxue de houxiandai wenhua qingjie" 网络文学的后现代文化情结. *Theory and Criticism of Literature and Art* 文艺理论与批评 no. 2 (2003): 38–43.

Ouyang, Youquan 欧阳友权. "Yiyi zhixiang yu jiazhi chengzai 意义指向与价值承载." *Renmin ribao* 人民日报 (Beijing), Apr. 25, 2014.

Pushkin, Alexander. "On Criticism." In *The Critical Prose of Alexander Pushkin, with Critical Essays by Four Russian Romantic Poets*, 75–76. Edited and translated by Carl A. Proffer. Bloomington: Indiana University Press, 1969.

Sartre, Jean-Paul. *"What Is Literature" and Other Essays*. Cambridge, Mass.: Harvard University Press, 1988.

Su, Shanshan 苏珊珊. *Rongyi pilao* 容易疲劳. Douban豆瓣, 2006. http://book.douban.com/review/1089896.

Taxue feihong 踏雪飞鸿. *Cong chuzhong kandao shuoshi biye gongzuo, shiduonian lao shuchong zhengli jiyi de tuishudan* 从初中看到硕士毕业工作, 十多年老书虫整理记忆的推书单. Youshu wang 优书网, 2015. www.yousuu.com/booklist/567e58393dbf228b483c67bb.

Yimeng 怡梦. "Wangluo wenxue xuyao shenmeyang de zhuanye piping? 网络文学需要什么样的专业批评？." *Zhongguo yishu bao*中国艺术报 (Beijing), Jul. 15, 2013.

Zhang, Ying 张英. *Wangshang Xunhuan* 网上寻欢. Changchun: Times Literature and Art Publishing House, 2002.

Zhao, Huiping 赵慧平. "Wangluo shidai de wenxue piping wenti" 网络时代的文学批评问题. *The Journal of Humanities* 人文杂志 no. 2 (2005): 101–106.

Zhao, Limei 赵李梅 and Fu, Zonghong 傅宗洪. "Chuantong wenxue piping ruhe yingdui wangluo wenxue de tiaozhan" 传统文学批评如何应对网络文学的挑战. *Journal of Mianyang Teachers' College* 绵阳师范学院学报 no. 7 (2010): 69–71.

9 Changes in the Constitution of Cyber Literary Critics

As mentioned, cyber literary critics fall roughly into three categories: scholars, whose studies of individual works or cyber literature as a whole are published in academic journals or at academic conferences; mass media, mainly newspapers, magazines, television, radio, and portal websites, which aim mostly to promote works and have a strong influence on readers' choice; netizens, who can be further divided into "critics of cyber literature" and "critics on the Internet." While "critics of cyber literature" concentrate on cyber literature itself, "critics on the Internet" attend to the peculiar nature of the Internet that has given distinctive features to literature online. Overall, the three categories of critics overlap as the boundaries between media are far from clear-cut.

Questions like "is cyber literature worthy of criticism?" and "is cyber literature real literature?" still trigger debates now and then. Besides its literary attributes, cyber literature also has the attributes of mass culture. It means more than the written texts online—published books, graphic and animated adaptations, film and TV screenplays, and IP licensing for games, all fall under the topic of cyber literature. Critics of cyber literature must take into consideration all the diverse texts, and how to define cyber literature, therefore, remains an interesting question.

This chapter traces the development of cyber literary critics by recounting the three phases during which the groups of critics connected and mixed with each other.

The Early Stage: The Coexistence of Multiple Groups

Overlaps and Separation

Shortly after the emergence of cyber literature, scholars began to study it. As early as the late 1990s, Chinese literary researchers had noticed this new literary form. Studies of cyber literature were mostly published in journals accessed via computers and on the Internet, focusing on the current development of cyber literature and criticizing the "dregs" in the works.

DOI: 10.4324/9781003428480-12

In 1998, when *The First Intimate Contact* (Diyici de qinmi jiechu) became popular on the Internet, the *Guangdong Sea Wind* (Yuehai feng) magazine published an article entitled, "Zebra Crossing in Postmodern Literature: A Web Novel and More" (Houxiandai wenxue de banmaxian—cong yibu wangluo xiaoshuo tanqi), which criticized *The First Intimate Contact* and treated it as an inevitable product of the Internet under the influence of postmodernism. Another article, "The Rise of Cyber Literature" (Wangluo wenxue de xingqi), was published in *Fiction World* (Xiaoshuo shijie) in 1999. It summarized several characteristics of cyber literature at the beginning of its development, including the author's anonymity, the openness and the virtuality of the text, and the immediacy of its popularity. In the fall of 1999, Qian Jianjun published a paper titled "The Xth Wave: Chinese Cyber Literature."[1] The article summarized the development of overseas Chinese cyber literature at that time. It pointed out that cyber literature served to express writers' emotions in an unrestrained yet skillful way. It also argued that cyber literature had unique advantages in expressions, creations, and interactions. The author predicted: "Cyber literature that is multi-dimensional will become the mainstream in the future. The prosperity of Chinese electronic literary publications is gradually changing the ways of thinking and living of overseas Chinese and even all Chinese people. The impact on the Chinese social and cultural structure will far exceed people's expectations."[2] This profound foresight made the article the most important contribution to the early scholarly criticism of cyber literature.

At about the same time, some mainstream periodicals, such as *Guangming Daily* (Guangming ribao), also published articles, including "The Aesthetics of Cyber literature"[3] and "Questioning Cyber literature,"[4] which expressed distrust of this new literary form. As the authors of these articles were scholars, the academics and the mainstream media shared their perspectives as observers. They would not rush to a conclusion. As cyber literature was a new phenomenon, they had a discreet and continuous observation of it, combined with prompt revisions to previous research findings.

But if we look at cyber literature in its very early years, we will notice a very interesting fact: cyber literature and cyber literary criticism came into being almost at the same time. The birth of Chinese cyber literature had to do with overseas Chinese people's efforts to make communication easier. In 1992, Wei Yagui of Indiana University founded the alt.chinese.text (ACT), a website for news and information sharing. With the popularization of the Internet and the increase of overseas students, ACT began to include more than just news, and posts of various kinds emerged. Literary contents took up some of these posts, marking the birth of Chinese cyber literature. The immediacy of posting catered for netizens' anxious desire to communicate and the literary works were replied to and commented on soon after they were published. The replies on those message boards are undoubtedly the original form of cyber literary criticism.

The earliest literary websites have long disappeared, but we know that the critics of cyber literature were often authors at the same time. Back then, it was not easy for people to access the Internet, and most users were overseas students, employees of Internet companies, and research scientists in China. This group had received relatively higher education, so their criticism tended to be calm and rational. Because of the group's exclusivity, cyber literary criticism at this stage remained a product of internal exchange among cyber writers on forums and websites. It seldom spilled over to influence the offline literary circle. The exclusivity left the websites with many good works but few good reviews.

At that time, the different groups of critics were largely separated from each other. Articles written by scholars or published by the mass media hardly attracted the attention of cyber writers, whose discussions, in turn, were rarely noticed by the academic circle. Scholars' academic papers and netizens' casual commentaries simply belonged to two worlds that were isolated from each other, and cyber literary criticism was groping its way forward in such a state.

Seizing Discursive Power: Revelry of Mass Criticism Online

At the turn of the century, when the Internet was emerging in China, the literary boom of the 1980s had not completely receded. Since video and music streaming was not yet possible, the most fashionable place for "web surfing" was chat rooms and forums, where literature became one of the most popular topics.

Early literary criticism concentrated on professional literary websites such as *Under the Banyan Tree* (Rongshu xia) and the literary section of comprehensive websites such as *Skyline Forum* (Tianya luntan). Founded in 1999, *Skyline Forum* houses numerous sections, and its literary section is further divided into the history block called "History over Wine" (Zhu jiu lun shi), the suspense and horror block called "Ghost Talk of the Lotus Seedpod" (Lianpeng guihua), and so on. *Skyline Forum*'s long prosperous life makes it the "living fossil" of the forum era, when the later famous cyber literary critics and writers completed their original accumulation of popularity and writing ability.

Among the online reviews of traditional writers and works, the liveliest are those on martial arts fiction, a genre that was enormously popular from the late 1990s to the early 21st century. Discussions of martial arts fiction are usually divided into two categories, one about cyber literature, and the other on the classic novels by Jin Yong, Gu Long, and others. Most of the forums on martial arts fiction feature Jin Yong. The number reached dozens in their heyday, from websites devoted to the writer to those focusing on a specific novel or a character. Unfortunately, most of the reviews have disappeared as the websites closed down, but in some published collections of online reviews, we can still catch a glimpse of the old martial arts forum culture.

The attention paid by online critics to martial arts fiction and culture highlights the mass cultural attributes of "literary criticism on the Internet."

The critics write on a wide range of topics, and their motives generally fall into the following categories.

(1) A "blasphemous" rebellion that stands against the mainstream ideology. Any authoritative concepts or authority figures in the mainstream discourse should be opposed, mocked, and parodied, even if only for the sake of opposing. There are many examples. Take a look at this comment on Lu Xun in the review, "Lu Xun on the Altar and the Minor Demons below" (Shentan shang de Lu Xun he shentan xia de xiaogui):

> When people talk about Lu Xun, they treat him as some legendary figure, like a clay statue of a god enthroned on the altar. Many people, especially those who live off this godlike writer, strive to be the first to worship him. All kinds of people gravitate to this giant shrine. Their hidden motives are all different, but they perform the same grand ritual of kneeling and kowtowing, with all the solemnity and clumsiness. When the ceremony is over, they grab their share of the cold pork and head home in a cheerful mood. No stirring outside the shrine attracts their attention; even if it does, it will be smothered by this group of worshippers, who see their action as justified and righteous.[5]

For another example, see these words about Jin Yong in the article, "A Sharp Warning to the Fame-Seeking Machines, Jin Yong, Yu Qiuyu, and Jia Pingwa" (Banghe Jin Yong, Yu Qiuyu, Jia Pingwa zhe sange shengming jiqi):

> Jin Yong, this old and inferior writer, with peace written on his face, disgusts young people just like that Yu Guangzhong in Taiwan, who writes embarrassing, clumsy phrases. ... we don't want Jin Yong's Matthew effect (also known as the celebrity effect). Those snobbish media scramble for the rubbishy writings by the big names, and that is why the true rising stars, like some promising youths in the medical field, are unable to stand out.[6]

We might as well take another look at a short paragraph about Yu Qiuyu in "My Opinion of Yu Qiuyu" (Wo kan Yu Qiuyu) by the same author:

> As if in a moving fairy tale, this guy has become famous. He has transformed from a most inferior literary contestant into a cultural celebrity. I have always wondered: does Yu, who has been a media celebrity, blush at his ironic title?
> And anyone who can't blush may not be worthy of the name of a writer. However, shameless literati abound in this age ...
> I have always been disgusted by Yu Qiuyu's collections of essays like *A Sigh in One Thousand Years* (Qiannian yi tan). He really has strong opinions, but his writings are as dry as some bird's breast. I can't help yawning. The stories he tells are boring, too.[7]

(2) The urge to relieve one's repressed desires through sexually suggestive metaphors and expressions.

Cyber writer "Ning, the God of Wealth" (Ning caishen) wrote the following words in "A Cup of Wine is Worth More than Fame after Death: Delving into the Significance of Cyber Literature" (Qie le shengqian yibei jiu, he xu shenhou qianzai ming—wang shenle tan wangluo xiezuo zhi yiyi):

> In the past, writers wrote to make a living. They were only forced to crank out words when they were out of money for the next meal. Just think about it: who wouldn't have complaints and opinions when their life was fucked up like that? After pondering on it for a bit, they reached the ultimate truth: joy in hardship and tears in laughter, whatever generates the greatest conflict with our stereotypical expectations will touch people the most. Isn't that true? These forefathers nailed it because they fucked literature, deflowering it without over-tipping. But now the situation has become a bit embarrassing. The brothers, with their saved wages, vow to find a virgin in a brothel to do it no matter how much money and energy it costs them. But the problem is you can't fuck if you don't have enough money, and if you do, you don't need to go to a brothel to find a virgin, do you? You'll end up ruining your own health instead of deflowering any virgins. Even worse, you may get yourself some serious disease. When you're stripped naked and pressed down in the bed, all you can do is cry out, with tears in your eyes, that this is too much to bear. You'll be fucked up by literature.[8]

Another reader wrote in "*Shanghai Baby* and Internationalism" (Shanghai baobei yu guojihua):

> I leafed through some pages of *Shanghai Baby* at the Sanlian Bookstore 720 days ago, without paying much attention to it, let alone expecting that day to be the eve of the book's sensational success. Soon it was met with enthusiasm on and off the Internet, and even the Shanghai Baby's boobs were put on a show across the country. What was supposed to be the exclusive privilege of "foreign guests" is now used to tantalize the Chinese people. Unfortunately, these were not met with passionate praises.[9]

(3) Liberation of emotions. When the critic's personal experience is echoed in the story, the boundary between fiction and reality is removed, and the critic exchanges roles with the author or the protagonist in the story. By commenting on the text, the critic sets free his/her true feelings. This type of criticism almost always targets romance novels. For example, a reader wrote in "Annie Baby, A Wandering Dream" (Anni baobei, yige liulishisuo de meng):

> Many people are reading her stories and writing about their enthusiasm for her. But what I want to write about is not just her; it has nothing to do

with love or attachment. The Annie Baby that I have always wanted to write about is a dream, a wandering, homeless dream.

The first work I read by Annie was "Fireworks" (Yichang yanhua) in a literary magazine bought by a female friend. I merely leafed through the pages, but when I finished reading, I was moved by the story. It was not because of the attractiveness of the story itself or the vivid loneliness and loss of the characters. It was because I saw myself in her words.

...

I continued to read her books, from *Farewell to Vivian* (Gaobie Wei'an) to *August Never Ends* (Bayue weiyang), and to *Beautiful Reborn Flower* (Bi'an hua). I bought her books one by one. I wasn't obsessed, but just moved again and again. She wrote the love stories that I have always wanted to write but never did. In her stories, there are my favorite images: fireworks, butterflies, subways, perfume, Faye Wong, IKEA furniture, a girl with seaweed-like hair wearing a cotton coat, a boy in a video store... Too many noisy images, and they lured me to involuntarily identify with them. So, I began to fantasize about passing her by in some city, and then with an understanding smile, bidding farewell to her in a crowd of people and continuing to dream the same wandering, homeless dream.[10]

(4) The display of one's thoughts or writing skills. The author or work that the review seems to focus on is merely an excuse for the reviewer to show off his/her thoughts or writing style. For example, a reader wrote in "Annie Baby: A Gloomy Witch" (Anni baobei—yinyu de nüwu):

This is exactly the reason why I don't like her: her gloominess. I can't help but speculate about the lack of luminosity in her heart, which gives me fear and horror not to be overcome. Gloominess is not melancholy. The latter is divine, but the former is demonic. I can perhaps only accept the divine.[11]

Another reader wrote in "Some Women and Their Writings" (Yixie nüren yiji zhexie nüren de wenzhangmen):

They love literature. They love music. They love art. They love sports. They love everything, as long as these can help them meet a rich man. They hold their heads high and look straight ahead, looking restrained, elegant, and dignified. They never fart in public. They are delicate, piteous, and sensitive. They pale in front of men when there's a cockroach, but they fight cockroaches with all their might when they're alone at home. They're usually pretentious, narcissistic, fanciful, lonely, neurotic, lacking sleep, and unwanted by men. They usually love socializing, partying, meeting celebrities, leaving phone numbers, and moaning in their writings, "I'm lonely!" They're usually shy and ladylike, with their lips tightly pressed together. They're usually not virgins. They're restrained in their upper body, coquettish in their lower one. They dress up as girls and do women's things. They have had many relationships and made love many times, but they tell others, all I want is true unforgettable love once in a lifetime. They advocate the protection of the environment. They love nature, show sympathy, and care about African refugees and all mankind—except the beggars on the roadside.[12]

The quality of literary criticism published on the Internet is unstable, and the management of the online platforms can be confusing at times, unable to satisfy readers' needs for searching and indexing. But at the turn of the century, online critical reviews undoubtedly blew some fresh air into the rigid circle of China's literary criticism.

To sum up, the psychological mechanism of online literary criticism is not complicated. After reading a work, readers usually have a desire to express themselves and share with others. Under the previous media conditions, there were some prerequisites for people who would participate in literary criticism. For instance, they had to have a specific knowledge background and writing skills that met professional expectations. These preconditions created a hindrance to ordinary literature lovers who did not major in literature. In addition, whereas literary researchers can easily find someone around to share their views, for ordinary readers, it is difficult to find like-minded friends. In terms of resources, researchers have access to various literary journals, critical articles, and lectures, but for an ordinary reader living before the Internet era, these things were almost a luxury. Fortunately, the Internet removed many obstacles and provided a channel for ordinary readers to express themselves.

The Boom: Division and Competition among Critics

Division and Opposition

Around the turn of the century, academic research on cyber literature remained lukewarm and cyber literary criticism was relevantly quiet. This had much to do with the environment of cyber literature. In 2001, the government increased its control over online forums and imposed new regulations on cyber literature that just started to grow. A number of new literary websites were shut down. At about the same time, China's first Internet economic bubble burst, and investors withdrew from Internet companies one after another. A large number of literary websites went bankrupt as a result. Left with some inefficient websites, cyber writers relocated to other platforms or moved their bases to Taiwan in the hope of reaching back to the mainland in the future. Some others went back to offline publishing through traditional channels, and still others simply gave up writing. While there were some works worth mentioning, this period can be regarded as a cold winter for Chinese cyber literature.

The situation improved in 2003, when the cyber writer "Zhonghua Yang" co-founded China's first paid literary website, "Ming Yang • Global Chinese Book Network" (Ming Yang quanqiu zhongwen pinshuwang). On the website, readers can pay to become members and get early access to the latest novel updates. Soon afterward, literary websites such as *Starting Points Chinese Net* (Qidian zhongwen wang), *Book Union for Swordsmen's Legends* (*Huanjian shumeng*), and *Dragon's Sky* (Long de tiankong) all adopted similar pricing models. This pioneering move led to the rise of cyber literature in the new century and ushered in the commercialization of cyber literature. It not only changed the mode of web publication but also profoundly impacted cyber literary criticism.

During this period, cyber literary criticism displayed the following characteristics. First, as literary forums developed slowly, some mature platforms, such as *Skyline Community* (Tianya shequ) and *Maopu* began to set up sections for cyber literature, where both creative writing and criticism became professionalized and specialized. Second, the emergence of literary websites led to the birth of exclusive review blocks for each literary work. Readers with paid subscriptions can post comments in a block and communicate directly with the author. This kind of online criticism is highly interactive and well-targeted, and it is still the best way for web writers to get reader feedback in the first place.

Third, online criticism was popularized as computers and the Internet became common in China's big cities. Internet cafes became one of young people's favorite pastimes, and easy access to the Internet brought more audiences to cyber literature. Most new Internet users who participated in online criticism had received only a moderate education and were ready to use harsh words, lambasting works that failed to live up to their expectations. It was from this period that cyber literary criticism came to be known as rough and crude. In short, the rise of online critics is the most noteworthy feature of cyber literary criticism in this period.

With its comprehensive cyber literature database and access to many authors' works, *Dragon's Sky* surpassed some old websites like *Skyline Community* to become the most prestigious venue for publishing online literary criticism. At the same time, users of *Baidu Post Bar* (Baidu tieba) increased and discussions about web novels flourished. Although critical articles were few and the quality of the reviews was uneven since *Baidu Post Bar* was mainly managed by netizens, the platform accumulated influence thanks to the sheer number of its users. It was also easier to register for an account and post comments on literary works on *Baidu Post Bar* than on specialized forums, where one had to follow many rules.

Massive investment in literary websites after 2003 gave cyber literature a larger share of the market. Meanwhile, the publication of some outstanding web novels as books also attracted more attention to cyber literature. Scholars began to attach importance to the study of cyber literature, initiating a research boom that has lasted for many years. Wang Xiaoying and Zhu Dong's book, *Looking Back and Examining: Ten Years of Cyber Literature Research* (Huiwang yu jianzhi: wangluo wenxue yanjiu shinian), summarizes some important themes of research on cyber literature during this period, which include cyber literature's legitimacy, literariness, industrialization, writing and reading, circulation, specific groups of people, and subgenres. This period also witnessed the publication of thousands of research articles and dozens of monographs. I alone published many books, including *An Outline for the Discussion on Cyber Literature* (Wangluo wenxue lungang, 2003), *The Ontology of Cyber Literature* (Wangluo wenxue bentilun, 2004), *Studies of Literature and Art in the Context of Digitalization* (Shuzihua yujing zhong de wenyixue, 2005), *Online Communication and Social Culture* (Wangluo chuanbo yu shehui wenhua, 2005), *An Academic Review of Cyber Literature* (Wangluo wenxue de xueli xingtai, 2008), *An Introduction to Cyber literature* (Wangluo wenxue gailun, 2008), *A History of Cyber Literature* (Wangluo wenxue fazhan shi, 2008), *Poetics in the World of Bits* (Bite shijie de shixue, 2009), and so on. As a result, I not only won the Lu Xun Literature Prize but was recognized as the pioneer of cyber literature research. It is worth pointing out that since the 21st century, not only cyber literature but also its criticism has become a subject for scholars to study.

While Internet media paid close attention to cyber literature and took part in literary criticism with an aim at making profits, traditional media such as newspapers, magazines, television, and radio showed little interest, and the meager reports that were relevant to cyber literature focused on the business and the profession rather than on literature itself. The "fantasy fever" (xuanhuan re) in 2005 was the only major phenomenon that attracted the attention of traditional media, and with the exception of a few excellent works such as *Chengdu, Please Forget Me Tonight* (Chengdu, jinye qing jiang wo yiwang) and *The Story of Wukong* (Wukong zhuan), cyber literature was largely overlooked by traditional media, whose audiences and writers alike showed little interest in the works published online.

Thus, criticism in this period featured the tripartite division among 1) individual readers on the Internet, who based their reviews on personal tastes; 2) the traditional media and the new media, which were already separated from each other; and 3) the academia, which emphasized theories and scholarship.

The division was also manifested in the different subjects of criticism. Scholars showed less interest in the literary texts than in cyber literature as a social phenomenon. So far, web novels that have served as subjects of literary studies are all from an earlier period, and these include *The First Intimate Contact*. This must be due to the lack of "literariness" in cyber literature. The novels' fast release speed and the increased but less educated audiences have led to a reduced quality of literary creation. Prompted to write a certain number of words (usually 3,000 Chinese characters per chapter, and one to two chapters per day) to guarantee their income, authors often cobbled up chapters with insipid plots, further watering down the literariness of cyber literature.

In contrast, online readers paid more attention to literary texts. Book review sections of literary websites abounded in discussions about popular works, and many of the reviews were quite well written. As mentioned above, many online critics were themselves writers, and even today, with a much-enlarged readership, cyber writers still constitute a significant part of online critics. Writers like "Where Has All This Gone" (Jin hezai) and Ma Boyong have produced high-quality works and enjoyed steady popularity as critics. The online reviews guided readers in selecting their next read, but critics' conflicting views also led to debate, which was a common form of cyber literary criticism. Unlike literary scholars, online critics favored straightforward expressions, and instead of digging into the meaning of a text, they showed more interest in the characters. When recommending works, those critics would list the features of a text and attach labels for readers' convenience.

New media tended to pay more attention to the development of cyber literature as an industry, and critics relied on tools such as online rankings to evaluate works. Rankings, usually created collaboratively by literary websites, well-known web literary editors, cyber writers, and online forum members, held sway over readers who had just started to read cyber literature. The click-through rate from a ranking list was a good indicator of a literary website's rate of return.

Competition among the three groups of criticism for the right to speak has often led to conflicts. The famous dispute between Han Han and Bai Ye mentioned in Chapter Five is one example. Although the dispute nearly developed into a gang fighting in cyberspace, its focus remained clear. Bai Ye's point was, as he put it, "from a literary point of view, what the 'post-80s generation' writers wrote in general is not yet literature but is amateurish at best." He argued:

> The "post-80s generation" writers and their works have made it into the market, but they have not entered the literary world (wentan). This is because the "star authors" among them have rarely appeared in literary magazines and are known by the literary circle only by their names and not their works. They also seem to be satisfied with their success and have no intention to leave the market and enter the literary world.[13]

In Bai's article, the "literary world" (wentan, literally "literary altar") apparently refers to the institutionalized circle of mainstream literature, and for that reason, it became the primary target of Han Han's attack. Han wrote:

> What has been sacralized will all fall, and all that has been treasured as "exclusive circles" will vanish in the end. As I said long ago, the true martial arts master is without company, or at most he allows a beauty with moderate martial skills to tag along. Only the inferior underlings like to flock.[14]
>
> These people form a so-called literary circle to take control of the right to speak, so they can talk nonsense and confuse right with wrong. They let money talk and plan publications, while they sit back and flaunt their pedantry and seniority, resisting any tendency to change... The so-called mainstream literature and literary pedigree are no more than a stain on literature.[15]

260   Part II

The "literary world" as Han understands it is very different from Bai's idea, due to their opposing understandings of literature. When subversive texts like Han's accumulate, they create pressure on the mainstream and force adjustments to traditional literary concepts by challenging the very definition of literature. Han wrote words in different blog posts as such:

> Literature needs to be cultivated, not taught. Those self-righteous hypocrites look down upon the younger generation and think, you'll need me to teach you what literature is.[16]
>
> Literature does not need anyone's guidance. Anyone willing to be guided by others cannot become a good writer. Literature is not dictated by anyone.[17]
>
> Every scribbler is a writer, and every writer scribbles.[18]
>
> Literature belongs to the masses. It belongs to the grassroots.[19]

As a typical conflict between cyber literary critics, the dispute is important not for who won it but for the social and cultural significance of Han's posture as a challenger. A netizen has summarized the dispute acutely: the two sides of the debate belonged to two different ecosystems, just like a llama raised in a pen encountering a llama from the wild. The captive llama says food is in the same place every day, but the wild one says food has to be found somewhere out there in the wild. Each believes that itself is the sole defender of truth. Later, the captive llama finds out the truth about the wild, which is just what the wild llama has told it. The captive llama then goes back to the pen.[20]

The Rise of Netizens' Discursive Power in an Orderly Way

In 2003, *Baidu Post Bar* was founded. It can be seen as an extension of forums. Any keyword, from "literature" to "realism," from "mystery" to "Lu Xun," "Jin Yong," and "Guo Jingming," can be the subject of a post. As a platform, *Baidu Post Bar* makes it significantly easier to open new forums and greatly simplifies the rules of posting, so people can write literary criticism online more conveniently. But its shortcomings remain the same as those of a BBS— literary works and their criticism only circulate within a closed system that relies on the management of a site supervisor. Many good reviews are buried deep beneath mountains of "highly rated posts," unknown to people who do not bother to visit the site and dig them out.

The founding of *Douban* in 2004 made a difference. As the best representative of the Web 2.0 Era, *Douban* was originally designed to facilitate users' exchange of comments on books and movies. The website only provides a basic framework, leaving content building to the users, who can add various items such as books, movies, and music, and select their status from "read/seen," "reading/watching," and "want to read/watch" under each item. They can also write a comment on the item or recommend it to others. Besides a large number of primary content entries, users also contribute a vast array of reviews, which are gathered under the reviewed works, making it convenient to find items and comment on them. Those who leave reviews range from professional scholars to book/movie lovers.

Take a book as an example. Users can upload a picture of the book cover, fill in the author, translator, publisher, ISBN number, and other information, provide an introduction or a list of contents, or add information about the book series. As *Douban*'s influence grew, many publishing houses began to collaborate with it. Over the past ten years, the accumulation of users helped *Douban* build a huge database of books, music, and video files, allowing physical books to be reborn in cyberspace.

The greatest contribution of *Douban* is to provide a convenient platform to those who love to write literary criticism on the Internet. There are not a lot of restrictions on the content of the reviews and no requirement of any professional qualification for posting them. The order of the reviews is determined by users who click the "useful" or "useless" button to rate them. High-quality scholarly reviews and reviews demonstrating online critics' personalities are usually the most popular.

Literary criticism on the Internet used to be scattered and closed, not easily accessible to the public before *Douban* came into the scene. The once isolated literary circles, like self-contained islands with meager communication with each other, are now joined by *Douban* into one continent to reach a broader audience.

Another advantage of *Douban* is its stability. In the past, a review only reached a small audience before it sunk into oblivion, but *Douban*'s catalog makes it possible to trace the reviews under a book entry over the years. A modest comment written years ago may still trigger widespread discussion today, which is unimaginable in other online forums. Undoubtedly, such stability attracts more readers to write serious literary criticism on *Douban*.

However, because *Douban* requires an ISBN number to add a book, cyber literary works not published in book form and privately funded fanzines cannot be added, which is a major drawback. As only a small number of works originally posted online can be published offline, *Douban* cannot well accommodate literary criticism on cyber literature. On the other hand, as reviews have to be attached to individual book entries, they cannot go in-depth on various literary schools or phenomena as traditional literary reviews do.

The boom in blogs in 2005 was a sign of the rising discursive power of netizens' literary commentaries. The popularity of blogs lasted for five years, during which blogging sites, including *Bullog* (Niubo wang), *Blogbus* (Boke daba), *Sina Blog*, *Tencent Blog*, and *NetEase Blog*, competed for users by promoting popular bloggers. *Sina Blog*, famous for its posts of professional literary criticism, registered a large number of writers and literary critics with their real names. Literary critics on the Internet used to attract attention by posting extraordinary topics in forums, but now they could win admiration like never before with their professional knowledge, writing skills, and unique personality.

Development: Confluence of Groups and the Ethics of Cyber Literary Criticism

The End of Separation

After 2008, new development of network technology and changes in the layout of literary websites brought some major changes to cyber literary criticism. Academic research of cyber literature acquired more depth and directions, while the use of various social media, such as microblogs and WeChat, made online literary criticism take on diverse forms. The division between scholars' criticism and netizens' criticism was disappearing. At the same time, as portal websites and other new media gradually replaced traditional media, almost all cyber literary criticism written by media workers now appears online.

Book reviews on popular websites used to be less about serious criticism than about the introduction and promotion of the works published on those sites, whereas scholars, under the influence of postmodernism, paid more attention to the hypertextuality of cyber literature and the use of new media. As artistic breakthroughs in cyber literature were scarce after 2008, there were only a few academic monographs or papers on specific works.

But new platforms brought about changes. Although *Fanfou*, the Chinese imitator of Twitter appeared as early as 2007, it never gained much influence. It had to wait until 2010, when *Sina Weibo* came on the scene, for the situation to be completely changed. *Weibo* users can post short texts to comment on what they read at any time. At the same time, the social network enables timely responses to and reposting of comments, further facilitating the circulation of opinions. In addition, compared with the earlier blogs, Weibo is easier to use, and many university professors and media employees have Weibo accounts, allowing professional criticism to appear online.

Another notable medium is WeChat, which allows users to create an "official account" (gongzhong hao), post a review article there, and share it to "moments" (pengyou quan) with their friends. WeChat friends generally know each other in real life, so articles shared to "moments" usually have a better-targeted audience. Users can subscribe to the "official accounts" they are interested in, motivating those accounts to become more professional. Some "we media" have professional teams and produce high-quality articles comparable to those published by academic journals.

Despite the confluence of reviews written by scholars and those by media workers, critics writing online can still be divided into several types.

There are professional recommenders, well-read in cyber literature and familiar with the sub-genres. Most of them are also authors, sometimes on good terms with the more famous cyber writers, which grants them a better grasp of the works they recommend. They are often senior members of a forum, where their words hold sway and the works they recommend are highly regarded. They typically do not analyze a work in depth unless they like or hate it very much. Instead, they prefer to write a list of recommended books and give their reasons for the recommendation.

Some critics are also fan writers, who base their creative writing on their favorite web novels. Although not everyone agrees that fan writers should be considered critics, such secondary creation constitutes an important way of critiquing and interpreting the original work. Compared with the first type of critics, fan writers pay more attention to the extension of the original work and their subjective interpretation, and are more tolerant of opposing viewpoints.

The third type consists of ordinary readers, who account for the majority of cyber literature audiences. They leave occasional comments and, instead of consciously contributing to literary criticism, prefer to use simple phrases such as "a fun read" or "boring." They also show a herd mentality, reading recommended works and giving favorable evaluations without hesitation. In this sense, they may be the least critical of cyber literary critics. Nevertheless, because of their large number, these critics play a pivotal role. If a work is well-received among the general readership, it will be a quick success.

The fourth group consists of rational opponents, who, like the first type, read extensively and have extensive social networks. But unlike the first type, these critics tend to offer negative comments—with cyber literature, it is not difficult to find faults. These critics are also fans of cyber literature, but with the expansion of the market, the loss of good authors, and the mass production of shoddy works for quick consumption, their provocative criticism often points to the roots of the problems. The negative comments are not necessarily hostile but are usually well-founded and highly readable.

Finally, there are malicious opponents, or "trolls." Different from the fourth type of critics, who focus on a work's logical structure and style of writing, these people's comments are filled with emotional expressions capable of stirring up antagonism. They have brought a lot of bad influence to criticism online and are no doubt the main target of ethical regulation.

Contending for Discursive Power: Extension of Netizens' Online Criticism

In 2010, while the system of book profiles on *Douban* was being perfected, *Zhihu* used a tree structure to instill new vitality into literary criticism on the Internet.

A question-and-answer website, *Zhihu* allows all questions worth discussing to be asked, and literature is one of its important topics. Here literary schools and phenomena are well sorted out, and the tree-structured classification system helps knowledge to be effectively organized. Under the category of "literature," topics as broad as "what is the essence of literature," or as specific as "how to evaluate the popularity of *Tiny Times* (Xiaoshidai)," are discussed, and specialized questions are asked targeting academics, such as "who are the representative figures of Romantic literature?" Each question may be answered by multiple people, and some popular ones have hundreds of answers, with the longer answers reaching tens of thousands of words. Well-written or long answers tend to get more attention, and the rational, analytical ambiance is conducive to the dissemination of literary criticism. Users can rank the answers by clicking "Agree" or "Disagree." Unlike the other question-and-answer websites such as *Baidu Knows* (Baidu zhidao), which focus on results only, *Zhihu* advocates rational investigation and attaches more importance to the process of finding truth through discussion.

To professional literary researchers, answering questions on *Zhihu* provides the opportunity to share their research findings or experience and improve their presentational skills. They also get to communicate with peers. The non-professional literary researchers on *Zhihu* can be divided into two groups. One consists of enthusiasts and amateur writers, who are often opinion leaders of cyber literary criticism. Whereas book reviews on *Douban* hardly get wide attention, answers to the hot issue questions on *Zhihu* can get hundreds of people's attention, which is an important motivation for the contributors. The other group consists of readers and learners, who find it a convenient and reliable way to learn about a subject by reading the answers.

Also born in 2010, *Sina Weibo* attracted widespread attention as soon as it was launched. Each message on Weibo has a word limit of 140 characters, meant to grab attention with its conciseness. It reinforces the mode of production that demands cyber literary criticism to become fast-food-like: a message on Weibo has to be short and fragmented, so readers can read the words quickly and casually. Speed reading and writing, the characteristics of this era, make it difficult for literary criticism to be in depth. Later, *Sina Weibo* enabled users to post longer messages, but it was just like a return of the blog. Literature and literary criticism are still needed, but people are no longer simply satisfied with "good" criticism; they want to seize "more" criticism in the information explosion.

As new media's right to criticism was endorsed by capital, the discursive power of online criticism also grew. As a result, the competition for the right to "write literary criticism on the Internet," once between netizens and scholars, became a rivalry between netizens and the mass media, which included literary websites and publishers. This can be seen in the chain reaction triggered by *Douban*'s book evaluation system.

On *Douban*'s "Reading" section, book reviews are divided into long reviews, which can run to 10,000 Chinese characters, and short comments, which are limited to 350 characters. To write a review, one is asked to give a star rating, with five stars meaning "highly recommended" and one star "very poor." In addition to bad translation, plagiarism, and other flaws, the reason for a one-star rating is usually the reader's emotional dissatisfaction with the work—or worse, with the author. Less subjective but critical evaluations usually settle with two or three stars. Sometimes, a five-star rating can become an expression of protest against the one-star ratings. *Douban* calculates the average of all ratings and gives each book a score using a 10-point scale.

For a reader who wants to know if a book is good before reading it, looking at the book's ratings and reviews on *Douban* is a convenient option. The profile on *Douban*, therefore, becomes crucial to a book: dozens of negative reviews can make the score of a less-read book plunge, hurting its reputation and sales. Conversely, if a book is highly praised by a famous critic, both its rating and sales are likely to rise. *Douban* ratings are therefore an important indicator to both readers and publishers.

Quantifying the quality of a book through scores is, of course, not a perfect solution. For one thing, book ratings fluctuate. Publishers often use four methods to promote new books and improve their ratings. First, they hire what is known as the "water army" (shuijun), a group of people paid to post ratings and reviews and confuse readers. However, because *Douban* has become stricter in calculating book scores in recent years and more accurate in detecting fake accounts, hiring the "water army" has lost its previous efficiency. Nevertheless, when malicious negative reviews show up, publishers or authors may still employ paid posters to fight back and create pressure on the trolls.

Another way to boost sales is to send out books as gifts, an activity usually announced by prestigious accounts on *Douban*. Those who would like to receive the book are asked to mark it as "want to read" and post their reasons for the recommendation of the book. The publisher then selects or draws winners from the participants and awards them the book. Books marked by many people as "want to read" within a certain period of time will be put on the front page of *Douban Reading* as popular new books. This promotion method can achieve publicity at a lower cost. Because participants are real readers, the recommended books' ratings are reliable and likely to stay high in the future.

As a third method, booksellers may invite professional book reviewers, usually well-trained and popular among readers, to review and recommend books. Although reviewers are paid for their work, most of them are careful with the quality of the books, for praising a book that will prove to be poorly written will ruin the reviewer's reputation. Reviewers, therefore, are not passively chosen; instead, they often choose booksellers to work with.

Last, the author, translator, or editor of a book may be invited to the book's profile page and write down their experience of producing the book. This brings the author, translator, or editor closer to readers and allows them to exchange their views. Highlighting the efforts put into the book production can also win sympathy from readers, who may then show more "mercy" when rating the book. However, if the author, translator, or editor appears condescending in their testimonies and the book itself is not excellent, this practice will be ridiculed and even incur many one-star ratings.

It is evident that "literary criticism on the Internet" has become increasingly involved in the technical fields of business, communication, psychology, and so on. A subtle rivalry is going on among publishers, book reviewers, and readers around *Douban*'s evaluation system, threatening to get out of control now and then and causing a series of problems. The notorious "One Star Movement" is a good example.

Negative reviews can be contagious when friends are invited to join the one-star rating spree even if they have never read the book. Hence the "One Star Movement," a performance art about taking an opposing position through book rating.

The most representative case occurred in 2013, when Tianjin People's Publishing House invited Li Jihong, a young translator, to retranslate several books in the public domain, including *The Great Gatsby*, *The Old Man and the Sea*, *Animal Farm*, and *The Little Prince*, to form the hardcover series, "Li Jihong's Translation of World Classics." When the new edition of *The Little Prince* was released, the publisher launched a large-scale promotion and called Li Jihong the "young talented translator." On the belly bands of the books, there were blurbs, including "the best translation so far" and "[This series] corrected over 200 errors in the other 56 Chinese translations of *The Little Prince*, and more than 1,000 errors in the other 50 versions of *The Old Man and the Sea*, bringing to you the purest, most graceful, and most faithful translation…" That was virtually saying all other translations were worthless and Li's translation was orthodox. A "water army" was hired to give high ratings on *Douban Reading*, helping *The Little Prince* to score a rare 9.3 points in a short time.

The publisher's eager attempt to put the translator on a pedestal backfired. He Jiawei, a translator and editor of French literature, took the lead in the attack. He published an article on *Douban*, entitled "Error Correction Is Not What I Like, But I Have to Do It" (Jiucuo bushi wo xihuan de shi, cici budeyi erweizhi), listing more than 20 flaws in Li Jihong's translation. The publishing house did not respond, but a "one-star movement" against the water army started, quickly plunging the rating of Li Jihong's translation of *The Little Prince* from 9.3 points to 3.7 points. Even after a long period of recovery, by the end of June 2016, when there was a total of 6,463 ratings, of which five-star ratings accounted for 45.7%, the score was still only 6.9 points.

Another incident happened in July 2015. Zhejiang Literature and Art Publishing House published Rabindranath Tagore's *Stray Birds*, translated by writer Feng Tang. The publisher stated in the blurb, "*Stray Birds* was first translated into Chinese by Mr. Zheng Zhenduo in 1922. Perhaps because the original flavor was lost in the English translation from Bengali [by Tagore himself] … So, we have invited the poet Feng Tang to re-translate the poems, believing his mature and concise style will help retrieve the original artistic mood and rhythm and make the poems more agreeable to modern Chinese readers."[21]

However, Feng's translation turns out to be vulgar and not free of errors. The publisher's panegyric only provoked more resistance, and the book's score dropped to 4.1, with one-star ratings accounting for 55% of the total.

The "One Star Movement" not only showcases the rivalry between online readers and the mass media, but to a certain extent, it also functions as online critics' regulation of writers. A quantitative evaluation system gives the reader a first impression of a book, and a low score can lead to the book's failure in the market. Therefore, giving a low rating to a badly written book can be seen as a declaration of war against the author and the publisher. However, since everyone can rate a book, how to limit malicious ratings and ensure fairness has become a tough issue.

Malicious reviews often include insulting language, such as slander on the work or author, verbal attacks, and doxing. Anonymity has fueled such cyber violence. Substantial harm to victims is rare, which also makes it difficult for victims to use legal weapons to defend their rights.

But order is needed in cyberspace. A chaotic platform means inefficient management and low-grade audiences. If debates in cyber literary criticism are allowed to escalate into slanging matches, personal attacks and other more dangerous situations will ensue. Therefore, it is crucial for the administrators of literary websites and forums to maintain order.

A very common means to enforce order is by deleting the posts culpable of verbal violence. The administrator can decide to delete a single reply or close the entire discussion. This approach is very effective in preventing disputes and showing the attitude of the site. Moreover, in most slanging matches, there is no feud between the quarreling parties, and once the post that caused the incident is deleted, the people can be expected to shake hands and make peace.

Another common method is to suspend or close accounts. The period of suspension varies, ranging from days to months, during which the suspended account cannot participate in or start discussions. Suspension is a more severe punishment than deleting posts and only applies to users who do not abide by the regulations after repeated warnings. However, banning a user's account amounts to the deprivation of his or her right to speech, and whether it is proper to do so is still under debate.

Why does cyberbullying persist in literary criticism? I believe it has to do with the characteristics of the audiences: cyber literature readers are relatively young, and they are more willing to spend their time defending their favorite works. When a popular web novel receives negative reviews, its supporters are likely to fight back, often adopting abusive language. These readers do not feel responsible for their words, and when they gather in large numbers, they can cause considerable damage. The current regulatory measures can check the escalation but cannot stop similar violence from happening now and again.

The age of unrestrained freedom for literary criticism on the Internet is gone. Literary critics are expected to be responsible for their words, for the works they review, and for other readers. A healthy cyberspace for literary criticism depends on the self-regulation of every critic online.

Notes

1 Qian, Jianjun 钱建军, "Di X ci langchao—huawen wangluo wenxue" 第X次浪潮——华文网络文学, *Journal of Huaqiao University: Philosophy and Social Sciences Edition* 华侨大学学报（哲学社会科学版） no. 4 (1999): 74.

2 Qian, Jianjun 钱建军, "Di X ci langchao—huawen wangluo wenxue" 第X次浪潮——华文网络文学, 74.
 3 Chen, Shuiyun 陈水云, "Wangluo wenxue de shenmei pinwei 网络文学的审美品位," *Guangming Daily* 光明日报 (Beijing), Oct. 5, 2000.
 4 Liu, Li 刘莉, "Zhiyi wangluo wenxue" 质疑网络文学, *Art Panorama* 艺术广角 no. 4 (2001): 17–21.
 5 Tan, Dejing 谭德晶, *Wangluo wenxue piping lun* 网络文学批评论 (Beijing: CFLAC Publishing House, 2004), 130.
 6 Tan, Dejing 谭德晶, *Wangluo wenxue piping lun* 网络文学批评论, 102.
 7 Tan, Dejing 谭德晶, *Wangluo wenxue piping lun* 网络文学批评论, 130.
 8 Tan, Dejing 谭德晶, *Wangluo wenxue piping lun* 网络文学批评论, 100–101.
 9 Tan, Dejing 谭德晶, *Wangluo wenxue piping lun* 网络文学批评论, 214.
10 Tan, Dejing 谭德晶, *Wangluo wenxue piping lun* 网络文学批评论, 92–93.
11 Tan, Dejing 谭德晶, *Wangluo wenxue piping lun* 网络文学批评论, 171.
12 Tan, Dejing 谭德晶, *Wangluo wenxue piping lun* 网络文学批评论, 102–103.
13 See: Bai, Ye 白烨, "'Baling hou' de xianzhuang yu weilai" "80后"的现状与未来, *Documents and Information for Research on Contemporary Literature* 当代文学研究资料与信息 no. 3 (2005). He published the article on his Sina blog on February 24, 2006, which triggered Han Han's response on March 2 and the subsequent dispute.
14 Han, Han 韩寒, *Wentan shige pi, shui doubie zhuangbi* 文坛是个屁, 谁都别装逼, Han Han boke beifen 韩寒博客备份, 2006b. https://hanhan.aaronfang.com/2006/03/blog-post_7510.html.
Translator's note: for some reason, all blog posts on Sina Blog, including Han Han's, are now inaccessible to the public. The links given here and below are to a personal website established to save all Han Han's posts.
15 Han, Han 韩寒, *Wenxue qun'ou xueshu zaojia dajieju, zhuyao daibiao jianghua* 文学群殴学术造假大结局, 主要代表讲话, Han Han boke beifen 韩寒博客备份, 2006c. https://hanhan.aaronfang.com/2006/03/blog-post_3118.html.
16 Han, Han 韩寒, *Wenxue qun'ou xueshu zaojia dajieju, zhuyao daibiao jianghua* 文学群殴学术造假大结局, 主要代表讲话.
17 Han, Han 韩寒, *Dui shijie shuo, shenme shi guangming he leiluo* 对世界说, 什么是光明和磊落, Han Han boke beifen 韩寒博客备份, 2006a. https://hanhan.aaronfang.com/2006/03/blog-post_14.html.
18 Han, Han 韩寒, *Youxieren huacaolibucao, youxieren huabucao rencao* 有些人,话糙理不糙;有些人, 话不糙人糙, Han Han boke beifen 韩寒博客备份, 2006d. https://hanhan.aaronfang.com/2006/03/blog-post_04.html.
19 Han, Han 韩寒, *Dui shijie shuo, shenme shi guangming he leiluo* 对世界说,什么是光明和磊落.
20 Zeng, Fanting 曾繁亭, *Wangluo xieshou lun* 网络写手论 (Beijing: China Social Sciences Press, 2011), 38.
21 Translator's note: see book description on the book's *Douban* profile page, https://book.douban.com/subject/26560166.

Bibliography

Bai, Ye 白烨. " Baling hou de xianzhuang yu weilai " "80后"的现状与未来. *Documents and Information for Research on Contemporary Literature* 当代文学研究资料与信息 no. 3 (2005): 14–20.

Chen, Shuiyun 陈水云. "Wangluo wenxue de shenmei pinwei 网络文学的审美品位" *Guangming ribao* 光明日报 (Beijing), Oct. 5, 2000.

Han, Han 韩寒, *Dui shijie shuo, shenme shi guangming he leiluo* 对世界说，什么是光明和磊落. Han Han boke beifen 韩寒博客备份, 2006a. https://hanhan.aaronfang.com/2006/03/blog-post_14.html.

Han, Han 韩寒, *Wentan shige pi, shui doubie zhuangbi* 文坛是个屁，谁都别装逼. Han Han boke beifen 韩寒博客备份, 2006b. https://hanhan.aaronfang.com/2006/03/blog-post_7510.html.

Han, Han 韩寒, *Wenxue qun'ou xueshu zaojia dajieju, zhuyao daibiao jianghua* 文学群殴学术造假大结局，主要代表讲话. Han Han boke beifen 韩寒博客备份, 2006c. https://hanhan.aaronfang.com/2006/03/blog-post_3118.html.

Han, Han 韩寒, *Youxieren, huacaolibucao; youxieren, huabucao rencao* 有些人，话糙理不糙；有些人，话不糙人糙. Han Han boke beifen 韩寒博客备份, 2006d. https://hanhan.aaronfang.com/2006/03/blog-post_04.html.

Liu, Li 刘莉. "Zhiyi wangluo wenxue" 质疑网络文学. *Art Panorama* 艺术广角 no. 4 (2001): 17–21.

Qian, Jianjun 钱建军. "Di X ci langchao—huawen wangluo wenxue" 第X次浪潮——华文网络文学. *Journal of Huaqiao University: Philosophy and Social Sciences Edition* 华侨大学学报（哲学社会科学版） no. 4 (1999): 65–74+127.

Tan, Dejing 谭德晶. *Wangluo wenxue piping lun* 网络文学批评论. Beijing: CFLAC Publishing House, 2004.

Zeng, Fanting 曾繁亭. *Wangluo xieshou lun* 网络写手论. Beijing: China Social Sciences Press, 2011.

10 The Impact of Cyber Literary Criticism

By the impact of cyber literary criticism, I mean the positive influence it has on writers, works, and the development of cyber literature, as well as the development of our society and culture in general. The structure of such an impact includes critics, the ecology of criticism, and the effect of criticism. An analysis of its significance and limitations will not only help chart the history of cyber literary criticism but also help preserve the heritage of classic cyber literature.

The Structure of Cyber Literary Criticism's Impact

The impact of cyber literary criticism consists of three layers. The heated collisions and collusions among critics constitute the first layer. Such collisions and collaborations between diverse forces accelerate our society's recognition of cyber literature as a field of study. The interaction among readers constitutes the second layer of the influence of cyber literary criticism. By taking part in the "carnivalesque" activities of literary criticism, readers abandon their identities as passive onlookers and receivers to exert their influence in a wide circle. The subversion and reconstruction of the "criticism ecology" constitute the third layer. The high-speed and multi-directional communication platform offered by the Internet has transformed the ecosystem of traditional criticism and promoted the decentralization of power. As everyone can now write critical words online, a new order in literary criticism has been created.

The Collision and Collaboration Between Different Groups of Critics

As mentioned above, literature amateurs gained their influence by posting on literary websites, and their criticism lacked authority. However, the openness of the Internet helped this group to pool their voices into a Bakhtinian "public square," where the critics' carnivalesque activities eventually led to the strengthening of this group to the degree that their views on literary events challenged the authoritative voices.

While ordinary netizens started to write literary criticism online, scholars began to defend their privilege and cultural capital by defining the boundaries of literature. Literary scholar Xi Yunshu published an article, declaring that web publication "has changed the content and form of cyber literary criticism" and diminished the voice of professional writers: "The system of discourse that conventional critics like us have relied on has lost its power, and all the doctrines and in-depth analyses have become meaningless in the era of cyber literature."[1] He cautioned that cyber literature "is devoid of 'aesthetic significance' and 'utilitarian significance,'" and believed that it was "reasonable" that cyber literary works were not recognized by traditional writers. Liu Li, a scholar, was more blunt. She declared: "Just like writers are divided into classes, there is a hierarchy for literature... Is this (cyber literature) literature at all?"[2] I discussed this issue in an article as follows:

> Some people regard the computer network as the savior of literature, some others deem cyber literature the new star, and still others think that the Internet will become the nemesis of literature... Before cyber literature can win people's respect with improved quality, it is not unreasonable to doubt its value and prospects.[3]

Mo Yan, a famous writer, compared the disorder and vulgarity of cyber literature to the scribbling of big-character posters: "The authors say whatever they like, showing no scruples about style or content, and the crudity of their writing ruins readers' appetite."[4] According to Li Jingze, some people doubted the legitimacy of the term "cyber literature":

> Literature comes from human minds, not from the Internet. The particular problem we face now is that a shocking illusion leads people to regard the Internet—instead of human minds—as what produces the content and form of literature. It is because of this that we have so-called "cyber literature" today.[5]

Among the critical voices, those of Bai Ye and Tao Dongfeng were particularly notable. As already mentioned, Bai Ye argued that the post-80s generation writers and their works had made it into the market, but they had not entered the "literary world" (wentan). Tao compared cyber literature with classic literature to show that the writing of fantasy novels, or *xuanhuan xiaoshuo*, which was popular as a genre of cyber literature, led literature into an era of mystification. "There has never been an accurate definition of *xuanhuan* literature," Tao wrote, "*xuanhuan* literature not only defies natural laws (laws of physics), the way in which our society operates based on people's rational capacity, and the rules of everyday life, but subverts the very norms of the natural and social worlds."[6] This comment led one scholar to remark, "Tao negated the legitimacy of cyber literature by denying its moral significance."[7]

As we know, professional critics usually have solid cultural and social capital and influence over the production of literature in the traditional sense. These scholars were seldom found to be in dialogue with grassroots critics. But the questions they asked show that the "collective unconscious" of grassroots criticism has infiltrated the traditional field of literature and begun to have an impact on literary criticism as a whole. The dispute between Han Han and Bai Ye ended with Bai Ye shutting down his blog in response to the attacks by Han Han and Han's followers, while Tao Dongfeng was criticized by cyber writers such as Xiao Ding.

Such debates testify to the changes in literary criticism's discursive power and structure of influence. It is worth mentioning that many scholars entered cyberspace through those debates, gained popularity, and interacted with common readers on an equal footing. It shows that popular cyber literary criticism began to influence the traditional modes of criticism. Scholars participated, though maybe unintentionally, in the building up of cyber literary criticism's impact. The debates epitomized the power contest between the rising online literary criticism, which strove to guard its territory in a decentralized online world and exert influence on academia, and scholarly criticism, which also had to defend its territory while trying to enter cyberspace through digital media. Early cyber literary criticism encountered the same identification dilemma as cyber literature itself did, and debate was an indispensable means through which it overcame the dilemma and optimized its influence in the literary field.

At the same time, some scholars, seeing the potential of cyber literature and the inevitability of cyber criticism, began to focus their research on those subjects. Unlike the early critics, such as Fang Zhouzi and Wu Guo, who were literature amateurs on the Internet, these scholars were better at theoretical interpretations of cyber literature and its criticism from a holistic perspective. Yang Xinmin's observation is representative of the scholarly intervention: "Cyber literature has surfaced with strong momentum. In contrast, its theoretical interpretation has been absent."[8] In an article, I summarized the characteristics of cyber literature as follows: "writers are also netizens"; "literary creation is done through interaction"; "literary texts are in digital forms"; "works are circulated online"; "readers read on computers and other electronic devices."[9] I also pointed out: "To develop a correct view of cyber literature, we need to cultivate a reasonable outlook on the ecology of literature in the information age, as well as an open and tolerant idea of 'literature in the board sense' and 'para-literature.' It is also necessary to get rid of elitism and promote grassroots values."[10]

Another scholar, Huang Mingfen, affirmed the historical significance of "computer literature and art," arguing that it is the "manifestation of the humanist spirit under new historical conditions," which "focuses on the new things in social life that have a promising future." Huang wrote: "It is the efforts of the numerous ordinary writers and artists who try to surpass the masters that have made possible the progress of literature and art." He also remarked on the purpose of the studies of "computer literature and art" and contended that "theoretical innovation must be based on hands-on, fresh experience in the creation and appreciation of cyber literature."[11] Although only a handful of scholars paid attention to cyber literary criticism in the early days, their trailblazing efforts opened up new space for its study.

The influence of these scholars can be seen in two places. First, their expertise in logical reasoning, such as deduction and induction, enables them to see the true condition of cyber literature, clarify the way in which cyber literature works, and draw useful lessons from such views and experiences. In this way, they help to construct a system of theories on cyber literature, and their efforts are conducive to the improvement of cyber literature and the general environment of cyberwriting. Scholars working in universities and research institutions help develop theories on cyber literature and guide the healthy development of literature through their research. Second, the elitist identity of scholars helps cyber literary criticism garner influence in academia, while the scholars also assume the responsibility as "coordinators" between academic literary criticism and its counterpart in cyberspace. Despite the obstacles, academic critics have made a great contribution to the growth of cyber literary criticism, securing the "positive evaluation" of cyber literature by "the mainstream voice of mainstream literature."[12] I raised an example in an article to illustrate this point:

> In October 2007, the Lu Xun Literature Prize, China's highest government award, which was reviewed by China Writers Association, was awarded to Ouyang Youquan's monograph on cyber literature, *Literature and Art in a Digital Context* (Shuzihua yujing zhong de wenyixue, 2005). It was the first high commendation for the academic study of cyber literature from the society of the mainstream culture and literature.[13]

The debate between different groups of critics does not mean the contradictions are beyond reconciliation. As mentioned above, the convergence of critics reinforced the impact of cyber literary criticism. Academics like Ge Hongbin, Zhang Yiwu, and Chen Dingjia began to test the waters in cyberspace, and critics such as Bai Ye and Tao Dongfeng also tried to moderately incorporate cyber literature into their discussions. Even Mo Yan, who used to see the writing of cyber literature as "the scribbling of big-character posters," wrote in an article published in *People's Daily*, acknowledging that "cyber literature is a good thing."[14] Media workers, such as Shu Jinyu, who worked for *China Reading News*, took notice of cyber literature and its criticism, and more reviews of cyber literature were published in print media. At the same time, netizens became less confrontational toward scholarly critics and were having more friendly, in-depth exchanges with academics. Some were even assimilated by the mainstream. For example, in 2005, China Writers Association recruited writers such as "Annie Baby" (Anni baobei) and Zhang Yueran, who wrote both online and offline. In 2010, more than 20 popular cyber writers, including "Bright Moon in That Year" (Dangnian mingyue), "Watch the Rise of Clouds with a Smile" (Xiaokan yunqi), and "The Third Young Master of the Tang Sect" (Tangjia sanshao), were recruited as members of the China Writers

Association, signifying the acceptance of cyber writers by the society of mainstream literature.

In 2010, the 5th Lu Xun Literature Prize included works of cyber literature as contestants for the first time, and soon the Mao Dun Literature Prize also accepted cyber literature for the first time. The web novel, *The Mighty River Flows Eastward* (Dajiang dongqu) won the Five-One Project Award (Wugeyi gongcheng jiang), and in 2013, the web novels, *The Code of the Classic of Mountains and Seas* (Shanhaijing mima) and *Dictionary: Southern Industrial Life* (Cidian: nanfang gongye shenghuo) won the 9th Lu Xun Literature and Art Award of Guangdong Province (Guangdong Lu Xun wenxue yishu jiang). Another outcome of the collaboration among critics is the expedited recognition of the academic significance of cyber literature. People begin to see cyber literature not as old literary works circulated on the Internet, but as a new category of literature with distinct features. As such, cyber literature requires new approaches of criticism, which should not only help cyber writers recognize the strengths and weaknesses of their own works, but also help readers appreciate and understand texts of cyber literature both as cultural commodities and artworks.

Cyber Readers as Spectators and Participants in Cyber Literary Criticism

The anonymity, freedom, and egalitarianism of the virtual space dissolve the barriers between readers of cyber literary criticism, making their interactions more frequent and unrestrained. The writing and reading of cyber literary criticism thus become a Bakhtinian carnivalesque activity in a public space and have a unique kind of social influence.

Bakhtin's theory of the carnival is predicated on the distinction between an "orderly world" and a "travestied world," the latter being accessible only to those who can give up their power, identity, and status of the "orderly world."[15] "The carnivalesque crowd in the marketplace or in the streets," writes Bakhtin, "is not merely a crowd. It is the people as a whole, but organized in their own way, the way of the people. It is outside of and contrary to all existing forms of the coercive socioeconomic and political organization, which is suspended for the time of the festivity."[16] Similarly, the readers who flock to the online marketplace of literary criticism are not merely a crowd who simply follow the trend without critical thinking. They are outside of the serious, hierarchical, and orderly world of criticism and have given up their power and identity in the real world to form a carnivalesque crowd and to have an impact on cyber criticism.

Readers, as spectators and participants in cyber literary criticism, exert their influence first through the inclusiveness of the "carnival," which "does not acknowledge any distinction between actors and spectators."[17] Unlike academic publications, which are written by elites and expect readers to be mere spectators, netizens' critical commentaries posted online allow their readers to select, respond to, and publish opinions, thus turning recipients into participants. Readers of online literary criticism not only participate in the production of criticism but show independence from the guidance of elite criticism, substituting the mundane and absurd for the serious and elegant in the carnival where they remain anonymous. The voices of authorities, celebrities, and leaders in academia are drowned in the heteroglossia in cyberspace, and the language endorsed by the "orderly world" is discarded. In this carnival, "everyone participates because its very idea embraces all the people. ... life is subject only to its laws, that is, the laws of its own freedom."[18]

The influence of these readers also lies in the simultaneity of multitudinous interactions in cyberspace—a carnival marketplace. Congestion in the real world is non-existent in cyberspace. Online readers, free from the restriction of time and space, gather around the same topic and make continuous revisions to comments and reviews, conducting a criticism of criticism. These spectators' participation is at once individual and collective, synchronic and diachronic, fractured and cumulative, as successive readers can always add to the previous conclusions.

For example, in 2007, Xia bu'an, a reader of the web novel, *Attack of Heaven* (Zhu xian), posted a review praising the marvelous imagination of the novel and complaining about the disappointing ending in the eighth book of the series, asking "if [the author] Xiao Ding's talents are really exhausted."[19] The review was enthusiastically liked and responded to, kindling a discussion that continued into 2015. It shows that the influence of cyber literature as a kind of "online carnival" goes far beyond one critical review. It lies in the collective and cumulative activities of the spectators and participants, who can make their existence felt by merely clicking "like" or sending an emoticon. This is why cyber literary criticism can have an enduring and widespread impact.

Subverting and Restructuring the Ecology of Criticism

Cyberspace generates new possibilities for the production and consumption of cyber literature and criticism, attracting a huge number of consumers with diverse terminals and transmitting literary criticism across regions and cultures. The subversion of the old ecology of criticism and the construction of the new constitute cyber literary criticism's social influence in a unique sense.

To begin with, the number of critics and readers both increased, and the mode of dissemination changed. With print media, the content was strictly controlled and disseminated in a small circle, whereas the development of network technology promoted high-speed and multi-dimensional dissemination of information. As of the end of June 2016, China's Internet users reached 710 million, with a 21.32 million increase in half a year, and the rate of Internet usage was 51.7%, an increase of 1.3% from the end of 2015. The number of mobile network users reached 656 million, and the percentage of mobile network users among all Internet users increased from 90.1% at the end of 2015 to 92.5% by the end of 2016.[20] In the decentralized cyberspace where literary criticism is popular, readers with a moderate education level are the primary audience, which was unimaginable in the past when literary criticism only appeared in print media. Among the huge number of Internet users, those who had middle school and high school (including specialized secondary school) degrees accounted for 37.4% and 29.2%, respectively. In terms of age, users aged 10–19 accounted for 20.1% of the total; the 20–29 age group was the largest, taking up 30.4%; and those aged 30–39 accounted for 24.2%. Among the new Internet users in the first half of 2016, 14.3% had only gone to primary school, 37.0% had a middle school education, 28.2% had a high school or secondary specialized school degree, 8.9% graduated from specialized postsecondary colleges, and 11.5% held a bachelor's degree or above. Moreover, 43.8% of the surveyed users said they liked to post comments on the Internet, among which 6.7% liked it very much and 37.1% liked it quite well. More than 108 million users actively posted comments in forums, accounting for 15.2% of the total users.[21] The large number of users with a secondary education brought great potential to cyber literary criticism, promising wide coverage and accessibility.

With the "compression of time and space by the network and the view of the world as a 'global village' following global integration,"[22] an "imagined community" was formed, featuring the simultaneous transmission and reception of information across a wide range of regions. The exclusivity of literary criticism was eliminated, and a new ecology was created, in which literary criticism was accessible to all, with wide coverage and deep penetration into people's daily life. As we have seen, discussions about literature and arts have never been so widespread and diverse as they are today. Criticism becomes a way of public communication as producers and consumers of cyber literary criticism participate in it through a variety of terminals and media.

People's view of literary criticism has also changed under the influence of cyber criticism. The digital platform fosters a powerful spirit of popular criticism, benefiting from the decentralization of power to challenge the monopoly of information by traditional media. As Negroponte puts it, being digital means decentralizing and empowering.[23] The empowered individuals enjoy more freedom. Liu Ji and Jin Wulun made such a discussion:

> In cyberspace, any computer can communicate with any other computer, no matter where it is located. No one has more privileges than anyone else; neither IBM nor the President of the United States has more power than a teenager in cyberspace. Power, class, hierarchy, and even geographic location are of no significance at all in cyberspace, where everyone can be the center and where people are equal, not controlled by a hierarchical system. Although the Internet was established with the support and funding of the US government, it has become an independent network since the 1990s. The decentralization of power has become the most basic spirit in cyberspace.[24]

The spirit of popular criticism thus prospers in cyberspace thanks to this shared freedom.

Significance and Limitations of Cyber Literary Criticism

Significance of Cyber Literary Criticism

Literary criticism has a long and solid tradition bolstered by vibrant theories. Ever since the emergence of cyber literature, there have been debates over whether cyber literary criticism can count as criticism at all and how it fits the actual condition of cyber literature. The validity of cyber literary criticism continues to be a topic of discussion today. Fortunately, the rich experience accumulated with the growth of cyber literature has expanded the boundaries of literary criticism and given cyber literary criticism more importance.

Since the 1990s, with the decline of literature's influence on people's life, literary criticism has suffered great loss and received a lot of criticism. Meanwhile, the growth of cyber literature further revealed the unbalanced relationship between literary criticism and emerging literary forms, the former being stretched too thin by the fast increase of cyberwritings. Nan Fan pointed out: "Many rising writers hardly receive any attention from literary critics. In other words, criticism is no longer involved in the current development of literature. It does not take the responsibility to guide writers and readers. Criticism has left literature behind to go on a vacation."[25] The general public could not participate in literary evaluation since they were "not in the mainstream," let alone participate in the construction and optimization of the criticism system, while professional critics found it difficult to win common readers and guide literary evaluation. The effectiveness of criticism was in crisis. Authors and ordinary readers lost their sense of respect for literary criticism, which had become an exclusive activity. As a result, both literature and literary criticism had to seek out new opportunities on the Internet.

As early as the beginning of cyber literature's rise in the late 1990s, critics like Fang Zhouzi and "Stupid Raccoon" (Benli), who were literature amateurs on the Internet, tried to summarize the characteristics of cyber literature. In an article titled "Networked Literature" (Wangluohua de wenxue) published on the Chinese literary website *New Threads of Thought* (Xin Yu Si), Fang Zhouzi named "openness" and "the use of multimedia" as the characteristics of this new literature and considered it an unorthodox literature because it "takes advantage of the Internet" to be "open to change, indefinitely unfinished, and interactive, presenting different versions to different readers on different dates, or created collectively by a group of people."[26] Early critics of cyber literature witnessed its birth and growth, but their criticism in cyberspace hardly sparked any in-depth discussion in the literary circle due to people's limited access to the Internet. Early cyber literary criticism, similarly, lacked the recognition and financial support from scholars, whose research hardly touched upon the systematic formulation of cyber literature. Nonetheless, early critics' attention to cyber literary criticism still signifies the need to adapt literary criticism to the changes brought about by cyber literature. Developing on its own, cyber literary criticism is the historical product of the impact of technology and is charged with the mission to revolutionize criticism and grasp the literary trend in the new century.

As communication grew between the "literature within the circle of mainstream writers" and the literature that grew freely in the market, the view of criticism as an individual monologue was discarded and the critic was no longer seen as a solitary, high-ranking judge. "All else is the means; dialogue is the end," says Bakhtin, "A single voice ends nothing and resolves nothing."[27] Cyber literary criticism turned criticism into a dialogue between authors, readers, and critics, bringing about more equality and diversity. The once much-neglected criticism flourished, with ordinary readers freely expressing themselves, scholars contributing their academic findings, and the media creating hot topics to draw wider attention.

As mentioned in previous chapters, cyber literary criticism expanded the spectrum of criticism, allowing popular literature into the game. It accelerates the dissolution of elitism in literary criticism and empowers ordinary people to choose any works to critique. Cyber literary criticism also enriches the language and form of literary criticism and makes it more accessible. The easy, unpretentious style stimulates public enthusiasm, attracting more people to write and read literary criticism online. Furthermore, cyber literary criticism allows critics to be involved in the process of cyberwriting, fostering interactions between criticism and creation. One notable example is *Innocent and Dubious* (Henchun hen aimei) by "Fisherman the Second" (Yuren erdai), which was extended from the original two to three million Chinese characters to four million in response to readers' feedback. As Chang Shuxing, a cyber writer, put it, "whereas traditional novel writing involves only one person, web novels are written through the interaction between authors and readers, the latter being tens, or even hundreds of people."[28] In sum, cyber literary criticism has changed the way of literary creation and widened the scope of criticism.

Limitations of Cyber Literary Criticism

Cyber literary criticism inevitably has its flaws and weaknesses due to the uncertainty and incompleteness of cyber literature.

First, the evaluation criteria will be difficult to pin down. With the diversity among critics and the influence of postmodern culture, the voices defying a series of ideas, including authority, enlightenment, self-discipline, rationality, center, and meaning, are growing. Traditional standards and authoritative concepts are ignored or questioned, while the rapid development of cyber literature makes any new criteria insufficient. The different groups of critics disagree with each other. Most online critics tend to give intuitive perceptions rather than rational analyses, whereas scholars' theoretical interpretation often falls short at the sheer volume of unsorted web works. As one researcher put it: "The open space of cyber literary criticism gives critics the freedom of identity, freedom of speech, and freedom of publication, which frees criticism from uniformity and gives it a distinct personality. However, this popular open platform also makes it difficult to create evaluation criteria."[29] Reviews are numerous and scattered in this borderless space. At the same time, literary genres are frequently crossed with the adaptation of web novels into TV dramas, movies, and radio dramas. All this adds up to the difficulty of evaluating and regulating criticism. In addition, the fast production and consumption of cyber literature make it hard for people to distinguish good works from bad ones. Cyber literary criticism is thus trapped in a dilemma among diverse critics and works with a lack of criteria for criticism. While some people proposed that "pleasure and beauty" should be used as the basic criterion for evaluating cyber literature, some others advocated decentralization and replacement of depth with emotion. A consensus has not been reached.

In contrast, scholarly critics share some universal criteria. They may evaluate a work according to their individual tastes, but their judgments are usually made against the yardstick of literary theories that have withstood the test of time. Lacking the heteronomy made possible by such normative theories, cyber literary criticism is easily led astray by the pursuit of pleasure, generating fragmented, superficial, and irresponsible expressions. Criticism runs wild without regulation.

As an example, Ta Ai (Han Weibing) posted a series of reviews on *Skyline Forum* (Tianya luntan) entitled "A Critique of Ten Beauty Writers" (Shi meinü zuojia pipanshu) in 2004, in which he evaluated ten female cyber writers, including "Annie Baby" (Anni baobei) and Chun Shu, and their works. The reviews were published as a book by Hualing Publishing House in 2005 and were reposted on many other websites. Many readers praised the author's "pungent remarks," and some said these reviews "reached the pinnacle of criticism with penetrating analyses."[30] However, as the book does not use traditional evaluation criteria to examine these works, it has been criticized by many in academia. Literary critic Bai Ye pointed out:

> These are not professional reviews but are a kind of "scathing criticism" (kuping) that aims at venting out the reviewer's feelings. The reviewer says things professional critics dare not or care not to say, but he also commits the fatal mistake of conflating works with authors, ending up attacking the author when critiquing the text.[31]

Professor Liu Anhai published an article criticizing the book for its lack of "analytical study of the works and characters," saying that the book "distorts the original meaning of literary criticism to a very serious degree" and "deviates from the true meaning of literary criticism."[32] Another scholar observed that "criteria for literary and art criticism must be detailed, clear, and easy to grasp in order to guide and regulate literary and artistic creation."[33] The lack of criteria leads to irrational judgments based on subjective perception that is unreliable and cannot withstand the test of time.

At the same time, critics are faced with a cognitive dilemma. Unlike literary scholars, who usually choose their primary texts from the repertory carefully screened and reviewed by editors and publishing institutions and give objective and rational analyses, netizens who write literary commentaries find themselves surrounded by tons of unreviewed texts. They must quickly identify valuable and representative works from the infinitely expanding stock—a goal that may only be reached after many delays and setbacks. Meanwhile, the information overload and temptation of online media keep interfering with the selection process, disrupting progressive thinking and leading to fragmentation, which exacerbates the netizens' cognitive dilemma.

In addition, in the absence of reasonable criteria, a few indices, such as the click-through rate, the volume of publications, and the rate of intellectual property transfer, become the yardstick for the evaluation of cyber literary works. This is a market-centered mechanism not founded reasonably on aesthetic values but on commercialization and the public need for entertainment. The commercial model of cyber literature—the simultaneity of its creation, dissemination, and consumption, as well as readers' participation in the production—further confuses critics. Yang Liquan discussed such an issue:

> When a critic keeps clicking on links in cyberspace, he/she will be in a continuous state of schizophrenia. The nonlinearity of the links not only brings up endless images ...but also damages the linear logical structure and cancels out the "function of sentences." The critic's perceptual experience becomes fragmented and disconnected, and he/she cannot unify the past, present, and future of spiritual life to form a cohesive intention.[34]

There is, furthermore, the incompatibility between academic critics and the cyber literature they critique. Scholars, as the cultural elite, are often unable to let go of their elitist attitude when researching cyber literature, and this mindset proves incompatible with a literature written and read by ordinary netizens. As a result, these critics end up talking about theories to themselves and their criticism loses its power. As Hong Zhigang put it, "when a critic critiques any past or present work from a professional point of view, the criteria he/she uses, although to some extent influenced by personal tastes and ways of thinking, cannot completely deviate from the accepted values or violate the established aesthetic system."[35] At the same time, cyber writers rarely subscribe to traditional academic journals, or hardly know about them, which makes it difficult for scholarly ideas to be conveyed to cyber writers. This lack of communication widens the gap between literary scholars and ordinary readers and creates a barrier for anyone who tries to approach literary criticism.

In fact, most scholars have never written any cyber literature, and their reading experience is limited too. Some of them, knowing little about the literary scene on the Internet, find it difficult to comprehend the present situation and development of cyber literature and are therefore unable to fully understand the texts they critique, which makes their criticism incompatible with the writing and reading of cyber literature and their literary theories widely questioned. In 2011, Zhang Jiong, a literary scholar, reposted a blog post, criticizing cyber writers for their "lack of an awareness of literary classics in cyber literary creation" and suggested that literary criticism should assist in the "examination and improvement of cyberwriting."[36] This suggestion was rebuffed by cyber writer "BLUE Angel" (BLUE Anqi'er). She retorted, "you can't have read more than a couple of classic web novels carefully," "so you just don't fully understand."[37] The criteria, scope, and techniques of literary criticism must be based on the reading of literary works. Using unsuitable theories or imposing preconceived ideas can only turn literary criticism into an unrealistic elaboration. Some scholarly research tends to focus on theoretical interpretation to the extent of ignoring the vibrant texts online, severing the connection between cyber literature and cyberculture, and dissociating theories from works.

In the living world of cyber literature, impractical criticism has no place to thrive. Unfortunately, recent years have witnessed very few influential critical reviews of web novels. There have been some well-written articles, such as Zhou Zhixiong's "Looking Back and Evaluating: *First Intimate Contact* and the Development of Web Literature" (Huigu yu pingpan: *Diyici de qinmi jiechu* yu wangluo wenxue de fazhan), Hu Yan's "Grotesque and Romantic: On the Web Fantasy *The Attack of Heaven*" (Qigui huangdan zhi qing zhi xing: ping wangluo xuanhuan xiaoshuo *Zhu xian*), and Zhu Yulan and Xiao Weisheng's "The Irresistible Second World: Using the Web Fantasy *The Attack of Heaven* as an Example" (Wu ke kangju di'er shijie de meihuo: yi wangluo xuanhuan xiaoshuo *Zhu xian* wei li), but they were all published only after the web novels they reviewed had been released in book form. Very few participated in the online discussion of those works, despite the fact that it is the duty of cyber literary critics to keep abreast of web publications, read carefully, and offer their evaluations and advice. Cyber literary criticism must "begin with reading online and stay in touch with the literary scene,"[38] because "with literature irreversibly transformed by new media, cyber literary criticism must also make a theoretical turn and choose a methodology for more effective communication. The choice made will affect the construction of cyber literary theory and the development of cyber literature."[39]

The Literary Canon in the Internet Era

As the embodiment of the "accumulated literary criteria over time,"[40] a literary canon represents the elite culture and offers a set of values for society to follow. The publication of literary classics through print media is controlled and limited, as most authors have to write under their real names and as publishers maintain high standards for publication. Through such a process, inferior works are eliminated, and a canon is formed. However, as the Internet extends public access to information, speeds up dissemination, and makes anonymous communication the norm, the traditional way of canon formation is challenged, and the right to criticism is moved down to the ordinary reader. The status of literary canons is inevitably changed and will continue to be challenged with the decentralization in literary criticism. In this reshuffle of critics, primary texts, and methodologies, classic works will get the cold shoulder as they never did. That is perhaps one of the negative byproducts of cyber literary criticism.

What, exactly, has caused the indifference to literary classics and their criticism in the era of Internet media?

The Mechanism of Cyber Literary Criticism that Blocks Deep Thoughts

Online criticism hinders critics from reflecting on the significance of literary classics. Whereas with print media, critics are "called on" by classics to repeatedly read, appreciate, decode, and eventually understand, this sequence of activities is disrupted with the mode of cyber literary criticism that goes straight from "online reading" to "online critiquing." The latter mode is inherently flawed. In this simulated world of digital media, what we have are only symbols that can infinitely reproduce, and things evolve into visual representations that have nothing to do with reality. The author's emotions, personality, and other humanistic features disappear in this mass reproduction of symbols. At the same time, information expands exponentially, making it difficult for the reader to read and think in-depth. As Michael Heim put it, "Infomania erodes our capacity for significance. With a mindset fixed on information, our attention span shortens. We collect fragments. We become mentally poorer in overall meaning. We get into the habit of clinging to knowledge bits and lose our feel for the wisdom behind knowledge."[41] The fragmentation interferes with humanistic aesthetics, depriving the reader of the opportunity to repeatedly experience and think about the text. As I pointed out in an article, "the poetry, aesthetics, techniques, and spiritual touch are all lost in the powerful flow of audio-visual information."[42] Canonical works consequently lose their charm.

Postmodernism's Deconstruction of the Literary Canon

As mentioned in previous chapters, the birth of cyber literature coincided with postmodernism in China. The postmodern character of cyber literary criticism fostered disregard for the sublime and sacred, dispelling the significance and authority of the literary canon. For Derrida, it is unreasonable to treat reason as a universal paradigm, for "an inverted hierarchical order" is sometimes the best strategy for deconstructing binary oppositions.[43] Cyber literary criticism, especially online criticism, is a postmodern product that disregards reason and the authority of the binary oppositional paradigm. It exemplifies the characteristics of postmodernism summarized by Jean-François Leotard, including de-legitimation, decentralization, heterogeneity, plurality, dissatisfaction with the status quo, disregard for rules, and constant innovation.[44] It is capable of deconstructing and subverting the concept of classic literature with "spoofing," a trick brimming with the postmodern qualities of intertextuality and decentralization.

Spoofing, as a way of criticism, still pays attention to characters and other key elements in works, but it also exaggerates or makes fun of serious issues, disrupting the relationship between the signified and the signifier. Its rewriting of traditional rules perhaps has more to do with the critic's perception of his/her living condition than with any significance of the work itself, but its playfulness can nevertheless dissolve the sublimity of the literary classic.

As an example, a spoof review titled "*Journey to the West*: A Past Classic or A Portrayal of Present Officialdom" (*Xiyouji* shi lishi juzhu, haishi dangdai guanchang xiantai) was published on *Skyline Community* (Tianya shequ) in 2012. It gives satiric and sarcastic discussions about characters—legendary figures in Taoist and Buddhist myths—and their power struggles in two ancient Chinese classics, *The Investiture of Gods* (Fengshenbang) and *Journey to the West* (Xiyouji), to subvert and reconstruct the theme of *Journey to the West*: the reviewer criticizes contemporary Chinese officialdom and concludes that "*Journey to the West* is an all-time classic that reflects the strife in today's officialdom."[45] The author converted various titles and positions of these figures in the mythological hierarchy into positions in the modern administrative system in China and infers that "The Supreme Venerable Sovereign" (Taishang Laojun) has committed adultery and has been keeping it a secret. The essay thus dissolves the mythological charm and authority of the two works as literary classics.

Consumerism's Challenge to Classics

Consumerism, which started to rise in China in the 1990s, approximately at the same time when the Internet was also developing, posed another challenge to the endurance of literary classics. For many people, consumption became a prerequisite for realizing their life's purpose and determining their social status. The desire for material and cultural goods surged across different cultural strata, stimulating the mass production and consumption of films, TV shows, cyber literature, and even literary criticism. Literary classics were thus marginalized and eclipsed by mass culture. As a result, literary criticism shifted its focus from literary classics toward various literary forms that were intended to entertain the public and were even vulgar in style and content.

Consumerism affects not only the production and consumption of popular cultural commodities but also people's choices, causing them to identify with the consumer culture. "The truth of consumption," says Baudrillard, "is that it is not a function of enjoyment, but a *function of production* and, hence, like all material production, not an individual function, but *an immediately and totally collective one.*"[46] One of the effects of the consumer culture is the formation of a morality and a system of exchange that underrate any delayed use value of cultural commodities and emphasize the social distinction and immediate pleasure as a result of consumption. Modern media represented by the Internet offers more and more instant cultural products at an ever-faster speed, encouraging the pursuit of immediate and short-term enjoyment.

The importance of literary classics to spiritual life and cultural construction declines, while shallow and entertaining expressions that used to be despised take the central stage in the new forms of literature and its criticism on Weibo, WeChat, and so on.

Young Internet users emphasize "hedonism, the pursuit of pleasure here and now, the cultivation of expressive lifestyles, [and] the development of narcissistic and egoistic personality types."[47] Literary classics cannot satisfy their need for immediate cultural and aesthetic entertainment, and the values proselyted by canonical works seem irrelevant to those young people's life. Spiritual depth is no longer an element of literary success; instead, sensational reviews become key to the popularity of literary works. As shallow expressions of strong emotions that intend to curry favor with the public have replaced deeper analyses of the meanings of works, there is no room for literary classics. Since it is hard for common readers to acknowledge and appreciate the aesthetic and cultural values of literary classics, it is also hard for the reader-as-critic to give adequate interpretation and evaluation of the aesthetic and cultural values of such works.

The Retirement of the Old Canon and the Construction of a Cyber Literary Canon

While the influence of literary classics is limited by the Internet culture, this does not mean the end of canonization. On the contrary, many websites, especially large portal websites, have opened forums for classic writers, and classic literature still seems to attract the attention of online critics. For example, after Mo Yan won the Nobel Prize for Literature in 2012, "the entire online world was in an unprecedented carnival as Mo Yan's receipt of the award became the most trending topic on both *Tencent Weibo* and *Sina Weibo*, far ahead of the second trending topics. Comments on Mo Yan's works and writing style abounded."[48]

Yet the limited attention cannot change the situation that literary classics still do not attract much public attention. This confirms what Tong Qingbing once pointed out in an article: "The literary canon is constantly changing. It is not formed once and for all after being determined by people of a certain era but is constructed in an ongoing process."[49] The predicament of literary classics in cyber literary criticism does not mean the loss of meaning of the canon. As we know, classics play an irreplaceable role in the education of readers and in the passing on of national and cultural heritage. But the status of classics is challenged and the means of its inheritance has been changed. Therefore, we need to re-examine classics and find an effective way to interpret them in the Internet age, so as to give them new vitality as they are read online.

Canon formation on the Internet has to rely on the combined forces of writers, readers, and critics. For cyber writers, to write a work that can be passed down to future generations, they need to show reverence for literature, have a sense of responsibility for society and history, and relentlessly pursue artistic innovation. This can by no means be achieved by writing more words, increasing the click-through rate of the works, or earning high royalties. Cyber literature, just like traditional literature, must rely on reputation, as readers are the ultimate judges of a literary work's worthiness. Not all the works loved by readers make it into the canon, but works not loved by readers will never become a classic. Shao Yanjun once said:

> Classics in the Internet age are no longer certified by any authority, but by fans. There is no longer a mysterious "river of classics" that just happens to pass through every classic work—the popular canon of any era has been the result of a collective push, and the cyber literary canon is even more so, a "collective creation" promoted by the majority of fans through continuous support. … In the circle of cyber literature, if a work not only attracts many followers immediately after its release, but also is drawn on, imitated, or parodied by succeeding writers in the following years, then it will most likely be canonized.[50]

For critics, the influence of cyber literary criticism on Internet canon formation should not be underestimated. The influence is exerted through two means: reviews and promotion of works, the latter including author recognition, literary awards, rankings, web seminars, and so on. If "the 'classic quality' of literature usually means exemplarity, transcendence, inheritance, and originality," which serve as the criteria for the evaluation of literature,[51] then the awards and recognition are aimed to highlight such qualities so that readers can appreciate and future writers can emulate. This is how literary classics were created and recognized, and how a cyber literary canon should be formed.

In recent years, more and more cyber writers have been recognized (by being recruited to China Writers Association, for example) and awarded (with the Mao Dun Literature Prize, Lu Xun Literature Prize, and others), and more works have been advertised. To name just the most influential events in 2015 alone: China Writers Association created the web novel rankings (quarterly and annually); the State Administration of Press, Publication, Radio, Film and Television recommended 21 outstanding web novels; Zhejiang Writers Association sponsored a Chinese Cyber Literature Biennial Award, and *Yangcheng Evening News* (Yangcheng wanbao) named its annual list of web novels for the "Huadi Literature Awards." Seminars about web literature held by organizations at all levels, ranging from China Writers Association to some online research societies, also speeded up the canonization process of cyber literature, in which cyber literary criticism played an indispensable role.

Notes

1 Xi, Yunshu 席云舒, "Wangluo de jueqi yu wenxue de kuisan 网络的崛起与文学的溃散," *Zhongguo wenhuabao* 中国文化报 (Beijing), Sep. 9, 2000.
2 Liu, Li 刘莉, "Zhiyi wangluo wenxue" 质疑网络文学, *Art Panorama* 艺术广角 no. 4 (2001): 21.

3 Ouyang, Youquan 欧阳友权, "Wangluo wenxue de meiti tuwei yu biaozheng beilun" 网络文学的媒体突围与表征悖论, *Social Science Front* 社会科学战线 no. 4 (2002): 90.
4 Xu, Miaomiao 许苗苗, "Teliduxing de wangluo wenxue 特立独行的网络文学," *Wenyi bao* 文艺报 (Beijing), Mar. 20, 2001.
5 Li, Jingze 李敬泽, "Wangluo wenxue: yaodian he yiwen 网络文学：要点和疑问," *Wenxue bao* 文学报 (Shanghai), Apr. 20, 2000.
6 Tao, Dongfeng 陶东风, "Zhongguo wenxue yijing jinru zhuangshennonggui shidai? 中国文学已经进入装神弄鬼时代？," *Zhonghua dushu bao* 中华读书报 (Beijing), Jun. 21, 2006.
7 Li, Yangquan 黎杨全, "Shuzi meijie yu wenxue piping de zhuanxing" 数字媒介与文学批评的转型 (PhD dissertation, Central China Norman University 华中师范大学, 2012), 31.
Translator's note: people used big-character posters during the Cultural Revolution as a way to struggle against each other.
8 Yang, Xinmin 杨新敏, "Wangluo wenxue chuyi" 网络文学刍议, *Literary Review* 文学评论 no. 5 (2000): 87.
9 Ouyang, Youquan 欧阳友权, "Wangluo wenxue: tiaozhan chuantong yu gengxin guannian" 网络文学：挑战传统与更新观念, *Social Science Journal of Xiangtan University* 湘潭大学社会科学学报 no. 1 (2001): 36–37.
10 Ouyang, Youquan 欧阳友权, "Wangluo wenxue: tiaozhan chuantong yu gengxin guannian" 网络文学：挑战传统与更新观, 36.
11 Huang, Mingfen 黄鸣奋, "Nüwa, weinasi, yihuo mogui zhongjiezhe?—diannao, diannaowenyi yu diannao wenyixue" 女娲、维纳斯，抑或魔鬼终结者？—电脑、电脑文艺与电脑文艺学, *Literary Review* 文学评论 no. 5 (2000): 85.
12 Ouyang, Youquan 欧阳友权, "Wangluo wenxue: cong 'caogen shuchu' dao zhuliu renke" 网络文学：从"草根庶出"到主流认可, *Study & Exploration* 学习与探索 no. 2 (2010): 179.
13 Ouyang, Youquan 欧阳友权, "Wangluo wenxue: cong 'caogen shuchu' dao zhuliu renke" 网络文学：从"草根庶出"到主流认可, 179.
14 Mo, Yan 莫言, "Wangluo wenxue shige haoxianxiang 网络文学是个好现象," *Renmin ribao* 人民日报 (Beijing), Dec. 1, 2008.
15 Hu, Chunyang 胡春阳, "Wangluo: ziyou ji qi xiangxiang—yi Bahejin kuanghuan lilun wei shijiao" 网络：自由及其想象—以巴赫金狂欢理论为视角, *Fudan University Journal: Social Sciences Edition* 复旦学报（社会科学版）no. 1 (2006): 116.
16 Mikhail Bakhtin, *Rabelais and His World*, trans. Helene Iswolsky (Bloomington: Indiana University Press, 1984b), 255.
17 Bakhtin, *Rabelais and His World*, 7.
18 Bakhtin, *Rabelais and His World*, 7.
19 Xia bu'an 夏不安, *Zhuxian cengjin dailai de gandong he jieju de shiwang* 诛仙曾经带来的感动和结局的失望. Douban 豆瓣, 2007. http://book.douban.com/review/1185836.
20 China Internet Network Information Center (CNNIC), "The 38th Statistical Report on Internet Development in China," *CNNIC*, last modified September 28, 2016, www.cnnic.com.cn/IDR/ReportDownloads/201611/P020161114573409551742.pdf.
21 CNNIC, *The 38th Statistical Report*.

22 Liu, Ji 刘吉 and Jin, Wulun 金吾伦, *Qiannian jingxing: xinxihua yu zhishi jingji* 千年警醒：信息化与知识经济 (Shanghai: Shanghai University of Finance and Economics Press, 1998), 21.
23 Nicholas Negroponte, *Being Digital* (New York: Vintage, 1996), 229.
24 Liu, Ji 刘吉 and Jin, Wulun 金吾伦, *Qiannian jingxing: xinxihua yu zhishi jingji* 千年警醒：信息化与知识经济, 269.
25 Nan, Fan 南帆, "Piping paoxia wenxue xiang qingfu qule 批评抛下文学享清福去了," *Zhonghua dushu bao* 中华读书报 (Beijing), Mar. 12, 2003.
26 Fang, Zhouzi 方舟子, *Wangluohua de wenxue* 网络化的文学. Xin Yu Si 新语丝, 1999. www.xys.org/xys/netters/Fang-Zhouzi/Net/webcmt22.txt.
27 Mikhail Bakhtin, *Problems of Dostoevsky's Poetics*, ed. and trans. Caryl Emerson (Minneapolis: University of Minnesota Press, 1984a), 252.
28 Dong, Lilong 董立龙, "'Hulianwang jia' dianfu le shenme '互联网+'颠覆了什么," *Hebei ribao* 河北日报 (Shijiazhuang), Jun. 2, 2015.
29 Ouyang, Youquan 欧阳友权 and Wu, Yingwen 吴英文, "Wangluo wenxue piping de jiazhi he juxian" 网络文学批评的价值和局限, *Exploration and Free Views* 探索与争鸣 no. 11 (2010): 65.
30 Jiushi shengmeng 就是生猛, *Ta Ai: kuping shi yiba kuaiyi de dao—ping Ta Ai "Shi meinü zuojia piping shu"* 他爱，酷评是一把快意的刀——评他爱《十美女作家批评书》, Tianya 天涯, 2005. http://bbs.tianya.cn/post-210-5337-1.shtml.
31 Bu, Changwei 卜昌伟, "'Shi meinü zuojia piping shu' paohong danghong nü zuojia 《十美女作家批评书》炮轰当红女作家," *Jinghua shibao* 京华时报 (Beijing), Apr. 26, 2005.
32 Liu, Anhai 刘安海, "Women jiujing xuyao shenmeyang de wenxue piping—dui 'Shi meinü zuojia piping shu' de piping" 我们究竟需要什么样的文学批评——对《十美女作家书》的批评, *Journal of Shantou University: The Humanities & Social Sciences Edition* 汕头大学学报（人文社会科学版）no. 6 (2008): 14.
33 Jian, Ming 剑鸣, "Leng Quanqing: wenyi piping jiben biaozhun yinggai shi shenme" 冷铨清：文艺批评基本标准应该是什么, *Social Sciences in China* 中国社会科学 no.6 (1984): 211.
34 Li, Yangquan 黎杨全, "Shuzi meijie yu wenxue piping de zhuanxing" 数字媒介与文学批评的转型, 86.
35 Hong, Zhigang 洪治纲, "Xinxi shidai: wenxue piping de tiaozhan yu xuanze" 信息时代：文学批评的挑战与选择, *Southern Cultural Forum* 南方文坛 no. 6 (2010): 22.
36 Guo, Guochang 郭国昌, "Wangluo wenxue huhuan wenxue piping 网络文学呼唤文学批评," *Renmin ribao* 人民日报 (Beijing), Feb. 5, 2010.
37 Translator's note: the original post is on *Sina Blog*. However, for some reason, all blog posts on *Sina Blog* are now inaccessible to the public.
38 Ouyang, Youquan 欧阳友权, "Zhongguo wangluo wenxue yanjiu jidian jiqi yujing xuanze" 中国网络文学研究基点及其语境选择, *Hebei Academic Journal* 河北学刊 no. 4 (2015): 96.
39 Ouyang, Youquan 欧阳友权, "Zhongguo wangluo wenxue yanjiu jidian jiqi yujing xuanze" 中国网络文学研究基点及其语境选择, 96.
40 Ouyang, Youquan 欧阳友权, "Wangluo meiti dui wenxue jingdian guannian de jiegou" 网络媒体对文学经典观念的解构, *Social Sciences in Guizhou* 贵州社会科学 no. 12 (2007): 29.
41 Michael Heim, *The Metaphysics of Virtual Reality* (New York: Oxford University Press, 1994), 9.

42 Ouyang, Youquan 欧阳友权, "Hulianwang dui wenxuexing de jishu qumei" 互联网对文学性的技术祛魅, *Journal of Jishou University: Social Sciences Edition* 吉首大学学报（社会科学版） no. 3 (2004): 56.
43 Zhu, Liyuan 朱立元, *Dangdai xifang wenyi lilun* 当代西方文艺理论 (Shanghai: East China Normal University Press, 1997), 303.
44 Jean-François Leotard, *The Postmodern Condition: A Report on Knowledge*, trans. Geoff Bennington and Brian Massumi (Minneapolis: University of Minnesota Press, 1984), passim.
45 Gegewu ggw 格格巫ggw, *Xiyou ji shi lishi juzhu, haishi dangdai guanchang xiantai* 西游记是历史巨著，还是当代官场现态, Tianya 天涯, 2012. http://bbs.tianya.cn/post-187-560126-1.shtml.
46 Jean Baudrillard, *The Consumer Society: Myths and Structures* (London: Sage Publications, 1998), 78.
47 Mike Featherstone, *Consumer Culture and Postmodernism* (London: Sage Publications, 2007), 111.
48 Ke, Hanlin 柯汉琳, "Wangluo piping yu xueyuan piping: maodun yu hubu" 网络批评与学院批评：矛盾与互补, *Journal of South China Normal University: Social Sciences Edition* 湖南师范大学学报（社会科学版） no. 3 (2015): 163.
49 Tong, Qingbing 童庆炳, "Wenxue jingdian jiangou zhu yinsu ji qi guanxi" 文学经典建构诸因素及其关系, *Journal of Peking University: Philosophy and Social Sciences Edition* 北京大学学报（哲学社会科学版） no. 5 (2005): 78.
50 Shao, Yanjun 邵燕君, "Wangluo wenxue de 'wangluo xing' yu 'jingdian xing'" 网络文学的"网络性"与"经典性," *Journal of Peking University: Philosophy and Social Sciences Edition* 北京大学学报（哲学社会科学版） no. 1 (2005): 148.
51 Shao, Yanjun 邵燕君, "Wangluo wenxue de 'wangluo xing' yu 'jingdian xing'" 网络文学的"网络性"与"经典性," 143.

Bibliography

Bakhtin, Mikhail. *Problems of Dostoevsky's Poetics*. Edited and translated by Caryl Emerson. Minneapolis: University of Minnesota Press, 1984a.
Bakhtin, Mikhail. *Rabelais and His World*. Translated by Helene Iswolsky. Bloomington: Indiana University Press, 1984b.
Baudrillard, Jean. *The Consumer Society: Myths and Structures*. London: Sage Publications, 1998.
Bu, Changwei 卜昌伟. "'Shi meinü zuojia piping shu' paohong danghong nü zuojia 《十美女作家批评书》炮轰当红女作家." *Jinghua shibao* 京华时报 (Beijing), Apr. 26, 2005.
China Internet Network Information Center (CNNIC). "The 38th Statistical Report on Internet Development in China." *CNNIC*. Last modified November 14, 2016. www.cnnic.com.cn/IDR/ReportDownloads/201611/P020161114573409551742.pdf.
Dong, Lilong 董立龙. "'Hulianwang jia' dianfu le shenme '互联网＋'颠覆了什么." *Hebei ribao* 河北日报 (Shijiazhuang), Jun. 2, 2015.
Fang, Zhouzi 方舟子. Wangluohua de wenxue 网络化的文学. Xin Yu Si 新语丝, 1999. www.xys.org/xys/netters/Fang-Zhouzi/Net/webcmt22.txt.
Featherstone, Mike. *Consumer Culture and Postmodernism*. London: Sage Publications, 2007.

Gegewu ggw 格格巫ggw. *Xiyou ji shi lishi juzhu, haishi dangdai guanchang xiantai* 西游记是历史巨著，还是当代官场现态. Tianya天涯, 2012. http://bbs.tianya.cn/post-187-560126-1.shtml.

Guo, Guochang 郭国昌. "Wangluo wenxue huhuan wenxue piping 网络文学呼唤文学批评." *Renmin ribao* 人民日报 (Beijing), Feb. 5, 2010.

Heim, Michael. *The Metaphysics of Virtual Reality*. New York: Oxford University Press, 1994.

Hong, Zhigang 洪治纲. "Xinxi shidai: wenxue piping de tiaozhan yu xuanze" 信息时代：文学批评的挑战与选择. *Southern Cultural Forum* 南方文坛 no. 6 (2010): 19–24.

Hu, Chunyang 胡春阳. "Wangluo: ziyou ji qi xiangxiang—yi Bahejin kuanghuan lilun wei shijiao" 网络：自由及其想象——以巴赫金狂欢理论为视角. *Fudan Journal: Social Sciences Edition* 复旦学报（社会科学版） no. 1 (2006): 115–121.

Huang, Mingfen 黄鸣奋. "Nüwa, weinasi, yihuo mogui zhongjiezhe?—diannao, diannaowenyi yu diannao wenyixue" 女娲、维纳斯，抑或魔鬼终结者？——电脑、电脑文艺与电脑文艺学. *Literary Review* 文学评论 no. 5 (2000): 77–86.

Jian, Ming 剑鸣. "Leng Quanqing: wenyi piping jiben biaozhun yinggai shi shenme" 冷铨清：文艺批评基本标准应该是什么. *Social Sciences in China* 中国社会科学 no.6 (1984): 211.

Jiushi shengmeng 就是生猛. *Ta Ai: kuping shi yiba kuaiyi de dao—ping Ta Ai "Shi meinü zuojia piping shu"* 他爱，酷评是一把快意的刀——评他爱《十美女作家批评书》. Tianya 天涯, 2005. http://bbs.tianya.cn/post-210-5337-1.shtml.

Ke, Hanlin 柯汉琳. "Wangluo piping yu xueyuan piping: maodun yu hubu" 网络批评与学院批评：矛盾与互补. *Journal of South China Normal University: Social Sciences Edition* 湖南师范大学学报（社会科学版） no. 3 (2015): 163–167+192.

Leotard, Jean-François. *The Postmodern Condition: A Report on Knowledge*. Translated by Geoff Bennington and Brian Massumi. Minneapolis: University of Minnesota Press, 1984.

Li Yangquan 黎杨全. "Digital Media and the Transformation of Literary Criticism" (Shuzi meijie yu wenxue piping de zhuanxing). PhD dissertation, Central China Norman University 华中师范大学, 2012.

Li, Jingze 李敬泽. "'Wangluo wenxue': yaodian he yiwen '网络文学'：要点和疑问." *Wenxue bao* 文学报 (Shanghai), Apr. 20, 2000.

Liu, Anhai 刘安海. "Women jiujing xuyao shenmeyang de wenxue piping—dui 'Shi meinü zuojia piping shu' de piping" 我们究竟需要什么样的批评——对《十大美女作家书》的批评. *Journal of Shantou University: The Humanities & Social Sciences Edition* 汕头大学学报（人文社会科学版） no. 6 (2008): 14–18+91.

Liu, Ji 刘吉 and Jin, Wulun 金吾伦. *Qiannian jingxing: xinxihua yu zhishi jingji* 千年警醒：信息化与知识经济. Shanghai: Shanghai University of Finance and Economics Press, 1998.

Liu, Li 刘莉. "Zhiyi wangluo wenxue" 质疑网络文学. *Art Panorama* 艺术广角 no. 4 (2001): 17–21.

Mo, Yan 莫言. "Wangluo wenxue shige haoxianxiang 网络文学是个好现象." *Renmin ribao* 人民日报 (Beijing), Dec. 1, 2008.

Nan, Fan 南帆. "Piping paoxia wenxue xiang qingfu qule 批评抛下文学享清福去了." *Zhonghua dushu bao* 中华读书报 (Beijing), Mar. 12, 2003.

Ouyang, Youquan 欧阳友权. "Wangluo wenxue: tiaozhan chuantong yu gengxin guannian" 网络文学：挑战传统与更新观念. *Social Science Journal of Xiangtan University* 湘潭大学社会科学学报 no. 1 (2001): 36–40.

Ouyang, Youquan 欧阳友权. "Wangluo wenxue de meiti tuwei yu biaozheng beilun" 网络文学的媒体突围与表征悖论. *Social Science Front* 社会科学战线 no. 4 (2002): 89–93.

Ouyang, Youquan 欧阳友权. "Hulianwang dui wenxuexing de jishu qumei" 互联网对文学性的技术祛魅. *Journal of Jishou University: Social Sciences Edition* 吉首大学学报（社会科学版）no. 3 (2004): 55–59.

Ouyang, Youquan 欧阳友权. "Wangluo meiti dui wenxue jingdian guannian de jiegou" 网络媒体对文学经典观念的解构. *Social Sciences in Guizhou* 贵州社会科学 no. 12 (2007): 29–32.

Ouyang, Youquan 欧阳友权. "Wangluo wenxue: cong 'caogen shuchu' dao zhuliu renke" 网络文学：从"草根庶出"到主流认可. *Study & Exploration* 学习与探索 no. 2 (2010): 178–180.

Ouyang, Youquan 欧阳友权. "Zhongguo wangluo wenxue yanjiu jidian jiqi yujing xuanze" 中国网络文学研究基点及其语境选择. *Hebei Academic Journal* 河北学刊 no. 4 (2015): 96–99.

Ouyang, Youquan 欧阳友权 and Wu, Yingwen 吴英文. "Wangluo wenxue piping de jiazhi he juxian" 网络文学批评的价值和局限. *Exploration and Free Views* 探索与争鸣 no. 11 (2010): 63–66.

Tao, Dongfeng 陶东风. "Zhongguo wenxue yijing jinru zhuangshennonggui shidai? 中国文学已经进入装神弄鬼时代？," *Zhonghua dushu bao* 中华读书报 (Beijing), Jun. 21, 2006.

Tong, Qingbing 童庆炳. "Wenxue jingdian jiangou zhu yinsu ji qi guanxi" 文学经典建构诸因素及其关系. *Journal of Peking University: Philosophy and Social Sciences Edition* 北京大学学报（哲学社会科学版）no. 5 (2005): 78–78.

Xi, Yunshu 席云舒. "Wangluo de jueqi yu wenxue de kuisan 网络的崛起与文学的溃散." *Zhongguo wenhuabao* 中国文化报 (Beijing), Sep. 9, 2000.

Xia bu'an 夏不安. *Zhuxian cengjin dailai de gandong he jieju de shiwang* 诛仙曾经带来的感动和结局的失望. Douban 豆瓣, 2007. http://book.douban.com/review/1185836.

Xu, Miaomiao 许苗苗. "Teliduxing de wangluo wenxue 特立独行的网络文学." *Wenyi bao* 文艺报 (Beijing), Mar. 20, 2001.

Yang, Xinmin 杨新敏. "Wangluo wenxue chuyi" 网络文学刍议. *Literary Review* 文学评论 no. 5 (2000): 87–95.

Zhu, Liyuan 朱立元. *Dangdai xifang wenyi lilun* 当代西方文艺理论. Shanghai: East China Normal University Press, 1997.

Coda
Three Follow-up Questions about the Historiography of Cyber Literary Criticism

We have witnessed how literary criticism with a long history was broken in by the new wave of ideas in the digital age. The new ideas are immature and messy, but they have infinite possibilities and room for growth. In this transitional period, it is important for us to trace the development of cyber literary criticism and try to give it a framework. To do so, we are faced with many challenges, and there are some more questions to be answered.

The Question about Historical Distance and the Theoretical Vacuum

Since we try to sort out a history for cyber literary criticism when China's cyber literature is only a quarter of a century old,[1] we are attempting something like urging Hegel's "owl of Minerva," who spreads its wings only with the falling of dusk, to take off at dawn.[2] That puts us in confrontation with many challenges.

To begin with, we are looking too "closely," and as a result, our field of vision is narrow and fragmented. Without a safe historical distance, the observer loses his/her objective footing and cannot see the forest for the trees. At the same time, the nascent cyber literature is in a volatile shape and is hard to pin down for evaluation. The show has just started, and any historiography must feel under-resourced. The research of cyber literature, as has been pointed out, "is still in its infancy, lacking a systematic structure and seriously outdated. It seldom focuses on the texts. Without a set of new evaluation criteria different from old ones, it cannot provide good guidance for the writing and reading of cyber literature."[3] In other words, there is very little to write about for a history.

Second, as mentioned above, critics are ill-equipped with the theoretical tools to approach cyber literature, which makes it impossible to write a well-balanced history. Criticism falls far behind the explosive production of web novels, and the limitations of both academic criticism and online reviews discussed in previous chapters only add embarrassment to the historiography of cyber literary criticism.

Nevertheless, in these disadvantages lies the opportunity. Since the time is short and we are looking closely, we are unlikely to miss out on anything and will have the details under control. With the participants of this history still around and the events fresh in our minds, it is possible to write a tangible, inclusive, and vivid history. As for the lack of criteria, we will have a lot to borrow from tradition and much more to create based on the new modes of writing, reading, and marketing. We will create, as Marx said of men's creation of history, not just as we please or under circumstances chosen by ourselves, but "under circumstances directly encountered, given and transmitted from the past."[4] From there, we can write a history of cyber literary criticism with an elucidation of both its roots and episodes.

The Question about Diversity and Standardized Criticism

As the most free and diverse mode of literary writing, cyber literature does not seem to be approachable with any fixed evaluation system. How are we to form a set of "criteria" and extract a clear "history" out of it? The key, I believe, is the distinction between the "changed" and the "unchangeable" of literature, literary criticism, and historiography.

What is the "unchangeable" of literature in the Internet age? Zhang Kangkang once said something illuminating when she participated in the "NetEase China Web Literature Awards Ceremony" (Wangyi Zhongguo wangluo wenxue jiang) in 2000: "Cyber literature will change readers' reading habits; it will also change writers' vision, mentality, way of thinking, and expression. But to what extent will it change literature itself? That includes literary elements such as emotion, imagination, conscience, and language." She also said, "Perhaps only after the information age has completely changed and reshaped human beings will it be possible for cyber literature to subvert 'traditional literature.'"[5] That is, as long as humanity and human society exist and human nature persists with its emotional needs, wishes, and ideals, the roots of literature will remain and the "literariness" will not be fundamentally changed regardless of its medium, technical component, and industrialized production. This is also true of literary criticism and its history, which depend on the core values of literature. These are the "unchangeable" in the new era.

The "changed," as elaborated on in previous chapters, involves various aspects of the digital age and requires us to have a more flexible attitude. As the literary critic Liu Xie (ca. 465–520) of the Southern Dynasties famously put it, "Literary subject matter and the form in which it is treated are conditioned by the needs of the times, but whether a certain subject matter or a certain form is emphasized or overlooked depends on the choice made by the writers."[6] Cyber literary criticism must respond to such changes and guide the development of literature, and the right way to do so is to "establish a set of evaluation criteria and a system for literary criticism … that accord with the traditions of literature, especially the traditions of popular literature, as well as the productive mode, readers' reception, market, and media of cyber literature." Chen Qirong suggested that the responsibilities of cyber literary criticism should at least include the following:

[Cyber literary criticism should] orient cyberwriting toward positive social values. It should clarify cyber literature's relationship with the people, the times, and the core values of socialism. Based on how cyber literary works follow the way of art and the principles of aesthetics and on their popularity among readers, cyber literary criticism should interpret and evaluate these works in terms of their intellectual connotations, artistic presentations, and aesthetic styles. Cyber literary criticism should then elucidate how such works fulfill their cognitive, educational, aesthetic, and entertainment functions. Through an analysis of the different genres, styles, schools, and texts of cyber literature, cyber literary criticism should make clear how various ways of writing, such as realism, romanticism, and modernism, are shown in cyber literature and find something universally truthful from this.[7]

This broad proposal has taken into consideration the "changed" aspects of literature, with faith in the positive role of cyber literary criticism. More specific guidance is still needed for practicing criticism. A history of cyber literary criticism must likewise respond to what has changed and identify the constructive values as well as recurring patterns.

The Question about Choosing Between the Old and the New

A history of cyber literary criticism must find a balance between the old and the new. "Every true history," said Benedetto Croce, "is contemporary history."[8] Historians interpret documents with an interest of the present life. For historians of China's cyber literary criticism, the history is a teleological one: it is about cyber literature and its criticism's development toward maturity. A considerable part of cyber literature (in particular novels) is the digitalized version of print literature, that is, works originally published in book form transferred onto the Internet to be read there, rather than originally published online. Such literature has not obtained its own aesthetic independence. Meanwhile, I agree with Shan Xiaoxi that "the aesthetic independence of cyber literature is embodied in its digital production, the multimedia cyber text, and the immersive aesthetic experience."[9] Since both cyber literature and cyber literary criticism are at a preliminary stage, the history of cyber literary criticism has to settle with the most conspicuous achievements so far.

Nevertheless, there have been groundbreaking studies in the field for historians to draw upon. For example, Professor Huang Mingfen from Xiamen University, who started his research in the field of cyber literature and digital arts in the 1990s, has edited the "Internet Hurricane Series" (Wangluo kuangbiao congshu) and published many important monographs. His trailblazing work has opened the space for future studies of cyber literature and literary criticism. The research team I have been leading at Central South University has published hundreds of research articles as well as monographs and edited collections on web literature. There are many other scholars whose efforts have advanced the field and enriched this history. Ma Ji and Chen Dingjia have both published books on the history of cyber literature, and scholars like Shan Xiaoxi and Zhou Zhixiong have written on cyber literature and cyber literary criticism, to name just a few.

Cyber literature and its criticism have come this far despite the skepticism from many people. With the increase of attention from both the general public and scholars, disapproving voices have dwindled. We can see the great potential in cyber literature and criticism and believe that they will be included in literary history. Today, the boundaries between cyber literature and traditional literature are disappearing, and it is inevitable that online and offline writers will become indistinguishable. As technology continues to serve the humanities and the media promote aesthetic values, we will eventually view cyber literature simply as a common type of literature. The names, "cyber literature" and "cyber literary criticism," will become obsolete, and the "history of cyber literary criticism" will simply be called a critical literary history.

Notes

1 In 1998, *The First Intimate Contact* shot to immediate fame, and the literary website *Under the Banyan Tree* (Rongshu xia) also became famous. An influential event commemorating the ten-year anniversary of cyber literature was sponsored by China Writers Association in 2008. The year of 1998 was therefore recognized as the first year of Chinese cyber literature.
2 The owl Hegel invokes is a symbol of wisdom and is associated with Minerva, who is the Roman goddess of wisdom and philosophy. The owl takes flight only at the end of the day, after witnessing the day's main events. Hegel uses this image to show that philosophy is a reflective activity and that we can only understand history's developmental logic at the end of history.
3 *Wangluo wenxue pingjia tixi xushitan* 网络文学评价体系虚实谈, ed. Creation and Research Department of China Writers Association 中国作家协会创作研究部 (Beijing: Writers Publishing House, 2014), 338.
4 Karl Marx, *The Eighteenth Brumaire of Louis Bonaparte* (Moscow: Progress Publishers, 1954), 10.
5 Zhang, Kangkang 张抗抗, "Wangluo wenxue zagan 网络文学杂感," *Zhonghua dushu bao* 中华读书报 (Beijing), Mar. 1, 2000.
6 Liu, Hsieh (Liu Xie) 刘勰, *The Literary Mind and the Carving of Dragons*, trans. Vincent Yu-chung Shih (Hong Kong: The Chinese University of Hong Kong Press, 1983), 318.
7 Chen, Qirong 陈崎嵘, "Zhubu jianli Zhongguo tese de wangluo wenxue lilun tixi, pingjia tixi he huayu tixi" 逐步建立中国特色的网络文学理论体系、评价体系和话语体系, in *Wangluo wenxue pingjia tixi xushitan* 网络文学评价体系虚实谈, ed. Creation and Research Department of China Writers Association 中国作家协会创作研究部 (Beijing: Writers Publishing House, 2014), 10.
8 Benedetto Croce, *History: Its Theory and Practice*, trans. Douglas Ainslie (New York: Harcourt, Brace & Co., 1921), 12.
9 Shan, Xiaoxi 单小曦, *Meijie yu wenxue: meijie wenyixue yinlun* 媒介与文学：媒介文艺学引论 (Beijing: The Commercial Press, 2015), 246.

Bibliography

Chen, Qirong 陈崎嵘. "Zhubu jianli Zhongguo tese de wangluo wenxue lilun tixi, pingjia tixi he huayu tixi" 逐步建立中国特色的网络文学理论体系、评价体系和话语体系. In *Wangluo wenxue pingjia tixi xushitan* 网络文学评价体系虚实谈, edited by Creation and Research Department of China Writers Association 中国作家协会创研部, 5–11. Beijing: Writers Publishing House, 2014.

Croce, Benedetto. *History: Its Theory and Practice*. Translated by Douglas Ainslie. New York: Harcourt, Brace & Co., 1921.

Liu, Hsieh (Liu Xie) 刘勰. *The Literary Mind and the Carving of Dragons*. Translated by Vincent Yu-chung Shih. Hong Kong: The Chinese University of Hong Kong, 2015.

Marx, Karl. *The Eighteenth Brumaire of Louis Bonaparte*. Moscow: Progress Publishers, 1954.

Shan, Xiaoxi 单小曦. *Meijie yu wenxue: meijie wenyixue yinlun* 媒介与文学：媒介文艺学引论. Beijing: The Commercial Press, 2015.

Wangluo wenxue pingjia tixi xushitan 网络文学评价体系虚实谈. Edited by Creation and Research Department of China Writers Association 中国作家协会创研部. Beijing: Writers Publishing House, 2014.

Zhang, Kangkang 张抗抗. " Wangluo wenxue zagan 网络文学杂感." *Zhonghua dushu bao* 中华读书报 (Beijing), Mar. 1, 2000.

Index

Note: Endnotes are indicated by the page number followed by "n" and the note number e.g., 89n33 refers to note 33 on page 89. Page locators in **bold** represents tables.

academic achievements 8–12; in cyber literary studies 18–19, 91–114
academic books, on cyber literature 91–2, **93–6**
academic journals, on cyber literature 11–12, **97–102**
academic papers, on cyber literature 92, **103–6**
aesthetics of literature 6, 183
Annals of Cyber Literature in China, The (Zhongguo wangluo wenxue biannianshi) 10
Annie Baby (Anni baobei) 38, 80, 112, 207, 240, 254–5, 273, 279
artificial intelligence 163–4, 186
artistic vocation 7
audiobooks 5–6

Baidu Post Bar (Baidu tieba) 40, 68, 194, 257, 260
Bai Ye 13, 21, 39, 80, 107, 160, 207, 259, 271–3, 279; debate with Han Han 152–3, 170; identity as a writer 171; "My Statement: Responding to Han Han" article 152
blasphemous: comment 132; tendency 23, 190–1
blog literary criticism 48–50
blogs 48–9, 60, 80, 124
Boke 48
Book of Illness and Forgetting, The (Bing wang shu) 49
Bowman, Shayne 47
Bulletin Board System (BBS) 39, 194–5

Cai Meijuan 213, 215
Cambridge History of Chinese Literature, The (Chang and Owen) 15
carnivalesque language style 187
casual and unrestrained discussions 130–2; on *Sina Weibo* 131–2; on *The World in the Sky* (Tianyu cangqiong) 130–1
Chen Cun 38, 80, 107
Chen Dingjia 24, 81–3, 110, 273, 294
Chen Haiyan 55
Chen Qirong 14, 79, 107, 157, 199, 202, 292
China Internet Network Information Center (CNNIC) 36, 52, 68
China National Knowledge Infrastructure (CNKI) **9**, 9–10, 56, 84, 92
China News Digest (Huaxia wenzhai) 21, 36, 67
China Writers Association 56, 75, 83–4, 155–7, 159–61, 230, 285
Chronicles of the Ghostly Tribe (Jiuceng yaota) 5
click-through rate 25, 68, 74, 123, 126, 131, 211, 241, 280, 285
Collected Entries of Major Academic Publications on Cyber Literature 10, 13
collective unconscious 272
Computer Fan (Diannao aihao zhe) 55
conceptualization of literature 161–8, 183
conceptual transformation in cyber literary criticism 183–5; aesthetics 185–6; hypertext 188–9; ironic and playful language style 187–8;

postmodernism 186–7; retention of traditional values 199–202; social and cultural context 185–9; *see also* notions in cyber literary criticism
consumerism, culture of 154, 283–4
contents of netizens' commentaries: casual and unrestrained discussions 130–2; direct and intuitive content 128–30; postmodern and deconstructive 133–6; subversive commentaries 132–3
copyright infringement 76
critics' anxiety, about the lack of evaluation criteria 213–14
cross-media *see* we media
cultural celebrities, cyber literary criticism by 77–80
cultural dimension of cyber literary criticism 2, 168–70; new folk culture 167
cyberculture 22, 28, 56, 58, 86, 120–1, 150, 168, 187, 192, 216, 281
cyber literary criticism 1, 36; academic achievements 8–9; adaptations 5, 11; "carnivalesque" activities of 28; characteristics 67, 109–11; competition between different critical voices 170–1; critics' interpretations 4; dissemination of 13; ecology of 12–14; editors' "on- site" criticism 77–8; elements 2–3; forms 13; functions 2, 25–7; groups of people involved 12–13; historical significance 2–8; impact of 27–8; influence on Internet 285; information-based criticism 74–6; major websites and forums 67–8; in mass media 74–80; mechanism 282; need and rationale 2–9; new media and 15–16; principles of 108–9; published in academic journals 13; rankings of works 68–9; reading preferences and textual details 69–70; research and 11; roles of market and technology in 211–13; scholars' contributions to 80–6; scholars' viewpoints 92; significance and limitations 28, 113–14, 173, 277–81; socio-cultural values 2, 5, 168–70; specific literary works and genres 111–13; types of 17–18, 37; visible criticism 77; by writers and other cultural celebrities 77–80
cyber literary criticism, in traditional media 55–61; development 55–7;
evaluation criteria 60; major issues discussed 57–9; significance and limitations of 59–61; values and drawbacks of 58
cyber literary criticism's impact 27–8; structure 270–6
cyber literary critics 27; collision and collaboration between groups 270–4; division and competition among 256–60; fan writers 263; grassroots critics 271; multiple groups 250–6; netizens 68–72; ordinary readers 67, 263; rational opponents 263; trolls 263
cyber literary research 56
cyber literary studies 18–19, 21, 23–4, 58, 81, 84–6
cyber literature 1; in academic journals and newspapers 56–7; commercial value of 7; critics of 7; deficiency of 4; demands for evaluation criteria 214–17; history of 4; massiveness of 4; positive and negative views of 206–9; texts of 6; theorization of 14; traditional and new ideas 209–11; values and dimensions of 220–2; *see also* evaluation system for cyber literature
Cyber Literature and Digital Culture Conference 56
cyber readers 27, 274–5
cyberspace 3, 5, 12, 28, 37, 67, 69–70, 72–4, 76, 79–80, 109–10, 112, 169, 171, 201, 208, 215, 217, 220–1, 228–31, 242, 259, 261, 267, 272–3, 275–7, 280; Chinese creative writing in 37–8; colloquial and vernacular expressions in 137–9; communication in 187; culture of 11; degree of freedom 8, 25–7, 114, 153, 162, 173, 189, 200; as dimension of reality 197; discursive power 28; disenchantment in 169, 190; effect of "heteroglossia" 12; electronic forms in 19; entertainment consumed in 167; features of 44; grassroots spirit 132; interactive criticism in 70; language used in 134; Martian language 136–7; Mu Zimei phenomenon 149; new media and 15–16; opinion leaders and public intellectuals 80; parody in 133; people's changing relationship in 212; purification of 76; pushing of information 18; rationality in 109; "salon- style" criticism 125; spam

298 Index

posts in 72–3; spoofs in 72; spread of feelings 193; virtual persona 195–6; voices in 67, 69; vulgar words usage in 192; writer-critics in 79
cyber technology 6, 155
cyber writers 17, 19, 27, 38, 55, 67, 76, 79, 82–3, 107, 112, 154, 160–1, 172, 198, 217, 221, 225, 240, 246, 252, 256, 259, 273–4, 280, 284–5; balance between the artistic and the commercial 58; blog articles written by 10, 39; China Writers Rich List 75; commentaries on 214; computer applications for cyberwriting 10; cyber literary criticism 207; degree of freedom and equality 25; fans of 73; first-generation 230; Internet publishing 8; literary creation 60; literary obligation 25; use of new technology 7; WeChat "official accounts" 51; writing abilities 3
cyberwriting 1, 13, 17, 19–20, 23, 27–8, 36–7, 45, 85, 112, 149–50, 156, 165–70, 172, 201–2, 219, 231, 243, 277–8, 281; aesthetics of 189; characteristics of 24; computer applications for 10; cyber literary criticism 8, 215; literary creation 7; practices of 2, 199; use of vulgar words 192; writing abilities 3–4

Dictionary of Words about Cyber Literature, A 10
digital information 35
digital poetics 6
digital technologies 6–7, 11, 15–16, 24, 35–6, 45, 47, 80–1, 114, 120, 139, 154, 164, 166–7, 184, 197–8, 208, 211, 219
direct and intuitive content of netizens' commentaries 128–30
disenchantment 23, 169, 190, 194, 232

Eagleton, Terry 188
ecology of cyber literary criticism 12–14, 275–6
editors' "on- site" criticism 77–8
electronic communication 35
Empresses in the Palace (Hougong Zhen Huan zhuan) 5
evaluation system for cyber literature 14, 24–5, 60, 107–8, 171–3; of commercialization 222; criterion for evaluating cyber literature 218–19; critics' anxiety 213–14; demand for 214–17; influence of new technologies 211–13; poetic and the commercial 218–19; positive and negative values 206–9; quality 233; scholars' criticism and netizens' criticism 262; traditional and new ideas 209–11; values and dimensions 220–2; ways of constructing 217–18
events of cyber literary criticism 21–3; cyber literature debate 153–5; debate between Han Han and Bai Ye 152–3, 170–1; "Mu Zimei phenomenon" 148–50; rankings of cyber literary works 155–9; seminars and discussions 159–61; Zhao's poems 150–1

Fanfou.com 49
Fang Zhouzi 37, 67, 71, 80, 272, 277
fantasy literature/fantasy novels 108, 113–14
First Intimate Contact, The (Cai Zhiheng) 21, 38, 55, 81, 161, 164, 206, 208, 251, 258
forms of netizens' commentaries: fragmentation of information 120–3; interactive commentaries 123–5; monologues 125–8
Forum for Cyber Literary Research 159
fragmentation of information 120–3; boundary between media and ordinary people 121; on Murong Xuecun's web novel 121–2; postmodernists views 121
free writing: colloquial and vernacular expressions 137–40; Internet language 142–4; in Martian language 136–7; use of vulgar words 140–2
functions of cyber literary criticism 2, 25–7, 228; breaking monopoly 229–30; changes and extension of 243–7; communication 230–3; diversity 241–2; establish criteria and paradigms 233–4; freedom 239–41; humanist concerns 242–3; promotion of openness and interaction 234–9

gatekeepers 3, 78, 242
Ge Hongbing 80–3, 207, 273
A General Survey of Cyber Literature Across Five Years: 2009–2013 9–10, 13, 92
genres in cyber literature 111–13
Ghost Blows Out the Light (Guichuideng) 5
Gillmor, Dan 46–7

Goldmark, P. 47
governmental regulations 76
grassroots, rise of 229–30
Grave Robbers' Chronicles (Daomu biji) 5
great leap forward 8
Guangming Daily 57–8, 77–8, 160, 251
Guo Chen 213, 215

hedonism 284
heteroglossia 12, 86, 275
history of cyber literary criticism: important events 21–3; representation of 15; review of academic achievements 9–12; theoretical discussions 15, 22–3
Huadi Literature Awards 285
Huang Mingfen 24, 55, 57, 81–2, 85, 109, 148, 163, 207, 210–11, 219, 272, 293
hypertext 25, 109, 121, 188–9, 210, 214, 221, 262; concept of 188; for creating virtual reality 198; creation of 23; in cyber literature 110; Hypertext Markup Language 188; non-sequential writing 188; use of 193

interactive commentaries 123–5; degree of plasticity 125
Internet 3, 5, 8, 10, 13, 27, 36, 48, 55, 57, 68, 70; celebrities 53, 73, 80; hypertextuality of 123; topological structure of 123
Internetization of literature 165
Internet language: evaluative, descriptive, and analytical expressions 143; postmodern context 144; style 142–3; thunderbolt points 143; writing skills and rhetorical techniques 143–4
Internet plus 27
intersubjectivity 23, 189

Jiang Fei 111
Jiang Shuyuan 107
Jing Wendong 165
Jinjiang Literature City (Jinjiang wenxuecheng) 39, 42, 44, 68, 71, 161
journalists' information-based criticism 74–6
Journey of Flower, The (Huaqiangu) 5

Kang Qiao 25, 79, 107–8, 201, 218

Lan Aiguo 83, 112–13
Li Chaoquan 83, 108, 110

Lin Huayu 111
literary canon 284; deconstruction of 282–3; formation on Internet 284–5; significance of 282
literary classics 60, 114, 132, 167, 193, 283–5; awareness in cyber literary creation 281; critics' attitudes toward 28; people's view of 28; publication of 281; significance of 282; as symbol of elite culture 28; traditional values 213
literary criticism: in academia 39; characteristics 23; in China 1–2; conceptual transformation 23–4; in cyberspace 39; in media 39
Literary Mind and the Carving of Dragons, The (Liu Xie) 2, 200
literary websites 3, 10–11, 26–7, 37, 39, 42, 48, 51, 55, 58, 67–71, 160, 219, 240, 252, 256; administrators of 267; emergence of 257; establishment of 207; interactive commentaries posted on 125; investment in 257; layout of 262; literary texts 258; rate of return 259
Liu Xiangning 218
Li Yuping 58, 108, 113, 206, 219
Love Is Not Blind (Shilian sanshisan tian) 5
Love Yunge from the Desert (Yunzhongge) 5
Luo Yong 216
Lu Shanhua 112
Lu Xun Literature Award 258, 273–4, 285

Ma Ji 55, 60, 77, 83, 111, 160, 200, 208, 212, 216, 219, 239, 294
Martian language 20, 225; texts in 136–7; used in netizens' literary commentaries 137; use of Mandarin phonetic symbols 136
McDonaldization of literature 165
McLuhan, Marshall 74, 120
media workers 1, 9, 12–13, 17–18, 27–8, 39, 65, 262, 273
mediocre, worship of 23, 189–90, 192
microblogs 13, 49–50, 60, 80, 124, 126, 242, 262; cross- media 47; evolution of 121; literary criticism 50, 74; messages posted on 19; posting of literary commentaries 26; social influence of 27
monographs, on cyber literary criticism 113

monologues: on *Blog China* 126–7; commentaries in the form of 19, 125–8; private 126
Mo Yan 79, 207, 271, 273, 284
multi-media works 6
MySpace.com 50

Nan Fan 81–3, 277
Negroponte, Nicholas 36, 276
Nelson, Theodor Holm 188
NetEase 37, 49, 80, 141, 261, 292
netizens 6, 12, 28, 58, 68–72; appreciative and critical reviews 70–2; dialogues and posts 69–70; expression of attitudes 68–70; power of 260–1, 263–7; short replies and clicks 68–9; stance of postmodernists 20
netizens' critical commentaries 19–21, 27; colloquial and vernacular expressions 20; language styles 20–1; netspeak 20–1; slang words, use of 20; in terms of content 19–20; types of texts 19; vulgar words, use of 20
networkedness 85, 89n33, 196–200
new media 5, 11, 56, 120, 135, 162–3, 166, 200, 208–9, 214, 221, 229, 258, 281; apps 68; concept of 47; development of 35–6; development of cyber literature 259; digital technologies 35; and the evolution of literary criticism in cyberspace 15–16; impact of 51; Internet as 21; literary criticism 16–17; platforms on the Internet 74; portal websites 27; power of 22; right to criticism 264; rise of 78; for transmission of information 13; use of 6, 262
New Threads of Thought (Xin Yu Si) 37, 67, 277
Nie Mao 112
Nie Qingpu 58, 111–12
Nirvana in Fire (Langyabang) 5
notions in cyber literary criticism: blasphemous tendency 190–1; disenchantment 194; intersubjectivity 189; mediocre 189–90; parody of classics 191–2; spoofing 193–4; spread of feelings 193; use of vulgar words 192

offline criticism 37
Olive Tree (Ganlan shu) 37, 67
online criticism 19, 37, 194, 228–9, 233, 257, 263–4, 282

online literary criticism 19, 69, 73–4, 83, 144, 148, 229, 239, 257, 262, 272, 275; characteristics of 21, 44–6; cyber literary criticism 68; forms of 39–44; important events in the history of 21–3; interactive 45; language used in 45; personal reflections 41; psychological mechanism of 256
Online Newsletter for Chinese Poems Written Overseas 36
oral communication 35
Ouyang Ting 7, 114, 167

parody 23, 72, 132–3, 135–6, 143, 150, 188, 191–2
People's Daily 14, 57–8, 76–8, 153, 160, 220, 273
photographic technologies 35
poetics 6
Poetics (Aristotle) 2
Popular Computer Weekly (Diannao bao) 55
pornography 76
postmodern and deconstructive contents 133–6
postmodernism in cyber literature 186–7, 234–42, **235–9**; deconstruction of literary canon 282–3
posts of critical reviews: based on argumentation 70–1; based on personal reflection 70; based on personal reflections 70–1; brick posts 70; excellent posts 70; for fun 70, 72; spoofs 70, 72
printing technology 35
professional critics and scholars 12–13

Qzone 80

Random Comments on Outlaws of the Marsh 49
rankings of cyber literary works: Chinese Web Novel Rankings 156, **157–8**; "*Promotion and Recommendation of Excellent Creative Cyberwritings in 2015*" 156–9; "*Review of Cyber Literature in the Past Ten Years*" 155–6
research projects on cyber literature 11
rewriting literary history project 5
right to literary criticism, through subversion: breaking the monopoly of elite criticism 229–30; building the

paradigm of cyber literary criticism 233–4; entrance of netspeak 230–3

"salon-style" criticism 125
scholars' contributions, to cyber literary criticism 80–6; graduate students and young scholars 84–6; in-depth research 82–4; influences and changes in conceptualization 161–8; pioneers 81–2; viewpoints 92, 161–74
Shanda Group 58, 219
Shao Yanjun 24–5, 83, 214, 285
Shu Jinyu 77, 273
Simulacrumization 187
Sina 49, 80
Sina Weibo 49–50, 54, 129, 131, 139, 143, 262, 264, 284
"site" of literary production 1, 3, 77, 208
Skyline Community (Tianya shequ) 38, 67, 71, 76, 130, 150, 194–5, 257, 283
Sohu 38, 49, 80
So Young (Zhi women zhongjiang shiqu de qingchun) 5
spam posts 73, 144, 196; for commercial purposes 12, 72–4; in cyberspace 72; posted in forums to flood screens 17; reasons for 73
spoofing 20, 23, 133, 151, 193–4, 282–3
spoofs 45, 70, 72, 83, 133
Starting Points Chinese Net (Qidian zhongwen wang) 39–40, 58, 68–70, 137, 155, 161, 245, 257
State Administration of Press, Publication, Radio, Film and Television (SAPPRFT) 156–7, 171
statistics of academic articles, books, research projects 11
subversive commentaries 20, 132–3
Sun Wukong 111

Tao Dongfeng 21, 80, 113, 194, 271–3
Tencent 50, 75, 80, 219, 261, 284
texts of cyber literature 6, 60, 86, 201–2, 274, 293
Theory of Literature (Wellek and Warren) 15
Tong Qingbing 284
travel-back-into-history novels 108, 164
trolls 263, 265

Under the Banyan Tree (Rongshuxia) 37–8, 67, 161, 252

virtual persona 23, 195–6
vulgar words 23, 140–2, 192; to make language more expressive 139; use as a language strategy 20; used in daily life 140; used in netizens' commentaries 140

Wang Yan 210–11
Wang Yichuan 24–5, 162–3
weakness of cyber literary criticism 28, 59–61, 113–14, 173; constructive reflections 173
WeChat 47–8, 80, 121, 124, 242, 262; fragmentation of information 121; literary criticism 48, 52–3; literature 11, 48, 50–2
Weibo 49–50, 139, 143, 262, 264, 284
Weixin 50–1
Welsch, Wolfgang 185
we media 46–51; application of 48; communication 48; freedom and autonomy 48; use of 47–8
we-media literary criticism 46–51, 126; characteristics of 51–5
Willis, Chris 47
World of Internet Information (Internet xinxi shijie) 55
writers associations 7, 56, 159–60
writers of cyber literary criticism 77–80
written communication 35
Wu Guo 38, 67, 79, 207, 272

Xici hutong 38, 149, 194
Xilu 38
Xing Yusen 38, 67, 72, 79, 207, 246
Xi Yunshu 271
Xu Miaomiao 112–13

Yahoo! 37
Yang Xinmin 55, 81–3, 88, 207, 272
Yang Yu 83, 112
Yan Zhen 83, 167
Yuan Chen 38, 67

Zeng Fanting 83, 111–12
Zhang Kangkang 25, 79, 163, 207, 292
Zhang Xianliang 127
Zhang Yiwu 80, 273
Zhang Yu 85
Zhang Yueran 273
Zhao Chenyu 107
Zhou Zhixiong 83, 173, 294

Taylor & Francis eBooks

www.taylorfrancis.com

A single destination for eBooks from Taylor & Francis with increased functionality and an improved user experience to meet the needs of our customers.

90,000+ eBooks of award-winning academic content in Humanities, Social Science, Science, Technology, Engineering, and Medical written by a global network of editors and authors.

TAYLOR & FRANCIS EBOOKS OFFERS:

- A streamlined experience for our library customers
- A single point of discovery for all of our eBook content
- Improved search and discovery of content at both book and chapter level

REQUEST A FREE TRIAL
support@taylorfrancis.com

For Product Safety Concerns and Information please contact our EU
representative GPSR@taylorandfrancis.com
Taylor & Francis Verlag GmbH, Kaufingerstraße 24, 80331 München, Germany

www.ingramcontent.com/pod-product-compliance
Lightning Source LLC
Chambersburg PA
CBHW050529300426
44113CB00012B/2009